Digital Transformation - Towards New Frontiers and Business Opportunities

Edited by Antonella Petrillo, Fabio De Felice, Monica Violeta Achim and Nawazish Mirza

Published in London, United Kingdom

Digital Transformation - Towards New Frontiers and Business Opportunities
http://dx.doi.org/10.5772/intechopen.97989
Edited by Antonella Petrillo, Fabio De Felice, Monica Violeta Achim and Nawazish Mirza

Contributors
Özlem Olgu Akdeniz, Elsadig Musa Ahmed, Bruno Daniotti, Alberto Pavan, Cecilia Bolognesi, Claudio Mirarchi, Martina Signorini, Iryna Kovshova, Arianna Bionda, Andrea Ratti, Bianca Christina Weber-Lewerenz, Peter Weiß, Markus Warg, Andreas Zolnowski, Akinniyi A. Adeleke, Joshua Onaade Ojo, Yemisi Ojokuku, Maria C.W. Peeters, Judith Plomp, Zhanna Mingaleva, Vladimir Postnikov, Kinda R. R Dahlan, Ali A Megahed, Ahmed A. Badawi, Francesco Calabrò, Maurizio Ceseri, Roberto Natalini, Attaphongse Taparugssanagorn, Kalapatapu Venkata Sai Krishna Raja Shiva Kumar, Arunya Prasantha Senadeera Senadiri Dumunnage

First published in London, United Kingdom, 2022 by IntechOpen
IntechOpen is the global imprint of INTECHOPEN LIMITED, registered in England and Wales, registration number: 11086078, 5 Princes Gate Court, London, SW7 2QJ, United Kingdom

British Library Cataloguing-in-Publication Data
A catalogue record for this book is available from the British Library

Additional hard and PDF copies can be obtained from orders@intechopen.com

Digital Transformation - Towards New Frontiers and Business Opportunities
Edited by Antonella Petrillo, Fabio De Felice, Monica Violeta Achim and Nawazish Mirza
p. cm.
Print ISBN 978-1-80355-762-5
Online ISBN 978-1-80355-763-2
eBook (PDF) ISBN 978-1-80355-764-9

Meet the editors

Antonella Petrillo, Ph.D., is a professor in the Department of Engineering, University of Naples "Parthenope," Italy. She received her Ph.D. in Mechanical Engineering from the University of Cassino and Southern Lazio, Italy. Her research interests include multi-criteria decision analysis, industrial plants, logistics, manufacturing, and safety. She serves as an associate editor for the *International Journal of the Analytic Hierarchy Process* and is an editorial board member for several other journals. She is also a member of the Analytic Hierarchy Process (AHP) Academy.

Fabio De Felice is a professor in the Department of Engineering, University of Naples "Parthenope," Italy. He received his Ph.D. in Mechanical Engineering at the University of Cassino and Southern Lazio, Italy. His current research focuses on multi-criteria decision-making analysis (with emphasis on the analytic hierarchy process [AHP] and ANP) and industrial, project, and supply chain management. Currently, he is a member of the Scientific Advisory Committee of the International Symposium on the Analytic Hierarchy Process (ISAHP). He is the founder of AHP Academy, which promotes the diffusion of the culture and methodologies of decision making, with particular reference to those based on the analytic hierarchy process. He is a member of the editorial boards of several international organizations and journals and has authored/co-authored numerous articles in the areas of decision science and business management.

Monica Violeta Achim is a full professor and doctoral supervisor in the field of finance at the Faculty of Economic Sciences and Business Administration, Babeş-Bolyai University, Cluj-Napoca, Romania. With more than 23 years of experience in academia, she has published as author and co-author of more than 150 scientific articles and 25 books. In 2020, she obtained the Award for Excellence in Scientific Research from Babeş-Bolyai University in recognition of her research. She has also attended many international economics conferences.

Nawazish Mirza is Professor and Director Academics of MSc International Corporate Finance at Excelia Business School, France. He is editor-in-chief of the *Journal of Risk Finance and Review of Accounting and Finance*. Dr. Mirza obtained his Ph.D. in Finance from the University of Paris Dauphine in 2010. He has more than 15 years of experience in consulting and teaching in Australia, Singapore, the United Arab Emirates, and France. His teaching and research interests include sustainable finance, financial intermediation, financial valuation, investments, and financial risk management. Before his career in academia, Dr. Mirza worked in investment banking, asset management, and credit ratings. He regularly contributes his opinions to popular media like Bloomberg, CNBC, China Daily, and more.

Contents

Preface

Digital transformation is characterizing the investigation of new business strategies and IT modernization of private and public companies, proposing the application of digital tools and technologies to the performance of normal work. However, not all organizations are yet clear about what digital transformation means and how it can be used fruitfully. Digital transformation should imply a redesign of processes and should be accompanied by a path of change management to overcome people's normal resistance to change. Today, information technologies fundamentally transform whole business models, products, and services. In fact, innovations are an opportune strategy for companies to compete in the digital age and to transform their business models, taking a service perspective on their value creation. In this scenario, digital transformation should be based on three essential components: people, company, and technology. Based on these premises, this book includes fourteen chapters that highlight companies that are successful in digital transformation and that are capable of changing mentality, strategies, and culture to keep up with continuously changing needs. The book analyzes business opportunities in different economic sectors.

Chapter 1, "Mastering Digital Transformation with Service Dominant Architecture" by Peter Weiß et al., presents insights from a longitudinal case study of an insurance company. Chapter 2, "Utilization of Fintech Applications during the Covid-19 Pandemic" by Özlem Olgu Akdeniz, is an empirical analysis evaluating a selection of the best FinTech-based investments in the Turkish banking sector using a hybrid DANP–fuzzy TOPSIS technique. In the current context, university education is one sector of national economies that is tremendously influenced by digital transformation. As such, Chapter 3, "Digital Maturity of University Libraries in Nigeria" by Adeleke Akinniyi et al., reports the findings of a survey of the level of digital maturity of university libraries in Nigeria. Chapter 4, "Modelling Digital Economy Implications on Long-Run Economic Development" by Elsadig Musa Ahmed, highlights that economics, like other social sciences, does not have one standard definition of the digital economy due to the subjective nature of the social sciences. Therefore, the chapter provides digital economy frameworks and policies to help in implementing digital transformation and to develop and use new technologies needed for sustainable economic growth through technological progress, human capital skills development, and environmental protection via green productivity technological progress. Chapter 5, "For Better or for Worse: The Impact of Workplace Automation on Work Characteristics and Employee Well-Being" by Maria C.W. Peeters and Judith Plomp, examines the consequences of implementing an automation technology (i.e., Robotic Process Automation [RPA]) for work characteristics and employee wellbeing. In the next years, perhaps more than ever before, a technological revolution will transform the construction sector in all its single aspects, greatly affecting services, production, and supplies. With building information modelling (BIM), as well as the concept of the digital twin, the innovation of tools has entailed a methodological innovation for the whole sector, owing to virtual reality simulations and actual dynamic real-time monitoring. Thus, Chapter 6, "Digital Transformation in the Construction Sector: From BIM to Digital Twin" by Daniotti et al., helps to understand the BIM phenomenon to achieve its mature use and future trends toward digital twin. Chapter 7, "New Approaches to Innovation Management in the Context of Digital Transformation" by Zhanna Mingaleva and Vladimir Postnikov, examines the impact of global trends on innovation activity as well as identifies new factors influencing innovation models. A conceptual approach to the analysis of the evolution of innovation models based on the transformation of information and communication technologies for innovation based on the bibliographic analysis and integration of existing concepts and theories of innovation, digitalization, and sustainable development in the world science is created. Chapter 8 "Digital Transformation: The Age of Innovations in Business and Society" by Iryna Kovshova, discusses the direction of innovative marketing management. In particular, it studies the opportunities of implementing artificial intelligence, neuromarketing, and augmented and virtual reality marketing technologies in company business processes. Chapter 9, "Perspective Chapter: Data as Currency - On the Impact of ICTs and Data on the Saudi Economy and Industrial Sector" by Kinda R. Dahlan et al., explores Saudi Arabia's digital readiness to further expound its industrial strategic goals. Chapter 10, "Yacht Digital Design: Technologies toward a Computational Morphology System" by Arianna Bionda and Andrea Ratti, investigates the role of digitally enabled technologies in modifying the disciplinary approaches to yacht design, a field of industrial design in which engineering and design approaches are mixed and overlapped. Chapter 11, "Applied Mathematics Tools in Digital Transformation" by Francesco Calabrò et al., presents mathematics tools that can help with digital transformation, along with some successful cases. It is clear that the digital age holds great potential for increased inclusion and closure of the gender leadership gap, especially in the construction industry. The construction industry, which is regarded as one of the most traditional and conservative male-dominated industries, serves as the best example of a long overdue need for dynamic restructuring and action related to women in leadership. Thus, Chapter 12, "Perspective Chapter: The Sovereign Way - How Diversity in Construction Is Key of Success in the Digital Age" by Bianca Christina Weber-Lewerenz, outlines the framework needed to redefine, recalibrate, and reshape the construction industry and increase women's roles within it. Chapter 13, "Education and Training in the Digital Era: A Compass for *Building Forward Better*" by Bianca Christina Weber-Lewerenz, emphasizes that digitization along with technological and social challenges requires a rethinking and adjustment of professional qualifications. The question is: "Are we ready for the technological challenges of tomorrow?" The research in this chapter found that there is significantly high potential for diverse teams, staffing the STEM fields with more female specialists, and fully using specialist knowledge and personal qualifications of both men and women. Finally, Chapter 14, "Virtual Internet of Things Laboratory Using Node-Red" by Kalapatapu V. S. K. R. Shiva Kumar et al., discusses how to implement virtual laboratory sessions for an IoT course. Due to the COVID-19 pandemic, attending the student laboratory session physically is difficult or even impossible. To overcome this problem, a virtual laboratory is implemented.

Based on the studies in this book, it is clear that a company is "digital" not only if it uses technologies but also if it thinks with the mentality of the digital world, in which both the way of creating and proposing its products are different and services is the way of working and collaborating between teams. This perspective shows how digital transformation affects every business activity as well as the economy and society. Thus, this book is intended to be a useful resource for anyone who deals with digital transformation. Furthermore, we hope that this book will provide useful resources ideas, techniques, and methods for future research on these issues. We wish to give special thanks to all the authors who contributed to the success of the project. We are very thankful to the contributing authors for their invaluable research as well as the referees who reviewed the contributions for their effort, time, and invaluable suggestions. Our special thanks to the staff at IntechOpen, especially Author Service Manager Ms. Martina Ivancic, for their support.

Antonella Petrillo and Fabio De Felice
Department of Engineering,
University of Naples "Parthenope",
Naples, Italy

Monica Violeta Achim,
Faculty of Economics and Business Administration,
Department of Finance,
Babes-Bolyai University,
Cluj-Napoca, Romania

Nawazish Mirza,
Excelia Business School,
La Rochelle France

Chapter 1

Mastering Digital Transformation with Service Dominant Architecture

Peter Weiß, Markus Warg and Andreas Zolnowski

Abstract

The paper presents insights from a longitudinal case study of an insurance company. Digital transformation requires companies to review their strategy. Today, information technologies fundamentally transform whole business models, products, and services. Innovations are an opportune strategy for companies to compete in the digital age and to transform their business models, taking a service perspective on their value creation. Service Dominant Architecture (SDA) offers practitioners a framework and environment to design and operate service systems and systems of engagement. Furthermore, it stimulates collaborative theorizing processes by involving decision-makers, managers, and practitioners in general as active participants in the research process (midrange-theory). Our focus is on evolving and applying our framework and IT artifact SDA. SDA provides guidance to practitioners and researchers, respectively, on how to build implementable and operable solution designs in real practice. Our research on SDA is primarily informed and guided by a Design Science Research (DSR) approach.

Keywords: digital transformation, engagement systems, service platform, service dominant architecture, service-dominant logic

1. Introduction

Digitization and digital transformation affect business in many companies. Companies are confronted with fast-changing markets and customer behavior because digital technologies affect the life events of consumers and producers [1]. Most practitioners perceive a gap and disconnect between the design of digital strategies and their execution. We will argue that building systems of engagement is central to key industries and evolve into a crucial role in service innovation. Service Dominant Architecture (SDA) aims to close this gap by translating the requirements of business initiatives into composable technical and business capabilities. SDA is implemented as a platform on top of existing IT infrastructures (systems of record) and offers new capabilities (systems of engagement) summarized as the foundation for strategy execution. SDA constitutes a conceptual framework and solution design, respectively. Management of actor engagement is seen as a key dynamic capability for companies to cope with the challenges of digital transformation. This research aims to expand the knowledge base and theoretical foundations of SDA.

The chapter provides an update on the current state of play of our ongoing research. We present new insights in relation to achievements and developments of previously conducted SDA research; both from a theoretical and practical point of view. We will provide an update of gained insights and will offer an outlook on future research challenges and the road ahead. We motivate the next steps and activities to evolve the SDA. The originality and value of SDA lie on the one hand in its concreteness and applicability and on the other hand in its link to the foundations of Service-Dominant Logic (S-D Logic) and Service Science.

The paper is structured as follows. The first two sections motivate our research and describe the research contribution, approach, and objectives. Then, we review and describe the digital transformation and its challenges highlighting in particular three decision areas. Next step, looks at required investments in new IT infrastructure capabilities building foundations for execution to realize envisioned digital strategies. Next, SDA is presented as a solution design and framework to guide strategy development and implementation of solutions in real practice. Finally, we summarize our research results and draw conclusions.

2. Research contribution, method and objectives

Our research on SDA is primarily informed and guided by a Design Science Research (DSR) approach [2–4]. Therefore, this chapter is organized according to the requirements and properties of a DSR project [4, 5]. Researchers have to understand the problems emerging in real-life projects and practice. Hevner et al. [2] have emphasized a design science approach that underscores a construction-oriented view of information systems (IS) research.

In particular, DSR puts emphasis on the relevance of research results to applications in business [3]. Accordingly, IS research is concerned with the development and use of IT artifacts in organizations [6]. Hence, the design, development, and evaluation of IT artifacts are at the core of the IS discipline [3, 5]. IS research deals with the development and use of information technology-related artifacts in human-machine systems [3]. DSR projects solve real-world problems involving the design of complex information systems. Hence, the IT artifact should be a focal point in most IS research [4]. Intervention activities are vital for building and evaluating effective systems designs in context as well as reflecting and generating design principles [4]. Suitably, presented research contributes to expand the knowledge of information systems design by technical action and making (**Figure 1**).

Conducted DSR projects covered both technical actions but as well generating a broader knowledge base about the phenomenon of digital transformation. In this way, we act in response to the requirements of DSR projects to advance existing knowledge in either a problem or solution domain [4]. Technical action is primarily focused on and determined by conceptualizing our IT artifact based on the purposed subsystems of SDA. Further, we concretize respective solution designs to meet the requirements of the given organizational context and the observable phenomenon of digital transformation [8]. SDA as a framework conceptualizes five distinguished subsystems. SDA solution design was developed and evolved incrementally and iteratively following an engineering (technical action) approach [7]. In addition, we have considered the requirements of Action Design Research (ADR) [6], service systems engineering [9],

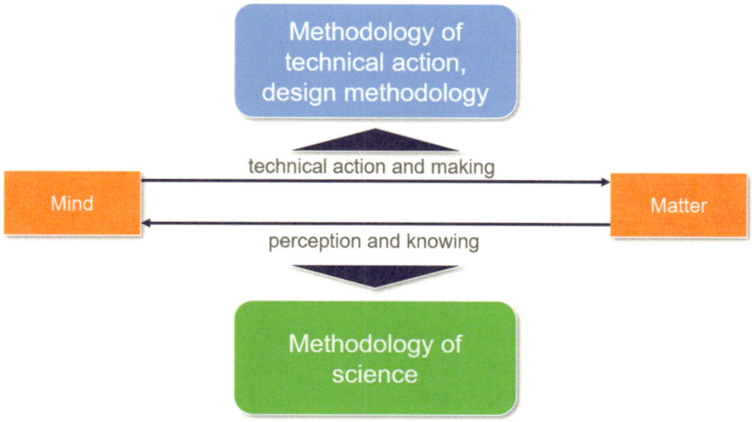

Figure 1.
Research approach and contribution: technical action [7].

and systems development [10, 11]. In order to develop the required understanding and generate knowledge about the state of the problem, we assessed current solutions and their efficacy in a selected organizational context [4].

Applying a longitudinal case study approach [12] allowed us to investigate the problem at hand, as well as to strive for a deeper and more comprehensive understanding of the given organizational context and its properties. This supports our ambition to generalize generated knowledge beyond the targeted application domain, namely the insurance business. We have been able to achieve the long-term commitment of participating organizations. Our case company is an insurance company with round about 12 thousand employees located in Germany.

In subsequent sections, we further concretize and determine the IT artifact's purpose, desired functionality, and its architecture as a base for technical action. Besides producing the novel artifact and instantiating respective processes and tasks, our DSR project aims to make in addition more general contributions to expand the knowledge base. This is achieved through elaborating on a midrange design theory about the phenomena of digital transformation [4].

As shown in **Figure 1** this relates to our evaluation activities which require a framework allowing to derive conclusions about created evidence. Our objective is to make a research contribution through the demonstration of the novel IT artifact. The IT artifact embodies design ideas and principles and theories which we aim to articulate on basis of our SDA framework. Our ambition is to reflect and generate design principles on basis of decisions made realizing the design proposal [4, 7]. Implemented use cases support evaluation activities comparing hypothetical predictions and facts with requirements [7].

We complement the DSR with an embedded single case study [12]. By analyzing different use cases within the longitudinal single case study of SDA and using more than one perspective, we broaden our scope aiming at a better understanding of the relevance of the solution design and long-term evaluation of the IT artifact created. Our research approach thus addresses the following pivotal research questions [13]:

1. How can digital strategies draw from a S-D Logic perspective and related principles to derive and build new capabilities to build unique value propositions based on service innovations?

2. What are respective capabilities to be derived to support business initiatives and strategic agility to design and operate co-creative business models incorporating digital technologies?

3. Digital transformation and insurance business

This section oversees digital transformation and describes the state of the problem. We start with a general description of the phenomenon of digital transformation. In a further step, we look then specifically into digital transformation in the context of the insurance business. We elucidate observable challenges and related problems. On this basis, we explain how we elaborated our solution design and derived relevant objectives for technical action (construction) and evaluation activities. An important step of the DSR process is to communicate the problem and its importance. This will be in the focus of subsequent sections before we describe our practical solution as a result of our DSR project [5].

3.1 Digital transformation: strategy, technology, value creation

Digital transformation can be defined as "[...] a process that aims to improve an entity by triggering significant changes to its properties through combinations of information, computing, communication, and connectivity technologies" [8, 14]. Hence, digital transformation needs to be understood rather as a process than as a state (**Figure 2**) [8].

Digitalization and digital transformation are the "[...] main driver of innovation and change in all sectors of our economy" and are taking place at a rapid pace [14–18]. The effect of digital transformation is discussed to be a revolution that unleashes and develops disruptive powers to change existing structures and systems [8, 15, 19]. Today, we face dramatic change in the business world through rapid digitization and new innovative business models breaking down industry barriers [19, 20]. Digital

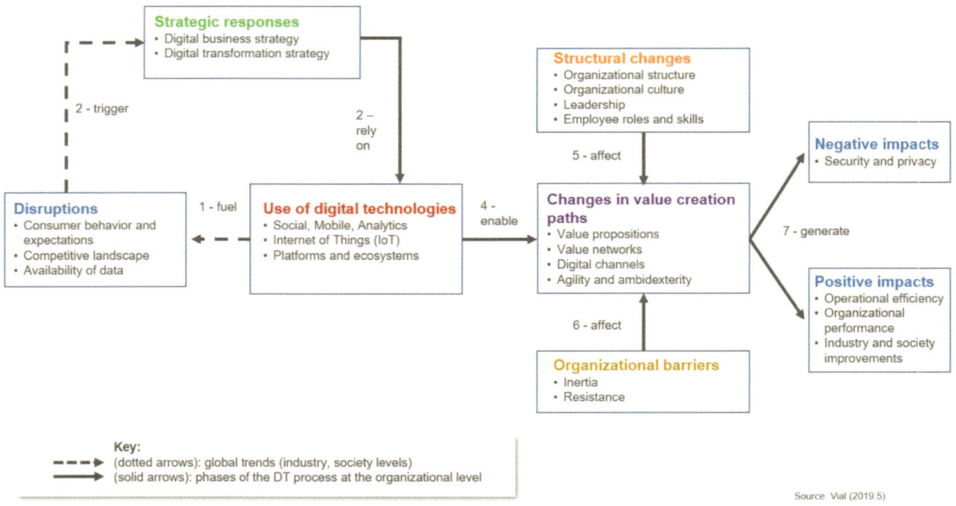

Figure 2.
Building blocks of the digital transformation process (own illustration based on [8]).

technologies are creating new opportunities but require a clear digital strategy [15, 21–23]. Based on a clear digital strategy, decisions concerning required IT investments and new infrastructure capabilities are achievable [1, 18].

Digital transformation is primarily about digital technologies and the conceptualization of their potential impact on a companies' current or future business. It is crucial for business leaders to understand the disruptive forces that digital technologies can unleash changing current business logic and value constellations [16, 17]. Digital disruption is a process, which creates dramatic change for industries or business branches based on the following attributes [19]: (1) rapidly digitizing, (2) breaking down industry barriers, (3) creating new opportunities, and (4) while destroying long-successful business models [1, 8].

In the remainder, we follow the proposed structure and elucidate related challenges in three particular areas shown in **Figure 2**, namely (1) strategy responses through digital strategy, (2) investment and use of digital technologies aligned with business strategy, and (3) changes in value creation activities and paths due to new business logics and changing markets.

3.2 Digital strategies and strategic responses

Digital responses to digital disruption encompass developing a digital business strategy and designing a digital transformation strategy [8]. Digital strategy is a business strategy inspired by the newly created IT infrastructure capabilities enabled by digital technologies (such as SMACIT: Social, Mobile, Analytics, Cloud, Internet of Things). The aim is to deliver unique, integrated business capabilities supporting strategic agility [23]. Hence, they have to be responsive to constantly change market conditions [23]. Thereby, companies seek ways to combine and augment existing capabilities with capabilities enabled by new digital technologies to create new value propositions [23].

Digital technologies remove long-established constraints of value creation activities, namely allowing new unprecedented reconfigurations of resources by applying new business logic such as platform-led strategies [24, 25]. Companies have to find appropriate strategic responses to resulting impacts and have to anticipate proactively future developments to be able to build required new digital capabilities.

Ross et al. [23] see in general two major directions to develop digital strategies, namely (1) customer engagement and (2) digitized solutions. Both directions allow to respond to described challenges [22, 23]. Digital business design relates to decisions oriented toward the support and realization of relevant business initiatives [15, 21]. Based on a vision of how the company will operate, business and IT have to agree and decide on key architectural requirements of the foundation for execution. Foundation for execution can be seen as a synonym for the Enterprise Architecture (EA). Each business initiative needs to highlight how it benefits from or contributes to the foundation for execution. Business initiatives can be either supplier-, customer- or internally oriented [26].

3.3 Digital technologies and new capabilities

Digital technologies constitute a central change driver fueling changes in value creation paths such as value propositions, value constellations or networks, digital channels, agility, and ambidexterity [8]. Digital technologies are linked in general to three types of disruptions: (1) change in customer behavior, preferences, and expectations, (2) new competitive landscape (new value constellations and removed barriers for competitors), and (3) availability of data [8].

Mastering the challenges of digital transformation, companies need to reflect and rethink their strategic positioning and by this their information systems and information technology strategy [23]. Enterprise architecture reflects the awareness that the design of information systems needs to be seen in a broader business and enterprise context. Business and IT need to be co-designed, and well-aligned to create foundations for execution [18, 27]. However, building foundations for execution requires companies to look at organizational design dimensions, which are often overlooked and not adequately considered in architectures that are aligned to the business strategy and the solution design [28]. Thus, digital technologies from our perspective open up new opportunity spaces for companies to interact in new ways with their customers and reach for new customer segments. However, this requires unprecedented levels of customer intimacy and a higher frequency of customer interactions. Digital technologies offer new strategic perspectives for companies to compete through service innovations substantiated in a shift from products to solutions to value-in-use. This translates into new practices of learning [4, p. 86] to arrive at more personalized, customized solutions and offerings, offering new strategic opportunities to operate as platform owner or "smart service provider".

Senior management has to make important decisions concerning infrastructure investments to introduce new strategic and operative capabilities for the company required to sustain in the digital age. Companies need to incorporate digital technologies to build new IT and business capabilities [18, 26] to achieve the required strategic agility and to create unique value propositions [15, 22].

Mastering digital transformation requires a clear understanding of the relationship as well as interdependencies between IT (infrastructure) capabilities of the enterprise and its "ability to implement its business initiatives" [26]. This relationship is addressed by an emerging discipline named EA Management (EAM) [21, 27, 29]. EA as discipline deals with "[...] controlling the complexity of the enterprise and its processes and systems" [29]. Hence, enterprise architecture defines principles, methods, and models resulting from the design of what constitutes the foundation for execution [21]. Weill et al. define strategic agility as "[...] set of business initiatives an enterprise can readily implement" [26]. Enterprise capability encompasses coordinating a respective set of elements such as customer base, brand, core competence, infrastructure, and employees, into an "integrated group of resources" [26].

Companies have to strive for strategic agility through building required IT infrastructure capabilities [18, 26]. However, what are the required IT infrastructure capabilities? Moore [30] motivates a new generation of enterprise IT systems based on interactive IT infrastructure capabilities which he summarizes as "systems of engagement" [13, 30, 31]. In essence, digital transformation requires a dramatic change in enterprise information systems (EIS).

3.4 Changes in value creation logics

Digital transformation is increasingly associated with a service imperative. However, this necessitates to establish respective mindsets and perspectives (**Figure 1**). Related developments are discussed increasingly as "digital servitization" [32–34] by augmenting existing offerings and value propositions with (digital) service elements. In the remainder, we argue a service perspective to overcome the challenges of digital transformation.

In this context, service innovations can be seen as an opportune strategy for companies to compete in the digital age [35]. Companies need to change their prevailing product-dominant mindset to a service-dominant one to develop digital strategies [15, 18, 22, 23]. New technologies introduce new capabilities, such as resource integration, that catalyze service innovations [18, 31]. Executing digital strategies is a major challenge for many companies as they rely on outdated, monolithic EIS. As a result, siloes prevent companies to mobilize and integrate valuable internal and external resources [36].

No doubt, the insurance business is currently undergoing dramatic change and is subject of digital disruptions (originating from new innovative service offerings and new market players ("digital attackers")) [1]. Consequently, insurers have to develop new visions of how to develop new value-adding offerings. This requires deeper customer insights and redesigning operations from the customer perspective. Incumbent insurers lack the required capabilities along with facing significant inertia and as a consequence are thus slow and not agile as their emerging competitors. Thereupon, incumbent insurers have launched new organizational entities freed from slowing and impeding restrictions such as compliance, regulations, and cultural barriers. Those new digital entities move faster, more agile, and adapt easier also more flexible to emerging changes such as customer preferences, behaviors, or new market segments (for example, car sharing, electric bikes, etc.) [37]. In consequence, incumbents have to find the right strategic responses to compete against digital attackers with more appealing, customer-centric, cheaper, more innovative products and services. To adapt and survive such digital Darwinism, insurers have to rediscover and renew their capabilities such as digitizing operations, imagining new customer journey, delighting their customers with excellent service, and reimagine their core systems and structures.

3.4.1 Service-dominant logic

As previously argued, digital technologies offer new opportunities for companies to innovate and to leverage their productivity. Taking a service lens on innovation and related processes is preferable, as it spurs new creative thinking through new mental models and creative business thinking by drawing from new perspectives on value creation activities.

Service-Dominant (S-D) logic [38–40] grounds on a resource-based perspective. It differs from broadly established goods-dominant (G-D) logic thinking through prioritizing "operant resources" (competence, skills, and knowledge) against "operand" resources (physical assets, goods) to achieve competitive advantage. Accordingly, S-D logic puts emphasis on cocreation, actor-to-actor networks, and interactive processes of learning. Service is defined as the application of resources (in particular knowledge, skills, and competencies) to make changes that have value for another [38–42].

Table 1 shows the S-D logic axioms and foundational premises (FP) which formalize related value creation logics and principles [38–41, 43, 44]. The value co-creation takes place in service systems. Service systems are defined as dynamic value-cocreation configuration of resources, including people, organizations, shared information (language, laws, measures, methods), and technology, all connected internally and externally to other service systems by value propositions [9, 45, 46]. Accordingly, a service system is an open system (1) capable of improving the state of another system through sharing or applying its resources, and (2) capable of improving its own state by acquiring external resources [47]. Overall, service systems [45–47] foster a systems

Axiom	Description	Capability
A1/FP1 FP2 FP3 FP4 FP5	Service is the fundamental basis of exchange Indirect exchange masks the fundamental basis of exchange Goods are a distribution mechanism for service provision Operant resources are the fundamental source of competitive advantage All economies are service economies	Service-for-service exchange Operand resources Operant resources Service provision Service economies
A2/FP6 FP7 FP8	Value is co-created by multiple actors, always including the beneficiary The enterprise can only make value propositions A service-centered view is customer-oriented and relational	Value cocreation Interaction Relationship Learning Customer orientation Value propositions
A3/FP9	All social and economic actors are resource integrators	Resource integration Resource orchestration
A4/FP10	Value is always uniquely and phenomenologically determined by the beneficiary	Value-in-use Value-in-context Service experience
A5/FP11	Value co-creation is coordinated through actor-generated institutions and institutional arrangements	Coordination Value cocreation Service Ecosystem Collaboration Actor-to-actor network Institution, institutional arrangements

Table 1.
Service-dominant logic: axioms and foundational premises (FP) [38–41].

perspective for studying and understanding service ecosystems and their influence on service-for-service exchange and emerging digital markets. S-D logic provides guidance through its systemic perspective on value creation activities, through service-exchanging entities and underlying logic. From S-D logic perspective, service innovation is embedded in an actor-to-actor network, which underscores the importance of common organizational structures and sets of principles to facilitate resource integration and service exchange among those actors [35].

As proposed by Lusch and Nambisan [35], service innovation can be conceptualized through a tripartite framework consisting of three major concepts, namely service ecosystem, service platform, and value co-creation. S-D logic showed high relevance for the later development of our framework and respective design patterns. S-D logic serves as the theoretical foundation of Service Science.

Of particular relevance is the concept service platform. Platform concepts create systems or environments to engage with other actors and resources in mutual value creation activities (systems of engagement) [18, 31]. In this context, to identify and know about resources external to the firm and the services they are able to render are of vital importance and constitutes a major incentive to search for new external knowledge.

3.4.2 Building systems of engagement

As previously motivated digital strategies are based on customer engagement and digitalized solutions. Understanding customer engagement or more general actor engagement is a pivotal capability to master successfully digital transformation. Systems of Engagement (SoE) relate to service platforms and digital platforms, respectively. Hereinafter, we summarize briefly relevant contents and refer to previous publications for further details and studies [1, 18, 31, 48–51]. SoE is seen as the next stage of enterprise IT which bring companies new communication and collaboration capabilities to engage with their customers and suppliers, and vice versa, with a focus on communication to enable collaborative business in real-time with all the benefits of mobility and speed [18, 30, 48, 50]. In summary, SoE brings companies new communication and collaboration capabilities. SoE brings S-D logic to the fore as this type of systems will foster interactions and relationships with communities and in more general resources that are outside the enterprise. Actor engagement [31, 48, 50–52] can be conceptualized as microfoundation for value cocreation within service ecosystems [9, 53]. Engagement platforms are an interesting field of research as the concept is not yet clearly defined. Engagement platforms are defined as multisided intermediaries that actors leverage to engage with other actors to integrate resources. Engagement platforms can be both intermediary or mediator. Hence, resource integration [54] turns into a core business capability to run what Moore [30] phrases as social business systems [48]. **Table 1** shows a list of elicited capabilities that need to be addressed by systems of engagement.

4. Digital transformation and insurance business

Trends such as connected cars, automated driving, smart home, connected healthcare are just a few examples representing change and new requirements for the insurance business. Incumbent companies possess customer insights and can rely on strong relational ties to their customers and business partners. However, this advantage is lost increasingly to new players entering their markets and targeting for their profitable customer segments. Those companies are named "digital attackers" [55]. Digital technologies are lowering the barriers for digital attackers to enter those markets to exploit new opportunities by using their digital capabilities and related key competencies as an advantage. Digital attackers are faster, more focused on customers, and responsive to their particular needs. Insurers risk to lose prosperous customer segments—foremost the younger generation—to new emerging competitors such as insurtechs [49, 50].

4.1 Building foundations for execution

Digital strategy outlines and details besides the business aspects the respective steps forward and targeted investments in IT infrastructure capabilities [18, 21, 26]. Ross et al. identify five building blocks for a digital transformation: (1) operational backbone, (2) digital platform, (3) external developer platform, (4) shared customer insights, (5) accountability framework [15]. "The advantage of approaching digital business design as a set of building blocks is that it allows leaders to focus on specific manageable organizational changes while implementing holistic design" [15]. Bonnet and Westerman propose and describe new elements as the foundation of new digital capabilities [14]. The new elements are grouped into five areas: (1) business model-related capabilities, (2) customer experience, (3) operations, (4) employee experience, and (5) digital platform.

Building a digital platform is fundamental for mastering the challenges of digital transformation [14, 56]. Digital platform contains three components: (1) core platform (operational and transactional systems), (2) externally facing platform, and (3) data platform [14]. The core platform is the company's technology backbone [14]. Detailed requirements of platform-related capabilities are discussed and analyzed in Weiß et al. [18] and are here not further detailed [18, 56, 57]. Secondly, the externally facing platform realizes customer-facing experiments and enables personalized experiences [14]. Finally, the third component, data platform, offers enhanced data analytics capabilities, build and test algorithms, and enables processing of huge amounts of unstructured data [14].

4.2 Service dominant architecture

In this section, we summarize and refer to previous research results and updates documenting the evolution of the IT artifact [13, 18, 31, 36, 58].

SDA was derived from the knowledge base of the domain theories Service Science, S-D Logic, and Institutional Economics with the aim of putting the findings, logic, and processes into practice by enabling actors in the process of value co-creation. Used in practice SDA enables entities to purposeful build up capabilities and to engage in the process of service exchange and value co-creation [55, 58, 59]. SDA can be viewed from a conceptual and an applied perspective:

(1) firstly, SDA a design pattern or virtual order in the understanding of a structure of five systems [58]. (2) secondly, SDA a tangible structure instantiated by at least one entity [60].

The instantiated structure consists of five systems including the recently added SDA service catalog as the fifth system focusing on shared institutional arrangements. SDA applied within an actor-to-actor network facilitates the process and coordination of service exchange and mutual value creation [38, 58]. SDA as architecture operationalizes the core elements of S-D logic by focusing on co-creation and resource integration. The aim of this development is to facilitate the before-motivated SoE [30] by introducing an additional architectural layer. SDA proposes to operationalize requirements and characteristics for the planning, designing, and building of customer-centric solutions, which are characterized by value in use.

4.2.1 SDA conceptual framework

In order to meet these requirements, the SDA conceptual framework defines the design patterns of four purposed subsystems and a Data Lake (**Figure 3**). In the following, respective design patterns are introduced.

1. *System of operant resources:* The system of operant resources is the heart of the SDA framework. It represents the workbench, where the various ingredients (resources) are brought together and processed. For this, this system applies certain logic or processes. An important target of this system is to achieve the required resource density. Solutions are dependent on the achievable level of resource density as a high level of resource density impacts positively the emergence and creation of innovative and valuable solutions [58].

2. *System of interaction:* The system of interaction, enables a bidirectional data flow between the provider and the customer. The aim is to achieve consistent customer-centricity across all customer channels in parallel, also known as omnichannel

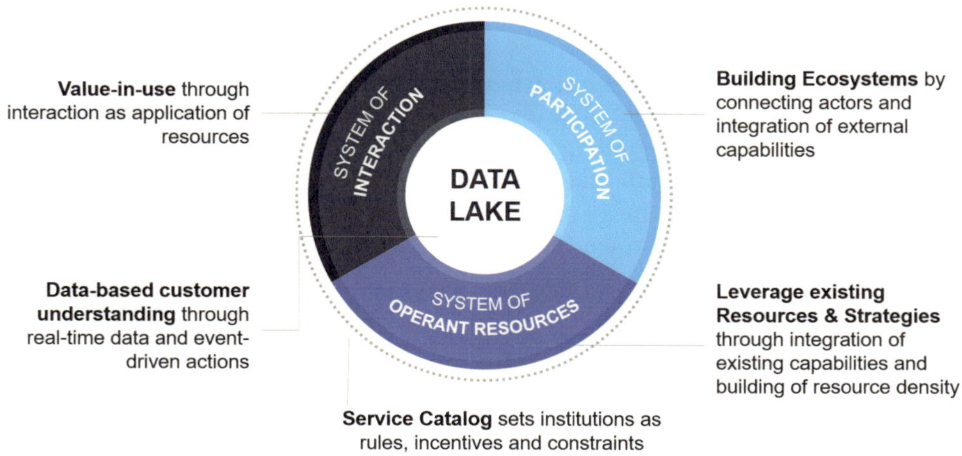

Figure 3.
Design pattern as architectural framework of service dominant architecture (SDA) (source: IfSD.Hamburg).

integration. In such an omnichannel integration layer is created, prerequisite for an interactive, uniform customer experience across all communication channels relevant to the customer.

3. *System of participation:* Ideally, the already presented concept of co-creation includes other co-producers in addition to the respective customer or more general actor. The system of participation enables actor-to-actor orientation and resource integration of third parties, i.e. other external resources.

4. *Data lake:* From a company's point of view, data received and generated by interacting with customers or in the value creation process should be systematically recorded and evaluated in real-time [58].

5. *System of institutional arrangements (service catalog):* As rules in use, institutions enable the coordination of actors as well as access to and use of resources. In conjunction with SDA design pattern, institutions enable the coordinated creation of solution designs by connecting actors and enabling the integration and application of resources [58].

4.2.2 SDA objectives and capabilities

In essence, SDA is the technical implementation of S-D logic (**Table 1**) and one of the most important elements for strategy execution to create valuable service experiences, called value in use. By combining a set of purposed subsystems, SDA provides a technical environment that combines external resources from customers and partners, for example, user data or market data, with internal resources, for example, customer relationship management data, or services.

Therefore, SDA links business architecture and IT architecture and achieves a shared understanding of EA and strategic priorities. Objectives of SDA design are reflecting business needs on technical side, including customer and service focus, collaboration, complexity containment, and agility [58].

5. Use case design, implementation and evaluation

The use cases of the first generation have been rather simple, but are essential to initiate learning processes and building required capabilities. **Table 2** displays the next generation of more demanding and advanced use cases. Each use case implements a set of respective capabilities operationalized by SDA. Selected use cases stem from the insurance business, namely an insurance company, which will be our application domain for experimenting and evaluating our developed IT artifact and solution design.

No.	Use case/service	Description	SDA capabilities/ S-D logic principles
1	Edith care	• Personal care assistant • Support for administrative activities • Application process: five minutes instead of six days	• Value cocreation • Resource integration • Resource density • Resource orchestration • Institutional arrangement/ rules in use
2	Claim notification	• Support services for managing claim requests and processes (focus on scalability requirements in case of natural catastrophe) • Integration of external services (e.g., Service/call centers, and AI-based services and partner (fraud management)	• Service ecosystem • Resource integration • Co-creation • Resource density
3	Stroke prevention (ai4medicine)	• Customer receives individual risk scoring and personalized recommendations and an action list • Personal health advisor app	• Value cocreation • Institutional arrangement/ rules in use • Resource integration • Resource density • Resource orchestration
4	Medicproof	• Assistance and information services for customers to manage medicamental treatments and drugs	• Co-creation • Resource integration • Service ecosystem
5	Cross carrier pension information	• Collected and aggregated data about customer status and forecast of pension request • Consolidation of data from various pension fonds based on historical data (career steps/status)	• Resource integration • Service ecosystem • Institutional arrangement/ rules in use • Value cocreation
6	Universally submission service	• Uploading and handing electronically documents and material by means of customer app • Supported by AI and chatbots.	• Value cocreation • Resource integration • Institutional arrangement/ rules in use

Table 2.
Evaluation: overview use cases (partly based on [13, 18, 58, 61].

5.1 Development and implementation

Before technical action is taken and concrete solutions are developed, DSR process foresees to determine desired functionality and architecture of actual solutions. S-D logic forms our core theory and allows us to derive objectives to design and develop the IT artifact [5]. Presented IT artifact aims to solve identified problems in the given organizational context. S-D Logic is used to identify new capabilities that are later operationalized through the IT artifact [4]. As previously stated, digital transformation necessitates to build new IT infrastructure capabilities to seize opportunities by launching business initiatives and to implement the company's digital business strategy [21, 26]. In this context, as already argued before business-IT alignment [62] plays a pivotal role to implement the foundation for execution. Nunamaker et al. [10] argue that systems development is one of the valid research methodologies and provides "proof-by-demonstration" [10]. Against this background, three stages of "last mile research" are eminent: (1) proof-of-concept, (2) proof-of-value, and (3) proof-of-use [11]. Researchers have to decide on the right balance of scientific rigor (formulation of design theories) and practical relevance (useful artifacts) [4, 11]. Nunamaker et al. [10] propose a multimethodological approach to IS research. Furthermore, we respond to corresponding research challenges as motivated by Böhmann et al. [9], foremost exploration of new and unknown service systems as well as call for "participatory design" and innovative "prototyping approaches".

5.2 Use case development

Table 2 overlooks selected use cases showing relevance as elaborated jointly with the case company. Shown use cases are used to evaluate produced IT artifacts in the given organizational context. Our aim is to strive for proof as motivated in the paragraph before. Continuous practitioner feedback and interaction with related organizational context is vital to adjust and find the right configuration of resources and people for aspired service systems.

Evaluation is considered a crucial task and will be conducted continuously. The evaluation depends on implementing exemplified use cases and derivable requirements by means of IT solutions based on SDA experimental prototypes. In this way, we will be able to launch appropriate experiments to strive for the required "proof of concept". Furthermore, our goal is to receive further feedback and data for next development iterations. Currently, SDA is evaluating various solution designs, various technologies, and SDA prototypes incrementally. At this stage of development, activities focus primarily on implementing SDA stable core. Purposed subsystems as described will be continuously expanded and further concretized through adding additional features and functionality. Various architectural paradigms have been tested and validated. As result, we foresee to launch further real-life experiments evaluating SDA in the context of available use cases, which stem from the digital transformation endeavors of our case company.

5.3 Example: use case stroke prevention

The following example is based on [58, 61]. SDA is reflected as a construction plan for microservices in respective technical stacks (as bundles of microservices). As motivated, SDA serves as medium, structure, and output for actor engagement.

SDA is implementable on various technology platforms. SDA instantiates processes of value co-creation in the given organizational context.

5.3.1 Implementing use cases: experimental designs

SDA provides ground for real-life experiments. SDA and related subsystems were implemented as experimental designs and prototypes (technical action). In this way, we aim to evaluate on basis of data and processes obtained from respective use cases. SDA informs about both required investments and how to build required new IT infrastructure capabilities. From a management perspective, SDA serves as a communication tool clarifying strategic directions. In addition, solution design has to meet required levels of agility enabling response to environmental changes. The central aim is to build a foundation for execution comprising an operational model, enterprise architecture/IS architecture, and related IT artifacts. Furthermore, this encompasses decisions concerning targeted investments to achieve required IT infrastructure capabilities. SDA provides guidance for the construction and planning of microservices in technical stacks (bundles of microservices). Current market competition enforces faster and more convenient development of solutions, strictly oriented toward customer requirements and embracing collaboration of business and IT within organizations [63]. Microservices and related technical concepts are not further detailed, we refer to previous publications and scientific literature [18, 63–65]. Microservices as a technical concept are associated with new development paradigms such as DevOps and agile development practices (such as SCRUM). Those new emerging paradigms allow us to build real-life solutions with a strong relation between business and information systems. This realizes required Business IT alignment and builds applications around business capabilities and use cases [63]. We provided a more detailed overview of the underlying conceptual base in Weiß et al. [18].

5.3.2 Institutional design and implementation: service catalog

Service Catalog is a new added system and element of SDA. Zolnowski and Frey [61] analyze requirements and develop relevant use cases such as ai4medicine comprising personal health advice service for stroke prevention in Germany (**Figure 4**).

The business model of ai4medicine is based on using an app to comprehensively assist customers in reducing potential stroke risk. Based on risk assessment, customers receive appropriate recommendations for behavioral changes contributing to reducing the risk of stroke. Solution develops recommendations based on customers' shared data aiming at adequate changes in customer behavior to prevent stroke. Service ai4medicine combines clinical and epidemiological data on stroke and generates domain knowledge to develop and train artificial intelligence models. Designed AI models and algorithms enable innovative, personalized value propositions and facilitate evidence-based, AI-powered stroke prevention guiding principles and strategies. Once customers have installed the respective mobile app on their devices, they can register and start using ai4 medicine application functionality. In addition, this application supports continuous consolidation of customers' historical health data accessible from partners' platforms (for example liaised insurance companies) and improves in this way continuously data quality and hence individual stroke prevention. Partner companies can seamlessly integrate ai4medicine into the application landscape, for example by offering additional functionality on run mobile apps.

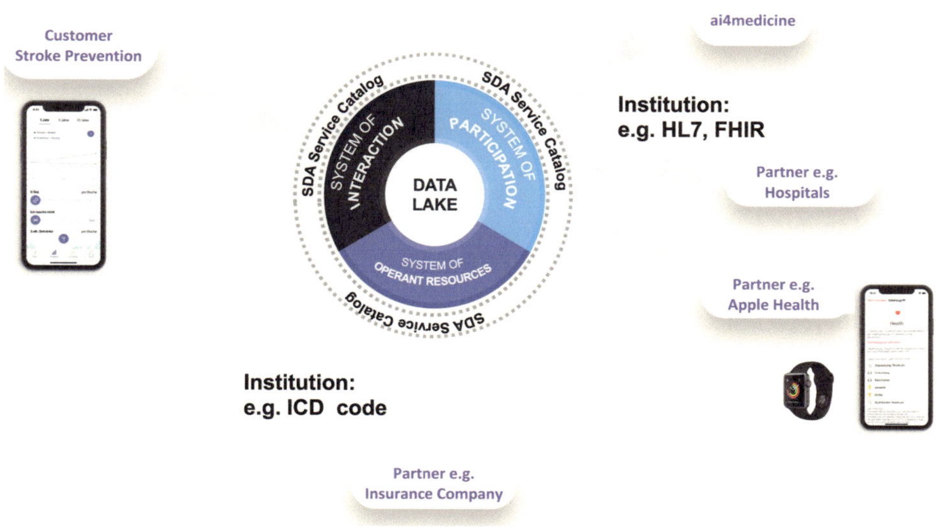

Figure 4.
Evaluation SDA: use case stroke prevention [58].

Furthermore, additional health data is supported to augment respective personal health data set, for example, data accessible from connected smart devices such as wearables, given appropriate interfaces and data interoperability. This reduces significantly additional efforts and pains related to manually entering data and keeping data updated [61].

6. Discussion

Design and execution of digital strategies [15, 21–23] are of utmost importance. New capabilities need to be built around emerging digital technologies and trends such as hybrid cloud, intelligent process automation, and artificial intelligence, in particular machine learning. Hence, building a robust digital platform turns into a core competence to be able to compete against digital attackers [37]. In response, companies alter their existing business models by incorporating digital technologies to arrive at new value propositions and new resource configurations [24, 32]. S-D logic [38–41, 66] offers valuable concepts and guidance on how to overcome the challenges of digital transformation. Executing and implementing digital strategies makes many incumbent companies struggle [23]. In the past, striving for higher efficiency and optimization for the foundation for execution has created a significant strategic advantage for incumbent companies against their competitors. In this way, those companies created an operational backbone based on a "[...] set of standardized, integrated systems, processes and data support a company's core operations" [15]. This constituted the main source of strategic advantage because smaller businesses or startups have not been able to rely on comparable resources and system performance, computing power as well as related IT infrastructure capabilities. However, nowadays, these historically grown and highly optimized systems are causing observable complexity in enterprise systems and are a reason for inertia to transform and react to rapidly changing market requirements and customer demands [15, 21, 67]. Investments in IT infrastructure capabilities should be driven by initiatives and business value. Strategic agility expresses the ability of a company to readily implement respective business initiatives. The more time and effort required to implement them indicates the existence of inconsistencies and reveals inappropriate alignment between business demand and previous investments in IT infrastructure capabilities. Hence, company's need to decide on the required capabilities to get future-ready [19, 20, 26] by investing in their foundation for execution [21]. Identified initiatives and measures are aggregated into a strategic roadmap. Initiatives are orchestrated through a high-level architectural vision shared and agreed upon by business and IT. In absence of an architectural vision explicated as EA, the company runs at risk to make isolated and siloed investments in its IT infrastructure, systems, and applications leading to "technical debt" [15, 68]. Technical debt is caused by previous pragmatic solutions or uncoordinated investments in IT infrastructure capabilities (often visible as "shadow IT"). Often new business initiatives had created demands which were solved through individual "rewiring" of system connections and creating uncoordinated on-demand interfaces to integrate systems. Consequently, the company's strategy development needs to clarify new capabilities required to compete in future digital markets, to exploit new opportunities and to nurture new customer segments.

7. Summary and conclusion

Digital transformation brings new requirements and challenges for companies to respond to market opportunities and take advantage of new digital technologies. We argued that the majority of companies aiming to address digital transformation, face challenges in developing appropriate digital strategies and struggle to shift from traditional goods-based to service-based focus [31].

Applying a DSR approach, SDA contains prescriptions for design and action in the form of a new design artifact, and in this way intends to formalize and generalize knowledge for the targeted problem and solution domain. Consequently, conducted research started with the developing of a novel artifact (namely SDA) in the given organizational context. We operationalized Service-Dominant Logic (S-D Logic) serving as descriptive or kernel theory that informs artifact construction [3]. Whereas S-D Logic is rather to be seen as a grand theory, SDA can serve as middle-range theory to overcome the perceived gap or disconnect between theory and practice [6]. However, this requires to fulfill respective requirements [3].

Following a DSR approach presented research aims to make clear contributions to real-world application environments [3]. Focus is set on technical action in the sense of an inside-out approach to stimulate and implement change [7]. In addition, we generate knowledge (outside-in) by studying the state of problem and current solutions and their efficacy. Our central aim was to create the artifactual solution in order to use it to solve identified problems not hitherto addressed [5]. Accordingly, we determined the artifacts desired functionality and its architecture. We created the actual artifact by applying S-D Logic and conceptualized offered concepts to move from objectives to solution design. Finally, we demonstrate and use the created IT artifact in a given organizational context [5]. DSR and ADR define concrete requirements and offer methodology for how this can be achieved. One particular effort can be seen in generalizing achieved outcomes and produced results. Our research objective is hence to further strengthen the theoretical foundations of SDA to transport design knowledge and guide digital strategy development as well investment decisions [3]. The IT artifact is a subject of continuous improvement and is being evolved primarily in its organizational context. In this way, we stimulate learning processes, create new knowledge and gain new insights studying the phenomenon of digital transformation.

Author details

Peter Weiß[1]*, Markus Warg[2] and Andreas Zolnowski[3]

1 Pforzheim University, Pforzheim, Germany

2 Institute for Service Design (IfSD), Hamburg, Germany

3 Signal Iduna, Hamburg, Germany

*Address all correspondence to: peter.weiss@hs-pforzheim.de

References

[1] Warg M, Weiß P, Zolnowski A, Engel R. Service dominant architecture based on S-D logic for mastering digital transformation: The case of an insurance company. In: Proceedings 26th Annual RESER Conference. Naples, Italy: RESER, University of Naples "Federico II; 2016. pp. 807-826

[2] Hevner AR, March ST, Park J, Ram S. Design science in information systems research. MIS Quarterly. 2004;**28**:75-105

[3] Gregor S, Hevner AR. Positioning and presenting design science research for maximum impact. MISQ. 2013;**37**:337-355

[4] Baskerville R, Baiyere A, Gergor S, Hevner A, Rossi M. Design science research contributions: Finding a balance between artifact and theory. JAIS. 2018;**19**:358-376. DOI: 10.17705/1jais.00495

[5] Peffers K, Tuunanen T, Rothenberger MA, Chatterjee S. A design science research methodology for information systems research. Journal of Management Information Systems. 2007;**24**:45-77. DOI: 10.2753/MIS0742-1222240302

[6] Sein MK, Henfridsson O, Purao S, Rossi M, Lindgren R. Action design research. MIS Quarterly. 2011;**35**:37-56

[7] Eekels J, Roozenburg N. A methodological comparison of the structures of scientific research and engineering design: Their similarities and differences. Design Studies. 1991;**12**:197-203. DOI: 10.1016/0142-694X(91)90031-Q

[8] Vial G. Understanding digital transformation: A review and a research agenda. The Journal of Strategic Information Systems. 2019;**28**:118-144. DOI: 10.1016/j.jsis.2019.01.003

[9] Böhmann T, Leimeister JM, Möslein K. Service systems engineering. Business and Information Systems Engineering. 2014;**6**:73-79. DOI: 10.1007/s12599-014-0314-8

[10] Nunamaker JF, Chen M, Purdin TD. Systems development in information systems research. Journal of Management Information Systems. 1990;**7**:89-106. DOI: 10.1080/07421222.1990.11517898

[11] Nunamaker JF, Briggs RO, Derrick DC, Schwabe G. The last research mile: Achieving both rigor and relevance in information systems research. Journal of Management Information Systems. 2015;**32**:10-47. DOI: 10.1080/07421222.2015.1094961

[12] Yin RK. Case study research: Design and methods. 5th ed. SAGE: Los Angeles, London, New Delhi, Singapore, Washington, DC; 2014

[13] Weiß P, Zolnowski A, Warg M. Service dominant architecture to master digital transformation: Case of an insurance company. In: Proceedings 15th International Research Symposium on Service Excellence in Management (QUIS 2015). Porto, Portugal: QUIS, School of Engineering of University of Porto (FEUP); 2017. pp. 638-643

[14] Bonnet D, Westerman G. The New Elements of Digital Transformation: The authors revisit their landmark research and address how the competitive advantages offered by digital technology have evolved. MIT Sloan Management Review. Cambridge, MA, USA: The MIT Press; 2020

[15] Ross JW, Beath CM, Mocker M. Designed for digital: How to architect your business for sustained success. Cambridge Massachusetts, London England: The MIT Press; 2019

[16] Kane GC, Palmer D, Phillips AN, Kiron D, Buckley N. Achieving digital maturity: Adapting your company to a changing world. MIT Sloan Management Review / Deloitte University Press. Cambridge, MA, USA: The MIT Press; 2017

[17] Kane GC, Palmer D, Phillips AN, Kiron D, Buckley N. Strategy, Not Technology, Drives Digital Transformation: Becoming a digitally mature enterprise. MIT Sloan Management Review and Deloitte University Press. Cambridge, MA, USA: The MIT Press; 2015

[18] Weiß P, Zolnowski A, Warg M, Schuster T. Service dominant architecture: Conceptualizing the foundation for execution of digital strategies based on S-D logic. In: Proceedings of the 51st Hawaii International Conference on System Sciences. Hilton Waikoloa Village, Kona, Hawaii, USA: HICSS-51 AIS (Association for Information Systems), AIS Electronic Library (AISeL); 2018. pp. 1630-1639. DOI: 10.24251/HICSS.2018.204

[19] Weill P, Woerner SL. Thriving in an Increasingly digital ecosystem. MIT Sloan Management Review. Cambridge, MA, USA: The MIT Press; 2015;**56**:26-35

[20] Weill P, Woerner SL. Is your company ready for a digital future? MIT Sloan Management Review. Cambridge, MA, USA: The MIT Press; 2018;**59**:20-26

[21] Ross JW, Weill P, Robertson D. Enterprise Architecture As Strategy: Creating a Foundation for Business Execution. Boston: Harvard Business Review Press; 2006

[22] Ross JW, Sebastian IM, Beath CM. How to Develop a Great Digital Strategy. MIT Sloan Management Review. 2017

[23] Ross JW, Sebastian I, Beath C, Mocker M, Moloney K, Fonstad N. Designing and Executing Digital Strategies. In: Thirty Seventh International Conference on Information Systems, Dublin, AIS Electronic Library (AISeL); 2016. pp. 1-17

[24] Normann R. Reframing Business: When the Map Changes the Landscape. Chichester: Wiley; 2001

[25] Chesbrough HW. Open Services Innovation: Rethinking Your Business to Grow and Compete in a New Era. 1st ed. San Francisco, CA, USA: Jossey-Bass; 2011

[26] Weill P, Subramani M, Broadbent M. Building IT Infrastructure for Strategic Agility. MIT Sloan Management Review. 2002;**44**:57-66

[27] Proper H, Lankhorst MM. Enterprise Architecture—Towards Essential Sensemaking. Enterprise Modelling and Information Systems Architectures (EMISAJ) – International Journal of Conceptual Modeling. Bonn, Germany: German Informatics Society (GI); 2014;**9**(1):5-21. DOI: 10.18417/emisa.9.1.1. ISSN: 1866-3621

[28] Warg M, Zolnowski A, Frosch M, Weiß P. From product organization to platform organization: Observations of organizational development in the insurance industry. In: Proceedings of The 10 years Naples Forum on Service. Ischia, Italy; 2019

[29] Lankhorst M. Enterprise Architecture at Work: Modelling, Communication and Analysis. 4th ed. Berlin, Heidelberg: Springer; 2017. Available from:

https://link.springer.com/book/10.1007/978-3-662-53933-0#about

[30] Moore G. Systems of Engagement and The Future of Enterprise IT: A Sea Change in Enterprise IT. Silver Spring, MD, USA: Whitepaper; AIIM International; 2011. Available from: https://info.aiim.org/systems-of-engagement-and-the-future-of-enterprise-it [last visit 21.02.2022]

[31] Weiß P, Warg M, Zolnowski A. Building systems of engagement to overcome the challenges of digital transformation. In: Gummesson E, Mele C, Polese F, editors. Service Dominant Logic, Network and Systems Theory and Service Science: Integrating three Perspectives for a New Service Agenda. Proceedings of The 10 years Naples Forum on Service. Ischia, Italy: SIMAS di Salerno for Naples Forum on Service; 2019. ISBN: 978-88-31622-19-6. Available from: http://www.naplesforumonservice.it/public/index.php?node=258

[32] Kohtamäki M, Parida V, Oghazi P, Gebauer H, Baines T. Digital servitization business models in ecosystems: A theory of the firm. Journal of Business Research. 2019;**104**:380-392. DOI: 10.1016/j.jbusres.2019.06.027

[33] Tronvoll B, Sklyar A, Sörhammar D, Kowalkowski C. Transformational shifts through digital servitization. Industrial Marketing Management. 2020;**89**:293-305. DOI: 10.1016/j.indmarman.2020.02.005

[34] Gebauer H, Paiola M, Saccani N, Rapaccini M. Digital servitization: Crossing the perspectives of digitization and servitization. Industrial Marketing Management. 2021;**93**:382-388. DOI: 10.1016/j.indmarman.2020.05.011

[35] Lusch RF, Nambisan S. Service innovation: A service-dominant logic perspective. MISQ. 2015;**39**:155-175. DOI: 10.25300/MISQ/2015/39.1.07

[36] Zolnowski A, Warg M. Conceptualizing resource orchestration—The role of service platforms in facilitating service systems. In: Bui T, editor. Hawaii International Conference on System Sciences: Hawaii International Conference on System Sciences. Hilton Waikoloa Village, Kona, Hawaii, USA: HICSS-51 AIS (Association for Information Systems), AIS Electronic Library (AISeL); 2018. DOI: 10.24251/HICSS.2018.131

[37] IBM. 3 steps to reprogram Insurance Companies become future ready. 2021. Available from: https://www.ibm.com/blogs/digital-transformation/in-en/blog/3-steps-to-reprogram-insurance-companies-become-future-ready/. [Accessed: January 14, 2022]

[38] Vargo SL, Lusch RF. Evolving to a new dominant logic for marketing. Journal of Marketing. 2004;**68**:1-17. DOI: 10.1509/jmkg.68.1.1.24036

[39] Lusch RF, Vargo SL. Service-Dominant Logic: Premises, Perspectives, Possibilities. Cambridge: Cambridge University Press; 2014

[40] Maglio PP, Spohrer J. Toward a science of service systems. In: Handbook of Service Science. Boston, MA: Springer; 2010. pp. 157-194. DOI: 10.1007/978-1-4419-1628-0_9

[41] Vargo SL, Lusch RF. Service-dominant logic: Continuing the evolution. Journal of the Academy of Marketing Science. 2008;**36**:1-10. DOI: 10.1007/s11747-007-0069-6

[42] Michel S, Vargo SL, Lusch RF. Reconfiguration of the conceptual landscape: A tribute to the service logic of Richard Normann. Journal of the Academy of Marketing Science.

2008;**36**:152-155. DOI: 10.1007/s11747-007-0067-8

[43] Spohrer J, Maglio PP, Bailey J, Gruhl D. Steps toward a science of service systems. Computer. 2007;**40**:71-77. DOI: 10.1109/mc.2007.33

[44] Maglio PP, Spohrer J. Fundamentals of service science. Journal of the Academy of Marketing Science. 2008;**36**:18-20. DOI: 10.1007/s11747-007-0058-9

[45] Weiß P. Microfoundations for building systems of engagement: Enable actor engagement using service dominant architecture. In: Spohrer J, Leitner C, editors. Advances in the Human Side of Service Engineering. Cham: Springer International Publishing; 2020. pp. 116-122. DOI: 10.1007/978-3-030-51057-2_17

[46] Rittweger R, Kronibus A, Weiß P. Value co-creation as the core of service innovation: Impacts of a case study of a fully digitized health: Insurance company service dominant architecture. In: Spohrer J, Leitner C, editors. Advances in the Human Side of Service Engineering. Cham: Springer International Publishing; 2020. pp. 86-92

[47] Weiß P, Kronibus A, Riedel F, Rittweger R. Digital service innovation and actor engagement: A multilevel design perspective—Impacts from a case study of an insurtech. In: Leitner C, Ganz W, Satterfield D, Bassano C, editors. 1st ed. Cham: Springer International Publishing; 2021. pp. 273-279

[48] Bächtold N. Microfoundations of Value Cocdreation: Using a Multilevel Design Approach to Building Systems of Engagement by Utilizing Service Dominant Architecture [Masterthesis]. Ljubljana, Slowenia: University of Ljubljana; 2021

[49] Payne AF, Storbacka K, Frow P. Managing the co-creation of value. Journal of the Academy of Marketing Science. 2008;**36**:83-96. DOI: 10.1007/s11747-007-0070-0

[50] Grotherr C, Semmann M, Böhmann T. Using microfoundations of value co-creation to guide service systems design: A multilevel design framework. In: Proceedings of Thirty ninth International Conference on Information Systems. San Francisco, USA: AIS (Association for Information Systems); 2018. ICIS2018 Proceedings 978-0-9966831-7-3

[51] Peters LD, Löbler H, Brodie RJ, Breidbach CF, Hollebeek LD, Smith SD, et al. Theorizing about resource integration through service-dominant logic. Marketing Theory. 2014;**14**:249-268. DOI: 10.1177/1470593114534341

[52] Warg M, Engel R. Service-Dominierte Architektur (SDA): Kernkomponente digitaler Transformation. In: Zeitschrift für Versicherungswesen. Hamburg: Allgemeiner Fachverlag Dr. Rolf Mathern GmbH. pp. 391-395

[53] Hein A, Schreieck M, Riasanow T, Setzke DS, Wiesche M, Böhm M, et al. Digital platform ecosystems. Electron Markets. 2020;**30**:87-98. DOI: 10.1007/s12525-019-00377-4

[54] Parker GG, van Alstyne MW, Choudary SP. Platform Revolution: How Networked Markets Are Transforming the Economy and How to Make Them Work for You. New York: W. W. Norton & Company; 2016

[55] Warg M, Hans S. How to overcome organizational inertia by shaping institutions and value propositions: An analysis of the impact of

service-catalogs. In: Bienzeisler B, Peters K, Schletz A, editors. 31st RESER Conference, Fraunhofer IAO, Heilbronn. In: The Disruptive Role of Data, AI and Ecosystems in Services, Conference Proceedings of 31th RESER Conference. Heilbronn, Germany: RESER (European Association for Research on Services); 2021. pp. 61-79

[56] Warg M, Weiß P, Engel R. Whitepaper: Service Dominierte Architektur (SDA): Die digitale Transformation erfolgreich meistern. Wedel, Germany: University of Applied Sciences Wedel (Fachhochschule Wedel); 2015

[57] Giddens A. The constitution of society: Outline of the theory of structuration. 1st ed. Berkeley: Univ. of California Press; 1984

[58] Zolnowski A, Frey D. Analyzing the role of artificial intelligence in the development of human-centered service. In: Spohrer J, Leitner C, editors. Advances in the Human Side of Service Engineering. Cham: Springer International Publishing; 2020. pp. 123-130. DOI: 10.1007/978-3-030-51057-2_18

[59] Henderson JC, Venkatraman H. Strategic alignment: Leveraging information technology for transforming organizations. IBM Systems Journal. 1993;**32**:472-484. DOI: 10.1147/sj.382.0472

[60] Evans E. Domain-driven design: Tackling complexity in the heart of software. Upper Saddle River, NJ: Addison-Wesley; 2011

[61] Newman S. Monolith to Microservices: Evolutionary Patterns to Transform Your Monolith. Newton, MA: O'Reilly Media, Inc; 2019

[62] Burden A, van der Ouderaa E, Venkataraman R, Nyström T, Shukla PP. Technical debt might be hindering your digital transformation. MIT Sloan Management Review. Cambridge, MA, USA: The MIT Press; 2018;**60**:1-7

[63] Fritzsch J, Bogner J, Zimmermann A, Wagner S. From monolith to microservices: A classification of refactoring approaches. In: International Workshop on Software Engineering Aspects of Continuous Development and New Paradigms of Software Production and Deployment. Cham: Springer; 2018. pp. 128-141. DOI: 10.1007/978-3-030-06019-0_10

[64] Vargo SL, Lusch RF. The SAGE Handbook of Service-Dominant Logic. 1st ed. London: SAGE Publications; 2018

[65] Akaka MA, Vargo SL. Technology as an operant resource in service (eco)systems. Information Systems and e-Business Management. Berlin, Heidelberg: Springer-Verlag; 2014;**12**:367-384. DOI: 10.1007/s10257-013-0220-5. ISSN: 1617-9846

[66] Vargo SL, Lusch RF. Institutions and axioms: An extension and update of service-dominant logic. Journal of the Academy of Marketing Science. 2016;**44**:5-23. DOI: 10.1007/s11747-015-0456-3

[67] Vargo SL, Lusch RF. Inversions of service-dominant logic. Marketing Theory. 2014;**14**:239-248. DOI: 10.1177/1470593114534339

[68] Taneja H, Maney K. The End of Scale. MIT Sloan Management Review. 2018;**59**:66-73

Chapter 2

Utilization of Fintech Applications during the Covid-19 Pandemic

Özlem Olgu Akdeniz

Abstract

At the beginning of 2020, a new disease (Covid-19) has emerged and expanded swiftly all around the world. Currently, we are still living in unprecedented times in which we should have social distance from one another and mostly work from home to diminish the spreading speed of the Covid-19. While we are experiencing these limitations, businesses and organizations are expected to work without having any disruptions. At this point, entering new technologies into our lives was inevitable and in fact, these new technologies have helped us to eliminate the challenges caused by the precautions with fewer flaws. Even though Fintech applications have numerous advantages, nothing comes without its drawbacks. The empirical analysis in this chapter aims to evaluate selection of best Fintech-based investments in the Turkish banking sector with an application of a hybrid DANP-fuzzy TOPSIS technique. Empirical findings of the analysis indicate that Strategy 2 has the best rank among the alternatives, followed by Strategy 1 and Strategy 3, whilst Strategy 4 has the weakest importance among the strategy preferences. Our findings suggest that policy makers/bank managers should focus more to direct Fintech investments firstly to lending services followed by payment systems.

Keywords: Fintech, Covid-19, financial institutions, pandemic, Turkish banking

1. Introduction

> *"Ignoring technological change in a financial system based upon technology, is like a mouse starving to death because someone moved their cheese."*
>
> *Chris Skinne*

At the beginning of 2020, a new disease (Covid-19) has emerged and expanded swiftly all around the world. As the global spread got out of control, World Health Organization (WHO) announced the situation as a pandemic. Followingly, governments took numerous precautions such as closing boarders, banns on international transportation, restrictions on social distancing, mandatory face masks, and flexible working conditions such as working from home/online meetings. Although, these precautions were taken against the virus, it affected almost all industries. The use of technology and innovation has increased more to eliminate the challenges caused by the precautions. At this point, Fintech applications have stepped forwards to catalyze business and individual processes.

'FinTech' is a compound word of Fin(ancial) and Tech(nology). It is a general name to refer to new disruptive, revolutionary technological developments that are redefining the financial markets and changing the rules. Even though, the term has gained popularity in public not long ago, it has become one of the most researched topics as it has managed to influence almost every subsector ([1], p. 235). Fintech helps companies and consumers to operate their financial assets and processes in better conditions via using specialized software and algorithms by solely accessing through computers and smartphones. Alongside strengthening business and processing big data to meaningful data, Fintech is universal, cheaper, and more secure compared to conventional methods [2]. In addition, Fintech eliminates traditional intermediaries while offering financial services [3].

FinTech has many new and complex underlying technologies like blockchain, artificial intelligence, big data, and machine learning. With the new dynamics that these techs bring, FinTech offers various advantages that traditional institutions cannot compete with. Some of the most important advantages are the ability that Fintech start-ups can avoid intermediation costs and acquire minimum capital requirements usually associated with traditional banking services. On the other hand, big data analytics and data science transformed how data are captured, processed, and analyzed, which results in significant cost reduction [4]. Traditional ways of finance are being challenged continuously and long-established institutions should decide if they will embrace or fight it.

Artificial intelligence, machine learning, big data, data analytics, robotic process automation, and blockchain technologies have played and still are playing important roles in the creation of today's successful Fintech applications. These technologies have comprised the base for many Fintech applications, where they have enabled the creation of crowdfunding platforms, mobile payment systems, robo-advisors, insurance applications, budgeting applications, and Regulatory Technology (RegTech). As a result, financial markets, financial transactions, simpler money trade-offs, anything which can be thought on financial activities have become more convenient by the Fintech applications. Higher rates of convenience have brought also a higher number of new users and efficiency. Fintech applications also provide personalized services for people who require and want data and services. Indeed, personalization plays a subsidiary role for the enhancements of those Fintech applications; because via personalized services, the owners of the applications can learn what do their customers need. Those needs, afterwards, can be met by the new updates of the applications. Via the products of the new tech, the time it takes to make each of the transactions has lowered, encouraging people to be involved in more financial activities. Financial markets may benefit from new and more involved players.

According to Moden and Neufeld [5] the usage of Fintech applications increased by 72% in Europe since the first lockdown due to the Covid-19 pandemic. Fintech is one of the hottest topics in current finance and is thought to be the power that will shape the future. This chapter aims to investigate the utilization of Fintech applications during the COVID-19 pandemic, analyze the Fintech phenomenon, and show some of its main applications in financial markets such as cryptocurrency, crowdfunding, and mobile payments. Moreover, this chapter evaluates Fintech-based investments in Turkish banking with an application of the ANP and TOPSIS models. We aim to contribute to the existing literature by identifying the most important Fintech-based investment alternatives and to providing suggestions for policy makers to achieve higher financial performance in the Turkish banking sector. Our empirical findings illustrate that "payment" and "lending" systems are the most important Fintech-based investment alternatives. We recommend that Turkish banks should mainly focus on directing investments to Fintech applications on payment and lending services to attract more customers, decrease operational costs and achieve higher levels of customer satisfaction.

The rest of the chapter is organized as follows. Section 2 introduces a summary of the evolution of Fintech applications. Section 3 provides a literature review, followed by methodology and empirical findings. Lastly, Section 5 concludes the chapter.

2. Evolution of Fintech applications

The origins of Fintech go back to the mid-19th century. Although, it was initially designed for back-end systems of financial institutions, it has moved towards consumer-oriented services over time [6]. The development between finance and technology has always been hand to hand in history. A need, a deficiency in finance would provoke the technology to come up with a solution and the result would benefit both. Arner et al. [7] list the co-existence of financial services and technology in three eras as: Fintech 1, Fintech 2, and Fintech 3. The first period (Fintech 1) is between 1866 and 1967, which represents the period of transition from analog to digital applications. During this period, the foundations were laid for financial connections that would enable the rapid realization of financial information, transactions, and payments by means of telegraph, railways, canals, and transatlantic telegraph cables. In fact, laying of the transatlantic telegraph cable formed the infrastructure of the financial globalization process. Moreover, credit card applications started during this era and formed the basis for the next stage of Fintech development (Fintech 2).

The digitalization of technologies used in communication and commercial transactions triggered the Fintech 2 era, which refers to the 1967–2008 period. Products and services offered in the financial services sector started to be digitalized and internet banking applications (Wells Fargo-USA and ING Bank-Europe) and ATMs (1967-Barclays UK) were introduced over this period. The emergence of ATMs is accepted as the most important development revealing the relationship between finance and technology and as the first step towards digitalization of the financial services sector [8]. In addition, technology companies such as IBM emerged during this period [7]. Chronologically, over the following years, NASDAQ was established (1971), SWIFT application was commissioned (1973), Bloomberg was established (1981), the first mobile phones emerged (1983), and online banking applications started (1985). By 2001, the number of customers consuming these technologies reached to one million. In 2005, the first physically branchless banks such as ING Direct and HSBC Direct emerged in the UK. At the beginning of the 21st century, banks' internal processes, external systems, and interactions with their customers were completely digitalized [7].

Lastly, Fintech 3 era covers 2008 and beyond, which has the trigger point as the global economic crisis in 2008. Global economic crises caused distrust in financial markets and expanded the importance of Fintech applications. The public's anger with the banking system has created an excellent area of development for financial innovation. Taking advantage of the opportunity created by the crisis environment, Fintech providers offered services to their customers with low-cost, more transparent, and easier to use interfaces through well-designed platforms and mobile applications [9]. Although, Fintech 3 has emerged as a response to the financial crises in the West, similar Fintech developments were observed in Asia and Africa a bit later. The period in these two regions is described as Fintech 3.5 [7]. The elements that support the Fintech 3.5 era in these regions can be listed as high penetration of mobile devices among young and technology-savvy individuals, the growth of the middle class, unused market opportunities, lack of physical banking infrastructure, and low competition [7].

Fintech technologies are used in areas such as payments, digital currencies, insurance, investment management, credit, deposit, and lending. The cost of the services provided by this technology to the customer is low and easy to access. Fintech companies focus on the customer and take their actions in line with customer needs. According to a survey of BCBS, most Fintech services are in the category of payment, clearing and settlement; then, it was concluded that the activities of market support services and credit, deposit, capital-raising services respectively were high [10]. While Fintech companies operating on payment provide convenience to their customers in terms of payment, Fintech companies operating in the field of market support services are companies that provide financial support as the name suggests.

People who need a loan often go to banks; however, getting a loan is not that easy. Banks classify individuals according to their ability to pay, suspecting whether they can receive a refund. They expose individuals applying for loans to many questions such as income level, age, wealth status, illness status, credit rating, education level, and it becomes difficult to get a loan for someone with any disadvantage. However, for those who lost their jobs and lost their home; or for people who want to start a new venture but do not have capital, the situation is not very heartwarming. Besides, even if a loan will be given to the person applying for the loan, there may be a high-interest payment system. The Fintech industry has launched many technology applications and financial support services to create a new lending market, which will address all difficulties, support and meet most of the consumers' needs. To find solutions to such problems, Fintech developed its applications with its technological infrastructure and established its credit system, and even started to give loans to people deemed defective by banks. Unlike banks, some Fintech companies kept the interest on repayment low, did not ask long and detailed questions like banks. Instead, thanks to the algorithms developed, they started to use all the data that could be used, from the games played by the individuals who want to get a loan to the lifestyle they live, to get a preview.

Peer to Peer Lending, one of the models of these applications, served as a link between lenders and borrowers thanks to its highly developed technological infrastructure; In a way, it has undertaken the duties of other financial companies. Venmo app is a smartphone app used to make digital payments. Venmo, which was designed by targeting the Peer-to-Peer system, after some personal information is verified, personal bank accounts are connected to the application and allows individuals to easily transfer money among themselves. Another example of using Peer-to-Peer Lending systems is Sofi and Earnest. These two applications, help students to find individuals who give student loans.

Thanks to the technological applications developed by Fintech companies, making payments has now been transferred to the digital environment and requires easier and shorter transactions, which do not require physical transactions. People can now send money to another individual at the touch of a button, at any time and at any distance. For example, it used to be more difficult to send money to individuals living abroad. People who must go to the bank, answer a lot of questions, wait long lines, and deal with a lot of paperwork can now handle this issue much more comfortably. Mobile wallets are considered an Online Payment system. This system, which replaces the normal wallet, allows the use of most bank cards virtually with the technology it contains; It is designed for users to use comfortably and to save time, to avoid worries such as forgetting a wallet or shortage of cash. For this, the user only needs to download the application. There are mobile wallet applications such as Google

Wallet, Square Cash, Paypal, and it allows individuals to carry a virtual wallet. Also, Apple released Apple Pay using its technology and moved users' purchases and billing transactions to digital using only Touch ID (Truong, p. 20).

In addition, cryptocurrency is introduced as a virtual currency, which has no physical appearance, and allows customers to transfer money digitally. Cryptocurrencies are tools for investing, like gold or dollar, you can trade and sell it through various apps and websites. The high demand and big expectations helped these currencies to reach all-time highs and they are still rising. Furthermore, they are parts of major investment banks' portfolios even though some of the banks still question their future. JP Morgan had announced that it had made a 50-million-dollar investment in Bitcoin and explained that they believe it is an important asset. As if that was not enough, JP Morgan went a step further and explained it will release its cryptocurrency for payments, JPM Coin. Before JP Morgan, platforms such as Amazon, Craigslist, and eBay had already realized the advantage of cryptocurrency payments [11]. In addition to incredibly fast payments, they allowed it to reduce their costs in labor and documentation and eliminate intermediary fees. They use these savings to improve their services for the customers. Also, blockchain technology allowed companies to set "smart contracts" which are codes with conditions that are executed when certain conditions are met [11]. These helped companies to avoid mistakes, save time and overcome trust issues. For example, in trade finance parties can guarantee that they will get their payment as soon as the shipment has arrived at the buyer. With smart contracts, there is no need for confirmation calls or emails.

The first and most popular type of cryptocurrency is Bitcoin. Bitcoin is a virtual currency where people are traded among themselves, and it is tracked through online platform sites, whilst without any regulation. It is now in such a position in the lives of individuals that it can be received as Bitcoin payment in some businesses. To create a digital platform for Bitcoin transactions, Blockchain technology is introduced, which enables data to be organized in blocks and protects the data it collects. In simplest terms, blockchain is a decentralized and secure electronic ledger. This ledger is public and built around a P2P system where participants are anonymous and do not have to reveal any information. Each transaction is linked to the previous one like a chain and because entries are linked, tracking and verifying them become significantly easier. But, before transactions become a "block" of the chain, they must be confirmed. The striking point is the participants are the ones who confirm them instead of a central power who charges fees and has the power to call off a transaction. Blockchain aims to replace authorities by creating a safe environment that is based upon the secure nature of cryptography and the trust participants have for each other. So, the transactions will be cheaper and irreversible.

Especially, the Crowdfunding system which combines individuals who are looking for capital for a project or a start-up but who have difficulty in finding them with their future investors, is a tool to find the desired financial support using P2P, and no fees are required to use this system. Thus, individuals or small companies in need of financing save time and could find an investment that they normally cannot find. At the same time, it enables the investor to receive commission after a certain period. In addition, Fintech application such as Virtual Saving Jars belonging to the investment area enable people to make savings by transferring their budget, expenses, and income to digital. This development, made especially by focusing on the young audience, is perfect for those who cannot save. Another application type made by Fintech companies is portfolio management. These applications such as Acorns and Betterment measure the risk level using the investor's data and match the suitability against which assets. In creating a portfolio, Robot-Advisor can be used which uses the investor's data and tells the investor how to make a portfolio. The system uses questions that are designed to get to know the investor, then it recognizes the investor and offers suitable portfolio options through its algorithms.

Fintech companies also help personal finance transactions to be carried out more efficiently. Despite each company's own technological infrastructure, customers who are suspected of being defrauded feel compelled to check many websites at the same time. For this purpose, websites such as Mint.com and CreditKarma were enabled to see individual transactions and to reach different banks with free of charge from a single platform. Thus, customers were able to manage their finances and have access to transaction, banking and credit activities much more easily. In this respect, LearnVest is an online platform that supports its users to manage their finance and investment.

Likewise, Asset and Wealth Management (AWM) is another financial service that is expected to be revolutionized by Fintech. Since 2008, there has been a constant rise in the number of AWM start-ups, which aim to stand out from the traditional advisors by incorporating artificial intelligence and new data analytic techniques in the game. Lopez et al. [12] list the major innovations that are making a difference as:

1. 'Well-designed platforms focused on simplicity, speed, and intuitive workflows through digital and mobile offerings',

2. 'Compelling editorial content and financial education distributed openly online with focus on human connection, constant feedback on client's financial health',

3. 'Average fees between 25 and 50 basis points; free tools to analyze fees across accounts while offering cost-saving alternatives'.

One of the most important inventions in the process of automatizing and digitalizing investment management is robo-advisory. 'Robo-Advisors are digital platforms comprising interactive and intelligent user assistance components that use information technology to guide customers through an automated advisory process' ([13], p. 1). The new alternatives that were born with this technology can be divided into two branches as: (i) Fully-Automated and (ii) Advisor-Assisted ([12], p. 4). Betterment and Wealthfront are two of the Fully-Automated management firms where there is zero human elements. On the other hand, firms like Personal Capital—an important Advisor-Assisted system—a more comprehensive analysis of assets, and more detailed tracking and advisory on investments are offered with real human advisors who are evaluating and reporting the process. Eliminating the extra employee-based costs such as food, transportation and monthly salaries allow robo-advisory start-ups to accept customers without minimum investment limit. That's why especially the fully-automated firms have gained traction with millennials, which have an average account size of \$20,000–\$100,000 [12].

Small and Medium Enterprises (SMEs) and business ventures used to get financial support from banks. However, with the beginning of the 2008 financial crisis, banks decreased loan amounts and frequencies in order not to take risks in a non-growing economic condition. This becomes the revolutionary standpoint for crowdfunding [14]. Loans taken from banks are no longer being used, instead crowdfunding is used with the help of financial technologies for loan practices. Crowdfunding practices are fulfilled via internet crowdfunding websites and social media. These platforms ease lending transactions by eliminating difficult negotiations and time-consuming paperwork. Since crowdfunding platforms are easily usable and accessible, crowdfunding continues to develop.

Last but not the least, the mobile payment system is a monetary payment made through an electronic environment. This environment is mostly a smart device like a phone, tablet, laptop, etc. In the traditional payment model, there is a direct link with financial institutions; however, with FinTech, payments are connected to financial institutions via Information Technologies (IT) companies. Even if IT is also used in traditional services, it is not easily adaptable to FinTech payment services [15]. For each financial institution, different payment methods should be used because traditional payment services were not developed as user-specific. Several companies give mobile payment services. Apple, Samsung, and Google developed mobile applications named respectively as Apple pay, Samsung pay, and Google pay. These applications are implemented to ease payment procedures and enable instantaneous purchasing by using barcodes. Another well-known platform is PayPal, which is mostly used by small stores instead of traditional equipment such as barcode readers and Point of Sales Terminal (POS). Mobile payment enables easy purchasing for stores that are not able to use traditional equipment and provides paying options other than cash [15].

3. Literature review

When the literature about Fintech applications in the finance industry is investigated it has been identified that studies were completed by countries, and mainly focused on (i) how consumers can react to Fintech applications, (ii) what are the challenges and barriers of Fintech applications for a specific country, and (iii) how Fintech applications can be popularized in the target country.

Starting with the challenges faced by countries on Fintech applications, Narayanasamy et al. [16] explored factors affecting the adoption of Fintech applications with a dataset of 100 participants who use Fintech applications. They identified that security, income, and cost are the main concepts that affect the adaptation of Fintech. Saksonova and Kuzmina-Merlino [17] studied the usage level of Fintech applications in Latvia compared to Europe and offered several recommendations to managers of Fintech enterprises. The study revealed that people in Latvia are not very aware of the applications. Furthermore, they made several suggestions to populate Fintech applications in Latvia such as forming impressive marketing campaigns to enhance the public's awareness, offering tax initiatives to attach investment to the sector, training human resources to specialize in Fintech applications, and further informing the population. Moreover, Harrison and Jürjens [18] examined the factors which affect the expectations of both users and organizations to adopt Fintech. Their study showed that data security, customer trust, and user design interface have an impact on adopting Fintech applications and can be a challenge.

Fintech applications provide cost-effective and more efficient transactions and have a crucial role in the banking industry since it is beneficial for customers [19]. Rizvi et al. [20] studied factors that enable penetration and growth of Fintech applications in Pakistan. Prominent suggestions to popularize the Fintech applications in the banking industry are promoting the Fintech applications, establishing an ecosystem where Fintech providers and consumers trust each other and the government's support. In another study, Nguyen et al. [21] investigated Fintech applications' development in the Vietnamese banking industry alongside identifying challenges to promote

Fintech applications in the banking and finance systems in Vietnam. Legal corridor, infrastructure, Fintech companies, customers, and human resources are the main barriers that the Vietnamese banking industry deals with. Main solutions to overcome these problems are finalizing the regulatory framework, encouraging the research and implementation of block-chain technology, training human resources for gaining Fintech application specialty, and constant promotion about Fintech applications.

Ratten [22] investigated the factors determining the intention of users to adopt Fintech applications. The research focused on the effects of users' entrepreneurship and learning disposition on marketing and information related to mobile banking. The results obtained are aimed to reduce the risks faced by users of financial institutions in e-finance applications.

Another popular subject on Fintech is money laundering, which is a global problem that authorities have been desperately trying to prevent but still fail. Banks must follow protocols such as "Know-your-Customer," "Anti-Money Laundering," and "Combatting the Financing of Terrorism" [23]. So, the fact that participants of a blockchain are anonymous, drew criticism from all over the world as money laundering could get much easier. While it is true that following someone on the blockchain is impossible, blockchain can help fighting frauds as you must justify the source and destination of each transaction, and all transactions can be followed publicly. HSBC, OCBC Bank, IMDA and Mitsubishi Financial Groups are working on a pilot blockchain system to reduce duplication and increase transparency [23].

From the robo-advisory function of Fintech services, the operations are based on calculations and algorithms which minimize error and risk. First, you must fill out a form and survey for the system, so that your investor profile can be figured out. Then, a recommended portfolio is created according to your profile, which consists of different asset classes in risk and liquidity. There exist many different approaches for determining the portfolio weights, but most robo-advisors use modern portfolio theory [24]. Following the investment, algorithmic rebalancing provides stability of the portfolio weights and therefore the risk-level by shifting investments among asset classes to revert towards its predefined risk long-term equilibrium, when the weights of the portfolio change [24]. The speed and precision of artificial intelligence (AI) is incomparably higher than a human's capability and there is no emotional decision-making involved. Based on the advantages it creates, AI and Fintech applications have been the focus of financial institutions. For instance, banking is one of the leading sectors that digitalization is applied for saving time, diminishing operational costs, increasing profitability and simplifying transactions for customers [25]. Therefore, it usually requires renovation of financial structure (Yoo et al., 2010). The main aim is to extend customer satisfaction and outline future customer needs [26].

Digitalization in banking is also used to improve service quality and introduce new financial products. To catch up with this global trend is crucial for banks as new market participants like Fintechs are a great threat to their effectiveness. Fintech applications in the banking sector are applied in various fields such as payment and collections systems, money transferring, savings, budgeting and borrowing. Loebbecke and Picot [27] stated that the first Fintech applications were designed for payment services such as Paypal. However, introducing Fintech applications on lending services provided a competitive advantage for conventional banks. With new technologies, customer expectations of the banking system have changed. Thus, banks face the challenge of improving their efficiency with the boosted competition. Philippon [28] illustrated that Fintech applications increased productivity in financial services (outputs) and lowered operating costs (inputs).

In a recent study, Kou et al. [29] analyzed Fintech investments in European banking with an application of interval type-2 fuzzy DEMATEL and interval type-2 fuzzy TOPSIS models. Empirical findings illustrate that 'payment and money transferring systems' are the most important Fintech-based investment alternatives. It is suggested that the European banks should mainly direct their investments into these channels for higher customer satisfaction and improved profitability.

According to Fu and Mishra [30], the number of mobile app downloads across major categories has increased and finance applications download rates increased both in the first and second lockdowns during the Covid-19 pandemic. This might be expected as, during the first lockdown in Europe, people were discouraged to use banknotes and were encouraged to contactless payment methods [31]. In addition, people were also encouraged to stay at home, therefore they were motivated to complete their financial transactions via financial applications. Saraogi [32] listed countries that were most affected by Covid-19 as Belgium, Brazil, China, France, Germany, Italy, Netherland, Spain, Switzerland, Turkey, the United Kingdom, and the United States. Considering the implemented social distancing and other precautions against the Covid-19, it was expected to see the number of downloads of Fintech applications to increase. Recent research conducted by MasterCard revealed that 79% of people worldwide and 91% in the Asia Pacific prefer to use tap-and-go payments due to safety and cleanliness reasons [32].

To sum up, Fintech applications make a significant contribution to the financial system by reducing costs, providing higher quality services and increasing customer satisfaction. Since the beginning of the pandemic, the speed of applications has boosted significantly. However, due to the short time span on the availability of detailed data in numerous industries and countries, new studies play an essential role to identify the needs of individual sectors and improve Fintech investments.

4. Empirical analysis

The aim of the analysis in this chapter is to evaluate the selection of best Fintech-based investments in the Turkish banking sector with an application of a hybrid DANP-fuzzy TOPSIS (Technique for Ordering Preference by Similarity to Ideal Solution) technique. DANP determines the weights of the SWOT factors and the fuzzy TOPSIS selects the best strategy for the Turkish banking sector. We identified the best strategies for decision-makers using an integrated model of the fuzzy TOPSIS technique with SWOT and DANP. To achieve a competitive advantage with growing Fintech applications, banks should identify targeted financial activities for prioritized Fintech investments. **Table 1** presents the proposed strategies based on feedback from the experts in the banking industry and academia.

4.1 Hybrid model construction

The integrated model has been built to select the best Fintech investment strategies for the Turkish banking sector by using the DANP (a combination of Decision-Making Trial and Evaluation Laboratory (DEMATEL) method and Analytical Network Process (ANP) method) technique to determine the weights of the SWOT factors followed by the fuzzy-TOPSIS (Technique for Order of Preference by Similarity to Ideal Solution) technique to select the best strategy. In determining the criteria for strategy formulation in this study, four banking experts with 15–20 years of experience cooperated to design a

Proposed strategies	Explanation
Strategy 1	Directing investments to Fintech applications in payment systems
Strategy 2	Directing investments to Fintech applications in lending services
Strategy 3	Directing investments to Fintech applications in collection services
Strategy 4	Directing investments to Fintech applications in asset and wealth (investment) management
Source: Authors' own table.	

Table 1.
Formulating strategies.

set of strategies. Then, three academics constructed the problems and modified strategies based on the expert scales and linguistic variables to evaluate the relative importance of the criteria and to select the strategies. First step of the analysis begins with the DANP technique to create the averaged initial direct relationship matrix with results presented in **Table 2**. The relationship among the SWOT factors is based on experts scales evaluated by the decision-makers.

Strengths are identified as increased service speed, improved customer satisfaction and cost reduction while weaknesses are customer adoption to no human transactions, physicological factors such as trust, technological capacity of customers. On the other hand, opportunities cover speedy international transactions, being part of Open Banking which may help in credit scores and providing alternative instruments/services. And finally, threats are identified as high initial investment costs, security and coping with foreign bank competition.

The second step is the application of the fuzzy TOPSIS technique to rank the proposed strategies. After constructing the fuzzy decision matrix, we normalized and weighted the matrix with DANP. **Table 3** introduces the findings in ranking the

	ri	*yi*	*(ri + yi)*	*(ri – yi)*
S (strengths)	6.37	5.36	11.73	0.94
W (weaknesses)	5.01	5.78	10.81	−0.77
O (opportunities)	5.92	5.51	11.43	−0.31
T (threats)	5.43	5.91	11.34	−0.48
Source: Authors' own table.				

Table 2.
Impact-relationship degrees of dimension.

Strategies	*Di+*	*Di-*	*CCi*	Ranking
Strategy 1	9.585	1.531	0.132	2
Strategy 2	9.443	1.583	0.156	1
Strategy 3	9.649	1.449	0.112	3
Strategy 4	9.896	1.216	0.108	4
Source: Authors' own table.				

Table 3.
Selection of the best Fintech investment strategy.

proposed strategies. $Di+$, $Di-$ and CCi are the values indicating distances of each strategy alternative from the positive and negative ideal solution.

Empirical findings of the analysis indicate that Strategy 2 has the best rank among the alternatives, followed by Strategy 1 and Strategy 3, whilst Strategy 4 has the weakest importance among the strategy preferences. Our findings suggest that policy makers/bank managers should focus more to direct Fintech investments firstly to lending services followed by payment systems.

4.2 Empirical findings

We applied a hybrid DANP-fuzzy TOPSIS technique to evaluate the selection of best Fintech-based investments in the Turkish banking sector. Ranking of the strategies helps us to identify the importance/priority of the proposed strategies on directing Fintech investments to various activities of Turkish banks. Empirical findings illustrate that among the financial activities of Turkish banks, lending services are identified to signal the highest need for Fintech investments. Payment services also show a priority in attracting Fintech investments being ranked as the second strategy. Receivable collection services and investment management services are not categorized as prioritized as others. These results should be interpreted carefully as customer satisfaction and expectations may differ from one country to another based on cultural and economic differences as well as the level of education and access to technology. To sum up, empirical analysis in this chapter suggests that policy makers/bank managers should focus more on direct Fintech investments firstly to lending services followed by payment systems.

5. Conclusions

Life has started to flow very quickly with the advancement of technology and the financial sector has also followed these developments with Fintech applications. Financial activities can be done faster and more effectively than traditional methods. With the Fintech applications, operations can be handled at the desired place and time because smart devices and online platforms eliminate the need of going to a bank. With the decrease of trust in traditional order due to the unethical attitudes displayed by traditional intermediaries, the Fintech sector has gained quick popularity in our lives [33].

Besides its advantages, there are also several disadvantages of Fintech applications. The Fintech industry is still developing faster than expected and there is no distinct transition to Fintech industries from traditional intermediaries. Therefore; the governmental regulations are tailored according to traditional companies [33]. As a result, Fintech companies may act through their desires and consider the requests of customers freely since some Fintech companies did not become legalized. The replacement of humans by artificial intelligence has negative effects on people's attitudes. In some circumstances, personal interaction becomes a need for customers. Researches show that only 11% of persons trust on robo-advisors and 49% of people do not prefer to use robo-advisory without getting consultancy from a real person [24].

Every invention brings along questions about the future and Fintech is no exception. Small ventures and entrepreneurs have concerns because they may lose their brand value, popularity, and the likelihood of the company in the future when they prefer crowdfunding instead of traditional banks to obtain capital. Since the crowdfunding process requires an online platform, all the investors and by extension the public may get quick notifications about the companies' failures and successes. Thus, even if the project has a future, if there is less demand or interest to project for a little time, investors who are expected to continue to invest may reduce their support or even cut their support completely.

Currently, we are living in unprecedented times in which we should have social distance from one another and stay at home. While these are happening, still businesses and organizations are expected to work without having any disruptions. At this point, entering new technologies into our lives was inevitable and in fact, these new technologies have helped us to get over this process with fewer flaws. One of these technologies was Fintech applications. Although, we used these technologies beforehand, with the Covid-19 precautions, the frequency and intensity of the usage of Fintech applications increased enormously. A recent study conducted in Singapore revealed that 80% of the consumers will probably continue to use Fintech applications even after the pandemic [34]. As one of the most affected countries from Covid-19, Turkey follows a similar trend for the utilization of Fintech applications.

Considering the challenges that other countries are dealing with while adopting Fintech applications, they are solutions to their problem. For instance, Saksonova and Kuzmina-Merlino [17] identified that during the utilization of Fintech applications, tax-related issues can appear. Therefore, governments should form related laws and regulations to regulate Fintech applications. Furthermore, Harrison and Jürjens [18] revealed that security is another important issue during the adoption of Fintech applications. Thus, awareness about security must be improved by both governments and businesses, which use Fintech applications. Finally, Nguyen et al. [21] illustrated that both employees and consumers might not understand the Fintech applications fully. Thus, training can be offered to them to explain the abilities of the Fintech applications.

Author details

Özlem Olgu Akdeniz
College of Administrative Sciences and Economics, Koç University, Istanbul, Turkey

*Address all correspondence to: oolgu@ku.edu.tr

References

[1] Alt R, Beck R, Smits MT. FinTech and the transformation of the financial industry. Electronic Markets. 2018;**28**:235-243. DOI: 10.1007/s12525-018-0310-9

[2] Lee I, Shin YJ. Fintech: Ecosystem, business models, investment decisions, and challenges. Business Horizons. 2018;**61**:35-46

[3] Thakor AV. Fintech and banking: What do we know? Journal of Financial Intermediation. 2020;**41**:100833

[4] Iman N, Tan AWK. The rise and rise of financial technology: The good, the bad, and the verdict. Cogent Business & Management. 2020;7:1. DOI: 10.1080/23311975.2020.1725309

[5] Moden N, Neufeld P. How Covid-19 has sped up digitalization for the banking sector. 2020. Available from: https://www.ey.com/en_gl/financial-services-emeia/how-covid-19-has-sped-up-digitization-for-the-banking-sector

[6] Kagan J. Financial technology—Fintech. 2020. Available from: https://www.investopedia.com/terms/f/Fintech.asp#:~:text=%E2%80%8B%E2%80%8B%E2%80%8BAt%20its,combination%20of%20%22financial%20technology%22

[7] Arner D, Barberris J, Buckley R. The evolution of Fintech: A new post-crisis paradigm? University of Hong Kong Faculty of Law. Research Paper No. 2015/047. 2015

[8] Nicoletti B. The Future of Fintech: Integrating Finance and Technology in Financial Services. Cham: Palgrave Macmillan; 2017

[9] Menat R. Why we're so excited about Fintech. In: Chishti S, Barberris J, editors. The Fintech Book. London: John Wiley and Sons; 2016. pp. 46-51

[10] Bank of International Settlements. Promoting Global Monetary and Financial Stability. Annual Economic Report; 2018

[11] Ertz M, Boily E. The rise of the digital economy: Thoughts on blockchain technology and cryptocurrencies for the collaborative economy. International Journal of Innovation Studies. 2020;**3**:84-93. DOI: 10.1016/j.ijis.2019.12.002

[12] Lopez JC, Babcic S, De La Ossa A. Advice goes virtual: How new digital investment services are changing the wealth management landscape. 2017. Retrieved from: https://papers.ssrn.com/sol3/papers.cfm?abstract_id=3084057

[13] Jung D, Dorner V, Glaser F, Morana S. Robo-Advisory: Digitalization and Automation of Financial Advisory. Business and Information Systems Engineering. 2018;**60**(1):81-86. DOI: 10.1007/s12599-018-0521-9

[14] Fenwick M, McCahery J, Vermeulen E. Fintech and the financing of entrepreneurs: From crowdfunding to marketplace lending. 2017

[15] Kang J. Mobile payment in Fintech environment: Trends, security challenges, and services. Human-centric Computing and Information Sciences. 2018;**8**:32. DOI: 10.1186/s13673-018-0155-4

[16] Narayanasamy K, Rasiah D, Tan TM. The adoption and concerns of e-finance in Malaysia. Electronic Commerce Research. 2011;**11**(4):383

[17] Saksonova S, Kuzmina-Merlino I. Fintech as financial innovation—The possibilities and problems of implementation. European Research Studies Journal. 2017;**20**(3A):961-973

[18] Harrison S, Jürjens J. Data security and consumer trust in Fintech in

innovation in Germany. Information and Computer Security. 2018;**26**(1):109-128

[19] Cheng MA, Wu Q, Yang B. How valuable is FinTech innovation? The Review of Financial Studies. 2019;**32**(5):2062-2106

[20] Rizvi SKA, Naqvi B, Tanveer F. Is Pakistan ready to embrace Fintech innovation? The Lahore Journal of Economics. 2018;**23**(2):151-182

[21] Nguyen DD, Dinh HC, Nguyen DV. Promotion of Fintech application for the modernization of banking-finance system in Vietnam. Journal of Asian Finance, Economics and Business. 2020;**7**(6):127-131

[22] Ratten V. Entrepreneurship, e-finance and mobile banking. International Journal of Electronic Finance. 2012;**6**(1):1-12

[23] Suominen K, Chatzky A, Reinsch W, Robison J. (Rep.). Center for Strategic and International Studies (CSIS). 2018. DOI:10.2307/resrep22491

[24] Jung D, Glaser F, Köpplin W. Robo-advisory: Opportunities and risks for the future of financial advisory: Recent findings and practical cases. 2019. DOI: 10.1007/978-3-319-95999-3_20

[25] Bhutani S, Paliwal Y. Digitalization: A step from sustainable development. OIDA International Journal of Sustainable Development. 2015;**8**(12):11-24

[26] Valenduc G, Vendramin P. Digitalisation, between disruption and evolution. European Review of Labour and Reserach. 2017;**23**(2):121-134

[27] Loebbecke C, Picot A. Reflections on societal and business model transformation arising from digitization and big data analytics: A research agenda. Journal of Strategic Information Systems; 2015

[28] Philippon T. The Fintech Opportunity. BIS Working Paper No. 655. 2017

[29] Kou G, Akdeniz OO, Dincer H, Yuksel S. FinTech investments in European banks: A hybrid IT2 fuzzy multidimensional decision-making approach. Financial Innovation. 2021;7:39

[30] Fu J, Mishra M. Fintech in the time of Covid-19: Trust and technological adoption during crises. Swiss Finance Institute Research Paper No. 20-38. 2020. Available from: https://papers.ssrn.com/sol3/papers.cfm?abstract_id=3588453

[31] Cocheo S. More consumers prefer contactless payments for pandemic purchases. 2020. Available from: https://thefinancialbrand.com/101415/payment-contactless-card-mobile-wallet-digital-coronavirus-covid-19-pandemic-trend/

[32] Saraogi V. Contactless payments will be the new normal for shoppers in the post Covid-19 world. 2020. Available from: https://newsroom.mastercard.com/asia-pacific/2020/05/20/contactless-payments-will-be-the-new-normal-for-shoppers-in-the-post-covid-19-world/

[33] Pejkovska M. Potential negative effects of Fintech on the financial services sector examples from the European Unıon, Indıa and the United States of America. 2018. Retrieved from: https://www.theseus.fi/bitstream/handle/10024/148416/Maja_Pejkovska_Theseus.pdf?sequence=1andisAllowed=y

[34] Gene NK. 8 in 10 will continue banking online after pandemic: Survey. 2020. Available from: https://www.straitstimes.com/singapore/8-in-10-will-continue-banking-online-after-pandemic-survey

Chapter 3

Digital Maturity of University Libraries in Nigeria

Akinniyi A. Adeleke, Yemisi Ojokuku and Joshua Onaade Ojo

Abstract

This chapter reports the findings of a survey of the level of digital maturity of university libraries in Nigeria. Forty-eight university libraries responded to an online survey based on the framework for digital mature schools (FDMS). The findings reveal that the libraries are e-enabled but yet to attain digital maturity. The paper also shows that the dimensions of ICT planning, management and leadership, and ICT infrastructural development statistically predict the digital maturity status of university libraries.

Keywords: academic libraries, digital maturity, digital transformation, university libraries, Nigeria

1. Introduction

University education is one sector of national economies tremendously influenced by digital transformation. According to Fosu [1], "the 21st century global digital and knowledge-based economies evolution powered by the rapid advancement of ICT with its gadgets have brought about a global wave of change in the education sector". With the current COVID-19 pandemic speeding up the hitherto steady developments, university campuses become more innovative by using virtual learning environments and digital communication platforms for teaching and learning; and applying knowledge and business analytics for decision making.

The incursion of the digital revolution into teaching, learning and research presents university libraries with opportunities and challenges to cope with changing information behaviours, resources and sources of their patrons, majorly students and faculty members. The ICT evolution and revolution, on the one hand, present university libraries with the opportunities of:

- using various gadgets and applications to present information sources and resources to patrons;

- using multiple platforms to communicate, collaborate and cooperate with patrons and other libraries in resource sharing and networking.

On the other hand, university libraries are grappling with how users access and use information which warrants that every library content is on electronic platforms.

Such demands require deploying substantial human and capital resources that are scarcely available and accessible to university libraries, particularly in developing countries like Nigeria.

University libraries are organised to support their host institutions' teaching, learning, and research activities, and to satisfy the ever-changing needs of their patrons fully, they take steps to integrate digital technologies with their operations and services. However, the pace of digital transformation in university libraries varies from institution to institution, country to country and region to region. Hence the libraries are at different degrees of their abilities to respond and take advantage of technological developments in their operations and services, a phenomenon referred to as digital maturity.

This book chapter seeks to interrogate and report on the digital maturity of university libraries in Nigeria. It attempts to review the libraries' efforts to adopt digital technologies and techniques for creating and adding value to their services to understand their levels of abilities to respond to the environment created by the evolving digital economy. The whole essence of this adventure is to determine the existence in the libraries of the capabilities, competencies, tools and infrastructure required to understand and respond to the needs and desires of the information user in the unfolding digital environment. In the final analysis, the discourse would establish the reality or fallacy of the digital maturity of university libraries in Nigeria. It will help the institutions and their owners understand the statuses of their digital compliance and determine how commensurate with their digital technologies investments is their ability to respond to the digital economy's demands.

Although university libraries were doing amazing things with ICTs, the library and information science literature reports only few of university libraries in Nigeria making deliberate efforts to adopt, deploy and use digital technologies and strategies for the digitalisation of information services and resources to address some peculiar challenges. For instance, Adeleke [2] reported how Tekena Tamuno Library, Redeemer's University, Ede resolved staff-patron conflicts with digitising past examination questions. The paper reiterates the power of the digital economy to remove interpersonal conflicts and establish peaceful co-existence among members of a community. The dearth of reports about university libraries in Nigeria deliberately implementing digital solutions to address research, teaching and learning issues informs the present attempt to investigate the digital maturity of the libraries.

A digitally mature library uses appropriate information and communications technologies for efficient and transparent management of resources and services, develops the digital competence of its personnel for innovative services, and develops its users' digital capacity to be life-long users of information in any environment. In short, digitally mature libraries have a high level of integration of ICTs in their routine operations and services and systematically approach the deployment of ICT in supporting the teaching, learning and research mandates of their parent institutions to adapt to the evolving digital environment.

The concept of digital maturity refers to the formation of specific capabilities to manage digital transformation in an organisation. Digital maturity represents the degree of adoption and application of digital technologies in business models. Kane et al. [3] see digital maturity as a systematic way for an organisation to transform digitally. Digital maturity incorporates managerial aspects of ICTs to describe what a company has already done and will do in digital transformation efforts that involve products, services, processes, skills, culture and abilities regarding the mastery of change processes [4]. Westermann et al. [5] assumed that developing specific digital capabilities leads to higher digital maturity.

Digital maturity is a systematic way for an organisation to transform digitally [3]. An organisation can take on digital transformation, not only from the standpoint of digital technology but organisation-wide, including people, culture, and processes, to achieve business outcomes [6]. According to Westermann et al. [5], an organisation's digital maturity is its ability to use digital technologies to drive significantly higher profit, productivity, and performance. The digital maturity of university libraries will imply the power of a library to use digital technologies to conduct its services and manage its resources to productively engage, educate and empower its users who have different information needs and diverse behaviours. A digitally mature library will excel at developing digital capabilities to work differently and the leadership capabilities required to achieve a vision. Digital maturity is a journey. Therefore, as university libraries realise the power of digital technologies to expand access to collections and enable their wide use for research, teaching and learning, they gradually build capacities and competencies to harness the opportunities in the current technology market to transform their services.

University libraries are not ranked among the most digitally mature organisations in the business technology literature, even in developed countries. Therefore, it is pertinent to understand how technology is adopted and used in university libraries because of its significance in supporting their parent institutions' teaching, learning, and research activities.

The expectations of today's library users and the ubiquitous and evolving nature of technology compel university libraries to re-imagine and redesign their operations and services to support the curricula and mandates of their parent institutions. Anuradha [7] asserts that digital sophistication is a criterion for any academic library to remain a relevant part of the educational experience of its ever-changing users.

The National Universities Commission (NUC) is the institution saddled with the responsibilities of licencing and regulating the operations of both public and private universities in Nigeria. The NUC, by law, has in part the burden of establishing minimum standards for all academic programmes that lead to awards of degrees in universities in Nigeria. The Commission also ensures that quality is maintained in the Nigerian university system. Owing to its prime position in achieving a university's teaching, learning and research mandates, the NUC earmarks a whopping 70% of the total accreditation scores for library facilities as the minimum requirement for an academic programme to attain full accreditation status [8]. Part of the library facilities often assessed by the NUC accreditation teams includes physical library collection or holdings on the programme being visited, seating capacity, subscription to electronic information resources, internet connection, etc.

Recently, NUC accreditation panels emphasise digital collections and connections more before approving a university to proceed with an academic programme. The accentuation of the requirements shows that the Commission acknowledges the necessity of integrating university education with digital technologies. And that the university campus cannot isolate itself from the evolving digital economy. To identify with the digital revolution, the NUC established a digital library project that aimed at digitising information materials and making them available to both public and private universities in Nigeria. The initiative was to encourage universities to build capacities to harness the enormous advantages of the ICT to teaching, learning and research. Meanwhile, university libraries in Nigeria confront with enormous challenges that have hindered them from making the best of the opportunities extended to them by ICT and its applications.

Baro, Oyeniran, and Ateboh [9] identified challenges confronting university libraries deploying ICTs in Nigeria. The problems include unstable internet connection, irregular power supply, poor funding, incompetent personnel, etc. These challenges may hinder the libraries' efforts to attain maturity in their parent institutions' digital transformation. Maturity models are used widely in information systems research [10, 11]; and are developed with a particular focus on the conditions and implications of digital transformation [12]. However, applications in educational contexts are scarce [13]. The available models are limited to the management of information systems in educational organisations, which are still at the initial stage of development [14].

Rossmann [15] conceptualised and operationalised a theoretical understanding of digital maturity to develop a scale for analysing digital transformation and continuous control. The framework is an extension of the work of Westermann et al. [5] and others such as Isaev et al. [16] and Poruban [17], and it is more appropriate for business organisations.

Durek et al. [18] developed a digital maturity framework for assessing the maturity level of higher education institutions in Croatia [18]. Using the analytic hierarchy process/analytic network process (AHP/ANP), Durek et al. identified seven main areas and 43 elements prioritised by the framework. The seven areas are 1.) leadership, planning and measurement; 2.) quality assurance; 3.) scientific research work; 4.) technology transfer and service to society; 5.) learning and teaching; 6.) ICT culture; and 7.) ICT resources and infrastructure.

Similarly, Begicevic Redjep, Balaban and Zugec [19] proposed and validated a framework for digitally mature schools (FDMS). The framework recognises five different levels of maturity in the form of a rubric. Begicevic et al.'s FDMS collapsed Durek et al.'s [18] framework into five dimensions namely; 1) planning, management and leadership, 2) ICT in learning and teaching, 3) development of digital competencies, 4) ICT culture, and 5) ICT infrastructure. The framework and the ensuing instrument support educational institutions in assessing, promoting and integrating digital technologies in teaching, learning and organisational practices.

Love et al.'s [20] maturity model for ePortfolios recognises five levels of digital maturity of organisations, with each one providing a stepping-stone for the next one. However, Begicevic Redjep et al. [19] warned that we should not read the different levels as judgemental but consider them as stages of the maturation process since maturity is a journey.

Based on their common characteristics, Begicevic Redjep et al. [21], in their paper: Framework for Digitally Mature Schools, named and described the five levels of digital maturity as Basic, Initial, e-Enabled, e-Confident and e-Mature. Basic is the school that is not aware of the possibility of using ICT in learning and teaching or management processes. Therefore, the school does not consider ICT when planning its growth and development. It does not use ICT in learning and teaching and does not provide ICT infrastructure yet, and computers are used only in a few classrooms in the school. Thus, online communication with the school is generally not possible.

At the initial stage of digital maturity, the school is aware of the possibility of using ICT in learning, teaching and management processes, but it has not yet been implemented. A small number of teachers use ICT in learning and teaching. There is awareness of the need to enhance the digital competencies of teachers and students. However, the system for the professional development of digital competencies still does not exist. The ICT infrastructure is generally undeveloped, with limited access to ICT resources and internet access available only in a few classrooms.

The school that is e-Enabled is aware of the possibility of using ICT in all its activities. It participates in small ICT-focused projects and guides the development of its strategic documents and integration of ICT into these documents. It uses ICT for working with students with special educational needs. Teachers can advance their digital competencies, develop digital content, and introduce innovative teaching methods. The school provides access to different ICT resources in most classrooms and gives special attention to equipment maintenance and the control of software licencing.

Begicevic Redjep et al. [21] described an e-Confident school as recognising the advantages of ICT usage in its activities and integrating the ICT implementation into strategic documents and everyday activities such as ICT projects. Teachers use ICT for advanced teaching and assessment methods and develop their own content and protect the same by copyright. It plans and performs the continuous professional training of teachers to acquire digital competencies. Students are encouraged to develop those competencies. The school provides access to different ICT resources in most classrooms, with shared repositories for all participants and plans the procurement and maintenance of the ICT resources. The school is also very active online in content presentation and communication. It controls software licencing and considers the security aspects of ICT use.

An e-Mature school very clearly recognises and requires ICT in all activities in its strategic documents and development plans. The management practice relies on integrating and obtaining data from all school information systems. The approach to enhancing the digital competencies of teachers and students is systematic, and professional training for teachers and additional course activities for students are available. Teachers use ICT within advanced teaching methods to develop new course content and assess student achievements. The school independently plans and acquires ICT resources available in nearly all classrooms and other rooms in the school. The entire school has a developed network infrastructure. An information security system has been designed, and software licencing is systematically controlled and planned. The school is characterised by varied ICT project activities and cooperation between teachers and students and other schools and stakeholders.

Just as it is uncertain if any university library in Nigeria can claim digital maturity because of the apparent challenges confronting them, no study in the extant literature reported any model or framework used to assess libraries' digital maturity. The study reported in this chapter attempts to address this gap in the literature using the framework for digital mature schools by Begicevi Redjep et al. [21]. The specific objectives of the study are to:

1. gauge the level of digital maturity in the university libraries in Nigeria;

2. determine the dimensions of the digital maturity framework that predict the level of digital maturity of university libraries in Nigeria and

Based on objectives two and three, three null hypotheses are tested in the paper. They are:

1. The dimensions of the digital maturity framework do not significantly influence the level of digital maturity in university libraries in Nigeria.

2. There is no significant relationship between the digital maturity and age of university libraries in Nigeria.

2. Methodology

The paper adopts a quantitative approach to determine the stage attained by university libraries in their digital transformation efforts to be in tune with the realities of the digital economy using an online structured questionnaire to collect data. The questionnaire has seven sections. Section A elicits information about the institution and the responding personnel.

Since university libraries support their parent institutions to achieve the mandate of teaching, learning, and research, this study adopts Begicevic Redjep et al.'s [19] framework to determine the digital transformation status in university libraries in Nigeria in Sections B to F of the questionnaire. The 38 items distributed among the five dimensions of the framework from Sections B to F are re-worded to reflect digital technology applications to library operations and services. Dimensions 1–4 of the framework in Sections B to E have seven times each, while the fifth in Section F has 10 items. The final instrument requests the participants to confirm or otherwise how applicable the questionnaire's statements the five sections are to their libraries on a scale of five (1 = does not apply to 5 = totally applies). The mean score of the responses represents the level of digital transformation in the library (where 1 = very low, 2 = low, 3 = moderate, 4 = high, 5 = very high).

The section G requires the respondents to categorically rate the level of maturity of their libraries on a scale of five (5) (1 = basic, 2 = initial, 3 = enabled, 4 = confident, and 5 = mature) based on how well they believed the statements in Sections B to F apply to their libraries.

The researchers used the Googe Form app to prepare the questionnaire and sent it to participants via social media platforms, including Whatsapp, Facebook and Telegram. The researchers sent the link to the survey to the email addresses of some heads of university libraries. The survey was on for four weeks. The study used the Statistical Package for Social Science (SPSS) version 16 to analyse the data collected, and the results are presented in the results section.

3. Results

Forty-eight universities (64% public and 36% private) responded to the online survey. About 37% and 33% of the libraries are between 25 and 50 years old and 10 to 24 years old. The respondents are heads of the libraries and library personnel in charge of the deployment and management of ICT facilities (59% females and 41% males), most of whom have worked in the libraries for more than ten years (59.6%). The participants are purposively selected for the study because they are believed to implement and drive the digital transformation of their respective libraries.

University libraries, in general, adopt digital technologies for meeting the diverse information needs of clients and creating inspiring spaces and innovative services to support the teaching, learning and research mandates of their parent institutions. The assertion may explain why all the university libraries that participated in this study integrate ICTs into their operations and services. All the universities integrate ICTs with their services and processes at different times but not less than five years ago. **Figure 1** presents the history of ICT integration in university libraries in Nigeria. The mean age of ICT implementation in all university libraries is between 5 and 15 years ago; meaning that most of the libraries started integrating ICT with their operations and services less than 20 years ago.

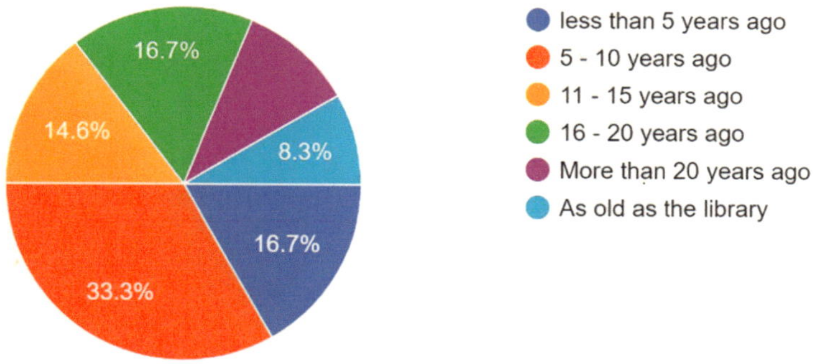

Figure 1.
History of ICT integration in university libraries in Nigeria.

3.1 Digital maturity of university libraries in Nigeria

The study's first objective is to gauge the digital maturity of university libraries in Nigeria. To achieve the purpose, the survey requests the participants to rank their libraries on a scale of five (1 = basic, 2 = initial, 3 = e-enabled, 4 = e-confident and 5 = e-mature). **Figure 2** shows the response distribution of the participants with a mean of 3.25 and a standard deviation of 1.06. The chart shows that most libraries are e-enabled, meaning that they are aware of the possibility of the libraries being e-enabled, meaning that they are aware of using ICT in all their activities. They participate in small ICT-focused projects and use ICT for working with patrons with special

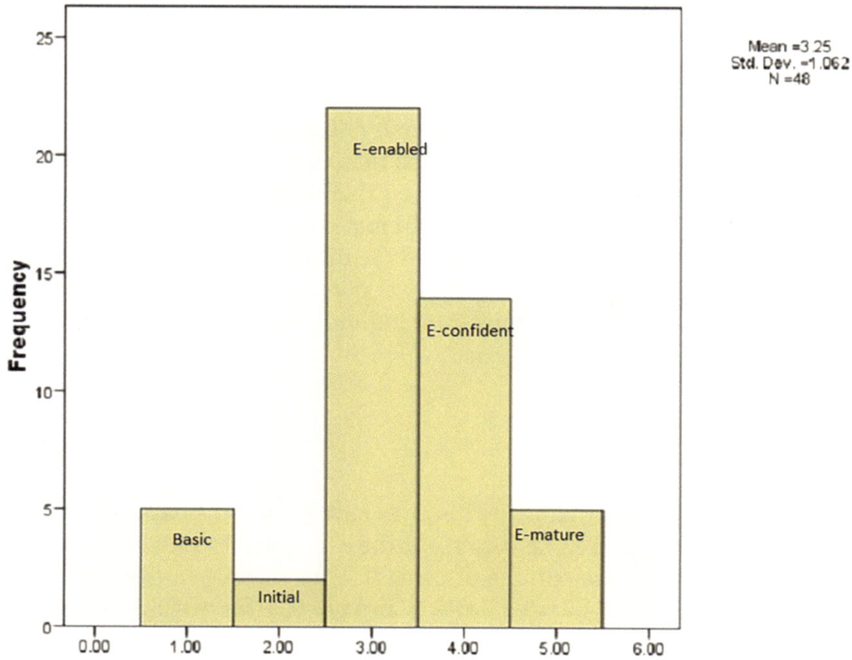

Figure 2.
Level of digital maturity of university libraries in Nigeria.

Variables	N	Mean	Standard deviation	df	R	R^2	F	Sig
Level of Digital maturity	48	3.27	1.07	5	0.85	0.73	22.68	0.00
ICT planning, management and leadership	48	3.79	0.90					
ICT Use in Library operations and services	48	4.06	0.85					
ICT competence development	48	3.42	0.93					
ICT culture	48	3.75	0.87					
ICT infrastructure	48	3.54	0.94					

Source: Data Analysis from the Study.

Table 1.
Relationships between the level of digital maturity and ICT dimensions in university libraries in Nigeria.

information needs. Also, the librarians can advance their digital competencies, develop digital content, and introduce innovative services by providing different ICT-based resources and giving special attention to equipment maintenance and the control of software licencing. The finding supports the report of Makori and Mauti [22]. They noted university libraries in Kenya (public and private) implement various technological approaches to provide for the information needs of their users. Such practices include social computing, internet and web-based services, information portals and digital repositories. Others are modern information environments, social media networks and multimedia applications. Although, the present study did not investigate the types of digital technologies and strategies used by university libraries in Nigeria, one may infer that their experiences are not different from their Kenyan counterparts.

The study's second objective is to determine the dimensions of the ICT framework that predict the digital maturity of university libraries in Nigeria. **Table 1** presents the result of the Regression analysis to explain the relationships among the level of digital maturity and the ICT dimensions in the university libraries.

There is a strong correlation between digital maturity and ICT dimensions in university libraries. The result presented in the Table shows that the five dimensions jointly predict 73% of the changes in the digital maturity of the libraries ($R^2 = 0.73$; $F = 22.68$ at $p < 0.05$). The study also finds that the dimensions of ICT planning, management and leadership ($\beta = 0.34$, $t = 2.40$ at $p < 0.05$) and ICT infrastructure ($\beta = 0.55$, $t = 3.68$ at $p < 0.05$) have significant individual effects on the level of digital maturity in university libraries in Nigeria.

4. Discussions

The study's finding shows that many libraries have passed the basic and initial stages of digital maturity, and a majority are at the e-Enabled level. This implies that the libraries are aware of the possibility of using ICT for their operations and services. They participate in small ICT-focused projects and use ICT for working with patrons with special information needs. Librarians can advance their digital competencies, develop digital content, and introduce innovative services by providing different ICT-based resources and giving special attention to equipment maintenance and the control of software licencing.

The dimensions of planning, strategy and leadership and building ICT infrastructure are positively significant to the level of maturity of the libraries in their efforts towards digital transformation. The observed statistical relationship implies that the libraries must consciously and deliberately pay attention to including strategic ICT implementation in their organisational planning and development. The libraries also must build capacity for leadership to drive their digital transformation agenda and acquire appropriate infrastructure for its successful implementation.

As illustrated by **Table 2**, the dimension of planning, management and leadership in ICT integration predicts the level of digital maturity in university libraries in Nigeria by 34% ($\beta = 0.34$). This finding suggests that developing leadership capabilities in planning and management is crucial to successfully integrate digital technologies and strategies into library operations and services. The result confirms the significant role of planning, management and leadership in the digital transformation of organisations as espoused in the literature, such as Begicevic Redjep et al. [19]. However, it was uncertain if the university libraries have formal documents stating their vision and guidelines towards digital transformation because the researchers did not include this aspect in the study. It will be worth the while for future studies to visit the physical location of the libraries to review their organisational structures to confirm the existence of actual policy documents, leadership drive and specific roadmap designed for deploying and implementing digital strategies and technologies in the institutions. The researchers' personal experience shows that implementation of ICTs in most university libraries is always dependent on the ICT strategies of their parent institutions, implying that the libraries do not usually have control over the planning and management of technology infrastructure. The development may take a toll on their efforts towards attaining digital maturity.

In their book, *Leading Digital: Turning Technology into Business Transformation*, Westermann, Bonnet, & McAfee [5] assert that "technology can remove obstacles and extend organisational capabilities, but it is not an end in itself." For an organisation to attain digital mastery, it needs to focus on its business and not the technology to enhance customers' experience, streamline operations or transform business models. As observed in the study, university libraries in Nigeria are well aware of the possibilities of using ICTs in their activities and management processes and also recognise the immense benefits of digital technologies. However, not many university libraries are at

Model	Unstandardized coefficients		Standardised coefficients	t	Sig
	B	Std Error			
(Constant)	−0.80	0.43		−1.88	0.07
ICT planning, management and leadership	0.41	0.17	0.34	2.40	0.02
ICT Use in Library operations and services	0.16	0.21	0.14	0.85	0.40
ICT competence development	−0.12	0.16	−0.10	−0.73	0.77
ICT culture	0.01	0.20	0.00	0.03	0.98
ICT infrastructure	0.63	0.17	0.55	3.68	0.00
Dependent variable: Digital maturity of university libraries in Nigeria.					

Table 2.
Coefficients.

the strategic implementation of ICTs to operations and services. University libraries in Nigeria are still at a level of awareness and appreciation of ICT and not yet taking full advantage of its potential to enhance service delivery and extend operational capabilities. For instance, just about 40% of the survey participants agreed and strongly agreed to the claim that "the library personnel use ICT for advanced services". The observed response pattern corroborates the work of Idhalama and Ifidon [23]. They found only a few university libraries in Nigeria implementing cutting-edge ICT facilities to manage their library resources and services. This development is very much unlike what is obtainable in developed countries of Europe, North America and parts of Asia.

One of the major problems militating against digital transformation in many developing countries like Nigeria is the shortage of ICT infrastructure and facilities. Several authors across Africa, including Chizenga [24], Oketunji [25], Okiy [26], Gbaje [27], Akanni [28] and Okiy [29], lamented the problem which still lingers to date. The researchers' personal experiences reveal that many university libraries in Nigeria experience epileptic power supply, which is an essential requirement for the digital transformation agenda of any organisation. University libraries in Nigeria often consider ICT infrastructure as acquiring computer machines, installing library management software, internet access, and subscriptions to electronic information resources. Although many libraries invest in these facilities, particularly the public universities with access to the Tertiary Education Tax Funds (TETFUND), power failure hampers their functionality.

Another significant infrastructural deficit in the digital transformation efforts of libraries in Nigeria is the lack of provisions for physically challenged individuals. Iroeze et al. [30] report in their study of library services for the physically challenged in Nigeria that such services are inadequate, outdated and provided in poorly architectural designed facilities. The respondents to the current study corroborated the gloomy picture painted by Iroeze et al. [30] because only a few believe that their libraries have dedicated digital resources and facilities for unique users such as people living with disabilities. The finding is also similar to that of Lawal-Solarin [31], who noticed that the architectural designs of most academic libraries in Ogun State, Nigeria, did not consider the peculiarities of the physically challenged persons.

The digital transformation agenda of any organisation should be all-inclusive. It must not discriminate against any individual peculiarities. The effort should cater to every community member's disabilities, strengths, and weaknesses. Unfortunately, Martinez and Vemuru, in a blog post at World Bank.org, noted that "persons with disabilities in Nigeria persistently face stigma, discrimination, and barriers to accessing essential social services and economic opportunities" [32]. This assertion might explain why library services usually exclude physically challenged people in Nigeria. Therefore, if Nigerian university libraries would attain maturity in their digital transformation efforts, they need to invest in strategic, all-inclusive and robust ICT infrastructure to drive their operations and services.

A critical indicator of digital transformation is the development of digital competencies; however, it does not significantly affect the level of digital maturity of university libraries in Nigeria. Digital competence, according to the recommendation of the European Parliament on the critical competencies for lifelong learning, is the confident and necessary use of Information Society Technology (IST) for work, leisure and communication [33]. It encompasses a set of attitudes, knowledge, skills, awareness, and values that are of great importance when utilising disruptive digital technologies and tools in an organisation [34].

Digital technologies shape how organisations interact with their internal and external stakeholders. Thus, a new culture that influences organisational values and norms emanates from digital technologies and tools. Digital culture emerged with the process of shared experience in digital environments. Organisations with a robust digital culture use digital tools and data-powered insights to drive decisions and unlock value [35]. In a nutshell, digital culture helps organisations integrate environmental, social and governance commitments and action across the organisation.

The extent to which ICT shapes the environment and experience of work in university libraries is critical to the digital transformation journey of an organisation. According to Akintunde [36], "many libraries in Nigeria still operate in the traditional service pattern where librarians are in charge in main service points of circulation, reference, serials, acquisition, cataloguing and documents without any emphasis on academic disciplines". Akintunde's standpoint confirms the embryonic state of digital culture in Nigerian university libraries. The slow pace of imbibing the ICT culture is borne out of a lack of competencies among academic librarians, as Okiy [29] observed in her paper titled *Globalisation and ICT in academic libraries in Nigeria: the way forward*. For academic librarians to render more effective services in the new digital environment, Okiy submits that they need to brace up to the unique challenges of ICT competencies. Her submission corroborated Okorie and Ekere [37] that if information professionals do not keep abreast of the changing technologies, they will be unable to manage the different types of information resources and cope with the users' ever-growing information needs in this electronic age.

One limitation of this paper is that the researchers did not visit the libraries to have an on-site assessment of their work environment to understand the digital lifestyle of the community. However, our personal experiences as one-time students and current workers in two of the universities that participated in the survey confirm that ICT culture is underway in Nigerian university libraries. Therefore, assimilating digital culture in Nigerian university libraries is a function of the readiness of academic librarians to build capacities for effective ICT use.

5. Conclusion

This chapter establishes that the journey to digital maturity in Nigerian university libraries is ongoing and at the embryonic stage. For Nigeria to achieve its vision and mission for transformation to a digital economy that will promote prosperity and security, the collaboration between academia and the industry is of the essence. According to Inyene Ibanga,

> *"academia serves as the centre for generating new knowledge and imparting education to students. Industry focuses on applying skills and efficient management to address solutions that have commercial value. Combining these two can lead to accelerated advances in innovation and entrepreneurship. This will, in turn, yield economic growth, capital formation and other attendant benefits" [38].*

Nigerian universities need to continue developing staff and institutional capacities to meet with the fast-changing digital innovations to proffer solutions to societal problems and challenges. For the universities to be positioned for this role, researchers must access current and relevant information resources and services their libraries provide. Therefore, the digital transformation efforts in academia must include deliberate empowerment of the library institutions and personnel if the universities would fulfil their mandates of research, teaching, learning and community development services.

Although, university libraries in Nigeria are deploying various ICT equipment and solutions to render services and enhance their operations, our study's findings revealed that the majority are yet to attain digital maturity. As Nigeria transforms into a digital economy, capacity building for libraries of higher institutions should occupy a prime position in the country's digital transformation agenda. The infrastructural deficit in most public universities, particularly irregular power supply, needs urgent attention and fixing to produce the required and relevant workforce for the emerging digital economy.

Author details

Akinniyi A. Adeleke[1*], Yemisi Ojokuku[2] and Joshua Onaade Ojo[3]

1 Tekena Tamuno Library, Redeemer's University, Ede, Nigeria

2 Department of Library & Information Science, Federal Polytechnic, Ede, Nigeria

3 University Library, University of Lagos, Lagos, Nigeria

*Address all correspondence to: adelekea@run.edu.ng

References

[1] Fosu A. Readiness of Universities for the 21st Century digital economies: A look at selected lecturers from Universities in Buffalo City Metropolitan in Eastern Cape Province South Africa. International Journal of Community Development & Management Studies, 2019;**3**:65-77. Retrieved from: http://ijcdms.org/Volume03/v3p065-077Fosu5523.pdf

[2] Adeleke AA. Resolving staff-patron conflicts with digitization: 'One' 'library's experience. New York: Library Hi Tech News. 2019;**36**(2):17-20. DOI: 10.1108/LHTN-09-2018-0060

[3] Kane G, Palmer D, Devine G. Achieving digital maturity. In: Research Report Summer 2017. New York. MIT Sloan Management Review & Deloitte University Press; 2017

[4] Chanias S, Hess T. How digital are we? "Maturity models for assessment of a company" 'company's status in digital transformation. In: LMU Munich Management Report 2/2016. Munich, Germany: Munich School of Management; 2016

[5] Westermann G, Bonnet D, McAfee A. Leading Digital: Turning Technology into Business Transformation. Boston, Massachusetts: Havard Business Review Press; 2014

[6] Rutkowski D. Digital Maturity: What it Is, How to Achieve it, and the Digital Maturity Model to Drive Business Transformation. 2022. Retrieved from Performance Improvement Partners: https://www.pipartners.com/digital-maturity/

[7] Anuradha P. Digital transformation of academic libraries: Opportunities and challenges. IP Indian Journal of Library Science and Information Technology. 2018;**3**(1):8-10

[8] NUC. "Nigerian Universities Approved by the NUC", National Universities Commission. Switzerland. 2012. Available at: www.nuc.edu.ng/pages/universities

[9] Baro EE, Oyeniran GK, Ateboh B. Digitization projects in university libraries in Nigeria: The journey so far. Library Hi Tech News. 2013;**30**(9):21-26. DOI: 10.1108/LHTN-09-2013-0049

[10] Proença DB. Information security management systems - a maturity model based on ISO/IEC 27001. In: Proença DB, Abramowicz W, Paschke A, editors. Business Information Systems. Switzerland: Springer; 2018. pp. 102-114

[11] Proença DV. A maturity model for information governance. In: Proença DV, Fuhr LKN, editors. Research and Advanced Technology for Digital Libraries. Vol. 9819. Cham, Switzerland: Springer; 2016. pp. 15-26

[12] Remane GH. Digital maturity in traditional industries: An exploratory analysis. In: 25th European Conference on Information Systems. Guimaraes, Portugal: ECIS; 2017

[13] Ifenthaler DE. Development and implementation of a maturity model of digital transformation. Tech Trends. 2020;**64**:302-309. DOI: 10.1007/s11528-019-00457-4

[14] Carvalho JV. A comparative study on maturity models for information systems in higher education institutions. In: Carvalho JV, Rocha TA, editors. Digital Science. DSIC18 2018. Advances in Intelligent Systems and Computing. Cham: Springer. 2019;**850**:150-158. pp. 150-158

[15] Rossmann A. Digital Maturity: Conceptualization and Measurement Model. 39th International Conference on Information Systems. San Fracisco: Association of Information Systems; 2018. pp. 1-9. Retrieved from https://aisel.aisnet.org/icis2018/governance/Presentations/8/

[16] Isaev EA, Korovkina NL, and Tabakova MS. "Evaluation of the readiness of a company's IT department for digital business transformation," Business Informatics (44:2), 2018. pp. 55-64. https://doi.org/10.17323/1998-0663.2018.2.55.64

[17] Poruban S. "Achieving digital maturity," Oil & Gas Journal (115:7), 2017. p. 14

[18] Durek V, Kadoic N, Redep BN. Assessing the digital maturity level of higher education institutions. In: 41st International Convention on ICT, Electronics and Microelectronics. Varazdin: Objavljena verzija rada; 2018. pp. 747-752. Retrieved from https://urn.nsk.hr/urn:nbn:hr:211:384585

[19] Begicevic Redjep NP, Balaban I & Zugec B. Assessing digital maturity of schools: Framework and instrument. Technology, Pedagogy and Education. 2021;**30**(5):1-17. DOI: 10.1080/1475939X.2021.1944291

[20] Love D, McKean G, Gathercoal P. Portfolios to webfolios and beyond: Levels of maturation. Educause Quarterly. 2004;**27**(2):24-37. Retrieved from https://er.educause.edu/-/media/files/articles/2004/4/eqm0423.pdf?la=en%26hash=4FB40C07FBFB46A3DC3AE34FD938937856288E07

[21] Begicevi Redjep N, Balaban I, Zugec B, Klacmer Calopa M, Divjak B. Framework for digitally mature schools. In: Proceedings of the European Distance and E-Learning Network 2017 Annual Conference. Jonkopng, Sweden: European Distance and E-Learning Network; 2017. pp. 360-371

[22] Makori EO and Mauti NO. Digital technology acceptance in transformation of university libraries and higher education institutions in Kenya. Library Philosophy and Practice, 1;2016

[23] Idhalama O, Ifidon EI. Information and communications technology (ICT) use in libraries: A plus or minus to academic libraries in Nigeria? Sumerianz Journal of Social Science. 2019;**2**(6): 68-73. Retrieved from https://www.sumerianz.com/

[24] Chizenga I. Global information and libraries In sub-Sahara Africa. Library Management. 2000;**21**(4):174-187

[25] Oketunji I. Agenda for putting information technology to work In Nigerian libraries In the new millennium. In: Compendium of Papers Presented at Annual National Conference and AGM. Owerri: Nigerian Library Association; 2000. pp. 17-21

[26] Okiy RB. Towards improving the relevance of Nigerian academic libraries and librarians in the knowledge age. The Academic Forum. 2003;**4**(3):63-68

[27] Gbaje E. Provision of online information services In Nigerian academic libraries. Nigerian Libraries. 2007;**40**:1-4

[28] Akanni SB. Globalization: Challenges and opportunities for Nigerian libraries. In: Compendium of Papers Presented at the 46th Annual National Conference and AGM of the Nigerian Library Association. Kaduna: Nigerian Library Association; 2008. pp. 1-12

[29] Okiy RB. Globalization and ICT in academic libraries in Nigeria:

The way forward. Library Philosophy and Practice (e-journal). 2010;**501**: 1-11 (online). Retrieved from https://digitalcommons.unl.edu/libphilprac?utm_source=digitalcommons.unl.edu%2Flibphilprac%2F501&utm_medium=PDF&utm_campaign=PDFCoverPages

[30] Iroeze P, Umunnakwe GC, Eze JU. Library Services for the Physically Challenged in south-East Nigeria: Origin and challenges. International Journal for Advanced Library and Information Science. 2017;**5**(1):393-405 Retrieved from https://bit.ly/34hRMhw

[31] Lawal-Solarin EO. A survey of library and information services to physically-challenged students in academic libraries in Ogun state, Nigeria. Library Philosophy and Practice (e-Journal). 2012. Retrieved from https://bit.ly/3r8TcUp

[32] Martinez RM & Vemuru V. World Bank Blogs. 2020. Retrieved from World Bank.Org: https://blogs.worldbank.org/nasikiliza/social-inclusion-persons-disabilities-nigeria-challenges-and-opportunities

[33] European Union. Recommendation of the European Parliament and of the Council of 18 December 2006 on Key Competencesfor Lifelong Learning 2006/962/EC. Brussels: European Union: Official Journal of the European Union; 2006

[34] Dzingirai M. Demystifying corporate restructuring strategy through digital transformation: Lessons learned from the banking sector of Zimbabwe. Sandhu K. In: Emerging Challenges, Solutions, and Best Practices for Digital Enterprise Transformation Hershey, Pennsylvania: IGI Global. 2021. pp.164-181. doi:10.4018/978-1-7998-8587-0.ch009

[35] World Economic Forum. Digital Culture: The Driving Force of Digital Transformation. 2021. Retrieved from Digital Culture Guidebook: https://www.weforum.org/docs/WEF_Digital_Culture_Guidebook_2021.pdf

[36] Akintunde SA. State of ICTs in tertiary institutions in Nigeria: Window on the universities. In: Compendium of Papers Presented at the 44th Annual National Conference and AGM of Nigerian Library Association. Abuja: Nigerian Library Association; 2006. pp. 123-137

[37] Okorie AM, Ekere JN. Information professional and knowledge Management in Global Library and Information Service. In: Compendium of Papers Presented at the 46th Annual National Conference and AGM of the Nigerian Library Association. Kaduna: Nigerian Library Association; 2008. pp. 53-62

[38] Ibanga I. Promoting Universities and Tech Industry Collaboration. Lagos, Nigeria: Premium Times; 2021. Retrieved from https://bit.ly/3AQJ8TA

Chapter 4

Modelling Digital Economy Implications on Long-Run Economic Development

Elsadig Musa Ahmed

Abstract

This chapter develops frameworks and models to examine digital transformation into digital economies via digital technologies' applications at both the macro and micro levels via both positive and negative externalities generated by digital technologies and pollutant emissions. A productivity mixed method approach has been developed based on the chapter modified frameworks and models to be employed at both the macro and micro levels to utilise the digital technology applications that will help in transforming digital economies to sustain their economic development. The study provided digital economy frameworks and policies to help in implementing digital transformation and to develop and use the new technologies needed for sustainable economic growth through technological progress, human capital skills development and environmental protection via green productivity technological progress. The study contributes to the knowledge body via proposed productivity mixed method frameworks and models that examine digitisation processes. The aggregate economies, industries, companies and other businesses will be provided with frameworks and guidelines to implement digital technologies' applications that will help them to be transformed into digital sustainable economies. The most significant contribution of this study is treating digital technology cybersecurity negative externalities spill over effects similar to their negative externalities of pollutants' emissions counterparts, besides developing capital productivity framework and model that were ignored in most of the studies.

Keywords: digital economies, externalities, digital transformation, cybersecurity, green productivity, COVID-19 implications

1. Introduction

Economics like other social sciences has no one standard definition of the digital economy due to the subjective nature of the social sciences as has been mentioned by [1]. Conversely, a satisfactory definition must place importance on the generation and exploitation of digital knowledge over digital technology applications to create new value in the economy. Undeniably, knowledge is information that is put to productive work through digital technology applications. Knowledge includes information in any form, know-how and know-why among others. The digital economy is not confined to information and communication technology (ICT) digital applications. Before the evolution of the digital technologies, it was the knowledge that remained embodied in human beings' 'human capital' and technology that was embodied in the capital investment undertaken by the Asian economies that brought about the so-called Asian miracle [2].

In this respect, cybersecurity economics is the economics that discourses the concerns of protection of digital technology applications that premeditated to enable the economic activities that are ordinariness face cybercrimes that cost the individuals, companies and the countries enormous amount of money and interrupt the economic and financial activities around the world as it has been indicated in ICT-based sustainable development as reported in [ICT & Sustainable Development Goals (SDGs) report, 2015]. ICT-based sustainable development reports the ICT role in attaining SDGs that is presented by the United Nations (UN) for its members to achieve SDGs that are planned to be implemented comprehensively within 2030. Besides, the report points apprehension of the potential shortcomings of ICT-based sustainable development, these trace on at least six broad areas such as the online world will literally reshape brain development, possibly leading to a loss of human skills. Moreover, the virtual or online communities will somehow crow out, meaning that real human communities heading to a decline in human interactions, trust and sociality; this is will lead to what so-called 'bowling alone' phenomenon as assumed by sociologist Robert Putnam. Further, the robots are estimated to relocate human work to the point of initiating bulk unemployment and economic pessimism. This point faced the argument that there might be the sheen of truth in such arguments, but the central circumstance is that with suitable public policies, technological advances develop well-being as this is measured to be the positive externalities of digital technology that formed the digital economy around the world. Nevertheless, the negative externalities allied through the advance of this technology are the cybersecurity negative externalities and the disparity of the human skills to optimise the digital dividends created in terms of a long-run sustainable economic growth involvement via the digital technology contributions to produce economic well-being [2].

Meanwhile, the fourth concern, the digital economy is subject to network failures than a production-based economy that is overtaken by a knowledge-based economy due to ICT revaluation and currently by a digital economy via the emergent digital technologies such as giant performance catastrophes due to the Internet or power network could bring the economy to irresistible incursion. Additionally, the next concern is that the interruption of the networked economy will become deliberate turns of cyber-warfare or what so-called cybercrimes [1]. The last concern is of excessive nervousness as that the digital-technology-based economy is a surveillance economy, with worldwide snooping and detriment of privacy. The infiltration might be by government giant digital technologies organisations or a smart partnership of the two or a grouping both everywhere [2]. These depictions of cybersecurity externalities' uncertainties were offered disgraceful validation by Edward Snowden, as not of the least of which was the ambiguous and trickeries of endorsed institutions concerning their surveillance policies [2].

The abovementioned fears will be used in this study to corroborate the cybersecurity negative externalities' concerns associated with digital-technologies-based economic activities corresponding with their environmental externalities' complements that both created as unwanted output alongside the chief product that negatively impacted the economies worldwide and made vast economic mortalities and even formed uncertainty on the democracy and election results as the alleged Russian interruption in US Presidential election and the Chinese Giant mobile company products of Huawei that is prohibited from using the Google system for its 5G products concerning spying activities among others. The innovation made by the digital revolution led by digital-technologies-based accompanying by obstacles deliberated above that should be overwhelmed particularly the cybersecurity negative externalities correlated to security concerns that cost the economies and endangered them to innovate. Contradictory, the humankind's know-how with technology dating back to the commencement of the industrial revolution that disregards the unintended shortcomings of technology to unlimited peril, the digital revolution should offer responsible resolutions to overcome the cybersecurity negative externalities of these obstacles to progress in accomplishing the SDGs as planned to be flourished by 2030 [2].

Regarding the negative externalities associated with environmental damages, Ahmed [3] presents that the concept of Green Productivity (GP) is drawn from the incorporation of two central progressive strategies, namely productivity enhancement and environmental safeguard. Productivity offers the framework for boundless progress, whereas environmental precaution delivers the underpinning for long-run economic growth and sustainable development [3].

Consequently, GP is an approach for enhancing productivity and environmental performance for inclusive socio-economic development. GP is an influential strategy that can complement economic growth and environmental protection for long-run economic growth and sustainable development. It presents small and medium businesses with a methodology to attain a competitive advantage by existence of improved business models. It is consequently an accurate approach to upsurge productivity and safeguard the environment simultaneously [3].

Furthermore, the United Nations (UN) Sustainable Development Summit held in New York in September 2015 approved the goal of the sustainable development agenda by 2030 [4]. The UN summit proposed a new indicator framework, accompanying with global and collective indicators, for international partnership and cooperation to accomplish sustainable development for the period of 2015 and 2030, including 17 new Sustainable Development Goals (SDGs). In fact, every country should arrange these 17 SDGs based on its country need and development stages not only as arranged by UN. For example, some countries need to implement goal 16 (peace, justice and strong insinuations), other goals took place as the institutional failure, bad leadership and governance among others.

It should be recalled that before implementing the 17 SDGs, this study proposes that these 17 SDGs should be revised as some of them outdated due to the digital economy issues brought by industrial revaluation 4.0 digital technologies and new businesses models associated with COIVD-19 implications.

Meanwhile, changes in productivity considered are key concerns in any economy due to the connection between productivity and living standards [2–6]. The definitive aims of productivity improvement are countless competitiveness, greater profitability, upper living standards and well economic and social fortune. In this regard, Total Factor Productivity (TFP), labelled as the combined contribution of the factors of production qualities, is an indicator of the technological progress that displays the spillover effects that must transfer the technology to the hosting economy and upgrade the skills of its human capital, which is what is named productivity-driven. TFP can explain the growth in a digital economy since it captures endogenous technical change and other features of the digital economy, including diffusion of digital knowledge, organisation, restructuring, networking and new business models that would contribute to market efficiency and productivity [2, 3, 5].

According to [7], digital technology in the form of the Internet, mobile phones and all the other digital tools used to collect, store, analyse and share information digitally consumes and has grown swiftly everywhere in the world. It has been projected that 70% of the households have mobile phones than have access to electricity and clean water in developing countries. Moreover, Internet users' number has more than tripled in a decade appraised to be in the range of 1 billion in 2005, 3.2 billons by the end of 2015. This means businesses, people and governments are more connected than before the digital revolution. The digital divide displays the gap in access to ICT applications within nation or between nations. In this respect, digital dividends (the income generated via using digital technology applications) are the broader development that benefits from using digital technologies. In several occurrences, digital technologies enhanced growth, expanded opportunities and better-quality service delivery. The digital dividends aggregate effect has dropped little and is unequally disseminated. For the digital technologies to benefit everybody everywhere in the world, it would be needed to close the residual digital divide, particularly in Internet access as it has been shown during COVID-19, many countries and business are not able to run online during movement control orders. Though, countless digital adoption will not be enough if it has not created value-added digital dividends from the economic activities.

2. Digital economy flagships and pillars

Digital economy flagships and pillars should be established as the groundwork for the digital economy institutions and facilities needed for its activities. With respect to digital economy flagships and pillars, certain countries are in an advanced stage in establishing digital economy flagships and pillars, some are in the starting stage and some have not thought about it. For instance, Malaysia developed their knowledge economy master plan in 1996 and embedded the digital economy flagships in stages that should be completed in 2020. Some other countries are ongoing in developing the digital economy foundation, and some are in the initial stages of digital economy flagships and pillars progress. Reviewing the countries' experiences that scheduled and established their economies into digital economies, such as countries in America, Europe and Southeast Asia, this study found that Malaysia's experience is a upright sample to monitor as the country prearranged comprehensively for the digital economy foundations. Multimedia Super Corridor (MSC) was developed for knowledge economy flagships and pillars, among economic corridors in several Malaysian states that are upgraded to digital economy flagships and pillars with a revised digital economy master plan [6].

To acquire significant advantage from the digital technologies, countries also need to work on the analog matches; such as strengthening regulations that guarantee competition between businesses, by adapting workers' digital skills to the demands of the digital economy and by guaranteeing that institutions are accountable. It should be noted that increasing human capital (skilled workers) particularly digital skills is a perquisite of progressing and realising digital technologies' applications in economic sectors and companies. With the accurate digital human skills, digital technologies will enable economic activities, due to the fact that technology in general and digital technologies' applications in particular are architects that need the right human skills to function [6].

To develop a competitive edge in a digital economy would need a highly skilled digital human capital besides other skilled workers. Highly skilled and talented human capital is likewise energy to grow the digital economy. The 'know-how' that goes into the production of innovative products to enable companies, businesses, organisations and countries to be competitive in the global market habitation will be provided by their exceptional skills. Besides, out-migration drains the limited talent pool: several professionals and technical personnel and students overseas have migrated to the countries that provided chances to progress; achieve their mental satisfaction to contribute and to enjoy their achievements senses among other benefits missed in their home countries. Another chance is to bring in the indispensable skilled human from overseas to the home countries which is liberalising recruitment with chances and benefits equal to what have enjoyed overseas to progress in their home countries. The education institutions should play a significant role as the foundation of the human capital development that is considered to be one of the important pillars to develop a digital economy [8].

Additional significant challenge that will be faced in the determination to transfer to a digital economy would be the capability to construct an innovative capacity in the country; hence, innovative goods and services could be developed for the digital economy [8]. With amplified liberalisation of economies and the elimination of tariff barriers via trade agreements and economic unions, goods and services produced by companies and countries will have to compete with corporations and national companies in general and specifically Small and Medium Enterprises (SMEs).

Research and Development (R&D) present amount of financial and other resources allocated in most of the countries as a percentage of GDP is minor compared with other countries that developed their economies into digital economies. The governments must foster an environment where creative and innovative thinking are fulfilled. Encouragements should be prearranged to persons and companies who originated cutting-edge concepts, innovative technologies and products in recognition to such inventions, innovations and outstanding discoveries. These prizes and credit should be firmly for the contribution of an innovative products and processes that would enrich innovative capacity and competitive standing in the universal marketplace [7].

Particular countries are highly qualified to be education centres that attract students around the globe, with the existing condition, higher institutions graduates and technicians are the most important sources of Gulf countries' human capital. If the education institutions established well, graduates could compete around the globe through developing economies into digital economies with the right foundations to facilitate the economic activities and businesses. The current business model practiced should be refined to encounter digital economy foundations' requirements. The current business model's improvement to meet the COVID-19 implications most likely will contribute and complement economic value added to the economic progress and accomplish the anticipated digital economy if deliberate it well in a short period of time as the latter countries will catch up very fast to achieve their economic growth. SMEs are the backbone of the economies everywhere in the world; 90–99% of the companies in in most of the countries are SMEs that were not well classified define and are not existed in some countries. Further, SMEs are considered as the digital economy corner stone in transferring the technology and upgrading the local human capital skills through Foreign Direct Investment (FDI) spill over effects brought by the multinational companies to the host countries [1].

Furthermore, cyber laws should be familiarised to overwhelm the cyber complications allied with digital economy activities. Cyber-crimes may take place overseas, and in this respect, there is an urgent need for collaboration around the world to overcome cyber-crimes through smart partnerships. It should note that the conclusive currency of a digital economy is intellectual property rights (IPRs) implementation via the rule of law based on the World Trade Origination (WTO) agreements. IPRs includes copyrights, patents, trademarks, service marks and goods of geographical indication. It should be noted that IPRs are legal monopolies awarded to original owners of copyrights and patents to enable them to benefit from their discoveries and ensure the sustainable inventions and innovations [2].

Emergent digital economy master plan to address the policies and developing digital economy institutions to move to a digital economy is considered to be the first step. This study will be useful for digital technologies policy formulation as an underpinning of the digital economy development. In this background, an appraisal of the digital technologies and productivity growth contributions in each of advanced countries in general and in the East Asian countries specifically will afford guidelines for the policy-makers to articulate applicable national and international digital technologies policies. This study findings based on the study frameworks and models developed are expected to help formulating policies to stimulate digital technologies investment to clue in enlightening human capital and infrastructure needed to support active digital technologies usage. It is likely that it can capitalise the interaction within the countries and between other countries and make full use of the competitive advantages in of all countries to impressed its deficiencies. The countries will be capable of fast-tracking the association towards technology-savvy nations that has been attained by Japan, South Korea and China, among others [6].

According to United Nations (UN) [4], there is a need to discourse security concerns connected with digital technology applications, hence to warrant the accomplishment of the implementation of the digital technology applications. More precisely, the concerns that should to be addressed are to guarantee security and privacy of existing e-channels, such as automated teller machine (ATM) and electronic point of sale (EPOS) among others, and to resolve all network problems. Building individuals' and societies' consciousness and counselling the communities about the reimbursements and use of new digital technologies and digital services are required. Here should be rigorous promotions to teach the public, particularly directing the urban and rural populations; consequently, they are conscious of the digital economy concepts and scopes to build the knowledge of digital socialites that is vital on which a digital economy would be based. Moreover, Ahmed [2] presents an appropriate regulatory setting, concerning user guidelines, trusts, rights and protections, right integration and a smart partnership between telecommunications network operators and the economy sectors, suitable staff training and presenting client literateness for appropriate use, evolving reliable and drivable digital technology's structure and rigorous digital products and service design are crucial to implement digital economy applications. Besides, collaborations, cooperation and smart partnerships between private and public sectors within countries and between countries to construct digital economies are instantly required particularly the smart partnership within a country and between the countries as the digital economy is a universal phenomenon that connected the world economy.

Lastly, as [2, 3] show, the sustainability of higher economic growth will remain to be productivity-driven not input-driven as experienced by most of the countries. The input-driven caused the collapse of the Soviet Union in 1990s as a result of combining many countries and used their resources without technological progress to sustain the economic development and long-run economic growth. The productivity-driven that should sustain higher and long-run economic growth will be achieved through the enhancement of TFP as a technological progress that combined the three dimensions of sustainable development (economic development, environmental protection and social sustainable development via human capital development and digital technologies). Such amplification needs to strain the human capital quality, demand intensity, economic restructuring, capital structure, technical progress and environmental standards. In this respect, the green productivity through green TFP creates the sustainable development concept of progressing technologically, socially and environmentally that will relieve to realise the sustainable development dimensions required for long-run economic growth and to guarantee its sustainability. That is, it will maintain the privileges of the upcoming, as well as existing, generations for them to gain a better life span.

3. Literature review

Feyen et al. [9] address the important cybercrimes prevention via data protection and interoperability as addressed by [10]. The study suggested that cybercrimes become more important via cross-border spill overs of antitrust and data-governing ace decisions, as well as the potential to improve fintech, and the digital transformation of financial service will be through harmonisation of standards in areas of cybercrimes prevention, data protection and interoperability, among others. In this respect, collaboration and smart partnerships can help via regulatory consistency and peer learning within the countries and between the countries that will achieve the higher well-being of the entire population and around the globe.

Furthermore, [11] mentioned that the financial ecosystem digitisation will be centre to economic growth in overall and an enhancement in several economic activities with a certain effect on customer experiences. The study addresses the need of cybersecurity and cyber management resolutions accomplished of rapidly recognising threat circumstances, counting cyber-attacks on digitised services and products and counsel the users on the possible forthcoming threat.

Meanwhile, Sabău et al. [12] identifies the importance of corporate governance to increase the digitalisation process among companies. In this respect, corporate governance and social responsibility are required elements to develop digital economy and to achieve digital inclusion. The study findings can be used to improve the public governance, investors, companies, governments to highpoint good corporate governance role for increasing the overall well-being of the society within the digital economy. As well as to preserve transparency enlarged, in a digital ecosphere appears comparable an easy thing to do.

Smart partnerships are very important within and between the nations in this regard [13] appraise the convergence across the European Union (EU) 28 members in the digital economy arena grounded on the Digital Economy and Society Index (DESI) and its dimensions via the log t club convergence method. The study empirical finding found that during the study period (2015–2020), there was no inclusive convergence across EU 28 members in the digitalisation context.

Accordingly, [3, 14] explain that the methods used to measure productivity growth mostly ignore the pollutants that are produced by the production process as undesirable products and unpriced output. For instance, pollutant emissions produced as undesirable output in addition to the main output of production are omitted from the productivity accounting framework and other approach that estimated productivity growth. This chapter tries to incorporate green productivity methods by taking into account pollutant emissions into production functions as un-priced inputs. The pollutant emissions under consideration include carbon dioxide (CO_2) emissions (that measures air pollution), Biochemical Oxygen Demand (BOD) emissions (that measures organic water pollution) and their mixture in the formula of total pollutant emissions, that is, combined air and water pollutions' emissions. Though, other pollutants' emissions should be measured, such as noise pollution and all other types of pollutants' emissions. It should be mentioned that, in 2018, the Nobel Prize for Economic Sciences was awarded to William D. Nordhaus and Paul M. Romer for research undertaken in the 1970s. William D. Nordhaus was awarded the prize for his research that addressed negative externalities, such as pollutant emissions, whereas Paul M. Romer was awarded the prize for his research concerning the new factors of production inclusion in the production function such as digital technology in the form of ICT and human capital to achieving long-term economic growth through technical progress and green development that sustain long-run economic growth via what recently called digital economy. Moreover, Romer [15–19] emphasised how the economy can expand the boundaries, and thus the possibilities, of its future activities. In his focus on the fundamental challenges of climate change, Nordhaus [20–29] stressed the importance of the negative side, and thus the restrictions, of the endeavours in bringing about future prosperity.

Moreover, Ahmed's [14, 30, 31] studies indicated that the greatest apparent absence in the growth accounting models undertaken by preceding studies was found to be the exclusion of externalities, such as the pollutant emissions, which were generated by the manufacturing and other economic sectors. The mentioned studies intended to add to the accessible literature on the growth accounting and econometric approaches, in that these studies combined together both methods to calculate the total factor productivity (TFP) and TFP per unit of labour growth as residuals. This residual identified by Solow [32, 33] via internalising the pollutant emissions with the traditional factors of productions employed in conventional production functions. Accordingly, green TFP and green TFP per unit of labour growth became indicators of green productivity. That is taking into account economic development and environmental protection benefiting from the studies undertaking by [34–40]. Finally, [6] recalled that: 'It has been documented in the Solow [32, 33] empirical work on economic growth that after accounting for physical and human capital accumulation, something else accounts for the bulk of output growth in most countries. Together, physical and human capital accumulations are definitely critical for economic growth. The development becomes more complex with the role of knowledge in the economic growth procedure'.

As has been mentioned earlier, in many instances, digital technologies boosted growth, expanded opportunities and improved service delivery. Their aggregate impact has fallen short and is unevenly distributed. For digital technologies to benefit everyone everywhere requires closing the remaining digital divide, especially in Internet access. To develop a competitive edge in a digital economy would need a highly skilled labour force. Greatly skilled human capitals are the fuel to the digital economy engine of growth. Highly skilled workforces will offer the 'know-how' gained via learning by doing those energies into the production of innovative products that empower companies, businesses and countries to be competitive worldwide.

Thanks to COVID-19-positive economic impact that forced people to work from home to sustain economic activities that was not acceptable around the globe due to technophobia in the heart and minds of the decisions makers and governments' officials to accept online comprehensive activates. High involvement on online activities is allowed via the digital technologies' applications to run daily activities via digital governance. This study developed frameworks and models to be employed and empirically examined the impact of COVID-19 and the digital technology's role in sustaining the economic growth. Besides, the study offers recommendations and policy implications to transfer the economies into digital economies that would sustain economic development under any undesirable conditions, such as COVID-19 that triggered massive economic losses. In this respect, digital economic development is expected to diminish the economic fatalities related with forthcoming global pandemics.

The main objective of this research is to model and examine the digital economy's positive and negative externalities spill over effects on the sustainable economic growth through employing a mixed method approach, consisting of quantitative and qualitative analysis at macro and micro levels.

The study recommended foundations to transform public and private sectors into a digital economy to achieve the Sustainable Development Goals (SDGs) agenda and to overwhelm the COVID-19 and upcoming pandemics' negative externalities. It will likewise be used to moderate the COVID-19 and forthcoming pandemics' negative impact through enabling economic activities under disinclinations via using the proposed frameworks and models that modified productivity approaches to accommodate digital technologies' applications.

The study fills the gaps in growth theories through developing three different frameworks and econometric models, and internalising pollutants' emissions as private and unpriced inputs in the three models. Further, the green capital productivity model is the exclusive contributing model developed in this research; it has not been assumed and empirically examined in previous studies, with the exception of the studies undertaken by [2, 3, 5, 41].

The significant contribution of this study has modified the fundamental findings of Nobel Prize Laureates' research findings [29] to integrate innovation and climate change in the form of green productivity as well as existing studies in developing frameworks and models to measure digital economy indicators such as digital technology positive externalities and negative externalities such as cybersecurity shortcomings and negative externalities generated by pollutants' emissions. The role of these externalities on long-term sustainable economic growth has been ignored by several past studies undertaken in these areas. These three modified frameworks and models in a significant method articulate the technological progress issues and sustainable economic growth as one of the most important sustainable developments and long-run economic growth dimensions.

4. Methodology development process

This study employed digital economy's positive and negative externalities in unindustrialised study frameworks and models in this chapter. At both the macro and micro economic levels, this chapter anticipates to use a mixed approach of quantitative and qualitative analysis. In this subdivision, a parametric analysis based on a combined method of parametric analysis is developed. The method combines both growth accounting that is non-parametric approach and econometric that is parametric approach. This method was developed to be applied in two steps: the first step is an econometric approach to estimate the study parameters (explanatory variables coefficients), whereas the second step plugs these parameters into the models to calculate the productivity indicators. Three frameworks and models have been developed based on [1–4, 6, 30, 31, 42] modified extensive growth theory and intensive growth theory (labour productivity and capital productivity). The aforementioned mentioned studies modified and combined the production function and Solow's residual [32, 33] and refined by [43] to fill the gaps in both approaches that cast doubts on the results generated by both. The framework (**Figure 1**) is an extensive growth theory presentation of Model 1 that consists of the output (Gross Domestic Product [GDP]) as a function of capital, labour, digital technology and pollutant emissions for pollution are the explanatory variables based on their quantity. In addition, the framework presents TFP that combined the inputs quality contribution (explanatory variables) that indicated that technological progress to be transformed into sustainable digital economies.

This chapter suggests a digital productivity framework, a digital labour productivity framework and digital capital productivity framework (**Figures 1–3**) to be used at the country level. The frameworks will measure the' digital economy productivity implications via the collection of a primary data survey and the analysis of qualitative focus groups interviews with concerned experts. The qualitative approach will capture

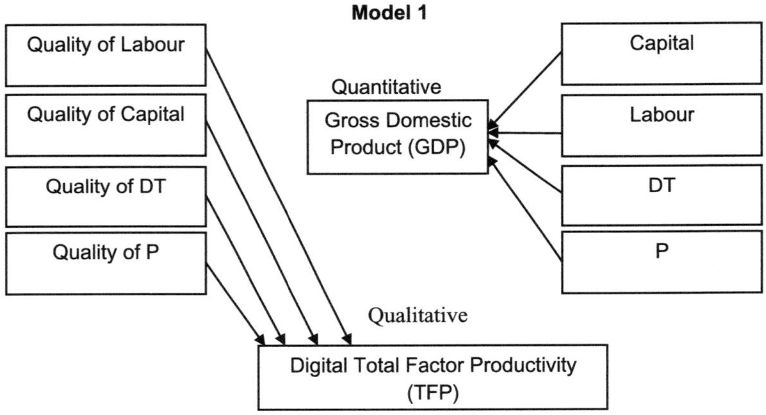

Figure 1.
Productivity framework, extensive growth theory. Source: Modified from [2].

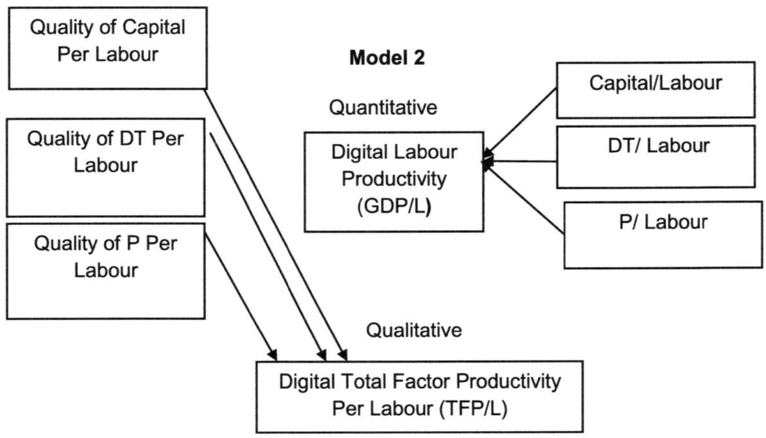

Figure 2.
Total factor productivity per worker framework, intensive growth theory. Source: Modified based on [2].

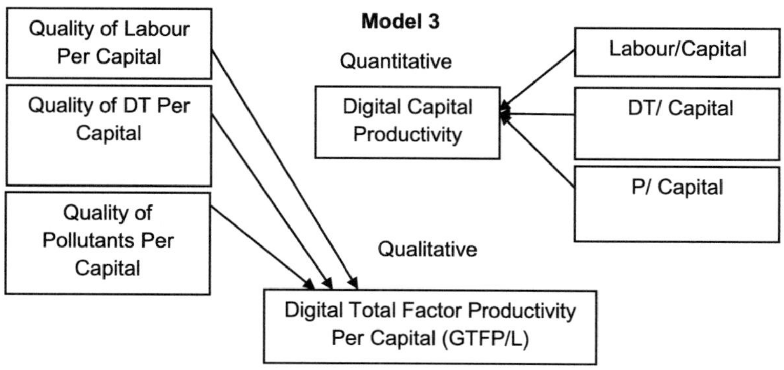

Figure 3.
Digital capital productivity framework, intensive growth theory. Source: Modified based on [2].

information and data that have not been published in the form of secondary data and information.

The production function for an economy can be categorised as follows:

$$\text{GDPt, i} = \text{F (Kt, i, Lt, i, DTt, i, Pt, i, Tt, i)} \quad (1)$$

where country i = 1, 2, ... in Years t, output real GDP is a function of real fixed physical capital input K, labour input L, DT for digital technology that includes digital technologies' variables including cybersecurity variables, while P represents the pollutant emissions, and time T proxies for TFP as a technological progress of the digital economies and sustainable development indicator.

4.1 Extensive growth theory

This subsection offers the extensive growth theory based on GDP that is decomposed into physical capital, employment, digital technology (DT) and pollutants' emissions (P). The chapter tries to fill the gap found in [30] research via modifying this model into a parametric model and providing statistical analysis for it in the first step, as follows:

$$\Delta\text{lnGDPt, i} = a + \alpha.\Delta\text{lnKt, i} + \beta.\Delta\text{lnLt, i} + \lambda.\Delta\text{lnDTt, i} + \theta.\Delta\text{lnPt, i} + \varepsilon t, i \quad (2)$$

t = Number of years and i is number of countries.
where.
α is the output elasticity with respect to capital
β is the output elasticity with respect to labour
λ **is** the output elasticity with respect to digital technology
θ is the output elasticity with respect to pollutants' emissions
a is the intercept or constant of the model[1]
ε is the residual term[2]
ln is the logarithm to transform the variables

[1] The intercept term, as usual, gives the mean or average effect on dependent variables of all the variables excluded from the model.

[2] The residual term proxies for the total factor productivity growth that accounts for the technological progress of the economy through the quality of input terms.

Δ is the difference operator denoting proportionate change rate.

The intercept (a) in Eq. (2) has no place in the calculation of the productivity growth indicators based on the estimated results of Eq. (2) by succeeding a second step. The second step computes the progression rates of productivity indicators, transforming Eq. (2) as an extension of the basic growth accounting framework. The production function is indicated in the parametric form of the above equation as follows:

$$\Delta \text{lnTFPit} = \Delta \text{lnGDPit} \ \text{-}[\ \alpha.\Delta \text{lnKit} + \beta.\Delta \text{lnLit} + \lambda.\Delta \text{lnDTit} + \theta.\Delta \text{lnPt, i}] \qquad (3)$$

Where the masses are assumed by the average value shares as follows:

$\Delta \text{lnGDPit}$ is the growth rate of output

$\alpha.\Delta \text{lnKit}$ is the contribution of the aggregate physicall capital

$\beta.\Delta \text{lnLit}$ is the contribution of the aggregate labour

$\lambda.\Delta \text{lnDTit}$ is the contribution of the digital technology

$\theta.\Delta \text{lnPit, i}$ is the contribution of the pollutants$'$emissions

$\Delta \text{lnTFPit}$ is the total factor productivity growth

The model decomposes the growth rate of GDP into the contributions of the rates of growth of the aggregate physical capital, labour, digital technology and pollutants' emissions, plus a residual term, typically referred to as the growth rate of TFP.

4.2 Intensive growth theory (labour productivity)

This subsection establishes an intensive growth theory framework (**Figure 2**) for Model 2, the labour productivity or output per labour (GDP)/labour as a function of capital per labour, digital technology per labour and pollutants' emissions per labour are the explanatory variables based on their quantity. Furthermore, the framework offers the total TFP per labour (TFP/L) that is expressed as the combined contribution of the quality of the explanatory variables.

This subsection demonstrates the decomposition of labour productivity into capital deepening, increased usage of digital technology per unit of labour and pollutants' emissions per unit of labour. Likewise, following [30, 31, 44–46], when constant returns $\beta = (1\text{-}\alpha\text{-}\ \lambda\ )$to scale is imposed, Eq. (2) becomes:

$$\ln GDPt,\ i = \text{a} + \alpha.\ln \text{Kt, i} + \lambda.\ln DTt, i + \theta.\ln Pt, i + (1 - \alpha - \lambda - \theta).\ln \text{Lt, i} + \varepsilon\text{t}, i$$
$$\text{t} = \text{Number of years} \qquad (4)$$

However, there are two options for dividing the variables by L:

1. Dividing the variables (data) by L before the analysis, in which the equation is given as: $\ln(\text{GDP/L})_\text{T} = \text{a} + \alpha \ln(\text{K/L})_\text{T} + \lambda \ln(\text{DT/L})_\text{T} + \theta.\ln(\text{P/L})_\text{T}$

   This will not be used in this study.

2. Dividing the variables by L during the analysis through programming the variables that will be used in this study, as follows

$$\ln(\text{GDP/L})_\text{T} = \text{a} + \alpha 1 \ln(\text{K/L})_\text{T} + \alpha 2[\ln\ (\text{K/L})_\text{T}]^2 + \lambda 1 \ln(\text{DT/L})_\text{T}$$
$$+ \lambda 2[\ln\ (\text{DT/L})_\text{T}]^2 + \theta 1 \ln(\text{P/L})_\text{T} + \theta 2[\ln\ (\text{P/L})_\text{T}]^2$$

The output elasticity is calculated with respect to capital per labour, digital technology per labour and pollutants' emissions per labour, i.e.$\alpha = \alpha 1 + \alpha 2$, $\lambda = \lambda 1 + \lambda 2$ and $\theta = \theta 1 + \theta 2$, respectively. Following [44, 30], the production function can be in the form:

$$\begin{aligned} &\Delta \ln (\mathrm{GDP/L})\mathrm{t,i} = \mathrm{a} + \alpha 1.\Delta \ln\ (\mathrm{K/L})\mathrm{t,i} + \alpha 2[\Delta \ln\ (\mathrm{K/L})\mathrm{t,i}]^2 + \lambda 1.\Delta \ln\ (\mathrm{DT/L})\mathrm{t,i} \\ &+\lambda 2[\Delta \ln\ (\mathrm{DT/L})\mathrm{t,i}]^2 + \theta 1.\Delta \ln\ (\mathrm{P/L})\mathrm{t,i} + \theta 2[\Delta \ln\ (\mathrm{P/L})\mathrm{t,i}]^2 + \varepsilon \mathrm{t}, i \\ &\mathrm{t} = \textit{Number of years} \end{aligned} \tag{5}$$

It then, follows that:

$$\begin{aligned} &\Delta \ln (\mathrm{GDP/L})\mathrm{t,i}\ \text{is the digital labour productivity contribution} \\ &\overline{\alpha}.\Delta \ln \overline{(\mathrm{K/L})} = \alpha 1.\Delta \ln (\mathrm{K/L})\mathrm{t,i} + \alpha 2[\Delta \ln\ (\mathrm{K/L})\mathrm{t,i}]^2 \\ &\text{is the contribution of the capital deepening} \\ &\overline{\lambda}..\Delta \ln \overline{(\mathrm{DT/L})} = \lambda 1.\Delta \ln (\mathrm{DT/L})\mathrm{t,i} + \lambda 2[\Delta \ln\ (\mathrm{DT/L})\mathrm{t,i}]^2 \\ &\text{is the contribution of the digital technology per labour} \\ &\overline{\theta}..\Delta \ln \overline{(\mathrm{P/L})} = \theta 1.\Delta \ln (\mathrm{P/L})\mathrm{t,i} + \theta 2[\Delta \ln\ (\mathrm{P/L})\mathrm{t,i}]^2 \\ &\text{is the contribution of the pollutants}'\ \text{emissions per labour} \\ &\varepsilon\mathrm{t,i}\ \text{is the residual term that proxies for TFP per labour growth}\ (\Delta \ln (\mathrm{TFP/L})\mathrm{t,i}) \\ &\Delta\ \text{is the difference operator denoting proportionate change rate} \end{aligned}$$

As mentioned in extensive growth theory, the intercept (a) has no position in the calculation of the productivity growth rate indicators. Consequently, it develops:

$$\begin{aligned} &\Delta \ln (\mathrm{GDP/L})\mathrm{t,i} = \overline{\alpha}.\Delta \ln\ \overline{(\mathrm{K/L})}\mathrm{t,i} + \overline{\lambda}.\Delta \ln\ \overline{(\mathrm{DT/L})}\mathrm{t,i} + \overline{\theta}.\Delta \ln\ \overline{(\mathrm{P/L})}\mathrm{t}, \\ &\mathrm{i} + \Delta \ln (\mathrm{TFP/L})\mathrm{t,i} \end{aligned} \tag{6}$$

Where $\overline{\alpha}$, $\overline{\lambda}$ and $\overline{\theta}$ indicate the dividends of capital per labour, digital technology per labour, the pollutants' emissions per labour. Total factor productivity per labour [(TFP/L) is the TFP per labour] contribution as an indicator of digital productivity and sustainable long-run economic growth spill over effect.

Besides, to calculate the TFP per worker, and other productivity indicators contributions, Eq. (6) transforms:

$$\begin{aligned} &\Delta \ln (\mathrm{TFP/L})\mathrm{t,i} = \Delta \ln (\mathrm{GDP/L})\mathrm{t}, \\ &\mathrm{i} - \left[\overline{\alpha}.\Delta \ln\ \overline{(\mathrm{K/L})}\ \mathrm{t,i} + \overline{\lambda}.\Delta \ln\ \overline{(\mathrm{DT/L})}\ \mathrm{t,i} + \overline{\theta}.\Delta \ln\ \overline{(\mathrm{P/L})}\ \mathrm{ti}\right] \end{aligned} \tag{7}$$

Subsequently, Eq. (7) guides the decomposition of digital labour productivity growth into the contributions of capital per labour, increasing the production rate of digital technology per labour and the pollutants' emissions per worker production as a by-product or unpriced products besides the main products, alongside the combined contribution of the stated inputs qualities. This is articulated as digital TFP per labour contribution that is indicated as the digital technology spill over effect.

4.3 Intensive growth theory (capital productivity)

The digital capital productivity framework for Model 3 (**Figure 3**) is a demonstration of the digital capital productivity or output per capital (GDP/capital) as a function of labour per capital, digital technology per capital and the pollutants' emissions per capital, considered to be the explanatory variables based on their quantities. Furthermore, the framework presents the digital TFP per capital (TFP/K) as the combined contribution of the qualities of the inputs demonstrated above in the capital productivity function.

Henceforth, the digital capital productivity decomposes into labour per capital, digital technology per capital and the pollutants' emissions per capital, as presented in [1–6]. When constant returns to scale $[\alpha(1\text{-}\beta\text{-}\lambda - \eta)]$, has been imposed, Eq. (2) becomes:

$$\ln GDPt,\, i = \mathrm{a} + (1-\beta-\lambda-\delta).\ln \mathrm{Kt,i} + \beta\ \ln \mathrm{Lt,i} + \lambda.\ln DTt, i + \delta.\ln Pt,\\ i + \varepsilon\mathrm{t}, it = \mathrm{N}umber\ of\ years \tag{8}$$

Accordingly, Eq. (8) has been transformed by dividing each term by K (capital input). The output elasticity was formerly calculated with respect to labour per capital, digital technology per capital and the pollutants' emissions per capital, i.e. $\beta = \beta 1 + \beta 2$, $\lambda = \lambda 1 + \lambda 2$, $\delta = \ \delta 1 + \delta 2$, correspondingly. Convening to [1, 2, 5, 6], the capital productivity production function can stand in the following formula:

$$\Delta \ln (\mathrm{GDP/K})\mathrm{t,i} = \mathrm{a} + \beta 1\Delta \ln\ (\mathrm{L/K})\mathrm{t,i} + \beta 2[\Delta \ln\ (\mathrm{L/K})\mathrm{t,i}]^2 + \lambda 1\Delta \ln\ (\mathrm{DT/K})\mathrm{t,i}\\ +\lambda 2[\Delta \ln\ (\mathrm{DT/K})\mathrm{t,i}]^2 + \delta\Delta \ln\ (\mathrm{P/K})\mathrm{t,i} + \delta\Delta \ln[\Delta \ln\ (\mathrm{P/K})\mathrm{t,i}]^2\varepsilon\mathrm{t}, i\\ \mathrm{t} = Number\ of\ years \tag{9}$$

It couriers in the following terms:

$\Delta \ln (\mathrm{GDP/K})\mathrm{t,i}$ is the digital capital productivity contribution capital productivty
$\overline{\beta}\Delta \ln \overline{(\mathrm{L/K})} = \beta 1\Delta \ln (\mathrm{L/K})\mathrm{t,i} + \beta 2[\Delta \ln (\mathrm{L/K})\mathrm{ti}]^2$
is the contribution of the labour per capital
$\overline{\lambda}\Delta \ln \overline{(\mathrm{DT/K})} = \lambda 1\Delta \ln (\mathrm{DT/K})\mathrm{t,i} + \lambda 2[\Delta \ln (\mathrm{DT/K})\mathrm{ti}]^2$
is the contribution of the digital technology per capital
$\overline{\delta}\Delta \ln \overline{(\mathrm{P/K})} = \delta 1\Delta \ln (\mathrm{P/K})\mathrm{t,i} + \delta 2[\Delta \ln (\mathrm{P/K})\mathrm{ti}]^2$
is the contribution of the pollutant emisssions per capital
$\varepsilon\mathrm{t,i}$ is the residual term that proxies for digital TFP per capital growth($\Delta \ln (\mathrm{TFP/K})\mathrm{t,i}$)
Δ is the difference operator denoting proportionate change rate.

It Following the output and labour productivity models' procedures, the intercept (a) has no value in the calculation of the productivity growth indicators as measuring other variables that are not considered in the models, subsequently it drives as follows:

$$\Delta \ln (\mathrm{GDP/K})\mathrm{t,i} = \overline{\beta}.\Delta \ln\ \overline{(\mathrm{L/K})}\mathrm{t,i} + \overline{\lambda}.\Delta \ln\ \overline{(\mathrm{DT/K})}\mathrm{t,i} + \overline{\delta}.\Delta \ln\ \overline{(\mathrm{P/K})}\mathrm{t},\\ \mathrm{i} + \Delta \ln (\mathrm{TFP/K})\mathrm{t,i} \tag{10}$$

Where $\overline{\beta}$, $\overline{\lambda}$ and $\overline{\delta}$ indicate the portions of labour per capital, the digital technology per capital, the pollutants' emissions capital and (TFP/K), is the digital TFP per capital contribution as a digital technology spill over effect indicator to transform the countries, sectors firms understudy into sustainable digital economies.

Finally, to compute the average annual growth rate contribution of the TFP per capital, alongside other productivity indicators' contributions in the model, Eq. (10) converts into the followings:

$$\Delta \ln (\mathrm{TFP/K})\mathrm{t,i} = \Delta \ln (\mathrm{GDP/K})\mathrm{t}, \\ \mathrm{i} - \left[\overline{\beta}.\Delta \ln \ \overline{(\mathrm{L/K})}\ \mathrm{t,i} + \overline{\lambda}.\Delta \ln \ \overline{(\mathrm{DT/K})}\ \mathrm{t,i} + \overline{\delta}.\Delta \ln \ \overline{(\mathrm{P/K})}\ \mathrm{ti}\right] \tag{11}$$

The digital capital productivity growth decompresses into the labour per capital contribution, increasing production of the digital technology per capital and the pollutants' emissions per capital as a desirable output in the form of unpriced products. Besides, the digital TFP per capital contribution as combined input qualities as reaffirmed in Eq. (11).

5. Discussion

It has been stated by World Bank [10] that beyond pandemic periods, the statistical capacity to yield and commendably employ fundamental economic and social data is inadequate. Numerous lower economic states are incapable to precisely track public finances, report on external debt or screening their development goals. Without such data, the capability to grasp regimes accountable and track progress shortcomings, as well as data governance preparations to enable countless data use while protecting against misappropriation stays in their beginning. It should be recalled that the legal and regulatory frameworks for data are inadequate in lower-income countries, which all too frequently have gaps in critical safeguards as well as shortages of data-sharing measures. There, the data systems and infrastructure that enable interoperability and allow data to flow to more users are incomplete. In this respect, less than 20% of low- and middle-income countries have modern data infrastructure such as colocation data centres and direct access to cloud computing facilities in same countries calls Department of Statistics that collected data via annual survey among others. Even where promising data systems and governance frameworks exist, a lack of institutions with the requisite administrative capacity, decision-making autonomy and financial resources holds back their effective implementation and enforcement. To discourse these worries, the World Development Report 2021 requests for a new social contract for data to permit the usage and recycle of data to generate economic and social worth, encourages unbiased chances to benefit from data and raises inhabitants' confidence that they will not be abused by misappropriation data provided. Nevertheless, in looking for such a social contract, lower-income countries are otherwise frequently deprived since they lack the infrastructure and skills to capture data and turn them into value. It should be noted that the scales and organisations to contribute rightfully in universal data marketplaces and their governance and the institutional and regulatory frameworks to build trust in data organisations.

Thanks to the World Development Indicators (WDI) of the World Bank and International Monetary Fund (IMF) financial database system for providing free access to their databases that assisted many researchers, scholars to conduct research around the globe. Thanks to other organisations such as International Telecommunications Union (ITU) of the UN, among others, if they provide free access to their databases to help those who are in need to this data and are not able purchase it due to financial constraints to conduct research worldwide.

The proposed quantitative data for this research ranging from GDP, gross physical capital, human capital proxies, air, water and other pollutants' emissions proxies, human capital index, human development, CO_2 emissions, the level of well-being, etc. which do not include only material/economic aspects will be obtained from the World Development Indicators (WDIs) of the World Bank, financial data system of International Monetary Fund (IMF) and other data sources including individual countries and institutions.

While digital technology proxies will be obtained from International Telecommunications Union and other sources provided this data include cybersecurity data.

The fundamental element is that with appropriate public policies, technological progresses foster the well-being that is deliberated positive externalities of digital technologies that have designed the digital economy everywhere in the world. Nonetheless, there are negative externalities accompanying with this technology progress in the form of undesirable output alongside the desirable output. These negative externalities associated with digital technology progress comprising cybersecurity and the mismatch of human skills in augmenting the digital dividends created by the new factors of production significant contribution to the long-run sustainable economic growth. Besides its counterparts' negative externalities generated as undesirable output by pollutants' emissions that this study based the digital technologies negative externalities assumption on it.

This chapter develops the innovation and climate change integration with economic growth. The Sustainable Development Goals (SDGs) agenda to achieve sustainability issues will be empirically examined via this chapter models and frameworks to realise the long-term economic growth based on a digital economy transformation that will allow to technologically progress and environmentally and socially sustainable. This advancement is essential to sustain long-term economic growth, protect the environment and sustain social evolution through innovation and the spill over effects carried about by the implementation of the SDGs agenda.

It should be noted that the supreme momentous impact in terms of the methodology is that three positive and negative externalities productivity frameworks were established and exhibited how to measure the apprehension variables through primary data (questionnaire) and qualitative analysis (interview and case studies). Furthermore, for the studies that will employ secondary data, this chapter closed the gaps of existing productivity models through three modified models to estimate and calculate digital technologies positive and negative externalities alongside traditional productivity indicators' contributions to industries, firms, sectors and the economies in a combined econometric and the traditional growth accounting methods to estimate explanatory variables' coefficients that is disregarded by growth accounting studies. Whereas in a second step, productivity indicators are proposed to be calculated through plugging of the estimated explanatory variables' coefficients into the models to calculate the productivity indicators that were ignored in the econometric method. In doing so, the study contributes significantly via filling extensive growth theory (output) and intensive growth (labour productivity) gaps. Furthermore, the most significant contribution of this study is treating the digital technologies cybersecurity negative externalities spill over effects equivalent to the negative externalities generated by pollutants' emissions and developing capital productivity framework and model that were ignored in most of the studies with the exception of [1–4, 41] studies.

Moreover, these frameworks and models can be applied at the microeconomic level for sectors, companies and other business based on the available data. Besides, the proposed qualitative method to capture the information and data that cannot be

DOI: http://dx.doi.org/10.5772/intechopen.102723

captured via quantitative method, this they will be in form of interviews with the experts and case studies among other qualitative methods such as focus groups among others. The proposed three frameworks and models can be employed to analyse secondary data through econometric estimation and the calculation of productivity indicators for the secondary data at the Macro and micro levels. A questionnaire survey to collect the primary data can be designed and distributed based on this chapter proposed frameworks. Likewise, a qualitative approach can be conducted via interviews with experts to capture the data and information that could not be captured via a quantitative approach.

6. Conclusions and policy implications

The research ideas and output are expected to contribute to and fill the knowledge gaps in the form of modified models and frameworks that examine the digital economy and digital inclusion at the macro and micro levels; these aim to achieve digital transformation. The empirical findings will be generated via employing this chapter proposed models and frameworks can help to develop recommendations based on the empirical findings will be generated and policy implications that will be generated based on the most expected significant empirical findings to be used by policymakers, industry and academics. It could also be used by international organisations and other concerned institutions around the world as a podium to implement the SDGs to sustainable digital economies and businesses around the globe.

To ensure enhanced coherence, it needs to utilise these study frameworks and models to empirically examine the SDGs sustainability issues in general and digital technologies in particular. In doing so, they could achieve long-term economic growth based on a digital economy transformation that will allow them to be transformed into the digital technological base required to sustain long-term economic growth. They would also protect the environment through the innovation and spillier effect brought by the implementation of the SDGs agenda related to the digital inclusion in general and financial inclusion in particular. This study's outcomes will provide a digital economy framework and policy implications and recommendations to enhance cooperation, collaboration and smart partnership between and within the countries in the fields of knowledge transfer, technological progress, digital assets and the development of intellectual property. Adopting the suggested frameworks could help sustain long-term economic growth to overcome the impact of COVID-19 and possible future pandemics. Digital technology applications can facilitate the economic activities needed to fight hunger and achieve food security, provide good health and well-being, quality education, clean water and sanitation, affordable and clean energy, industry, innovation and infrastructure.

It will provide recommendations, policy implications and solutions to the problems facing in implementing the digital technology applications to transform their economies into digital economies and to implement the new technologies in the future to achieve the SDGs.

The aggregate economy, economic sectors, industries and companies will be provided with solutions and guidelines to implement digital technology applications to transform into digital economies. The proposed frameworks and models will be empirically examined in the economies, sectors and companies to provide practical solutions to sustain the economic development via the digital solutions needed to overcome the problems and lessons learned in the post-COVID-19 era and to develop policies to be implemented by public and private sectors to achieve sustainable development.

This study proposed ideas based on frameworks and models that will be useful for digital technology policy construction as a foundation for the establishment and growth of a digital economy based on digital economy level. In this setting, a contrast of digital technology's contributions to productivity growth would provide guidelines for policy-makers to frame suitable national digital transformation policies in line with the digital transformation programme. The findings from this study will likewise support the construction of a digital technology investment policy and help the development of the human capital and infrastructure needed to support the effective use of the digital technology, this should be supported by good governance, implementation of corporate social responsibility.

It should be noted that the countries can capitalise on their synergy within and between the countries to fully practice the competitive advantages to overhaul their digital assets' deficiencies. In that circumstance, the countries will be able to accelerate the movement towards a digital technology-savvy nation that is accomplished by the members of the Organisation for Economic Cooperation and Development (OECD), such as Europe, USA, Canada, Australia, Japan and South Korea and non-OECD countries such as China.

This study proposed that a digital transformation programme should be taken by countries to narrow the digital divide and dividends brought by digital technologies and to improve digital technology dividends. This would contribute to the transformation of digital economies and make a difference for the nations to enjoy high living standards and well-being, like their OECD counterparts. In addition, classifying the lagging concerning the adoption of digital technology and human capital development delivers a standard to improve cooperation and a smart partnership within and between countries. In this respect, the first phase to relocation to digital economies is an emerging digital economy master plan to identify the policies and strategies to develop digital economy flagships and pillars to improve the existing digital economy flagships and pillars for the countries such as Malaysia, among others, including refining and developing digital economy institutions that needed to facilitate knowledge economy activities and governed them. In this respect, the guidelines are provided for developing a digital economy blueprint and policy implications for digitising the whole economies in general and Small and Medium Enterprises (SMEs) and Micro level in particular. A framework for a digital transformation and developing digital economies should be produced to serve as a guideline for digital economy implementation.

Author details

Elsadig Musa Ahmed
Faculty of Business, Multimedia University, Melaka, Malaysia

*Address all correspondence to: elsadig1965@gmail.com

References

[1] Ahmed EM. COVID-19 implications on IsDB member countries sustainable digital economies. International Journal of Innovation and Knowledge Management in Middle East and North Africa (IJIKMMENA). 2020;**8**(1&2): 12-37

[2] Ahmed EM. Modelling information and communications technology cybersecurity externalities spillover effects on sustainable economic growth. Journal of the Knowledge Economy. 2021;**12**(1):412-430. DOI: 10.1007/s13132-020-00627-3

[3] Ahmed EM. Modelling green productivity spillover effects on sustainable development. World Journal of Science Technology and Sustainable Development. 2019;**17**(3):257-267. Available from: https://www.emerald.com/insight/content/doi/10.1108/WJSTSD-01-2020-0009/full/html

[4] United Nations (UN). Transforming our World: The 2030 Agenda for Sustainable Development. United Nations: United Nations General Assembly, New York; 2015. p. 2015

[5] Ahmed EM. Are bio-economy dimensions' new stream of the knowledge economy? World Journal of Science Technology and Sustainable Development. 2018;**15**(2):142-155. DOI: 10.1108/WJSTSD-06-2017-0014

[6] Ahmed EM. ICT and human capital spillover effects in achieving sustainable east Asian knowledge-based economies. The Journal of Knowledge Economy. 2017;**8**(3):1086-1112

[7] World Development Report. Digital Dividends. Washington DC, USA: The World Bank-International Bank for Reconstruction and Development; 2016

[8] Ahmed EM, Anwar A. Achieving Sudan's sustainable development via microfinance Mobile banking. In: Ali AES, Ali KM, Azrag MH, editors. Enhancing Financial Inclusion Through Islamic Finance. Vol. II. Switzerland AG: Palgrave MacMillan, Springer Nature; 2020. pp. 297-325

[9] Feyen E, Frost J, Gambacorta L, Natarajan H, Saal M. Fintech and the Digital Transformation of Financial Services: Implications for Market Structure and Public Policy. Basel, Switzerland: BIS Papers; 2021

[10] Romer PM. Increasing returns and long-run growth. Journal of Political Economy. 1986;**94**(5):1002-1037

[11] Romer PM. Growth based on increasing returns due to specialization. The American Economic Review, Chapters and Proceedings. 1987;**77**(2): 56-62

[12] World Bank. World Development Report 2021: Data for Better Lives. Washington DC, USA: The World Bank; 2021

[13] Badea L, Rangu CM, Scheau MC. Fintech–financial innovation facilitators. Acta Universitatis Danubius, OEconomica. 2021;**17**(3):301-316

[14] Sabău AI, Achimb MV, Safta LI. Does corporate governance may enhance the digitalization process? A panel data analysis. In: RSEP Conferences. 23rd RSEP International Economics, Finance & Business Conference—Virtual/Online; 25–26 November 2021; University of Washington Rome Center, Rome, Italy. BC Publishing; 2021. p. 287

[15] Shapova M, Varbanov T, Ovchinnikov E. Digital economy across

EU: Convergence or club convergence? In: 23rd RSEP International Economics, Finance & Business Conference—Virtual/Online 25–26 November 2021. Rome, Italy: University of Washington Rome Center; 2021. pp. 357-368. Available from: www.rsepconferences.com. Conference proceedings/full papers ISBN: 978-605-70583-5-5/December 2021

[16] Ahmed EM. Green TFP intensity impact on sustainable east Asian productivity growth. Economic Analysis and Policy. 2012;**42**(1):67-78

[17] Romer PM. Crazy explanations for the productivity slowdown. NBER Macroeconomics Annual. 1987;**2**:163-210

[18] Romer PM. Endogenous technological change. Journal of Political Economy. 1990;**98**(5):S71-S102

[19] Romer PM. Two strategies for economic development: Using ideas and producing ideas. In: Proceedings of the World Bank Annual Conference of Development Economics 1992. Washington, DC: World Bank; 1993

[20] Nordhaus WD. Resources as a constraint on growth. The American Economic Review. 1974;**64**(2):22-26

[21] Nordhaus WD. Can we control carbon dioxide? Vienna: IIASA Working Chapter; 1975. p. WP-75-063

[22] Nordhaus WD. Economic growth and climate: The carbon dioxide problem. The American Economic Review. 1977;**67**(1):341-346

[23] Nordhaus WD. Managing the Global Commons: The Economics of Climate Change. Cambridge, MA: MIT Press; 1994a

[24] Nordhaus WD. Expert opinion on climate change. American Scientist. 1994b;**82**(1):45-51

[25] Nordhaus WD. Integrated economic and climate modeling. In: Dixon PB, Jorgenson D, editors. Handbook of Computable General Equilibrium Modeling. Amsterdam: Elsevier; 2013. pp. 1069-1131

[26] Nordhaus WD. Estimates of the social cost of carbon: Concepts and results from the DICE-2013R model and alternative approaches. Journal of the Association of Environmental and Resource Economists. 2014;**1**(1–2): 273-312

[27] Nordhaus WD. Projections and Uncertainties about Climate Change in an Era of Minimal Climate Policies, NBER Working Chapter 22933. Cambridge, MA: National Bureau of Economic Research; 2017

[28] Nordhaus WD. Evolution of modeling of the economics of global warming: Changes in the DICE model, 1992–2017. Climatic Change. 2018; **148**(4):623-640

[29] Nordhaus WD, Romer PM. Integrating Innovation and Climate with Economic Growth, Scientific Background on the Sveriges Riksbank Prize in Economic Sciences in Memory of Alfred Nobel 2018. Stockholm, Sweden: The Royal Swedish Academy of Sciences; 2018

[30] Ahmed EM. Carbon dioxide emissions, impact on Malaysia's manufacturing productivity growth. World Review of Science Technology and Sustainable Development. 2006; **3**(1):58-69

[31] Ahmed EM. The impact of biochemical oxygen demand emissions on Malaysia's manufacturing productivity growth. Global Economic Review. 2007;**36**(4):305-319

[32] Solow RM. The production function and the theory of capital. The Review of Economic Studies. 1955;**23**(2):101-108

[33] Solow RM. Technical change and the aggregate production function. The Review of Economics and Statistics. 1957;**39**(3):312-320

[34] Pittman RW. Multilateral productivity comparisons with undesirable output. Economic Journal. 1983;**93**:883-891

[35] Baumol WJ, Oates WE. The Theory of Environmental Policy. New York: Cambridge University Press; 1988

[36] Chaston K, Swinand G, Gollop F, Arontt R. A Welfare-Based Measure of Productivity Growth with Environmental Externalities. Department of Economics, USA: Boston College; 1997

[37] Gollop FM, Swinand GP. Total resource productivity: Accounting for changing environmental quality. In: Dean E, Harper M, Hulten C, editors. New Directions in Productivity Analysis. Conference on Research in Income and Wealth. Chicago, MI: University of Chicago Press; 2021

[38] Gollop FM, Swinand GP. From total factor to total resource productivity: An application to agriculture. American Journal of Agricultural Economics. 1998; **80**:577-583

[39] Gollop FM, Roberts MJ. Environmental regulations and productivity growth: The case of fossil fuelled electric power generation. Journal of Political Economy. 1983;**91**: 654-674

[40] Harchaoui T, Kabrelyan D, Smith R. Accounting for Greenhouse Gases in the Standard Productivity Framework Statistics. Canada: Micro-Economic Analysis Division; 2002

[41] Ahmed EM. Capital productivity determinants: East Asian perspectives. International Journal of Sustainable Economy. 2009;**1**(3):245-254

[42] Ahmed EM. Human capital and ICT per capita contribution to east Asian productivity growth. International Social Science Review. 2010;**85**(1-2):40-55

[43] Jorgenson DW, Gollop FM, Fraumenri B. Productivity and US Economic Growth. Amsterdam: North Holland; 1987

[44] Dollar D, Sokoloff K. Patterns of productivity growth in south Korean manufacturing industries 1963-1979. Journal of Development Economics. 1990;**33**(2):309-327

[45] Wong FC. Patterns of labour productivity growth and employment shift in the Singapore manufacturing industries. The Singapore Economic Review. 1993;**38**(2):231-251

[46] Felipe J. On the myth and mystery of Singapore's zero TFP. Asian Economic Journal. 2000;**14**(2):187-208

Chapter 5

For Better or for Worse: The Impact of Workplace Automation on Work Characteristics and Employee Well-Being

Maria C.W. Peeters and Judith Plomp

Abstract

This article examines the consequences of implementing an automation technology (i.e., Robotic Process Automation; RPA) for work characteristics and employee well-being. Based on the job demands-resources framework we examined to what extent the utilization of RPA was related to job resources (i.e., autonomy and task variety) and a job demand (i.e., information processing), and to what extent these work characteristics were related to work engagement and exhaustion. Data were collected among 420 employees working for a Dutch ministry where RPA was recently introduced. Structural equation modeling revealed that RPA use was negatively related to both autonomy and task variety, which formed a threat to employee work engagement. Contrary to our expectations, RPA use was unrelated to information processing and subsequent exhaustion. These findings put emphasis on the importance of designing new technologies with sufficient job resources to create and maintain a healthy and motivated workforce during and after implementing workplace automation.

Keywords: technological innovation, workplace automation, robotic process automation, work characteristics, employee well-being

1. Introduction

Technological innovations and work process automation play a key role in meeting the increased demands that organizations face in today's competitive and fast-changing market [1]. To become and remain efficient, automation and robotics offer many solutions for the potential optimization of work processes. Robotic Process Automation (RPA) is currently one of the most used tools in business process automation that stimulates higher organizational productivity [2]. RPA is a software robot that uses the interface of an already present computer system and mimics the actions of a human employee. RPA can automate work processes that are administrative, well-structured, and repetitive of nature [3–5]. Typical tasks that can be done by RPA entail, for example, processing incoming emails and orders, transferring data from one digital system to another, and searching for and communicating with potential new hires. Organizations greatly benefit from the implementation of RPA, mainly due to increased process speed and production growth, as well as error reduction [6].

However, although there are many advantages to the commissioning of RPA, it is estimated that between 30 and 50% of all RPA implementations fail [7]. This relatively high number of unsuccessful RPA implementations is in line with the general notion that digital transitions often do not result in desired outcomes, such as enhanced productivity and efficiency. A potential explanation for failing technological implementations is the lack of consideration for the employees who have to work with a new technology [8]. With this study we aim to gain more insight in this human-technology interaction [9] by investigating to what extent the implementation of an RPA technology impacts work characteristics and employee well-being.

In-depth knowledge on the consequences of digital transitions for the work characteristics and employee well-being is increasingly important, because both are to a large extent predictive of overall employee performance and organizational productivity [10, 11]. By studying this issue we contribute to the existing body of knowledge on workplace automation and information systems in two important ways. First, this study aims to address the research gap concerning the impact of workplace automation on individual work experiences. Whereas earlier research has mainly focused on the effects of technological innovations on employment and labor market composition, we argue that more understanding of the relationship between the implementation of an automation system and work characteristics, as well as well-being of those who have to work with these new technologies can contribute to the successful implementation of technological innovations. This can help organizations that want to innovate and invest in better designed jobs, as well as lead to better implementations of new technologies such that sustainable employee performance can be consolidated and organizational efficiency can be achieved. Second, we aim to contribute to the growing body of literature on workplace automation and the application of RPA technology [5, 6, 12, 13]. More specifically, we examine to what extent RPA influences the work experiences of employees and whether RPA technology results in the desired outcomes with regard to a decrease in job demands, an increase in job resources, and in turn enhanced employee well-being. In sum, with this research we want to achieve a better understanding of how employees experience working with RPA, so that such an innovation in the future actually contributes to what it is intended for and does not generate negative side effects. In the following sections, we will explain how RPA can influence work characteristics and how these work characteristics are related to employee well-being.

2. RPA and work characteristics

Work process automation changes the way work is performed and perceived by employees. For example, the use of robots that automate heavy manual labor can result in less physically straining job tasks for employees, while at the same time requires them to handle new machinery. Similarly, the use of chatbots can significantly decrease interpersonal interactions at work, but can potentially also result in employees to feel alienated from their original work role. Hence, the introduction of a new technology and workplace automation can have both simultaneously positive and negative influences on employees' work experiences.

The idea behind RPA technology is that administrative work processes become more streamlined and efficient, so that employees have to spend less time on performing repetitive work tasks [3]. Compared to traditional automation systems (e.g., BPM, CRM) RPA can automate many different work tasks, is easy to implement and use, and does not require modification of existing IT infrastructures [5]. As such, RPA is unique in a sense that it requires minimal human intervention, can be applied to a range of business applications, and is designed such that end users can make changes without the need to possess extensive programming skills. Although RPA does not automate and replace complete jobs, it does substantially change certain tasks and the way jobs are designed [9, 14]. Therefore, the implementation of RPA is likely to change the way employees (perceive their) work and thus can result in better or worse designed jobs, which likely has a profound impact on important outcomes related to employee work experiences and well-being [9].

From a work design perspective, the job demands-resources model states that all work characteristics can be divided into job demands and job resources [15]. Job demands, such as workload, time pressure, and role conflict, refer to all aspects of a job that require continuous cognitive or emotional effort and are related to physiological and/or psychological costs. Job resources are those aspects of a job that help employees cope with high job demands, attain work goals and performance, and stimulate professional growth. Examples of job resources are feedback, task variety, support, and autonomy [15]. In line with Demerouti [16] and Parker and Grote [9], we argue that during and after the implementation of a new technology and workplace automation both job demands and job resources are subject to substantial changes. A recent systematic literature review [17] on the impact of the implementation of technological innovations on core work characteristics, showed that the implementation of a new technology was associated with intensified job demands, including job complexity and workload. Additionally, the relationship between the implementation of a technological innovation and job resources was predominantly positive, especially with regard to autonomy and control. These findings suggest that although job demands tend to increase after the introduction of a new technology, job resources seem, at least to some extent, compensate for these increased demands. However, in finding an answer to the question which work characteristics are susceptible to change after the introduction of an RPA technology, it is important to take a closer look at the defining features of RPA.

Starting with job resources, as mentioned above, one of the main goals of RPA is to take over administrative and repetitive work tasks from employees [5]. This means that the use of RPA frees time that employees otherwise had to spend on monotonous tasks. Considering that RPA generates more time for other aspects of the job, this should allow employees to exert more control over their work structure and tasks. As such, we expect that RPA use relates to more autonomy at work for employees. This notion is also supported by a qualitative interview study of Engberg and Sördal [18], who found that the introduction of RPA enhanced the experienced freedom of employees to independently organize their work schedule and tasks.

Second, although RPA is useful in replacing structured and repetitive tasks, it is less suitable to take over complex work that requires more advanced problem-solving skills and abilities [3]. Taking into account that RPA technology releases employees from carrying out repetitive work duties, it simultaneously leaves more room to perform other and more challenging tasks. In line with this argumentation, several qualitative studies have shown that, overall, employees experienced that RPA enabled them to advance their skill set. In addition the introduction of RPA enabled them to devote time to their professional development and growth while performing new and challenging tasks [18, 19]. These findings suggest that RPA creates space for employees to focus on a variety of challenging work tasks. Therefore, we also expect that the use of RPA positively relates to task variety, which entails the extent to which employees experience variety in their job content and can perform a wide range of tasks that require different skills [20].

Turning to job demands, reference [21] indicates that RPA is able to take over and process up to 300% more information compared to human employees. This increase in productivity is due to the fact that RPA can complete a large range of administrative tasks in a fraction of the time compared to actual employees and can work throughout the night and weekend. Additionally, RPA is relatively easy to implement and configure, meaning that employees can use RPA, as well as make changes in how tasks are performed, without an extensive technical background [22]. This implies that employees are no longer bothered with continuously having to deal with processing and analyzing large amounts of information and are able to easily adjust the system during the implementation process based on the requirements and needs of their job. Information processing refers to the amount of data and information that employees are required to monitor and manage in their job [20, 23]. Considering that RPA takes over data and information processing tasks to a substantial extent, we propose that RPA completes a large range of administrative tasks in a fraction of the time compared to actual employees. Taken together, with regard to changes in job demands and job resources we formulate the following hypotheses:

Hypothesis 1:RPA use is positively related to (a) autonomy and (b) task variety.
Hypothesis 2:RPA use is negatively related to information processing.

3. Work characteristics and employee well-being

Employee well-being refers to a passive or active work-related affect and individual's evaluation of the quality of experiences at work [24]. In this study, we included work engagement and exhaustion as indicators of work-related well-being, considering that both are regarded as important factors in the operationalization of employee well-being [25, 26]. In relation to work-related well-being, the JD-R framework proposes two independent underlying processes [15]. First, a health impairment process, in which continued exposure to high job demands results in strain, burnout, and an overall decline in health-related outcomes. Second, a motivational process is proposed, in which access to sufficient job resources protects employees against high job demands and leads to motivation, work engagement, and increased productivity. Following these central assumptions, we argue that higher levels of autonomy and task variety associated with RPA use instigate the motivational process as proposed in the JD-R framework. To clarify, autonomy and task variety are key job resources, which consistently have been found to be predictive of work engagement and performance outcomes (for overviews see [27, 28]. Consequently, we propose that employees who can turn over their repetitive tasks to RPA are likely to experience more autonomy and task variety, and in turn feel more engaged. In addition, consistent exposure to high job demands, including workload and information processing, are linked to increased levels of exhaustion and burnout (e.g. [29]. With regard to information processing, we expect that employees who can transfer their administrative responsibilities to RPA and thus on a daily basis deal with substantially less repetitive job tasks, experience lower levels of information processing (see Hypothesis 2). In turn, lower levels of information processing are likely to relate to lower levels of exhaustion (i.e., a positive relationship). Therefore, we hypothesize the following:

Hypothesis 3:(a) Autonomy and (b) task variety are positively related to work engagement.
Hypothesis 4:RPA use is indirectly related to more work engagement through (a) autonomy and (b) task variety.
Hypothesis 5:Information processing is positively related to exhaustion.
Hypothesis 6:RPA use is indirectly related to less exhaustion through information processing.

4. Method

4.1 Sample and procedure

Data for this study was collected via an online questionnaire. We recruited data from employees within two large departments of a Dutch Ministry (N = 420). The response rate was 37.33%. In 2019 this Ministry introduced and implemented RPA in their organization. Employees working in the two departments typically hold office jobs, such as administrative workers, financial and legal experts, project managers and members, and HR representatives. We invited both employees who could turn over certain aspects of their work to RPA (i.e., RPA users, who make or control work processes and provide input for the RPA robot; N = 140) and employees whose work was not directly impacted by RPA (N = 280). In the questionnaire employees were asked whether their work was somehow impacted by the introduction of RPA and if so, in what way their work has changed and how they interacted with the robot. Based on these answers a distinction could be made between RPA users and non-RPA users. The group of RPA users consisted of employees from whom RPA took over one or several administrative and repetitive work tasks, such as scanning and filing emails and documents, extracting data, and generating (mass) emails. Additionally, this group also consisted of employees that made or controlled RPA work processes and output, as well as provided new input for the RPA robot. All employees received an email from the Ministry with information about the aim of the study, a link to the online questionnaire, and an explanation of the confidentiality was offered to all respondents. This study obtained approval of the Ethics Review Board.

In the total sample, 54.90% was male and the average age was 48.96 years (SD = 10.85). The mean job tenure was 14.61 years (SD = 11.22) and on average respondents worked for 33.48 hours a week (SD = 4.87). Most employees worked in jobs that required a Bachelor's Degree (48.10%) or an Associate Degree (12.10%). In terms of demographical variables (i.e., gender, age, weekly workhours, and contract type) RPA users did not differ significantly from non-RPA users. Additionally, we tested for differences between RPA users and non-RPA users on the study main variables by conducting independent samples t-tests in SPSS. **Table 1** shows the results

	RPA users		Non-RPA users		*t*-test
	M	SD	M	SD	
Autonomy	3.62	0.74	3.97	0.65	4.86**
Task variety	3.33	0.82	3.68	0.70	4.59**
Inform. Processing	3.83	0.65	4.02	0.67	2.82**
Work engagement	4.71	0.99	4.69	0.90	−0.22
Exhaustion	2.07	0.75	2.01	0.68	−1.15

*Note: n = 420. * p < 0.05, ** p < 0.01.*

Table 1.
Results of t-tests comparing RPA users (N = 140) and non-RPA users (N = 280) on the study variables.

of these analyses. RPA users reported significantly lower levels of autonomy, task variety, and information processing compared to non-RPA users.

4.2 Measures

Frist, autonomy was measured with a Dutch translation of three items of the Work Design Questionnaire (WDQ; [20]). An example item of this scale is: "The job allows me to make a lot of decisions on my own". Cronbach's α was 0.80. Task variety was measured with two items of the WDQ [20]. One of these items is "The job involves a great deal of task variety". Information processing was measured with two items of the WDQ. An example of these items is: "The job requires me to monitor a great deal of information". Work engagement was measured with the three-item version of the Utrecht Work Engagement Scale [30]. An example item of this scale is: "At my work, I feel bursting with energy". Cronbach's α for this scale was 0.82. Exhaustion was measured with three items of the Burnout Assessment Tool (BAT [31]). One of the items is: "I feel mentally exhausted at work". Cronbach's α for this scale was 0.81.

4.3 Strategy of analysis

First, we evaluated the measurement model using confirmatory factor analysis (CFA). Latent variables (i.e., autonomy, task variety, information processing, work engagement, and exhaustion) were modeled with scale items. The following fit indices were used to evaluate model fit: the Comparative Fit Index (CFI), the Tucker-Lewis Index (TLI), and the root mean square error of approximation (RMSEA). With CFI and TLI values above 0.95, and RMSEA below 0.06, model fit is acceptable [32]. Second, we tested the proposed research model using structural equation (SEM) with the AMOS software package [33]. To assess the specific indirect effects of autonomy and task variety in the relationship between RPA use and work engagement, as well as the specific indirect effect of information processing in the relationship between RPA use and exhaustion, we applied the phantom model approach [34]. In addition, to test the robustness of our proposed research model, we tested an alternative model, that proposed a relationship between RPA use and work engagement, and in turn, autonomy and task variety. Additionally, this alternative model proposed an indirect relationship between RPA use, exhaustion, and information processing.

5. Results

5.1 Descriptive statistics

In **Table 2** the descriptive statistics, including the means, standard deviations, and correlations of the variables in this study can be found. Job level was the only demographic variable that correlated significantly with several of the outcome variables (i.e., autonomy, task variety, and information processing). Therefore, we controlled for job level in our further analyses.

5.2 Testing the hypotheses

The measurement model, including autonomy, task variety, information processing, work engagement, and exhaustion as latent variables, showed a very good fit to the data: χ^2 = 144.00, df = 55, CFI = 0.96, TLI = 0.94, RMSEA = 0.06. All factor loadings loaded significantly on their respective latent factor and ranged between 0.63 and 0.97.

In Hypothesis 1a and 1b we predicted that RPA use was positively related to (a) autonomy and (b) task variety. Contrary to our expectations, our analysis showed an opposite relationship, namely that RPA use was significantly and negatively related to both autonomy ($\beta = -0.19$, $p < 0.01$) and task variety ($\beta = -0.13$, $p < 0.05$), thereby not supporting Hypotheses 1a and 1b.

In Hypothesis 2, we predicted that RPA use would be negatively associated with information processing. Although this relationship was indeed negative, it was not significant ($\beta = -0.06$, $p = 0.17$), and thereby not in support of Hypothesis 2.

In line with Hypotheses 3a and 3b, we found that autonomy ($\beta = 0.13$, $p = 0.01$) and task variety ($\beta = 0.26$, $p < 0.05$) were as expected indeed positively and significantly related to work engagement, thereby confirming Hypothesis 3.

Turning to Hypotheses 4a and 4b and the indirect relationship between system use and work engagement through both autonomy and task variety, the data showed that this combined indirect effect was negative and significant (estimate = −0.06, $p < 0.02$ with a bias-corrected confidence interval ranging from −0.10 to −0.02). To assess the specific indirect effects of autonomy and task variety separately in the relationship between system use and work engagement, the phantom model approach was applied [34]. The specific indirect effect of autonomy in the relation between system use and work engagement was indeed negative and significant (estimate = −0.10, $p = 0.02$), thereby not in support of Hypothesis 4a. The specific indirect effect of task variety in the relation between system use and work engagement was also negative and significant (estimate = −0.06, $p = 0.02$). As such, Hypothesis 4b was also not confirmed.

In contrast to Hypothesis 5, we found no significant relationship between information processing and exhaustion, ($\beta = 0.08$, $p = 0.17$). As such, Hypothesis 5 was not supported by the data.

Hypothesis 6, in which an indirect effect of information processing in the relationship between RPA use and exhaustion was hypothesized, was not supported by the data (estimate = −0.01, $p = 0.16$ with a bias-corrected confidence interval ranging from −0.02 to 0.00). As such, Hypothesis 6 was not confirmed.

Overall, the proposed structural model showed a good fit to the data: χ^2 = 210.235, df = 78, CFI = 0.94, TLI = 0.92, RMSEA = 0.06. **Figure 1** shows a schematic representation of all study's results.

	Mean	SD	1	2	3	4	5	6	7	8
1. Age	48.96	10.85	—							
2. Job level	2.72	0.68	−0.01	—						
3. System use	0.33	0.47	−0.08	−0.25**	—					
4. Autonomy	3.85	0.70	0.03	0.34**	−0.24**	—				
5. Task variety	3.56	0.76	−0.05	0.48**	−0.23**	0.47**	—			
6. Information processing	3.96	0.67	0.07	0.37**	−0.14**	0.36**	0.36**	—		
7. Work engagement	4.70	0.92	0.05	0.05	0.01	0.28**	0.32**	−0.14***	—	
8. Exhaustion	2.04	0.71	−0.04	−0.01	0.06	−0.14**	−0.13**	0.09	−0.27**	—

Note: $n = 420$. * $p < 0.05$, ** $p < 0.01$.

Table 2.
Descriptive statistics and inter-correlations of the study variables N = 420.

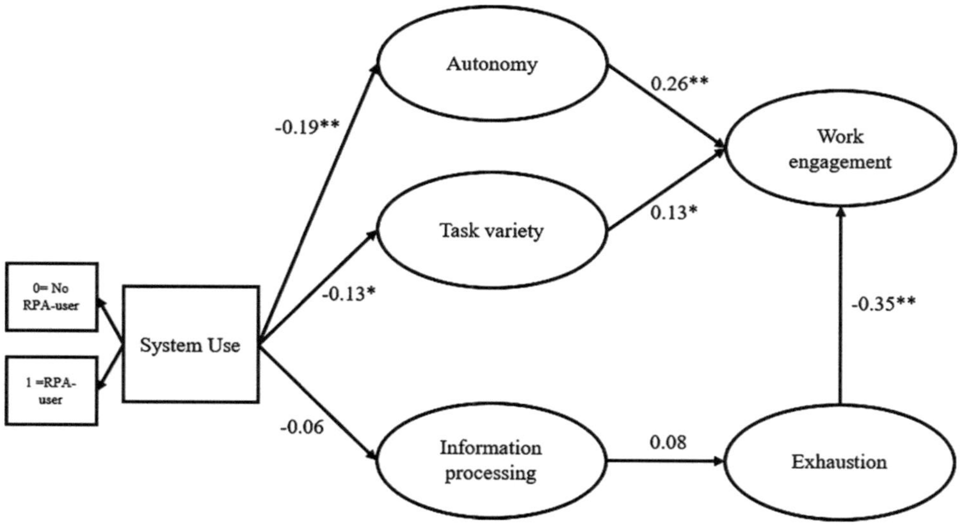

Figure 1.
Overview of results of structural equation modeling. Note: n = 420. $^{*}p < 0.05$, $^{**}p < 0.01$.

Last, we tested a plausible alternative model, in which system use was related to autonomy and task variety, through work engagement. Additionally, in this alternative model we proposed that system use was indirectly related to information processing through exhaustion. The alternative model showed a lower overall fit with the data ($\chi^2 = 248.549$ df = 80, CFI = 0.92, TLI = 0.90, RMSEA = 0.07). After comparison of the two models, the proposed research model yielded a significantly better fit ($\Delta\chi^2 = 38.314$, $\Delta df = 2$, $p < 0.01$).

6. Discussion

To gain a better understanding of the impact of workplace automation on the quality of work and employee well-being, we examined to what extent the introduction of RPA relates to work characteristics and subsequent work-related employee well-being. We drew on the JD-R framework [15] to argue for a positive relationship between RPA use (vs. non-use) and the job resources autonomy and task variety, and in turn work engagement. Additionally, we proposed a negative association between RPA use and information processing and subsequently exhaustion. Contrary to our expectations, the results showed that RPA use was negatively related to both autonomy and task variety, which in turn were positively related to work engagement. Moreover, the indirect effects of both autonomy and task variety were negative in the relationship between RPA use and work engagement. These results indicate that the introduction of a workplace automation, and more specifically the use of RPA, is at the expense of work engagement for employees who have to deal with this new technology through a decrease in job resources. Furthermore, we found no significant relationship between RPA use and information processing and in turn exhaustion, suggesting that job demands were not significantly affected by the introduction of a new workplace technology.

Unexpectedly and remarkably, the findings of this study demonstrate that working with RPA as a new technology is associated with lower levels of both autonomy and task variety. This is a worrying finding in itself, especially because autonomy and task variety are important predictors of work engagement, as also underlined by the results of this study. Moreover, many studies have demonstrated that a lack of job resources, including autonomy and task variety, is also associated with other negative work outcomes such as burnout, turnover intentions, lower levels of learning behaviors, as well as a decrease in motivation, proactivity, and performance [35–37]. This further underlines that it is very important to conserve job resources when introducing a new work process automation.

A possible explanation for the negative association between RPA use and autonomy and task variety - and thus the opposite intended effect of RPA - could lie in the ongoing implementation process of a workplace automation [9]. In this case, RPA was relatively recently introduced within the organization, meaning that the system was still in continuous adjustment to the specific demands of the organization and employees. Although RPA takes over well-structured and repetitive work tasks, the provided output still needs to be regularly checked by human employees. Therefore, it could be that employees working with RPA were still spending considerable time to examine and correct potential system mistakes and updating the robot to certain tasks and needs [38]. Considering that employees needed to search, report, and adjust RPA system errors, this could lead to a decreased sense of autonomy and control. Additionally, because this also requires a different set of work skills, room to engage in new and challenging tasks could be limited. Moreover, employees who had to work with RPA could not freely choose whether RPA took over certain work tasks they previously performed themselves. It could be the case that this lack of individual influence on the use of RPA resulted in a decreased feeling of control. As such, because employees were required to use and learn RPA and did not have a final say in whether RPA was implemented in their work or not, their autonomy may be threatened and thus reduced.

Taken together, the present study findings implicate that after the implementation of a work process automation technology, employee engagement, and thus well-being, is at risk due to a significant decrease in core job resources for RPA users. Additionally, the results of this study showed that RPA use is not related at all to information processing. A possible explanation for this finding may be that information processing simultaneously increases and decreases for RPA users, thereby canceling out any effects. More specifically, it could be that while RPA use relates to less administrative information that has to be analyzed and processed, employees do have to process more information associated with learning to work and getting familiar with RPA, as well as controlling and adjusting RPA processes. In that case, it would be useful to distinguish between different types of information processing related to a digital transition. For instance, information processing associated with the eventual effects of a new technology on individuals work content (and thus an expected decrease in simple and monotonous work tasks), and information processing related to the implementation process and learning a new technology.

Alternatively, other job demands than information processing could be taken into account when examining the impact of RPA on work characteristics. For instance, workload and role conflict could be potential interesting factors in light of the implementation of RPA, considering that the job content is likely to change due to the implementation of a new work process automation technology. Additionally, in the initial phase after a digital transition a new system requires new routines and knowledge, which is likely to have an impact on employees' workload [39].

Last, we did not found the expected positive relationship between information processing and exhaustion. Exhaustion is often regarded as a more distal outcome compared to work engagement, because employee exhaustion only develops after repeated exposure of (high) job demands [40]. Due to the cross-sectional design of this study that also was conducted only two months after the implementation of RPA, it could be that the health impairment processes, as proposed by the JD-R framework, had not been set in motion yet.

6.1 Theoretical contributions

A first important contribution of the current study is that it demonstrates that the relationship between the implementation of technological innovations at work and employee well-being via work characteristics is not straightforward. Our results show that, although RPA is often introduced with the intention to lessen the burden on employees concerning monotonous, repetitive work tasks, this goal is not necessarily achieved. Based on the present study, it seems that job demands do not decrease for those employees that work with the new technology. More importantly and also contrary to our expectations, the use of a new system at work was related to lower instead of higher levels of autonomy and task variety, meaning that job resources of system users seem to decrease after implementation of a work process automation. Thus, our findings demonstrated that the introduction of a new technology did not lower demands. In fact, it even generated less resources in that it created less space for employees to take control over their work and engage in challenging and a wider variety of tasks. Taken together, these findings provide support for the existence of a technology paradox, in that the potential of a new workplace technology does not necessarily results in desired organizational and individual outcomes. Specifically, the implementation of a work process automation should not be at the expense of employee job resources.

Second, the present study contributes to the emerging literature on RPA [5, 6] and offers more insight into workplace automation, and specifically the implementation of RPA, on employee experiences. Whereas earlier studies on the impact of workplace automation and RPA showed overall positive associations with job resources [18, 41, 42], the results of this study present a different picture. Our findings suggest that automation does not always result in a desired reduction of demands, and more importantly, that it poses a potential treat to well-being via a decrease in job resources. To the best of our knowledge this is one of the first papers that focusses on both job resources and a job demand following the implementation of a workplace automation. To gain a deeper understanding of the complex human-technology interaction, future research should place emphasis on changes in both challenging and hindering demands following a digital transition, as well as on job resources that can help employees cope and perform with automation and RPA.

6.2 Limitations and future research

This study has several limitations. First, due to the cross-sectional study design, we cannot draw conclusions about the causal relationships between RPA use, the examined job resources and demand, and work engagement and exhaustion. Although we carefully followed the core premises by the JD-R model [15], it could be the case that some proposed relationships are reciprocal. For instance, it might be that employees who experience high levels of work engagement also perceive more job resources in their work [43]. Earlier studies (e.g. [44, 45] indeed found that job resources and work engagement influence each other in both directions, suggesting a gain cycle in which the presence of job resources and work engagement reinforce each other reciprocally. These findings further underline the importance of more longitudinal research to investigate such bidirectional relationships in a digital transition context. Additionally, when investigating the influence of a technological implementation on employees' job quality and work experiences, future research could apply a longitudinal study design, in which users and non-users are compared at several measurement points, including pre- and post-implementation. Since employees included in the present study were not randomly assigned to use RPA, the selection of employees to use RPA could be correlated with their perceptions of task variety and job automation. For instance, some employees are more capable and can handle more task variety, so they may be more likely to be selected to use RPA. Thus, it is a challenge to determine the causal effect. Therefore, a within-group pre-post design would have been better and is recommended for future studies.

In addition, the use of self-reports could lead to common method bias [46]. However, additional to the good fit of the measurement model, we conducted Harman's single-factor test, which demonstrated that variance in the data was not due to a single underlying factor and thus indicating that common method bias was not a problem in this study. Moreover, it can be argued that constructs reflecting individual states, such as work engagement and exhaustion, as well as perceived work characteristics, can best be evaluated by the individual actor, and are not necessarily suitable to cross-validate with other-ratings.

Finally, in this study we focused on (only) three specific work characteristics that were likely to be influenced by the introduction and use of RPA, namely autonomy, task variety, and information processing. The choice of these work characteristics was based on earlier qualitative research findings on the impact of RPA on job resources [18]. Moreover, we reasoned that the implementation of RPA lessens the amount of information that needs to be processed by human employees, as well as generates more control and room for other challenging tasks. Considering that we found no relationship between RPA use and information processing, it would be particularly interesting to uncover if and how other job demands of system users are affected by the implementation of a workplace automation. For instance, future research could further differentiate between challenging and hindering job demands, were job hindrances (e.g., job insecurity, role conflict, and constraints) are associated with exhaustion and job challenges (e.g., workload and cognitive demands) with engagement [47]. It could be that the implementation of new technologies at work simultaneously incite hinderances and challenges for employees. More insight into how workplace automation affects these specific job demands could contribute to a better implementation of new technologies and optimize adaption among employees who have to work with these technologies [9]. Similarly, it would be relevant to examine what and how job resources can help employees to achieve their goals and stay motivated during the introduction of a new technology [16]. In sum, it is of key importance to design jobs in such a way that a digital transition involves both challenging and realizable job demands, as well as sufficient job resources to stimulate employee performance and well-being. A human-centered approach to workplace automation and job design with particular consideration for employee work experiences is of key importance in reducing the technology-paradox and optimizing the full potential of technology [8].

6.3 Practical implications

The present study connects to a broader debate on the quality of work in the rapid-changing contemporary world of work [48, 49]. Both employees and managers benefit greatly from a healthy and motivating work environment, especially in times of digital transition and widespread automation within organizations. The findings of this study provide further insight into how technological innovations relate to employee well-being through work characteristics and underline the importance of stimulating autonomy and task variety in order to safeguard employee motivation after introducing a workplace automation.

Facilitating a work environment in which employees have access to sufficient job resources that help them deal and work with technological advancements, as well as enabling good performance, is one of the most important implications for practice. Based on the results of this study and in line with the recommendations of reference [16], organizations and HR practitioners should take responsibility during and after the implementation of new technologies. One of the focal points should be to (re) design jobs in such a way that technological innovations turn into a resource itself by closely paying attention to the needs and concerns of users. Carefully identifying how job demands may change after a digital transition can also help organizations to offer appropriate job resources for employees to cope with changes in their job demands. For instance, access to sufficient training and education can help employees to become acquainted and more proficient in using a new technology, and thereby also reducing workload, anxiety, and job insecurity [50]. Additionally, providing feedback and support from the organization and managers are two main resources for employees that help them deal with the negative consequences of job demands [51]. Furthermore, another way to successfully gain and maintain well-being and motivation during a digital transition, is by facilitating employee job crafting [52] which refers to an individual proactive strategy to seek out relevant job resources that can help employees during technological change. Managers and organizations play a key role in creating a work environment in which employees feel encouraged to engage in job crafting and proactively seek out resources they need to adjust and perform [53].

In sum, during and following the implementation of a technological innovation, organizations and managers should be aware of changes in job demands and needs from employees, as well as focus on providing adequate resources for employees to cope with these demands and to stimulate optimal performance with a new technology.

7. Conclusion

The current study demonstrates that the introduction of a workplace automation system may have a profound negative impact on employee job resources. More specifically, the findings indicate that use of an automation system relates to lower levels of autonomy and variation in work tasks, forming a serious threat to the work engagement of employees who have to work with the new system. As such, this study shows that organizations should take a close look at and take into account potentially affected job resources due to the implementation of a workplace automation. Importantly, focusing on stimulating relevant job resources, such as autonomy and task variety, during and after digital transitions is necessary to maintain and promote employee well-being and motivation.

Acknowledgements

This research was funded by a grant from A + O fonds Rijk, an independent Dutch Foundation for innovation and research within the Dutch Government.

Author details

Maria C.W. Peeters[1,2]* and Judith Plomp[1]

1 Department of Social, Health and Organizational Psychology, Utrecht University, Utrecht, The Netherlands

2 Eindhoven University of Technology, Human Performance Management Group, Eindhoven, The Netherlands

*Address all correspondence to: m.peeters@uu.nl

References

[1] Schilling MA, Shankar R. Strategic Management of Technological Innovation. Chennai, India: McGraw-Hill Education; 2019

[2] Miers D, Kerremans M, Ray S, Tornbohm C. Gartner Magic quadrant for robotic process automation software. Market Research Report, no. G00379618. 2019.

[3] Asatiani A, Penttinen E. Turning robotic process automation into commercial success–Case Opus Capita. Journal of Information Technology Teaching Cases. 2016;**2**:67-74

[4] Kroll C, Bujak A, Darius V, Enders W, Esser M. Robotic process automation-robots conquer business processes in back offices. Capgemini Consulting. 2016:1-48

[5] Van der Aalst WMP, Bichler M, Heinzl A. Robotic process automation. Business and Information Systems Engineering. 2018;**60**:269-272

[6] Aguirre S, Rodriguez A. Automation of a business process using robotic process automation (RPA): A case study. In: Figueroa-García JC, López-Santana ER, Villa-Ramírez JL, Ferro-Escobar R, editors. Applied Computer Sciences in Engineering. Vol. 742. Cham: Springer International Publishing; 2017. pp. 65-71

[7] Herm LV, Janiesch C, Helm A, Imgrund F, Fuchs K, Hofmann A, et al. A Consolidated Framework for Implementing Robotic Process Automation Projects. In: Fahland D, Ghidini C, Becker J, Dumas M, editors. Business Process Management. Cham: Springer International Publishing; 2020. pp. 471-488

[8] Peeters MCW. Sustainable work performance in times of digitalization: From paradox to potency. Gedrag en Organisatie. 2020;**33**:163-183

[9] Parker SK, Grote G. Automation, algorithms, and beyond: Why work design matters more than ever in a digital world. Applied Psychology: An International Review. 2020;**69**:1-45

[10] Gayathiri R, Ramakrishnan L, Babatunde SA, Banerjee A, Islam MZ. Quality of work life–Linkage with job satisfaction and performance. International Journal of Business and Management Invention. 2013;**2**:1-8

[11] Warr P, Nielsen K. Wellbeing and work performance. In: Diener E, Oishi S, Tay L, editors. Handbook of Well-being. Salt Lake City: DEF Publishers; 2018

[12] Hofmann P, Samp C, Urbach N. Robotic process automation. Electronic Markets. 2020;**30**:99-106

[13] Madakam S, Holmukhe RM, Jaiswal DK. The future digital work force: Robotic process automation (RPA). Journal of Information Systems and Technology Management. 2019;**16**:1-17

[14] Osmundsen K, Iden J, Bygstad B. Organizing robotic process automation: balancing loose and tight coupling. Hawaii: Proceedings of the 52nd Hawaii International Conference on System Sciences; January 2019

[15] Bakker AB, Demerouti E. Job demands–resources theory: taking stock and looking forward. Journal of Occupational Health Psychology. 2017;**22**:273-285

[16] Demerouti E. Turn digitalization and automation to a job resource. Applied

Psychology: An International Review. 2020:1-6

[17] Plomp J, Peeters MCW. The impact of technological innovations on the quality of work and wellbeing: A systematic literature review. Gedrag and Organisatie. 2020;**33**:348-375

[18] Engberg S, Sördal T. Robotic Process Automation-Robotic Process Automation and its Effects on Job Characteristics [thesis]. Lund, Sweden: Lund University; 2019

[19] Johansson B, Engberg S, Lindgren I, Sordal T. Impacts of RPA on employees skill variety. Paper presentation at the Conference of the Association for Information Systems (AMCIS). August 2020

[20] Morgeson FP, Humphrey SE. The Work Design Questionnaire (WDQ): developing and validating a comprehensive measure for assessing job design and the nature of work. Journal of Applied Psychology. 2006;**91**:1321-1339

[21] Lamberton C, Brigo D, Hoy D. Impact of Robotics. RPA and AI on insurance industry, challenges and opportunities. Journal of Financial Perspectives. 2016;**4**:1-13

[22] Noppen P, Beerepoot I, van de Weerd I, Jonker M, Reijers HA. How to Keep RPA Maintainable? In: Fahland D, Ghidini C, Becker J, Dumas M, editors. Business Process Management. Cham: Springer International Publishing; 2020. pp. 453-470

[23] Daft RL, Macintosh NB. A tentative exploration into the amount and equivocality of information processing in organizational work units. Administrative Science Quarterly. 1981;**26**:207-224

[24] Warr P. The measurement of well-being and other aspects of mental health. Journal of Occupational Psychology. 1990;**63**:193-210

[25] Martínez-Iñigo D, Totterdell P, Alcover CM, Holman D. Emotional labour and emotional exhaustion: Interpersonal and intrapersonal mechanisms. Work and Stress. 2007;**21**:30-47

[26] Schaufeli WB, Taris TW, Van Rhenen W. Workaholism, burnout, and work engagement: Three of a kind or three different kinds of employee well-being? Applied Psychology. 2008;**57**:173-203

[27] Halbesleben JRB. A meta-analysis of work engagement: Relationships with burnout, demands, resources and consequences. In: Bakker AB, Leiter MP, editors. Work Engagement: A Handbook of Essential Theory and Research. New York: Psychology Press; 2010. pp. 102-117

[28] Schaufeli WB. Work engagement: What do we know and where do we go? Romanian Journal of Applied Psychology. 2012;**14**:3-10

[29] Bakker AB, Demerouti E, Verbeke W. Using the job demands-resources model to predict burnout and performance. Human Resource Management. 2004;**43**:83-104

[30] Schaufeli WB, Shimazu A, Hakanen J, Salanova M, De Witte H. An ultra-short measure for work engagement: The UWES-3 validation across five countries. European Journal of Psychological Assessment. 2019;**35**:577-591

[31] Schaufeli WB, De Witte H, Desart S. Manual of Burnout Assessment Tool (BAT). Leuven, Belgium: KU Leuven; 2019

[32] Hu LT, Bentler PM. Cutoff criteria for fit indexes in covariance structure analysis: Conventional criteria versus new alternatives. Structural Equation Modeling: A Multidisciplinary Journal. 1999;**6**:1-55

[33] Arbuckle JL. Amos for Windows. Analysis of Moment Structures, Version 6.0. Spring House, PA: AMOS Development Corporation; 2005

[34] Macho S, Ledermann T. Estimating, testing, and comparing specific effects in structural equation models: The phantom model approach. Psychological Methods. 2011;**16**:34-43

[35] Bakker AB, Demerouti E, Euwema MC. Job resources buffer the impact of job demands on burnout. Journal of Occupational Health Psychology. 2005;**10**:170-180

[36] Parker SK, Morgeson FP, Johns G. One hundred years of work design research: Looking back and looking forward. Journal of Applied Psychology. 2017;**102**:403-420

[37] Schaufeli WB, Bakker AB. Job demands, job resources, and their relationship with burnout and engagement: A multi-sample study. Journal of Organizational Behavior. 2004;**25**:293-315

[38] Montero JC, Ramirez AJ, Enríquez JG. Towards a method for automated testing in robotic process automation project. In: Proceedings of the 14th International Workshop on Automation of Software Test (AST). Piscataway, New Jersey, US: IEEE Press; May 2019. pp. 24-47

[39] Lundh M, Rydstedt LW. A static organization in a dynamic context: A qualitative study of changes in working conditions for Swedish engine officers. Applied Ergonomics. 2016;**55**:1-7

[40] Crawford ER, LePine JA, Rich BL. Linking job demands and resources to employee engagement and burnout: A theoretical extension and meta-analytic test. Journal of Applied Psychology. 2010;**95**:834-848

[41] Morris MG, Venkatesh V. Job characteristics and job satisfaction: Understanding the role of enterprise resource planning system implementation. MIS Quarterly. 2010;**34**:143-161

[42] Venkatesh V, Bala H, Sykes TA. Impacts of information and communication technology implementations on employees' jobs in service organizations in India: A multi-method longitudinal field study. Production and Operations Management. 2010;**19**:591-613

[43] Taris TW, Kompier MA. Cause and effect: Optimizing the designs of longitudinal studies in occupational health psychology. Work & Stress. 2014;**28**:1-8

[44] Schaufeli WB, Bakker AB, Van Rhenen W. How changes in job demands and resources predict burnout, work engagement, and sickness absenteeism. Journal of Organizational Behavior. 2009;**30**:893-917

[45] Xanthopoulou D, Bakker AB, Demerouti E, Schaufeli WB. Reciprocal relationships between job resources, personal resources, and work engagement. Journal of Vocational Behavior. 2009;**74**:235-244

[46] Podsakoff PM, MacKenzie SB, Lee JY, Podsakoff NP. Common method biases in behavioral research:

A critical review of the literature and recommended remedies. Journal of Applied Psychology. 2003;**88**:879-903

[47] Van den Broeck A, De Cuyper N, De Witte H, Vansteenkiste M. Not all job demands are equal: Differentiating job hindrances and job challenges in the Job Demands–Resources model. European Journal of Work and Organizational Psychology. 2010;**19**:735-759

[48] Adamson M, Roper I. Good' jobs and 'bad' jobs: Contemplating job quality in different contexts. Work Employment and Society. 2019;**33**:551-559

[49] Cazes S, Hijzen A, Saint-Martin A. Measuring and Assessing Job Quality: The OECD Job Quality Framework. Paris: OECD Social, Employment and Migration Working Papers 174; 2015

[50] De Witte H, Vander Elst T, De Cuyper N. Job insecurity, Health and Well-being. In: Vuori J, Blonk R, Price RH, editors. Sustainable Working Lives. Dordrecht, NL: Springer; 2015

[51] Xanthopoulou D, Bakker AB, Dollard MF, Demerouti E, Schaufeli WB, Taris TW, et al. When do job demands particularly predict burnout? The moderating role of job resources. Journal of Managerial Psychology. 2007;**22**:766-785

[52] Tims M, Bakker AB. Job crafting: Towards a new model of individual job redesign. SA Journal of Industrial Psychology. 2010;**36**:1-9

[53] Wang H, Demerouti E, Bakker AB. A review of job crafting research: The role of leader behaviors in cultivating successful job crafters. In: Parker SK, Bindl UK, editors. Proactivity at work: Making things happen in organizations. New York, USA: Routledge; 2016. pp. 77-104

Chapter 6

Digital Transformation in the Construction Sector: From BIM to Digital Twin

Bruno Daniotti, Alberto Pavan, Cecilia Bolognesi, Claudio Mirarchi and Martina Signorini

Abstract

In the next years, perhaps more than ever before, a technological revolution will transform the construction sector in all its aspects, greatly affecting services, production, and supplies. With BIM, and even more considering the Digital Twin topic, the innovation of tools has entailed a methodological innovation for the whole sector, owing to virtual reality simulations and actual dynamic real-time monitoring. This research, starting from an integrated analysis between the current research trends and some relevant national and European projects about the digitalization of construction sector, aims at providing a systematic analysis of some of the pillars that are guiding this phenomenon. In detail, the state of the art, activities, and trends of standardization and platform development in construction sector are considered and intersected to provide a clear background towards the future trends in the sector.

Keywords: BIM, digital twin, digital platforms, standardization, process management, construction

1. Introduction

In the next years, perhaps more than ever before, a technological revolution will transform the construction sector in all its single aspects, greatly affecting services, production, and supplies. Freehand drawing, drafting machines or CAD have represented innovative tools in graphic representations. In such cases, the evolution of tools for the productivity of the sector has improved and quickened the design, but not more than that. With Building Information Modeling (BIM), and even more considering the Digital Twin (DT) topic, the innovation of tools has entailed a methodological innovation for the whole sector. Around BIM and DT several technologies and topics needs to be analyzed including virtual reality simulations, dynamic real-time monitoring and controlling, data driven decisions, etc. Nowadays, several drivers can be identified in the evolution of both the research and the industrial applications. Hence the need to provide a systematic analysis that can provide a clear background useful for future research works. Among these drivers the standardization activities and the development of digital platforms for the construction sector represent key points for the understanding of the ongoing research and development in the digitalization of the construction sector. The work here presented has been developed starting from an integrated analysis between the current research trends and some relevant national and European projects about the digitalization of construction sector and considering a perspective view that comprehend the history and evolution of the BIM topic and its implications.

This research aims at providing a systematic analysis of these two pillars considering the intersection of both the research trends and the results obtained from the development of some key national and European projects. The results here proposed can inform future research paving the way for the development of new works around these two key drivers of the digital transformation in the construction sector.

Following these directions, this chapter is organized as follows. Section 2 reports a brief analysis of the main evolution points that shaped the change from CAD to BIM. Section 3 proposes an analysis of the standardization framework analyzing the existing works and the ongoing and future activities. Section 4 reports a presentation of some of the main projects that have been developed in the context of the development of digital platforms for the construction sector. Finally, Section 5 reports the conclusions of the chapter.

2. BIM: from CAD to BIM

2.1 The first steps

In the last two decades the work of designers has radically changed not only in relation to conceptual differences in the representation of the project [1], more and more oriented to 3D development as a model from which to derive two-dimensional drawings of plans, sections and elevations, but also in relation to the technical instrumentation offered by the software and hardware capabilities related to the representation and simulation of the project, with inevitable repercussions on the professionalism and responsibility of individual actors [2].

On the one hand, the ability to represent the project as classically occurred in the past has remained the same for centuries, delegating to the designer the realization skills of his own project, with responsibility for all parts of its development and the obligation to represent and describe every single piece of information destined to its best realization; on the other hand, the step change that occurred with the digital design processes was first slight with the introduction of the first two-dimensional CAD, then more and more involving with the transition to BIM [3].

The transition from manual drawing to CAD [4] takes place as for BIM starting from the mechanical and precisely automotive industries; the need for absolute precision in the design for production is required by the simulations related to the efficiency of vehicles as well as the hypothesis of making the house a machine for living is becoming more and more possible.

In a traditional design workflow, the designer generally worked on his single area of expertise and from a preliminary architectural content descended the structural and plant choices unless required by a state of necessity. The subordination of actions in the development of the project was very clear and the roles as well. With the advent of CAD and the use of different layers this position of absolute dominance over the project begins to waver, if only for the possibility of greater flexibility in the construction of variants compared to previous workflows. Coordination becomes part of the design routine, at least above a certain size, and a process of modernization of the workflows takes place. Coordination has very specific goals: smoothing out conflicts, introducing compatible variants, correcting layers. There remains a vast waste of forces and time to correct different layers, sections, up to a better coordination between the windows of the model space but still in two-dimensional and limited scope. The discordances between those who work in architecture and those who work in engineering remain also when we try to visualize the project: for an architect it's about evaluating the space and the perspective views or anyway the 3D sketches are the most used means; for an engineer the most adequate representation concerns plans and construction details.

In the early days of the BIM revolution [5], the first calculation applications linked to CAD tools, some first library of materials and objects, offered as blocks, mainly linked to price lists, came forward.

When BIM arrives, the revolution is disruptive; the designer's point of view changes from the setting, working primarily from the 3D model. The sub-units of the model are objects, parametric, informed, and offer rapid possibilities in their transformation, in the modeling of the whole [6]. The preliminary phase of the project already brings in itself more information than necessary, having the single objects parameters defined; some argue that this definition from the first phases of the project of the objects risks binding the less experienced to the design. Nevertheless, the obtained model results the only true DB of all the information on the project, through which we can build the base documentation and not only.

In addition, the parametric model combines the expectations of two worlds: the expectations of architects, who want to visualize the project at 1 m from the ground, and of engineers, who want to visualize what is in the project, such as in the walls or floors, finds a point of contact [7].

2.2 BIM model definition and introduction of a disruptive process

Once the backroom battles that accused BIM of deadening the creative process of designers have died down, process integration comes into its own. Geometric information alone does not allow the representation of the project necessary for the BIM process in its entirety, and therefore BIM proposes an object-based representation. In the case of construction, this translates into a representative schema modeled around the project entities and their mutual relationships.

In the definition of the floor object, for example, the geometry constitutes only one of the different properties of this building element; a room consisting of floors and walls, in addition to the geometric data will contain information such as connected walls and adjacent spaces. We speak not only of model set-up but of "building representation", considering the specific domain of information integrated in the objects.

As the structural principles of object modeling are reshaped, metrics are introduced to measure the actual application of BIM within production facilities; as the level of maturity of BIM adoption increases, so do the levels. Level 0 represents the initial form of the introduction process; generally, people still work in two-dimensional mode, with 2D drawings enriched by data without shared standards. We are in traditional procedures, prodromes of a real BIM and far from an object-based structure. In level 1 standardized structures and formats are introduced, certainly in the design phase there is a 3D phase enriched by 2D documents with design information; however the collaborative phase is still remote and federated models are not yet in progress so the strengths of BIM are not yet used. At Level 2, we are already thinking in a fully collaborative environment: all parties are using 3D CAD models, and collaboration comes in the form of how information is exchanged between the various parties through common file formats that allow anyone to create a investigable federated model. So, we are in a 3D environment with attachments where the starting disciplines are still on separate models that can be assembled. At level 3, sharing and collaboration between disciplines is total. There is a single design model allocated in an IFC-compliant repository referred to in the following lines. At Level 3, the design team has overall control over design and construction, and design optimization is achieved. In Level 3, we talk about a fully open process and data integration enabled for standards-compliant "web services." (**Figure 1**)

2.3 Federated models and shared environments

The need to deal with a common language, to share procedures and basic documents, to use interoperable and sharable software, a choice reinforced using BIM within the Public Administrations, together with the need to have reference figures for certain categories of work in the design flow, to be able to build environments of data sharing determine at first a disruption in the organization of work [8]. In BIM the information flows related to the project are integrated; there is a shift from a "document-centric" approach, to an innovative "data-centric" approach, with attention paid to the entire life cycle of the work; the BIM model therefore immediately guarantees the complex management of the building and distributed over time starting from the design, planning for the realization, estimation, up to the realization and management of the work.

The big step forward is about the ability to work synchronously on the same model as the key element; each project is modeled in relation to a number of models focused on specific disciplines. The models are associated with a federated model, a centralized repository of information for the entire project. In a typical construction project, the federated model may consist of the architectural model, the structural model, and other specialized models containing all the relevant information provided by the building owner, architect, structural engineer, mechanical engineer, plumbing

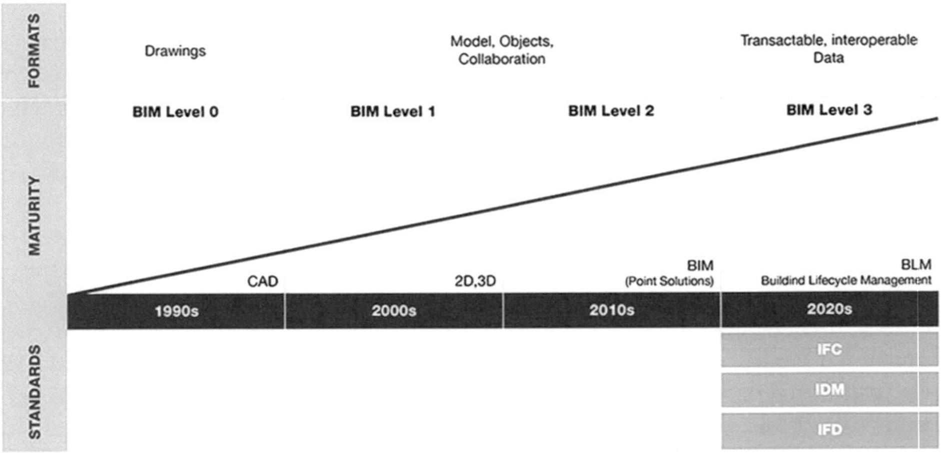

Figure 1.
Levels of insight into the use of BIM, from level 0 to level 3 objective, BSI PAS 1192–2.

engineer, and contractors. It is easy to understand how the possibility of cooperation between the different types of design and the consequent management of conflicts can be resolved through platforms, but not only; shared work imposes the sharing of procedures and requires a shared environment, favoring the construction of digital environments where information can be transmitted.

The sharing environment is CDE, in Italy, better known as Common Data Environment [9] abroad: it is an environment of organized collection and sharing of data related to models and digital works, referring to a single work or a single complex of works. The professional figure who deals with the management of the Data Sharing Environment and the information dynamics based on the introduction, exchange, management and storage of data is the CDE Manager. The Data Sharing Environment Manager is a figure who is in charge of the data sharing environment implemented by the organization to which they belong.

2.4 BIM dimension and new professionalisms

For the intrinsic properties of the models in BIM environment they lend themselves to simulation processes even complex enough; we can consider them as prodromal to the development of Digital Twins. To explain their natural inclination to the complex management of the built environment, a scale of dimensional values, from one to seven, has been coined to describe the intrinsic characteristics within the workflow; after the second and third dimensions of BIM, graphic representation of the work in 2D, function of the plan, or 3D, function of space, the fourth dimension 4D is introduced to simulate the work or its elements as a function of time, as well as space; the fifth dimension 5D [10] as a function of economic value; the sixth 6D as a function of simulating the work for management, maintenance and eventual disposal; the seventh 7D as a simulation of the work as a function of economic, environmental and energy sustainability of the intervention (**Figure 2**).

For the management of the whole process new roles are needed and different degrees of specialization are introduced, keeping the focus of the activity linked to the management of the model even if informed; also the UNI 11337–7 [11] standard

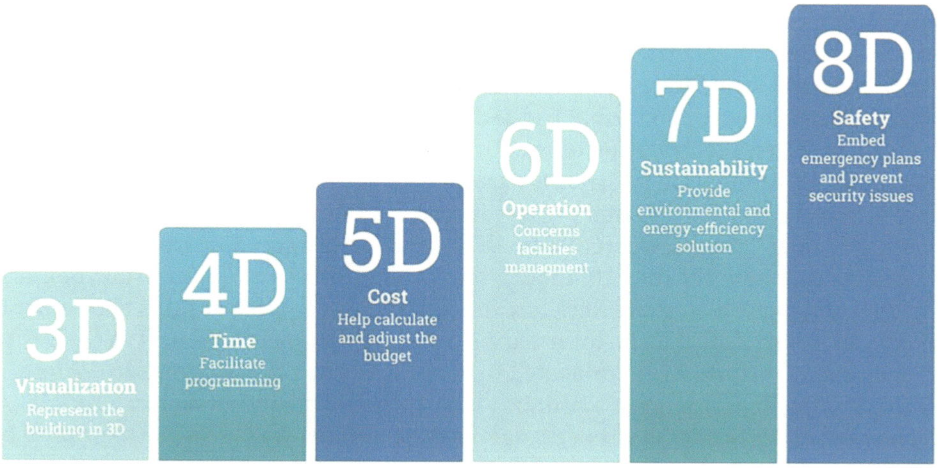

Figure 2.
BIM "3D-7D" graph [10].

identifies roles, knowledge and skills associated to the professional activities involved in the BIM information flow, aggregating the roles foreseen by previous British standards in the following four roles. The BIM manager is considered for the general supervision and coordination of the projects from the information point of view. This is the person who defines the BIM instructions and the way in which the digitization process impacts the organization and the work tools. The BIM Coordinator operates at the level of the single order, in agreement with the top management of the organization and on the indication of the BIM Manager. The BIM Specialist is the advanced operator of management and information modeling and usually acts within the single orders for authoring activities through digitization procedures and object modeling and management.

Generally, he follows the elaboration of the model and also interfaces with the CDE Manager. The BIM specialist must know the software for the realization of a BIM project, according to his own disciplinary competence (architectural, structural, plant engineering, road, hydraulic). He must understand and use the technical and operational documentation for the production of drawings and models (standards and procedures); he/she must "model the information" for the graphic and non-graphic models, interfacing with the supervision and coordination of the BIM Coordinator or the BIM Manager of the company or of the design group in order to elaborate the graphic models and the related objects and their libraries; he/she must extract data from the models, from the drawings and from the objects; he/she must modify the models and the objects derived from the coordination between models and from the project revisions. Its intervention is part of the digital workflow enhanced by the ability to analyze the contents of the information specification and the information management plan having full capacity to verify the information model, and to validate its consistency.

2.5 Interoperability standards and ongoing evolutions

The progressive transition to BIM has created an inevitable proliferation of software products related to information modeling [12] in which the model can find full expression of its geometry and related information. However, the coordinated work between different teams, as well as forcing the sharing of data in a common environment, imposes the solution of problems related to communication between software. The software is proprietary, with problems of communication between each other such as to require an open format whose purpose lies in neutrality towards commercial brands of software to share sets of projects and assets through standards of communication and data exchange. The attempt to standardize data transmission through the use of an open format has decades of history (**Figure 3**).

Over the years, the evolution of the data schema has added multiple degrees of complexity to its hierarchical structure based on the entity-relationship model, to provide a data transposition that preserves more and more information and the consequent relationships. Currently the IFC standard can standardize and codify different components of the BIM model: the recognition of the object in an automatic way, the information on characteristics and attributes, the relationships with other objects, all this to transmit the information model keeping the logic and the geometric-documental information connected to it. However, the IFC attempts to enclose in a predefined logical scheme a context, such as the construction sector, which is represented by a greater degree of complexity than is currently possible to unravel by computer and this particular points it is that one that renders still more important the geometric definition of the model like first interface with the consumer destined to the understanding of the model.

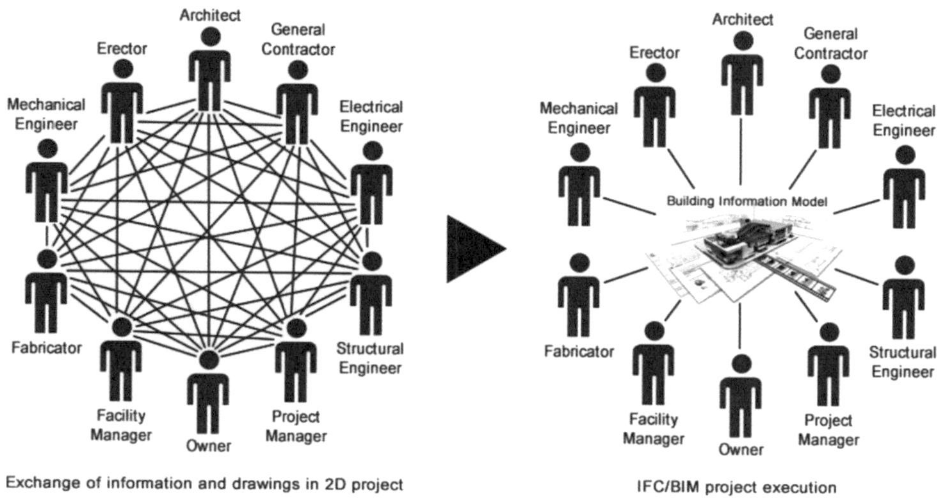

Figure 3.
Interoperability [12].

3. BIM standardization: UNI, CEN TC442, ISO TC59 SC17, buildingSMART

The evolution over time of Building Information Modeling can be traced back to three fundamental aspects:

- technological evolution;
- legislative developments;
- evolution of technical regulations.

The technological evolution can be traced back to the transition from CAD (Computer Aided Design) software systems also dedicated to the construction sector (from the early 80s) to Object-Oriented programming systems of the AEC (Architecture Engineering Construction) domain, also known as BIM Authoring software (starting from the late 80s and with considerable development since the late 90s—**Figure 4**).

The legislative evolution (laws, mandatory rules), especially in the European panorama, can be traced back to the strategy of relaunching the construction sector of the British government after the systemic crisis of 2007/2008 and the related PAS (2011–2013) which they achieved (**Figure 5**): the obligation of government BIM public procurement above 5 million pounds in 2016 in the UK; the introduction of BIM in voluntary form in the European Procurement Directive of 2014: the consequent transposition of BIM in the contract codes of the EU member states (by 2016) and, for example in Italy, the introduction of mandatory BIM from 2019 to 2025 (complex works greater than or equal to 100 million–2019; each works over 1 million euros–2025).

The regulatory evolution at the level of the practices and standards presents three fundamental moments, corresponding to the production of three reference documents (**Figure 6**): the PAS 1192–2 UK (2013), the BIMForum LOD Specifications USA (2013) the BIM Project Execution Planning–of the Pennsylvania University, USA (2010).

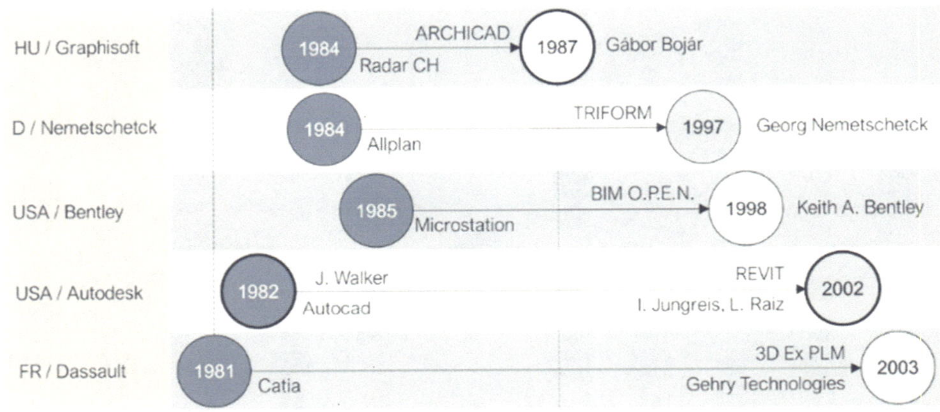

Figure 4.
Tools evolution to BIM (example).

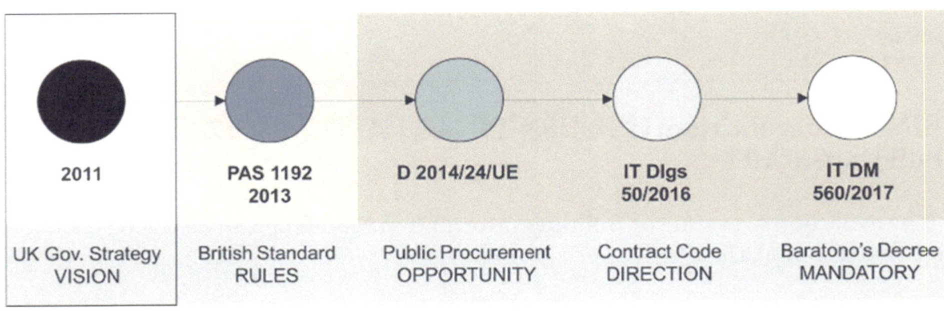

Figure 5.
Laws evolutions to BIM (EU).

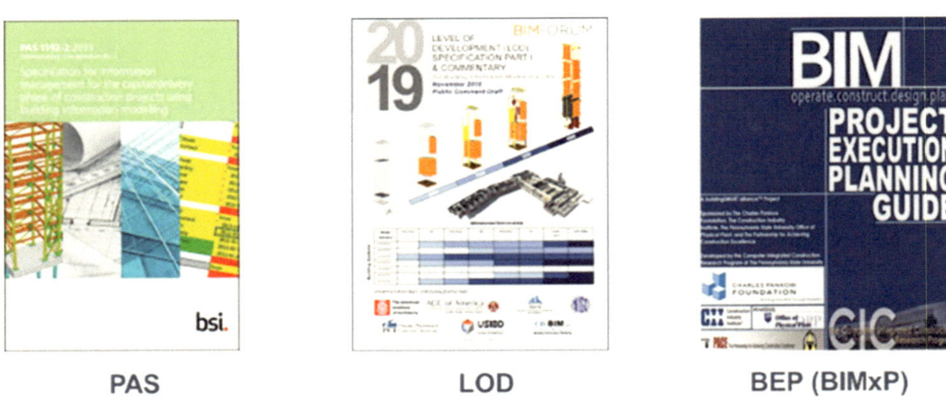

Figure 6.
Main technical specifications and reference practices for BIM.

These constitute, on the one hand, the arrival points of the first works and standards on BIM (ISO STEP 10303; ISO 16739—IFC), on the other hand, the principle of all voluntary technical regulations now in use (**Figure 7**): worldwide at ISO level, in Europe at CEN level and in each individual state (e.g., Italy, Great Britain and United States of America) at UNI, BSI, ANSI levels among others.

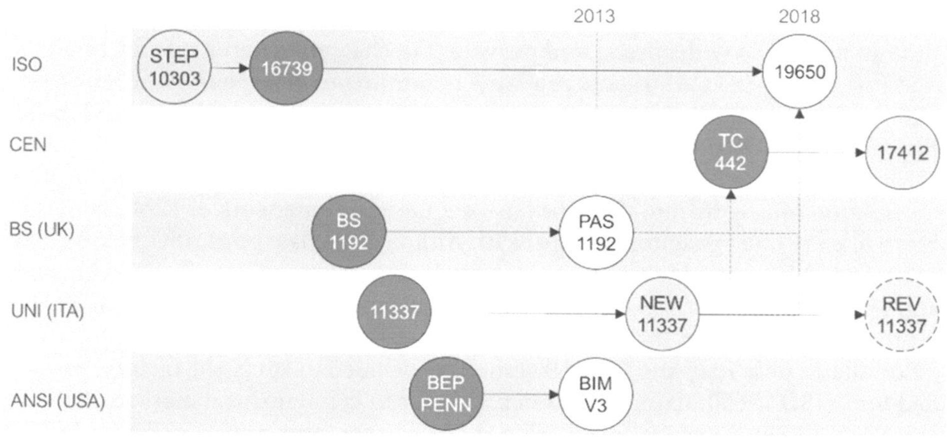

Figure 7.
BIM standard evolution in the world.

The voluntary technical standards are non-mandatory regulatory references that the market adopts to define a workspace–market–within whose boundaries all the actors concerned recognize common principles, shared, with which to operate to protect everyone and the market itself. The standardization body that operates internationally is the International Organization for Standardization (ISO), and its standards take the acronym: ISO. The standardization body that operates at European level (and some added states including Great Britain) is CEN, and its standards take the acronym: EN. CEN is part of ISO. For BIM there is an agreement called "Vienna Agreement" for which (from 2017) each ISO standard automatically becomes a CEN standard (without specific further adoptions). The ISO standards on BIM, after 2017, are therefore ISO EN standards. Finally, each state has its own national standardization body (for Italy the UNI, for Great Britain the BSI, for the USA the ANSI, etc.). They draw up the national rules valid in the specific territory in the national language. For the EU countries the EN standards are automatically adopted even at national level, therefore, in the BIM panorama, the ISO and CEN standards are for example: in Italy UNI EN ISO, and in Great Britain BS EN ISO (**Figure 8**).

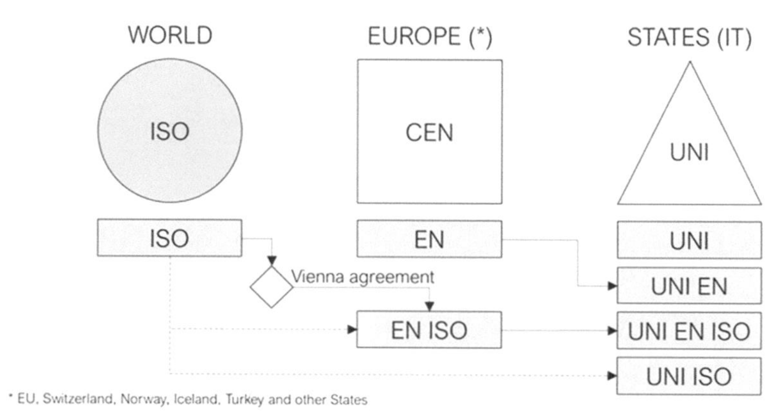

Figure 8.
Standard body structure in the world.

Analyzing the three normative levels (national, CEN and ISO) we see that BIM, although not yet so widespread and prevalent in the construction sector (compared for example to CAD), enjoys a large panorama of reference standards that actually allow a conscious and regulated use in every market, as illustrated in the following **Figure 9**.

With the publication of the first part of the package of standard ISO 19650: 2018 (Information Management—IM) the basic regulatory framework of BIM assume a picture like the one presented in **Figure 10**. Although the last born, ISO 19650 (in its various parts) becomes the reference standard, applicable in all markets. In Europe, it applies together with the subsequent CEN standards (of which, the first, is on the definition of the Level of Information Need: EN 17412:2021).

Nowadays, only Italy and Great Britain have decided to apply the faculty, provided for in ISO 19650, to insert national annexes to facilitate local markets in its application. Other states are considering adopting their own annexes (Spain, France, Germany, Morocco, etc.).

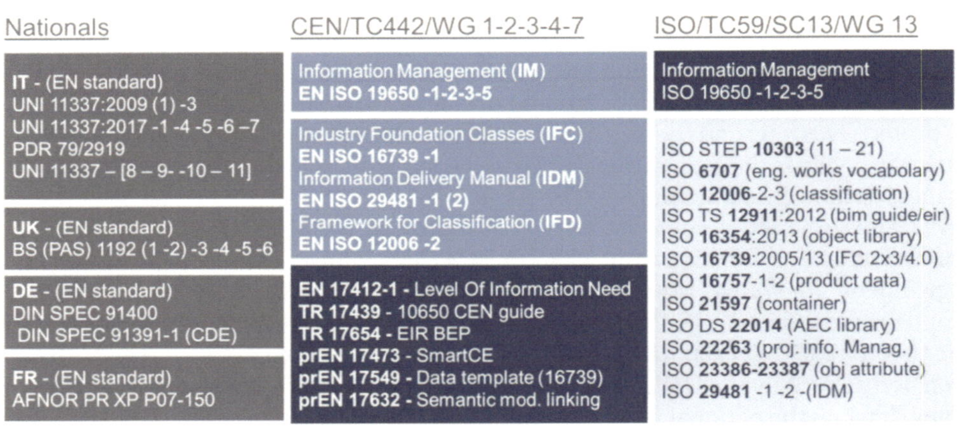

Figure 9.
Map of BIM standards in the world.

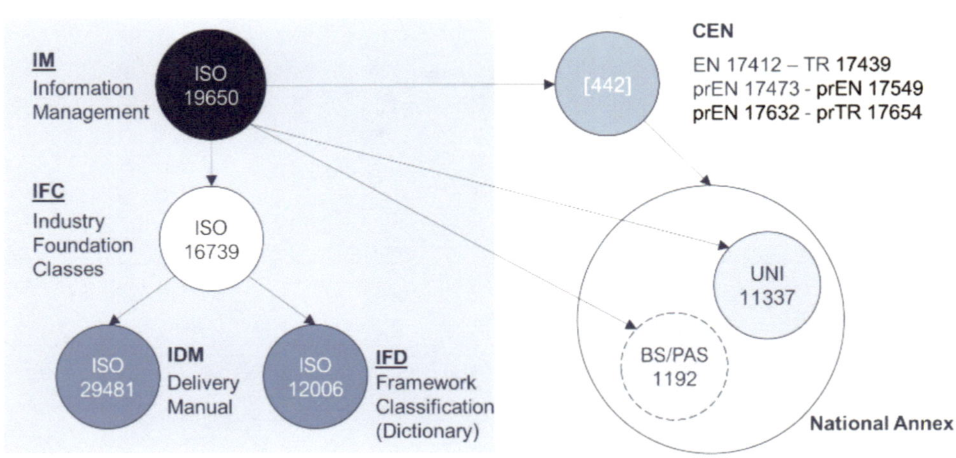

Figure 10.
BIM standard basic relationship.

In particular, while Italy has adopted the path of attaching the entire international package to national standards UNI11337, as a separate package, Great Britain has chosen to withdraw its standards and practices of group 1192 as the fundamental principles of these are assumed in ISO 19650 and insert the remaining parts not transposed at the bottom of the UK national version of ISO 19650 part 2 (in these regulatory annexes). For this reason, it should always be remembered that BS EN ISO 19650-2 (**Figure 11**) has a different conformation from the original version, which does not include annexes.

The Italian decision to keep in force the entire package of UNI 11337 standards is justified by the need to verticalize on the Italian market not only the ISO 19650 but all the most important ISO and CEN standards. In addition to stimulating the writing of other parts or standards necessary not only in the Italian market but also in the international or European scene (**Figure 12**).

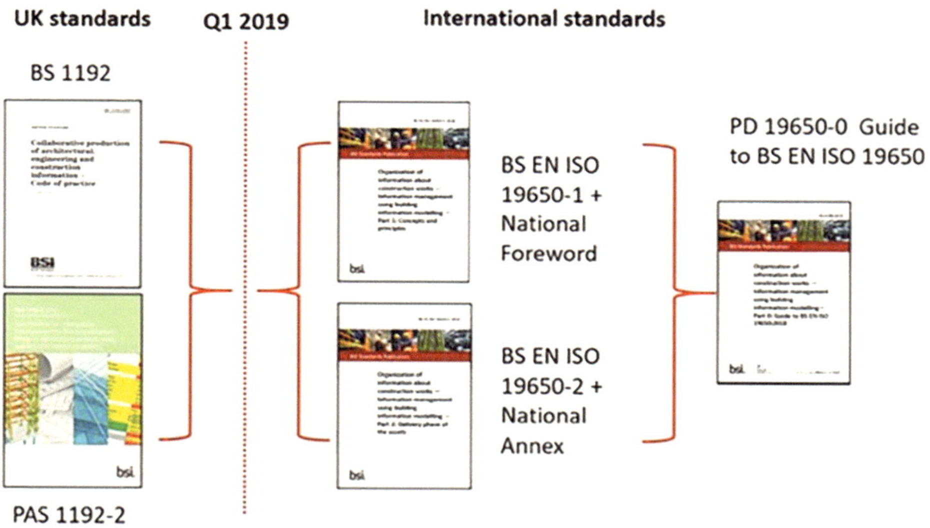

Figure 11.
ISO 19650 vs. BS EN ISO 19650.

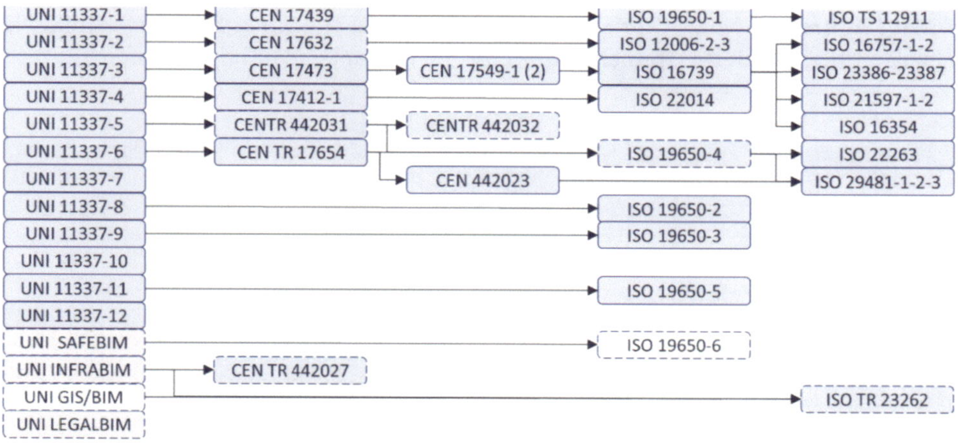

Figure 12.
Standard BIM map relationship.

For example, part 7 of the UNI 11337 (2017) is currently being studied at CEN 442 for the definition of BIM roles and figures at European level, in order to clarify the confusion currently present between BIM professionals, such as between these and those of Project Management (BIM Manager vs. Project Manager; **Figure 13**).

The BIM figures of UNI 11337–7:2017, are:

- **Common data environment manager (CDE manager):** the common data environment manager (CDE manager) is a figure who deals with the data sharing environment implemented by the organization to which it belongs or contractually provided for a specific order by another entity.

- **Manager of digitized processes (BIM manager):** The manager of digitized processes (BIM manager) is a figure that relates mainly to the level of the organization, as regards the digitization of the processes put in place by the same, possibly having the supervision or general coordination of the portfolio of orders in progress. Delegated by the top management of the organization, he defines the BIM instructions and the way in which the digitization process impacts on the organization and on the work tools.

- **Coordinator of the order information flows (BIM coordinator):** The coordinator of the order information flows (BIM coordinator) operates at the level of the individual order, in agreement with the top management of the organization and on the recommendation of the manager of the digitized processes.

- **Advanced operator of management and information modeling (BIM specialist):** The advanced operator of management and information modeling (BIM specialist) usually acts within the individual orders, collaborating in a stable or occasional manner with a specific organization.

An outline of BIM standards cannot fail to end without a quick mention of the IFC (Industry Foundation Classes) standard for open language and OpenBIM. IFC is curated and implemented worldwide by BuildingSmart International and is regulated by the ISO 16739 standard. IFC is both a data model (with definition of standard classes and relationships) and an open schema for generating exchange files in non-proprietary format (**Figure 14**). Non-proprietary formats guarantee the integrity and readability of data over time, which is extremely important, for example, in public procurement.

LEVEL	PM	BIM Management		
	ISO 21500	USA	UK	UNI
Organization	Proposal Manager	Information Manager	//	BIM Manager
Job order	Project Manager	BIM Manager	Information Manager	//
			Task Inform. Manager	
	PM Staff (Communication)	BIM Coordinator	Interface Manager	BIM Coordinator
		BIM Specialist	Information originator	BIM Specialist
		//	//	CDE Manager

Figure 13.
BIM figure and roles.

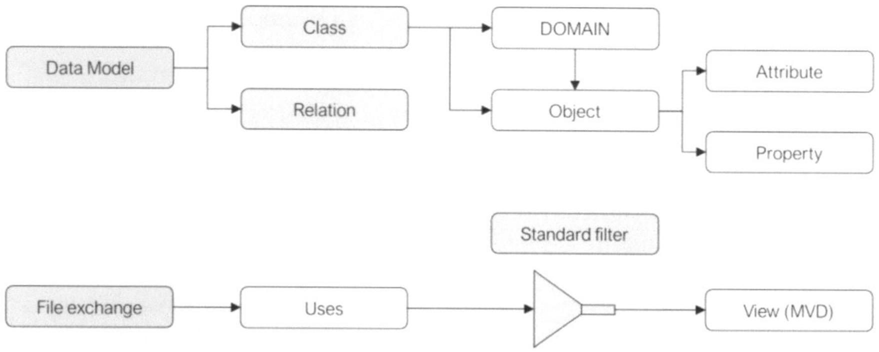

Figure 14.
BuildingSmart ISO 16739–IFC.

4. BIM-based platforms for building process management and research developments towards digital twin

The entire building process must deal with an ineffective information exchange between actors due to a data exchange still mainly based on paper-based transmission system, a variety of classification systems as well as on a use of disparate criteria and practices and a consistent number of stakeholders involved such as architects, engineers, services, and contractors from the design to operation phase. Each stakeholder possesses different set of skills, standards and tools, and thus the communication and the information exchange are characterized by a high level of complexity, as well as the knowledge and process management are often time-consuming [13].

The relevance of BIM in the Architecture, Engineering, Construction, and Operation (AECO) sector is worldwide recognized. Its implementation benefits the construction project reducing and avoiding errors, speeding up the process, improving the communication among the involved actors [14]. It integrates multidisciplinary data to create a digital representation of an asset throughout its life cycle from planning and design to construction and commissioning. BIM-based platforms such as INNOVance and BIMReL help in this direction enhancing data and information exchange along the building lifecycle.

The first BIM-based platform for the construction sector in the Italian context is INNOVance. It aims at collecting, processing and sharing data and supporting involved stakeholders by creating a unique code for the products, services, activities and resources used, a standardized datasheet and a web portal that allows users to use the information at every stage of construction [15].

BIMReL is an interoperable open-source BIM library for construction products that allows to associate all the technical information of the products to the BIM objects present in it. It supports the management of information throughout the entire life cycle of a building, based on the definition of information and technological needs. The added value lies in providing standardized datasheets conforming to UNI 11337–3 [13].

With the need to monitor and control assets all through their lifecycle and with IoT introduction and Artificial Intelligence (AI) diffusion, the birth and the growing affirmation of the Digital Twin has become more and more important [16].

The DT can be defined as "a realistic digital representation of assets, processes, or systems in the built or natural environment" [17] where data are synchronized from the physical to the digital [18], therefore it is seen as a technology that enables the physical and virtual space to communicate [19].

DT presents a new approach in the AEC sector: it is not only a building visual representation, but the latter can be enhanced with real-time data to diagnose the asset state and with the integration of statistic, probabilistic or AI models to allow predictive skills [20–22]. DT can be used for the following applications: real time monitoring, simulation, diagnosis, and performance prediction [16, 23–25].

BIM and DT are still mainly applied on new buildings, even though a growing consideration for the renovation requires their use and advantages.

In fact, since AECO sector and especially buildings are the cause of serious issues to the environment such as high level of energy consumption and CO_2 emissions, in recent times more attention is being paid to renovation phase [26–28].

Hence, the practice of renovating and re-using buildings needs to be stimulated. Nevertheless, improving the quality of renovations, reducing the time of building construction phase, minimizing the impact on tenants, and guaranteeing that cost/benefits targets are accomplished are typical barriers that need to be faced and overcome [29, 30].

Digitalisation becomes an instrument towards the construction sector to enhance the renovation process. Digital solutions can be adopted to manage information and data in a more ordered structure, with a consequent reduction of time and building waste and, an increased productivity and performance [31].

4.1 BIM in renovation context: The BIM4EEB project

To improve the building process efficiency towards the main renovation barriers, Europe is responsible for various initiatives for the promotion and dissemination of digital tools through policies (e.g., 'Renovation Wave' [28], funding (e.g., InvestEU [27]) and regulations (e.g., EU-level regulatory framework for the creation of the Single Market for Data for better data quality and data management [31]).

Also, it is responsible for several research projects aiming at exploiting digitals tools to make the renovation process more efficient and improve the performance of the building with attention to the sustainability aspect. The waste of time and the consequent waste of money caused by inefficiency is limited and reduced with the digitalisation that results in using resources more efficiently and responsibly.

In this respect, regarding technologies such as BIM and DT aiming at improving the building information management and communication there are different H2020 projects. Among these projects aimed at developing BIM-based tools for an efficient retrofitting [32], BIM4EEB can be mentioned.

The ongoing European project BIM4EEB, namely BIM based fast toolkit for Efficient rEnovation of residential Buildings, has the main goal to develop a BIM-based toolkit for improving renovation of existing residential buildings. The research activity developed within the project involves the use of IoT in residential buildings, the development of a platform for the share of information among the involved stakeholders and different kind of BIM-based tools implemented.

The BIM-based toolkit has been developed for different areas of renovation, such as: fast mapping of existing buildings, building information management, energy simulation of renovation scenarios, fast-track construction management, etc.

BIM-based tools are connected and can be accessed by the BIM management system (BIMMS), a platform where all the activities of the building process can be managed and the interested parties can exchange data from different sources.

BIM4EEB toolkit is characterized by the following tools, as showed in **Figure 15**:

- BIM Management System
- BIMplanner is a fast-tracking tool for renovation operations
- BIMeaser is a BIM assisted Energy refurbishment assessment tool
- AUTERAS and BIMcpd are tools to support decision-making and energy refurbishment assessment
- BIM4Occupants is a human machine interface tool
- Fast mapping toolkit is a tool for reducing the survey time

As part of the project, testing and validation of the developed toolkit are planned at three demonstration sites identified in existing residential buildings and located in different environmental contexts: Mediterranean (Italy), continental climate (Poland) and northern countries (Finland).

A social housing building owned by ALER has been selected for the Italian demonstration site and it is located in Monza (Lombardy). The building, dating back to

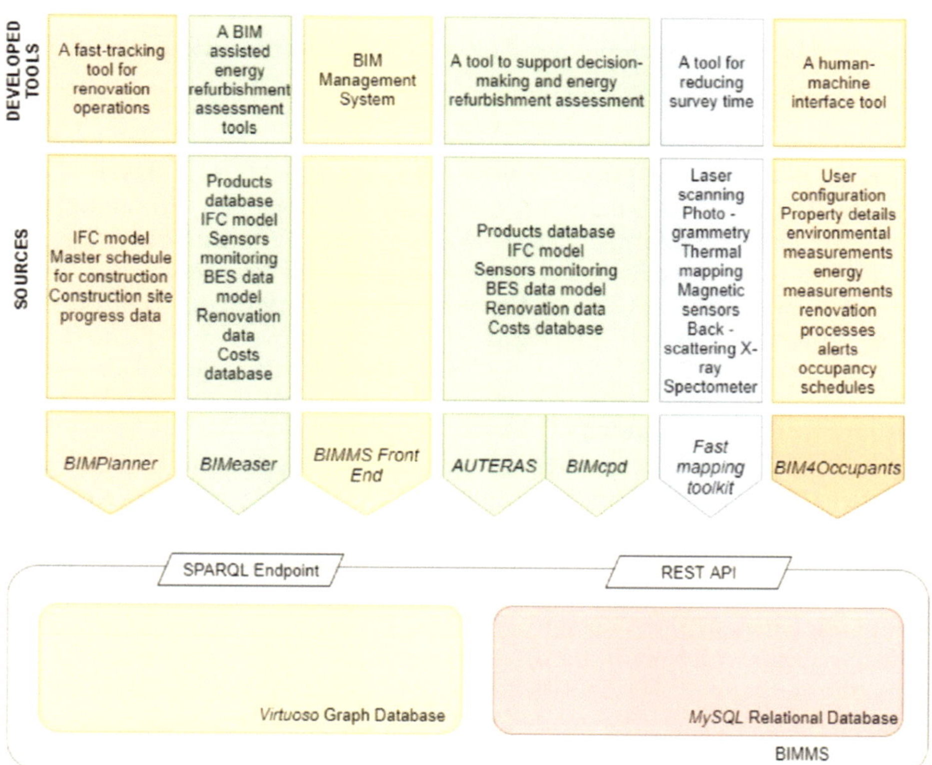

Figure 15.
BIM4EEB toolkit Daniotti et al. [33].

the 60s, presented a significant need for renovation measures. Hence, it has been subjected to two main renovation interventions such as the replacement of windows and the application of external thermal insulation.

The Poland demonstration site is placed in Chorzow, a town in the southern Poland, and it was built at the beginning of 1900.

The Finnish demonstration site instead is located in the city of Tampere.

The expected results of the project are the following:

- a time reduction by at least 20% compared to traditional methods,
- a cost reduction by 15%,
- a net primary energy use reduction by 10% for a residential apartment,
- working days reduction from 3 to 1.5 required for a deep energy audit.

The project, lasting 3 years, is now at its conclusion. The last part of the project consists in the demonstration of the BIM-toolkit feasibility to the previously mentioned case studies. In this regard, the achievement of the project is assessed by using Key Performance Indicators (KPIs) such as Renovation Process KPIs, Energy Performance KPIs, Human Comfort KPIs, Economic Performance KPIs, Social Related KPIs, Environmental and Safety KPIs evaluating objectives and stakeholders' requirements fulfillment.

4.2 Building information modeling adapted to efficient renovation: H2020 projects

Belonging to the topic "Building information modelling adapted to efficient renovation", in addition to BIM4EEB project, there are other Horizon 2020 projects: BIM4REN (BIM-Based Tools for Fast & Efficient Renovation) [34], BIM-SPEED (Harmonized Building Information Speedway for Energy-Efficient Renovation) [35], BIMERR (BIM-based holistic tools for Energy- driven Renovation of existing Residences) [36], ENCORE (ENergy Aware BIM Cloud Platform in a COst-Effective Building REnovation Context) [37]. Also SPHERE project (Service Platform to Host and SharE REsidential Data) [38], part of "ICT enabled, sustainable and affordable residential building construction, design to end of life" topic, is considered among BIM4EEB sister projects (**Table 1**).

All these projects have in common the study and development of solutions for a more efficient building renovation by using BIM. The main objectives are reduction of renovation working time of at least 15–20% compared to current practices; acceleration of the market uptake across Europe, by speeding-up industrial exploitation, among constructing/renovations companies with a target of 50% of their renovation business based on BIM; creation of best practice examples for the construction retrofitting sector with benefits for the operators and associated stakeholders.

If on the one hand BIM4EEB, BIM4REN, BIM-SPEED, BIMERR and ENCORE are all characterized by the development of BIM tools, on the other hand SPHERE project aims at improving the energy design, construction, performance, and management of building with the development of a BIM-based Digital Twin platform based on Platform as a Service (PaaS) approaching the concept of Digital Twin.

Programme	Topic	Project
Technologies enabling energy-efficient systems and energy-efficient buildings with a low environmental impact	LC-EEB-02-2018 Building information modeling adapted to efficient renovation (European Commission, Building information modeling adapted to efficient renovation (RIA), 2018)	BIM4EEB
		BIM4REN
		BIM-SPEED
		BIMERR
		ENCORE
	LC-EEB-06-2018-2020 ICT enabled, sustainable and affordable residential building construction, design to end of life	SPHERE

Table 1.
EU projects promoting digitalization in the built environment.

SPHERE is a Horizon2020 project that has developed a Digital twin environment based on Platform as a Service. The project aims at enhancing the performance and management of buildings, reducing construction costs and the environmental impact, starting from the design and construction phase but including also manufacturing and operational phase. It enables the integration of large-scale data, information and knowledge, and it facilitates decision making and the collaboration among involved users. SPHERE exploits the concept of Digital Twin for predictive and interrogative purposes. For the first the Digital Twin will be used for the prediction of future performance of the building, for the latter the Digital Twin will be investigated to get information about the current and past status [39].

5. Discussion and conclusions

This chapter proposes an overview of the main drivers that are guiding the digital revolution in the construction sector. The intrinsic changes that the entire construction value chain is experiencing are generating and will generate important impacts not only on construction but on the entire society and the people that will live in buildings and use infrastructure. Nowadays, the Digital Twin topic represents a key element of both research and practice innovation with enormous potential impacts considering the possibility to continuous monitoring buildings and infrastructure and the integration of controlling systems. This evolution will produce impacts on several scales, from the practical development of assets with a better quality up to the operation and maintenance with the possibility of creating data driven decision systems.

To provide a comprehensive overview on this area three main points are reported in the chapter. First, the movement from CAD to BIM is clarified to highlight the main key points that are driving the creation of digital simulation (information models) of buildings and infrastructures. Then a detailed description of the standardization context is provided. To clarify how standards are shaping the BIM context and will impact on its integration at the different levels (international, European, national) the standardization principles are presented and linked to the evolution that the standards have experienced in the last years shaping the BIM panorama. Finally, the so called "platformization" concept is proposed with the presentation of some key national (considering Italy) and European projects that have been developed or are under development and will shape the creation of the future platforms for the construction sector (DigiPLACE, BIM4EEB, INNOVance, BIMRel, Sister projects, SPHERE).

Platforms and standards represent two main axes of the digital transformation of the construction sector and are strictly intersected providing the backbone to enable the future of the digital constructions. Nevertheless, platform development is still an open research and industry topic that needs to be clarified and disseminate in the construction sectors considering the different levels that characterize it (European, national, regional, etc.). This dimension should be considering according to the standardization works that needs to be distributed in these different levels to guarantee, on the one hand a sufficient generalization for common topics, and on the other hand detailed focal points integrated in the national/local context to guarantee a practical applicability from the interested stakeholders. Researchers and industry stakeholders can start from the results here presented to have a clear picture of the standardization and platform development driver. Future research should work to integrate other trends and key topics in this picture to create a shared map of the drivers for a digital evolution of the construction sector.

Acknowledgements

The work detailed in this manuscript was carried out within the BIM4EEB project. This project has received funding from the European Union's Horizon 2020 research and innovation programme under grant agreement No. 820660.

Author details

Bruno Daniotti, Alberto Pavan, Cecilia Bolognesi, Claudio Mirarchi*
and Martina Signorini
ABC Department, Politecnico di Milano, Milan, Italy

*Address all correspondence to: claudio.mirarchi@polimi.it

References

[1] Scheer D. The Death of Drawing. Architecture in the Age of Simulation. 1st ed. New York: Imprint Routledge; 2014. p. 258. DOI: 10.4324/9781315813950

[2] Bernstein PG, Pittman JH. Barriers to the adoption of building information modeling in the building industry. In: Autodesk Building Solutions Whitepaper. San Rafael, CA: Autodesk Inc.; 2005

[3] Carmona J, Irwin K. BIM: Who, what, how and why. Building Operating Management. 2009. Available from: http://www.facilitiesnet.com/software/article/BIM-Who-What-How-and-Why–7546 [Accessed: August 21, 2009]

[4] Azhar S. Building information Modeling (BIM): Trends, benefits, risks and challenges for the AEC. Leadership and Management in Engineering. 2011;**11**(3):241-252. DOI: 10.1061/(ASCE)LM.1943-5630.0000127

[5] Pavan A, Giani M, Mirarchi C. BIM: metodi e strumenti Progettare, costruire e gestire nell'era digitale. 1st ed. Milan: Tecniche Nuove; 2017. p. 328

[6] Osello A. Il futuro del disegno con il BIM per ingegneri e architetti. 1st ed. Palermo: Dario Falccovio Editore; 2012. p. 324

[7] Dimyadi P, Parsanezhad J. Effective facility management and operations via a BIM-based integrated information system. In: CIB Facility Management Conference: CIB W070, W111 & W118: 21-23 May 2014. Copenhagen, Denmark; 2014. DOI: 10.13140/2122989764

[8] Ashworth S, Carbonari G, Stravoravdis S. How Facility Management Can Use Buidling Information Modelling (BIM) to Improve the Decision Making Process. Technische Universität Wien Published; 2015. pp. 55-69. DOI: 10.34749/JFM20152120

[9] Pavan A, Rota A, Mirarchi C, Romano A. I capitolati informativi con metodologia BIM. 1st ed. Milan: Tecniche Nuove; 2021. p. 232

[10] Charef R, Alaka H, Emmitt S. Beyond the third dimension of BIM: A systematic review of literature and assessment of professional views. Journal of Building Engineering. 2018;**19**:242-257. DOI: 10.1016/j.jobe.2018.04.028

[11] Mirarchi C, Spagnolo SL, Daniotti B, Pavan A. Structuring general information specifications for contracts in accordance with the UNI 11337:2017 standard. Digital Transformation of the Design, Construction and Management Processes of the Built Environment. 2019:103-112. DOI: 10.1007/9783030335700-0_10

[12] Borin P, Zanchetta C. IFC–Processi e modelli digitali openBIM per l'ambiente costruito. 1nd ed. Vol. 194. Palermo: Milan: Maggioli Editore; 2020

[13] Lupica Spagnolo S, Amosso G, Pavan A, Daniotti B. In: Daniotti B, Gianinetto M, Della Torre S, editors. BIMReL: The Interoperable BIM Library for Construction Products Data Sharing, in Digital Transformation of the Design, Construction and Management Processes of the Built Environment. Cham: Springer; 2020. pp. 37-47

[14] Build up, Digitalization in the construction industry. 2019. Available from: https://www.buildup.eu/en/news/overview-digitalisation-construction-industry

[15] Lupica Spagnolo S. Information integration for asset and maintenance

management. In: Integrating Information in Built Environments. From Concept to Practice. Routledge: Taylor& Francis Group; 2017. pp. 133-149

[16] Boje C, Guerriero A, Kubicki S, Rezgui Y. Towards a semantic construction digital twin: Directions for future research. Automation in Construction. 2020;**114**:103179

[17] Centre of Digital Built Britain. The Gemini Principles. 2018

[18] Batty M. Digital twins. Environment and Planning B: Urban Analytics and City Science. 2018;**45**:817-820

[19] El Jazzar M, Piskernik M, Nassereddine H. Digital twin in construction: An empirical analysis. In: EG-ICE 2020 Workshop on Intelligent Computing in Engineering, Proceedings. 2020. pp. 501-510

[20] Camposano JC, Smolander K, Ruippo T. Seven metaphors to understand digital twins of built assets. IEEE Access. 2021;**9**:27167-27181

[21] Mathupriya S, Saira Banu S, Sridhar S, Arthi B. Digital twin technology on IoT, industries & other smart environments: A survey. Materials Today: Proceedings. In press

[22] Sacks R, Brilakis I, Pikas E, Xie HS, Girolami M. Construction with digital twin information systems. Data-Centric Engineering. 2020;**1**:e14

[23] Errandonea I, Beltrán S, Arrizabalaga S. Digital twin for maintenance: A literature review. Computers in Industry. 2020;**123**:103316

[24] Fuller A, Fan Z, Day C, Barlow C. Digital twin: Enabling technologies, challenges and open research. IEEE Access. 2020;**8**:108952-108971

[25] Jafari MA, Zaidan E, Ghofrani A, Mahani K, Farzan F. Improving building energy footprint and asset performance using digital twin technology. IFAC-PapersOnLine. 2020;**53**(3):386-391

[26] European Commission, Renovation Wave: Doubling the Renovation Rate to Cut Emissions, Boost Recovery and Reduce Energy Poverty, 2020.

[27] BPIE. The European renovation wave: From words to action. 2020

[28] European Commission, A Renovation Wave for Europe–greening our buildings, creating jobs, improving lives. 2020

[29] IET and NTU. Scaling Up Retrofit 2050. 2018

[30] S. D'Oca, A. Ferrante, C. Ferrer, R. Pernetti, A. Gralka, R. Sebastian, P. o. t. Veld, Technical, Financial, and Social Barriers and Challenges in Deep Building Renovation: Integration of Lessons Learned from the H2020 Cluster Projects. Buildings, MDPI, Switzerland; 2018. pp. 1-25

[31] ECSO, Digitalisation in the Construction Sector. 2021

[32] European Commission. Building information modelling adapted to efficient renovation (RIA). 2018

[33] Daniotti B, Bolognesi CM, Spagnolo SL, Pavan A, Signorini M, Ciuffreda S, et al. An Interoperable BIM-Based Toolkit for Efficient Renovation in Buildings. Buildings, MDPI, Switzerland; 2021. pp. 1-16

[34] Building Information Modelling based tools & technologies for fast and efficient RENovation of residential buildings|BIM4REN Project. 2018. 1-9

[35] Harmonised Building Information Speedway for Energy-Efficient

Renovation|BIM-SPEED Project. 2018. 1-8

[36] BIM-based holistic tools for Energy driven Renovation of existing Residences|BIMERR

[37] ENergy aware BIM Cloud Platform in a COst-effective Building REnovation Context|ENCORE Project. 2019. 1-6

[38] Service Platform to Host and SharE REsidential data|SPHERE Project. 2018. 1-9

[39] Alonso R, Borras M, Koppelaar RHEM, Lodigiani A, Loscos E, Yöntem E. SPHERE: BIM digital twin platform. Proceedings. 2019;**20**:9

Chapter 7

New Approaches to Innovation Management in the Context of Digital Transformation

Zhanna Mingaleva and Vladimir Postnikov

Abstract

The previous decade is rightfully called the era of digital transformation. The purpose of the study is to assess the impact of global trends on innovation activity, as well as to identify new factors influencing innovation models. A conceptual approach to the analysis of the evolution of innovation models based on the transformation of information and communication technologies for innovation based on the bibliographic analysis and integration of existing concepts and theories of innovation, digitalization and sustainable development is created. With the help of the factor method, the analysis of the main innovation models is carried out and a promising innovation model is determined. It is found out that digital technologies are the technological basis of the modern model of the innovation ecosystem. The result of the research is the author's classification of modern factors of innovation activity that determine the directions and types of implemented innovations, as well as the role of innovation in society. The peculiarity of the study is that it has a conceptual nature, does not use the collection of empirical data, but is based on the integration of previously developed concepts and theories.

Keywords: digital transformation, model of closed innovations, model of open innovations, the innovation ecosystem model, innovation management

1. Introduction

From the end of the twentieth century, digital technologies are actively penetrating into all spheres of society. Scientists and researchers started talking about the transition to a new model of functioning based on digital technologies - Society 5.0 and Industry 4.0 [1–5]. At the same time, the influence of digital transformation is felt by many countries, as well as all sectors and industries of the economy and types of enterprises.

The impact of digital technologies has also been experienced by the key process of technological business development - the innovation process [6–8]. The use of modern supercomputers, robotic complexes, VR technologies, etc. in science, research, and production has led to significant changes in the system of organization of innovation activities. Digital technologies accelerate the flow of information, reduce the cost of obtaining and exchanging information, and provide a basis for applying the open innovation model. And in turn, innovations also affect the digital economy [9].

For the sustainable implementation of innovations, and their successful and effective participation in global transformation processes, it is necessary to take into account the influence of the main trends that take place in the economy and society. Including the widespread dissemination of the concept of sustainable development. The first attempts to analyze the relationship between industry 4.0, society 5.0, and sustainable development goals are made in the modern scientific literature [10–14].

However, the rapid development of digital technologies comes into conflict with the applied models and methods of innovation management. Moreover, a contradiction between the level of development of digital infrastructure and the effectiveness of innovation management methods already exists in a number of countries and regions. This requires a revision of a number of conceptual approaches.

The presented work is aimed at reducing the gap in the theoretical literature on the analysis of the evolution of innovation models, identifying modern factors of innovation activity, identifying promising areas and types of innovation, and assessing the complex role of innovation in the economy and society.

The structure of the work is formed in accordance with the goal and the objectives of the research.

Section 2 contains a bibliographic description of the available literature, concepts, and theories on the relationship between innovation models and the information and digital technological basis for innovation, as well as a list of the main factors influencing innovation. Section 3 contains a description of the methodological approaches to the research and the basic limitations of the study. The main results of the study are reflected in Section 4. This section also contains some controversial issues and research results that require further discussion and empirical verification. In conclusion, the main conclusions and further directions of research are presented.

The discussion of the hypothesis will make it possible to identify and evaluate new factors of innovation activity in the conditions of digitalization of the economy and create a theoretical basis for the formation of a new approach to innovation management that corresponds (adequate) to modern trends in the development of society.

2. Theoretical

2.1 Models of innovation in innovation theories

Schumpeter is rightfully considered to be the founder of innovation theory [15]. The mechanisms of creating new knowledge and innovations always influenced human life, especially during critical moments of economic development [16–19]. At the same time, innovations and the innovation process have the function of ensuring the competitiveness of the company by creating new products, new technologies for manufacturing new products, or new methods of organizing activities. Success in the competitive struggle is ensured by legal protection of innovations, which gave an advantage over other companies by providing a monopoly right to produce a specific product or possess a specific production technology, organization of activities, provision of services, etc.

At the same time, strict legal regulation of monopoly rights to innovation (discovery, new product, new technology, etc.) was the basis for a special approach to the organization of innovation activity, called the concept of "closed" innovation. We will not dwell on the characteristics of the closed innovation model in detail. But we would like to pay attention to only 2 points that are directly related to the topic of this study.

The first concerns the main characteristics and factors of innovation. On the basis of previous studies, the following success factors for innovation activity can be identified in the model of "closed" innovations [20–29]. They are:

- internal R&D and technological capabilities (investment in research and development, acquisition of capital assets, etc.),
- close cooperation with universities, research centers,
- availability of strong public funding,
- specific industry and production characteristics of the company, including such as energy intensity, material intensity, human capital, the absorption capacity of the industry market to adopt a new product, the size of the company, etc.,
- technical norms and standards defining the characteristics of a new product or new technology,
- the level and strength of competition in international markets,
- cooperation with other private firms (private co-financing of individual research projects)
- access to external knowledge (primarily in terms of checking innovation for patent protection), etc.

The main results of various studies show that internal R&D, acquisition of fixed assets, and technical regulations, are the main drivers of "closed" innovation. Large firms were more successful in introducing various innovations, including radical ones.

The second is the main information technology basis of innovation, which made it possible to achieve success. Computers, including supercomputers, were the information-technological and technical basis for the implementation of innovations within the framework of this model, the presence of which ensured advantage (winning) in research activities and competition [30–34].

However, it was the development of the information technology and technical basis for innovation that simultaneously became the reason for changing the innovation model, the basis for the transition to the open innovation model. Changes in the level of implementation of information and communication technologies in various processes of society's life became the key points of transition from one model to another. Digital transformation has had a big impact on innovation.

The transition from the closed innovation model to the open innovation model is provoked by the massive introduction of information and computer technologies into the communication environment of society and business management. Computers became not only a powerful means of processing large amounts of data but also a means of everyday communication for ordinary people, as well as a tool for promoting products in markets [35–38]. At the same time, strict legal support of monopoly rights to innovation was partially preserved in the open innovation model but led to certain transformations in the system of innovation diffusion and transfer.

As for the main factors for the success of innovation in the model of "open" innovations, the factors listed above are added to such factors as the active development of network interaction between companies and the regional community, other subjects of society, the emergence and accounting for side effects from other innovations, taking into account external effects from own innovations, more active consideration of environmental norms and standards, the emergence of requirements for social responsibility, ethics and morality [39–42]. Also, in the model of "open" innovation, the role and importance of the factor of access to external knowledge have significantly increased, (external knowledge became the main source of information for scientific and research activities), as well as the role of interaction with other companies, including private ones [43].

The next major step in changing the applied model of organizing innovation activity is the emergence of an innovation ecosystem and a model that describes it. The transition to the innovation ecosystem model is based on the strengthening of the processes of digitalization of society and the economy, which began with the mass digitization of various elements, data, and processes [44–50]. As a result, such characteristics of the information and communication environment as the openness of information, the speed and ability to transfer information in the external environment, the social effect, and significance of information have become the most important factors in the management of innovation activity.

Thus, there is a clear and direct connection between the information and digital technological basis for the implementation of innovation activities and the innovation model used by companies. Digital technologies become the technological basis of the modern model of the innovation ecosystem.

However, the emergence and formation of a modern innovation management system, built on the basis of the innovation ecosystem model, is also under the influence of another global trend - the increasing application (in society and economy) of the requirements of sustainable development and climate safety of human activities.

2.2 Sustainable development as a global factor in the transformation of innovation models

The second global trend in the development of modern society, which is influenced by the transformation of the innovation model, is the concept of sustainable development and climate security of society [51–53]. The widespread adoption of the provisions of this concept and its implementation in the practice of state regulation and corporate governance changed the role and importance of companies in modern business and economy and led to the formation of an environmental assessment of innovations [54–56]. To assess the socio-environmental consequences of business activities, more and more diverse social and environmental indicators are used, and the quality of innovation activity is assessed through the statistics of "green" innovations of all types and through the concept of sustainable innovation [57–61]. Moreover, in recent years, the provisions of the concept and ESG regulation and the assessment of ESG factors in the framework of business processes and innovation activities have been widely applied.

Without dwelling in detail on the characteristics of each of the types of innovations used today in the practical activities of various companies and organizations [62], it is important to highlight the changes in emphasis on the characteristics of innovations implemented in the innovation ecosystem model. These are, first of all, environmental or "green" innovations that ensure the achievement of sustainable development goals, elimination of climate consequences, and ensuring environmental safety [6–67]. In turn, the development of green innovations involves the formation of a new system of innovation management. The main factors of the innovation model are also changing. In the system of "green" innovations and in the innovation ecosystem model, new factors of influence appeared, such as the applied business model and value proposition as part of the company's innovation policy, consideration and use of ESG factors in innovation activities, and the application of ESG regulation, more comprehensive consideration of the long-term consequences of innovation for nature and society, the focus of innovation on meeting environmental norms and standards, social responsibility, ethics and morality in the framework of innovation [68–79]. The importance of such factors as the openness of information, the speed and possibilities of information transfer in the external environment, the social effect, and the significance of information, which appeared in the open innovation model, increased also.

So, an analysis of global trends occurring in the society of the XXI century showed that in modern conditions digitalization and sustainability became the two inextricably linked trends and fundamental factors that have a significant impact on innovation. It is these two trends that underlie the formation and development of the modern model of innovation.

In this regard, an important theoretical and practical question that arises is the problem of identifying and assessing the significance of new factors influencing the implementation of innovation activities within the framework of a new innovation model that corresponds (adequately) to modern trends in the development of society.

Within the framework of this scientific problem, the following hypothesis was formulated.

Hypothesis 1: *digitalization of the economy and the implementation of sustainable development goals make changes to the innovation management model, leading to the emergence of new factors influencing innovation.*

The results of the study will expand scientific knowledge about the factors and models of innovation in modern conditions, supplementing the theoretical base with an analysis of the evolutionary development of innovation models. Also, the results of the study will add literature on the impact of digitalization on specific processes in the economy and society - innovation and on the mutual influence of digitalization processes, sustainable development, and innovation.

3. Methodological note

The presented work is conceptual in nature and is based on the integration of concepts and theories previously developed by world science [80–85]. The study is based on a thorough review of the literature on the evolution of innovation models, on other conceptual ideas in the field of the development of innovation theory, on the integration of various points of view and analysis, which were combined to develop a conceptual framework and build an analytical model [3, 86–89].

The bibliographic base of the study is Web of Science, Scopus, Springer, and Google Scholar. The search was conducted on the following keywords: the AND model AND of "closed" innovations; innovation AND eco-system; the "open" innovation AND model; digital AND transformation AND of AND innovation AND activity; innovations AND in AND industry AND 4.0.; sustainable AND innovation; green AND innovation; sustainable innovation AND digital platforms.

The selection was carried out according to the following criteria: TITLE-ABS-KEY. An extended set of criteria was used, since checking only by the TITLE criterion did not give the required result in a number of cases. For example, checking by the search criteria "TITLE-ABS-KEY (digital AND transformation AND of AND innovation AND activity) AND PUBYEAR > 2009" in the Scopus system returned 470 articles, while checking only by TITLE (digital AND transformation AND of AND innovation AND activity) AND PUBYEAR >2009″ published only 1 article.

Similarly, checking with the search criteria "TITLE-ABS-KEY (innovations AND in AND industry AND 4.0) AND PUBYEAR > 2009" in the Scopus system returned 470 articles, while checking only with TITLE (innovations AND in AND industry AND 4.0) AND PUBYEAR >2009″ showed no publications with that title at all.

The literature review has a clear goal - to identify the main changes taking place in the implementation of innovative activities under the influence of digitalization processes and the implementation of sustainable development goals and to identify new factors influencing innovative activities in modern conditions.

For this purpose, scientific articles and books on the following topics were collected and analyzed: (1) the model of "closed" innovations; (2) the "open" innovation model; (3) the innovation ecosystem; (4) sustainable innovation; (5) green innovation; (6) factors of innovative activity; (7) digitalization and digital transformation of innovation activity; (8) innovations in Industry 4.0.

In total, 1659 different publications for the period 2010–2021 and January–February 2022 were studied.

Bibliographic analysis made it possible to develop a factorial model for the evolution of innovative systems based on their digital transformation. This work is strictly conceptual and does not involve the collection of empirical data. Future empirical studies carried out will make it possible to verify the reliability and accuracy of the proposed theoretical model. Also, in the process of future verification of the proposed theoretical model, it is possible to determine the quantitative values of the strength of influence of individual factors and their groups.

At the same time, in order to preserve the freedom of choice of scientific papers used for analysis, it was decided not to conduct a systematic review of the literature, similar to reviews in other conceptual studies, for example, describing Digital Platform Ecosystems for Sustainable Innovation [90–92].

4. Research results

4.1 Factor model of the innovation ecosystem

Currently, in the theory of innovation, there are three integrated models which characterize the organization of the innovation process in different information and communication basis and principles. Such as the *closed innovation model (CIM); open innovation model (OIM) and the innovation ecosystem model (IEM)*.

Over the past two decades, these models have been affected by two global trends: digitalization and the expansion of the scope of the sustainable development goals. The influence of these two global trends on the peculiarities of innovation activity at the present stage of development is manifested in turn through a set of factors underlying innovation management and the applied model of innovation activity [93–96]. **Table 1** demonstrates a list of factors affecting innovation activity in general, divided into 3 main innovation models: the closed innovation model (CIM); the open innovation model (OIM) and the innovation ecosystem model (IEM).

The list of factors and the author's assessment of their significance is compiled using the method of bibliographic analysis of scientific literature devoted to the study of factors of construction and implementation of innovative activities, as well as the method of comparative analysis of innovative models of various types [7, 97–102]. Modern factors (factors of the innovation ecosystem) are identified by the authors independently in the process of studying the issues of the formation of the digital economy and the creation of national innovation ecosystems [34, 103–106]. Also, to identify these factors, the results and conclusions of scientific research on the transformation of the open innovation model in the conditions of creating Society 5.0 were used [3, 107–109].

The factors are divided into 4 groups depending on their participation in innovation activities and depending on environmental conditions.

The order of factors in groups is given based on their importance in the closed innovation model - the list of factors is built as their importance decreases in this model. This order is chosen from the point of view of the historical context of the analysis since it is the first historical model of closed innovations and the analysis of the order of model construction and their transformation begins from the consideration of these factors. At the same time, it allows you to trace the change in the importance of particular factors in social development, as well as the transition of society to the new operating model based on digital technology – Society 5.0 and Industry 4.0.

Not going into detail on the features of the transformation of the model of closed innovation to the open innovation model, let us pay attention to the creation and development of innovation ecosystems, which mostly reflects the trends, requirements, and features of digital transformation.

Table 1 makes it possible to come to the conclusion that in the innovation ecosystem model, the influence and impact on the effectiveness of innovation activities are increased from all factors except the factor of internal R&D. However, this decrease is rather nominal and reflects not the absolute decrease in the value of the factor, but its relative importance compared to other factors, especially new ones.

Moreover, several factors have appeared in the innovation ecosystem model that is not typical of traditional models of closed and open innovations. The emergence of these factors was caused by the influence of digital technologies and modern computer and information and communication technologies, which radically changed approaches to understanding the fundamentals of the functioning of society, business, and innovation.

Further, we would like to focus in more detail on the characteristics of each specific factor in order to understand their role in the process of digital transformation of innovation activity.

Analyzing the directions and power of changes in the role and influence of factors, first of all, it is necessary to assess the impact of such a group of factors as "*Innovative resources*". These traditionally include investments in research and development (R&D), cooperation with public and private organizations, acquisition of capital assets and external knowledge. We also include such factors as side effects from other

Influencing factors	CIM	OIM	IEM
Innovation Resources			
Internal R&D and technological capabilities (investment in research and development, acquisition of capital assets)	+++	++	++
Cooperation with government organizations (state funding)	+++	+++	++
Cooperation with private organizations (private co-financing)	++	+++	+++
Access to external knowledge	+	++	+++
Network interaction (with universities, scientific centers, other subjects of society, etc.)	+	++	+++
Side effects from other innovations	—	++	+++
Industrial and market conditions			
Specific characteristics of the firm, including such as energy intensity, material intensity, human capital, absorptive capacity, industry affiliation, firm size, etc.	+++	++	++
Technical norms and standards	++	+++	+++
The level and strength of competition in international markets	++	+++	++
Environmental regulations and standards	+	++	+++
Applicable business model and value proposition	—	—	+++
ESG factors and ESG regulation	—	—	+++
Social and public factors			
Presence of external effects from own innovations	—	++	+++
Social responsibility, ethics, and morality	—	++	+++
Long-term consequences of innovation	—	+	++
Information and communication environment			
The speed and possibilities of information transfer in the external environment	—	+	+++
Openness of information	—	+	+++
Social effect and significance of information	—	+	+++

Source: compiled by the authors. Abbreviations: CIM - closed innovation model; OIM - open innovation model; IEM - the innovation ecosystem model.

Table 1.
The main factors of innovation activity in different innovation models.

innovations and networking in this group, since a side effect from another innovation can become a source (resource) of basic knowledge and ideas for new developments, and networking is the basis and a powerful resource for search and innovation activities. At the same time, it should be noted that the last two factors appeared only at the stage of the open innovation model and were developed and recognized in the innovation ecosystem model.

The first of these factors is a complex and multi-element factor of the level of development and scale of the company's internal R&D and its technological capabilities [110–115]. This complex factor is described by such indicators as investments in research and development (their volume, structure, sources), acquisition volumes, acquisition of capital assets, and qualitative indicators of R&D directions and structures. In the conditions of the closed innovation model, this factor was key to the effectiveness of the company's innovation activity. However, in the models of open innovation and innovation ecosystem, its role is decreasing, since now companies can attract R&D resources and technological capabilities of other companies based on the formation of external links within one or more innovative projects or within the framework of long-term scientific and technical cooperation with various private firms, science-based and market-based partners [116–119]. Such opportunities for external interaction have expanded especially strongly in the process of digital transformation.

The analysis of changes in the influence of the factor of cooperation with state organizations on public financing issues shows that under the conditions of applying the innovation ecosystem model, this factor acquires a specific orientation [120–124]. Thus, the directions of state support for research in the EU countries are currently focused on solving environmental problems and are largely associated with "green" innovations. Financing of non-"green" innovations has moved to the sphere of cooperation between private firms.

At the same time, the high importance of factors of internal investment in research activities, specialized equipment purchase, access to external knowledge, the development of cooperation with suppliers and universities was noted both in earlier studies in this area and in modern works devoted to stimulating various kinds of innovations and above all "green" innovations. Modern researchers have noted that these factors are more important for enterprises in the implementation of environmental innovation than other innovations [68, 125–127].

The following three factors of the given group (Access to external knowledge, Networking (with educational institutions, etc.), and the Side effects of other innovations) had no importance and influence in the framework of the model of closed innovation.

In the closed innovation model, access to external knowledge is of some importance, but it refers, first of all, to the analysis of patent information and data on scientific and technological research conducted by competitors concerning the development of new products and technologies, as well as their improvement. Innovations obtained by corporate research centers and laboratories are actively protected by means of patent law, and the dissemination of innovations to the external environment is carried out on the basis of licenses, patents, franchisees and other instruments for the transfer of property rights [112, 128].

In the open innovation model, based on the exchange of knowledge between different firms and their involvement in solving a single complex task, the role of the factor of access to external knowledge increased significantly [129–131].

As for the innovation ecosystem model, its functioning is impossible without broad and free access to external knowledge.

The factor of network interaction between various subjects of society in the model of the innovation ecosystem has acquired a special scope and significance [56, 116, 132–136]. If in the closed innovation model such interaction existed mainly between manufacturing firms and research centers and universities, then as the open innovation model and the innovation ecosystem model expanded, such networks began to cover an increasing number of economic entities and society as a whole, including not only business partners but competitors also. Modern research proved that companies involved in innovative cooperation with other firms of their industry affiliation and industry market are more actively developing and implementing "green" innovations.

Finally, as for the impact of side effects from other innovations, as can be seen from **Table 1** in the closed innovation model, this factor did not matter, since innovation activity had an internal basis and an internal orientation. In the open innovation model and the innovation ecosystem model, this influence appeared and intensified due to the openness of both models and the inevitable dependence on external phenomena and processes [119, 137–141].

The group of factors "*Industry and market conditions*" is also quite important and traditional for all models. Within the framework of the innovation ecosystem model, it includes six factors, four of which strongly influenced upon innovation activity in the closed innovation model and continue to play an important role in modern conditions.

As in the group of innovative resources, the first of the factors of the group "Industry and market conditions" is complex and multi-element. These are specific characteristics of the company, including such as energy intensity, material intensity, human capital, absorption capacity, industry affiliation, size of the company, etc. [142–144]. In the closed innovation model, all these characteristics were crucial for choosing the object of innovation activity, the mechanism of its implementation, directions of development, etc. In the models of open innovation and innovation ecosystem, these characteristics begin to lose their significance, as the transition of innovations between industries and activities becomes easier, more active, and broader. Nevertheless, the industry affiliation of companies, as well as the structure and national jurisdiction of capital are significant factors in the innovation ecosystem model in terms of the types of innovations being implemented. Thus, modern research proved that in the case of networking based on innovative cooperation within the same industry and market, the greatest effect is obtained when interacting between foreign companies. However, the positive effect of cooperation with competitors in the field of innovation is achieved by organizing a network between local firms, as well as between competing companies in the service sector.

The second traditional factor of this group – "technological norms and standards" has become increasingly important recently [9, 145–149]. This is determined by the fact that increasing the uniformity of products in accordance with international norms and standards makes it possible to ensure sales on global markets without additional adaptation of technical documentation and products to the national legislation of various countries. At the same time, technological norms and standards play a more important role in open innovation and ecosystem models than in closed innovation models, when the focus was primarily on internal corporate and national norms and technical standards.

Similarly, the influence of the third factor of this group ("the level and strength of competition in international markets") is also manifested. It becomes the most significant in the open innovation model. However, in the conditions of digitalization of production and the "erasing" national borders of many production processes, this factor loses part of its influence on innovation activity [150–152].

The factor "Applied business model and value proposition" is new in relation to the models of closed and open innovations [50, 153–160]. The transformation of many classical business models in all spheres of activity, which occurred under the influence of the widespread use of digital technologies and the general digitalization of production and business, means a reorientation of business to a value model of supply. Innovation activity, as one of the key business processes of the company, starts to focus on the value model of supply. At the same time, the influence of the factor of the applied business model within the framework of the innovation ecosystem model will be more pronounced in relation to local companies. This is determined by the fact that it is local firms that are more focused on creating value propositions for a specific end-user of a specific region (territory, city). Modern digital technologies make it possible to take into account the interests of the local community more specifically and to develop and promote new values more specifically, especially within the framework of product and process innovations.

Two more factors from the "Industry and market conditions" group - the factors "Environmental norms and standards" and "ESG factors and ESG regulation" are closely interrelated and are also the result of current trends [161–166]. At the same time, digitalization of all processes of environmental control, monitoring of the environmental situation, the possibility of rapid response to various events in society and nature, increasing the openness and transparency of corporate governance based on information and communication technologies, provide a technical and technological basis for the influence of these factors, which will increase over time.

The next group of factors *"Social and public factors"* concerns the assessment of the social consequences of innovation, the manifestation of externalities from innovation [138, 167, 168]. At the same time, the external effects factor includes only that part of the external effects that create our own innovations (external effects from other people's innovations are taken into account in the group of "innovative resources", which was already noted earlier). It is the presence of external effects and their significance for society as a whole that is becoming an increasingly important indicator of the social expediency of innovation. And in the model of the innovation ecosystem, this becomes a key factor in the implementation of a particular innovation. At the same time, the digital environment creates particularly favorable conditions for the widespread scaling of these effects (both positive and negative). This, accordingly, increases the importance of ethics, morality, and social responsibility of business for innovation [96, 169, 170].

In this group of factors, the factor of long-term consequences of innovations is also singled out as an independent one [140, 168]. In the digital society and the digital economy, the importance of this factor is increasing.

As for the last group of factors *"Information and communication environment"*, it is also new and specific primarily for the stage of digital transformation of activities. The widespread use of digital technologies has significantly increased the role and status of information and knowledge in the innovation system [101, 171–175]. At the same time, it is necessary to clearly distinguish the concept and factor of "external knowledge" and "information in general". In this case, external knowledge includes specialized scientific and technical knowledge (information) related to the specific activities of the company. This factor was singled out as an independent one in the group of "innovative resources" and analyzed in sufficient detail in this paper. The development of external knowledge and information is closely related to the innovation decision-making system.

As for information in general, as well as its characteristics such as openness of information, speed, and possibilities of information transmission in the external environment, various types of effects from the dissemination of information (economic, social, socio-political, etc.) in Society 5.0, in Industry 4.0, in the model of the innovation ecosystem become more significant. At the same time, it should be noted that in both cases, the information and communication environment and the level of digitalization of society and the economy are the key basis for increasing the importance of these factors [176–178].

4.2 Difficulties in the development of innovation models based on digital transformation

The emergence and wide distribution of innovation ecosystems at various levels confirm the conclusion that the digital environment is an important development factor and a condition that affects innovation.

However, the active introduction of the innovation ecosystem into the business model and its further development faces a number of fundamental issues related to the role of innovation as a competitive tool.

However, with the development and improvement of computer and digital technologies, the key factors of innovation activity are also changing, including the procedure for determining the copyright holder of innovation and the mechanism of protecting property rights. Thus, participation in the creation of an innovation and its practical application "erodes" the individual nature of rights, making legal protection and protection of rights more difficult and complex. Moreover, in recent years, there has been a broad discussion in the scientific community and society about who is the creator and copyright holder of the intellectual property rights in the case of participation in the creation of artificial intelligence. This is closely related to addressing the ethical issues of intellectual property protection [179, 180].

Artificial intelligence – a supercomputer with the help of which new knowledge is obtained - is beginning to be interpreted as a special subject of scientific and research activity, and not as a tool for obtaining new information and data about phenomena and processes. In the twentieth century, computers and computing technologies are perceived as a tool /technical means by which scientific research is facilitated, scientific results are obtained more accurately and quickly. However, with the development of digital technologies and the creation of self-learning and self-developing systems, ideas about protecting the intellectual property rights of a robot/artificial intelligence as an equal creator of intellectual property with human researchers began to spread. This can lead to a significant transformation of such an element of innovation activity

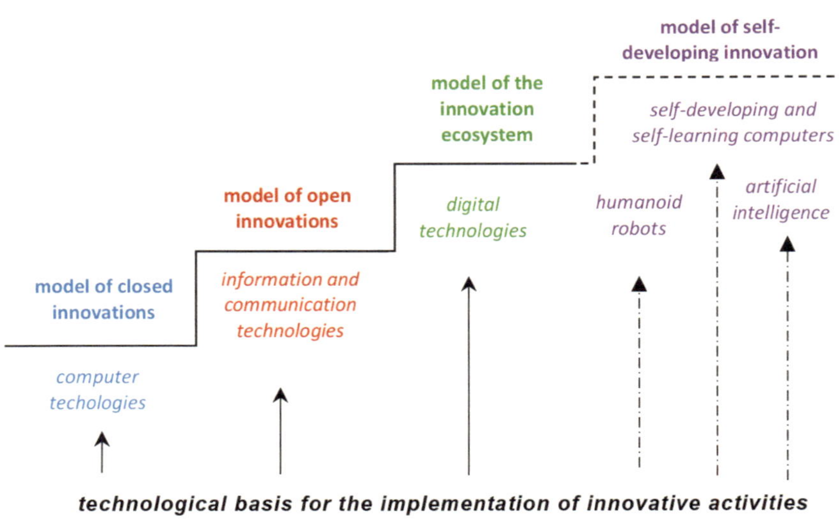

Figure 1.
Evolution of innovation models and their information and digital basis. Source: Compiled by the authors.

as the mechanism for determining the right holder of innovation and the mechanism for protecting property rights, and, accordingly, change the model of innovation activity itself.

Based on different studies in the field of forecasting the directions of development of information and digital technologies, it can be assumed that a new model of innovation will be formed in the future, which will be based on robots, artificial intelligence, and self-developing computer systems [181–185]. Conventionally, such a new model of innovation can be called a model of "self-developing" innovation.

The stages of transformation of models of innovation activity, including a new model, the characteristics of the information and digital basis of their existence, as well as their relationship are shown in **Figure 1**.

The diagram of the evolution of innovation models presented in **Figure 1** is the author's development and requires further research both of a theoretical nature and empirical verification in order to clarify the basic parameters of the model.

5. Conclusions

In general, summing up the characteristics of the process of evolution of innovation activity models under the influence of digital transformation, the following can be distinguished.

Digitalization has had a significant impact on the process of creating innovations and implementing innovative activities and has also led to the transformation of the innovation model. To date, the evolution of innovation activity models has gone through three stages - from the closed innovation model through the open innovation model to the innovation ecosystem model. However, it should be noted that all three models continue to be actively used in business, and the choice of model primarily depends on the specifics of the products (including market features), the industry specifics of the company, its size, capital structure, form of ownership, etc.

The second important trend that has influenced the transformation of the innovation model is the broad implementation of the provisions of the concept of sustainable development and climate security. However, in the modern world, sustainability can be ensured only based on universal consideration of all factors that affect the life of society, and not only on the specific conditions of doing business. That is why, within the framework of the modern model of the innovation ecosystem, greening factors and ESG factors have appeared and gained significant influence, the transition to the use of which in the regulation of activities has become a necessary element of any business.

It should be noted that the use of computer technology has posed a number of unexpected questions to society regarding intellectual property rights. The process of intellectualization of labor (i.e., an increase in the share of intellectual labor in human economic and economic activity), on the one hand, and the increasing use of a modern computer, information and communication, and digital technologies, on the other hand, naturally lead to a change in the model of innovation management and organization of innovation activities on a new technological basis.

Acknowledgements

The work is carried out based on the task on fulfilment of government contractual work in the field of scientific activities as a part of base portion of the state task of the Ministry of Education and Science of the Russian Federation to Perm National Research Polytechnic University (topic # FSNM-2020-0026). This research was partially supported by the Ministry of Education and Science of the Russian Federation to Perm National Research Polytechnic University as part of the development of the Technology Transfer Center (topic # 075-15-2021-1378).

Conflict of interest

The authors declare no conflict of interest.

Author details

Zhanna Mingaleva[1*] and Vladimir Postnikov[2]

1 Faculty of Humanities, Center for Research on Sustainable Development and Innovation Processes, Department of Economics and Industrial Management, Perm National Research Polytechnic University, Perm, Russia

2 Faculty of Humanities, Department of Economics and Industrial Management, Perm National Research Polytechnic University, Perm, Russia

*Address all correspondence to: mingal1@pstu.ru

References

[1] Bordeleau F-E, Mosconi E, de Santa-Eulalia LA. Business intelligence and analytics value creation in industry 4.0: A multiple case study in manufacturing medium enterprises. Production Planning & Control. 2020;**31**(2-3):173-185. DOI: 10.1080/09537287.2019.1631458

[2] Chen M, Sinha A, Hu K, Shah MI. Impact of technological innovation on energy efficiency in industry 4.0 era: Moderation of shadow economy in sustainable development. Technological Forecasting and Social Change. 2021;**164**:120521. DOI: 10.1016/j.techfore.2020.120521

[3] De Felice F, Travaglioni M, Petrillo A. Innovation trajectories for a society 5.0. Data. 2021;**6**(11):115. DOI: 10.3390/data6110115

[4] Ramírez-Montoya MS, Castillo-Martínez IM, Sanabria-Zepeda JC, Miranda J. Complex thinking in the framework of education 4.0 and open innovation—A systematic literature. Review Journal of Open Innovation: Technology, Market, and Complexity. 2022;**8**:4. DOI: 10.3390/joitmc8010004

[5] Żywiolek J, Rosak-Szyrocka J, Molenda M. Satisfaction with the implementation of industry 4.0 among manufacturing companies in Poland. European Research Studies Journal. 2021;**24**(3):469-479. DOI: 10.35808/ersj/2366

[6] Cusumano MA, Gawer A, Yoffie DB. The Business of Platforms: Strategy in the Age of Digital Competition, Innovation, and Power. New York: Harper Collins; 2019

[7] Ludbrook F, Michalikova KF, Musova Z, Suler P. Business models for sustainable innovation in industry 4.0: Smart manufacturing processes, digitalization of production systems, and data-driven decision making. Journal of Self-Governance and Management Economics. 2019;7:21-26. DOI: 10.22381/JSME7320193

[8] Yoo Y, Boland RJ, Lyytinen K, Majchrzak A. Organizing for innovation in the digitized world. Organization Science, INFORMS. 2012;**23**(5):1398-1408. DOI: 10.1287/orsc.1120.0771

[9] Teece DJ. Profiting from innovation in the digital economy: Enabling technologies, standards, and licensing models in the wireless world. Research Policy. 2018;**47**(8):1367-1387. DOI: 10.1016/j.respol.2017.01.015

[10] Ejsmont K, Gladysz B, Kluczek A. Impact of industry 4.0 on sustainability - bibliometric literature review. Sustainability. 2020;**12**(14J):5650. DOI: 10.3390/su12145650

[11] Birkel H, Müller JM. Potentials of industry 4.0 for supply chain management within the triple bottom line of sustainability – A systematic literature review. Journal of Cleaner Production. 2021;**289**:125612. DOI: 10.1016/j.jclepro.2020.125612

[12] Beltrami M, Orzes G, Sarkis J, Sartor M. Industry 4.0 and sustainability: Towards conceptualization and theory. Journal of Cleaner Production. 2021;**312**:127733. DOI: 10.1016/j.jclepro.2021.127733

[13] Piccarozzi M, Silvestri C, Aquilani B. Is this a new story of the 'two giants'? A systematic literature review of the relationship between industry 4.0, sustainability and its pillars. Technological Forecasting and Social

Change. 2022;**177**:121511. DOI: 10.1016/j.techfore.2022.121511

[14] Zengin Y, Naktiyok S, Kaygın E, Kavak O, Topçuoğlu E. An investigation upon industry 4.0 and society 5.0 within the context of sustainable development goals. Sustainability. 2021;**13**(5):2682. DOI: 10.3390/su13052682

[15] Schumpeter J. The Theory of Economic Development. Cambridge: Harvard University Press; 1934

[16] Ahn S. Competition, innovation and productivity growth: A review of theory and evidence. OECD Economics Department Working Papers. 17 January 2002;**317**:1-77. DOI: 10.2139/ssrn.318059

[17] Fagerberg J, Fosaas M, Sapprasert K. Innovation: Exploring the knowledge base. Research Policy. 2012;**41**(7):1132-1153. DOI: 10.1016/j.respol.2012.03.008

[18] Mingaleva Z, Deputatova L, Akatov N, Starkov Y, Mitrofanova E. Application of HADI-cycle for providing sustainability of processes of knowledge and innovation. Entrepreneurship and Sustainability Issues. 2019;**7**(2):1628-1640. DOI: 10.9770/jesi.2019.7.2(58)

[19] Mingaleva Z, Deputatova L, Starkov Y. Management of Organizational Knowledge as a basis for the competitiveness of Enterprises in the Digital Economy. Integrated science in digital age. ICIS 2019. Lecture Notes in Networks and Systems. 2020;**78**:203-212. DOI: 10.1007/978-3-030-22493-6_18

[20] Acharya R, Ziesemer T. A closed economy model of horizontal and vertical product differentiation: The case of innovation in biotechnology: A correction. Economics of Innovation and New Technology. 1997;**5**(1):91-92. DOI: 10.1080/10438599700000009

[21] Almirall E, Casadesus-Masanell R. Open versus closed innovation: A model of discovery and divergence. Academy of Management Review. 2010;**35**(1):27-47. DOI: 10.5465/AMR.2010.45577790

[22] Barge-Gil A. Open, semi-open and closed innovators: Towards an explanation of degree of openness. Industry and Innovation. 2010;**17**(6):577-607. DOI: 10.1080/13662716.2010.530839

[23] Felin T, Zenger TR. Closed or open innovation? Problem solving and the governance choice. Research Policy. 2014;**43**(5):914-925. DOI: 10.1016/j.respol.2013.09.006

[24] Parmentola A, Simoni M, Tutore I. Fast and furious: How the open vs closed dilemma affects the technology diffusion dynamic. Management Decision. 2018;**56**(4):867-890. DOI: 10.1108/MD-01-2017-0071

[25] Regenfelder M, Slowak AP, Santacreu A. Closed-loop innovation for mobile electronics - the business model innovation approach of the sustainably SMART project. Electronics Goes Green. 2016;**(EGG). 2016**:1-6. DOI: 10.1109/EGG.2016.7829847

[26] Ettlie JE, Pavlou PA T-b. New product development partnerships. Decision Sciences. 2006;**37**(2):117-147. DOI: 10.1111/j.1540-5915.2006.00119.x

[27] Malerba F. Sectoral systems of innovation and production. Research Policy. 2002;**31**:247-264

[28] Mingaleva Z, Bykova E, Plotnikova E. Potential of the network concept for an assessment of organizational structure. Procedia-Social and Behavioral Sciences. 2013;**81**:126-130. DOI: 10.1016/j.sbspro.2013.06.400

[29] Greenfield A. Radical Technologies: The Design of Everyday Life. London: Verso Books; 2017. p. 349

[30] Rojas MA, Saldanha TJ, Khuntia J, Kathuria A & Boh WF. Overcoming Deficiencies for Innovation in SMEs: IT for Closed Innovation versus IT for Open Innovation. International Conference on Information Systems, ICIS 2020 - Making Digital Inclusive: Blending the Local and the Global. Association for Information Systems (AIS), India. 2021. arr.no.167844

[31] Bardhan I, Krishnan V, Lin S. Business value of information technology: Testing the interaction effect of IT and R & D on Tobin's Q. Information Systems Research. 2013;**24**(4):1147-1161. DOI: 10.1287/isre.2013.0481

[32] Cainelli G, De Marchi V, Grandinetti R. Do knowledge-intensive business services innovate differently? Economics of Innovation and New Technology. 2020;**29**(1):48-65. DOI: 10.1080/10438599.2019.1585639

[33] Choi B. The role of firm size and IT capabilities in open and closed innovation. Asia Pacific Journal of Information Systems. 2019;**29**(4):690-716. DOI: 10.14329/apjis.2019.29.4.690

[34] Li C, Jiang Y, Fang P. Innovation in advanced manufacturing driven by supercomputing. Procedia CIRP. 2019;**83**:584-589

[35] Boudreau K. Does "Opening" a Platform Enhance Innovative Performance? Panel Data Evidence on Handheld Computers Working Paper. Boston, and HEC, Paris: Massachusetts Institute of Technology; 2006

[36] Christensen CM, Verlinden M, Westerman G. Disruption, disintegration and the dissipation of differentiability. Industrial and Corporate Change. 2002;**11**(5):955-993. DOI: 10.1093/icc/11.5.955

[37] Kesidou E, Narasimhan R, Ozusaglam S, Wong CY. Dynamic openness for network-enabled product and process innovation: A panel-data analysis. International Journal of Operations and Production Management. 2022;**42**(3):257-279. DOI: 10.1108/IJOPM-06-2021-0380

[38] Chesbrough H. The logic of open innovation: Managing intellectual property. California Management Review. 2003;**45**(3):33-58. DOI: 10.1177/000812560304500301

[39] Chesbrough HW. Open Innovation: The New Imperative for Creating and Profiting from Technology. Boston, MA: Harvard Business School Publishing; 2003

[40] Chesbrough HW, Vanhaverbeke W, West J. Open Innovation: Researching a New Paradigm. Oxford: Oxford University Press; 2006

[41] Saebi T, Foss NJ. Business models for open innovation: Matching heterogeneous open innovation strategies with business model dimensions. European Management Journal. 2015;**33**(3):201-213. DOI: 10.1016/j.emj.2014.11.002

[42] Bröring S, Herzog P. Organising new business development: Open innovation at Degussa. European Journal of Innovation Management. 2008;**11**(3):330-348. DOI: 10.1108/14601060810888991

[43] Boh WF, Huang C-J, Wu A. Investor experience and innovation performance: The mediating role of external cooperation. Strategic Management Journal. 2020;**41**(1):124-151. DOI: 10.1002/smj.30891

[44] Calabrese M, Sala AL, Fuller RP, Laudando A. Digital platform ecosystems

for sustainable innovation: Toward a new meta-organizational model? Administrative Sciences. 2021;**11**(4):119. DOI: 10.3390/admsci11040119

[45] Granstrand O, Holgersson M. Innovation ecosystems: A conceptual review and a new definition. Technovation. 2020;**90-91**:102098. DOI: 10.1016/j.technovation.2019.102098

[46] Helfat CE, Raubitschek RS. Dynamic and integrative capabilities for profiting from innovation in digital platform-based ecosystems. Research Policy. 2018;**47**(8):1391-1399. DOI: 10.1016/j.respol.2018.01.019

[47] Jackson DJ. What Is an Innovation Ecosystem? (2011). Available from: https://erc-assoc.org/sites/default/files/topics/policy_studies/DJackson_Innovation% 20Ecosystem_03-15-11.pdf (Accessed: January 7, 2022)

[48] Jacobides M, Cennamo C, Gawer A. Towards a theory of ecosystems. Strategic Management Journal. 2018;**39**:2255-2276. DOI: 10.1002/smj.2904

[49] Mingaleva Z, Mirskikh I. The problems of digital economy development in Russia. Advances in Intelligent Systems and Computing. 2019;**850**:48-55. DOI: 10.1007/978-3-030-02351-5_7

[50] Smorodinskaya N, Russell M, Katukov D, Still K. Innovation ecosystems vs. innovation systems in terms of collaboration and co-creation of value. In: 50th Hawaii International Conference on System Sciences. AIS Electronic Library (AISeL), Village, HI, USA; January 4-7, 2017

[51] Abdelkafi N, Täuscher K. Business models for sustainability from a system dynamics perspective. Organization & Environment. 2016;**29**:74-96. DOI: 10.1177/1086026615592930

[52] Colglazier W. Sustainable development agenda: 2030. Science. 2015;**349**:1048-1050. DOI: 10.1126/science.aad2333

[53] Hall J, Vredenburg H. The challenges of sustainable development innovation. MIT Sloan Management Review. 2003;**45**:61-68

[54] Brunnermeier S, Cohen M. Determinants of environmental innovation in US manufacturing industries. Journal of Environmental Economics and Management. 2003;**45**:278-293

[55] Jaffe AB, Palmer K. Environmental regulation and innovation: A panel data study. The Review of Economics and Statistics. 1997;**79**:610-619

[56] Kirschten U. Sustainable innovation networks: Conceptual framework and institutionalization. Progress in Industrial Ecology, An International Journal. 2005;**2**(1):132-147. DOI: 10.1504/PIE.2005.006781

[57] Boons F, Lüdeke-Freund F. Business models for sustainable innovation: State of the art and steps towards a research agenda. Journal of Cleaner Production. 2013;**45**:9-19. DOI: 10.1016/j.jclepro.2012.07.007

[58] Cillo V, Messeni Petruzzelli A, Ardito L, Del Giudice M. Understanding sustainable innovation: A systematic literature review. Corporate Social Responsibility and Environmental Management. 2019;**26**:1012-1025. DOI: 10.1002/csr.1783

[59] Godin B, Gaglio G. How does innovation sustain 'sustainable innovation'? In: Handbook of Sustainable Innovation. Cheltenham: Edward Elgar Publishing; 2019

[60] Schaltegger S, Wagner M. Sustainable entrepreneurship and sustainability innovation: Categories and interactions. Business Strategy and the Environment. 2011;**20**:222-237. DOI: 10.1002/bse.682

[61] Schaltegger S, Lüdeke-Freund F, Hansen EG. Business models for sustainability: A co-evolutionary analysis of sustainable entrepreneurship, innovation, and transformation. Organization & Environment. 2016;**29**:264-289. DOI: 10.1177/1086026616633272

[62] OECD/Eurostat. Oslo Manual. 2018: Guidelines for collecting, reporting and using data on innovation, 4th Edition, The Measurement of Scientific, Technological and Innovation Activities, OECD Publishing, Paris/Eurostat, Luxembourg. 2018. doi:10.1787/9789264304604-en (Accessed: January 14, 2022)

[63] Adams R, Jeanrenaud S, Bessant J, Denyer D, Overy P. Sustainability-oriented innovation: A systematic review. International Journal of Management Reviews. 2016;**18**(2):180-205. DOI: 10.1111/ijmr.12068

[64] Carrillo-Hermosilla J, del Río P, Könnölä T. Diversity of eco-innovations: Reflections from selected case studies. Journal of Cleaner Production. 2010;**18**:1073-1083. DOI: 10.1016/j.jclepro.2010.02.014

[65] Bossle MB, Dutra De Barcellos M, Vieira LM, Sauvée L. The drivers for adoption of eco-innovation. Journal of Cleaner Production. 2016;**113**:861-872. DOI: 10.1016/j.jclepro.2015.11.033

[66] Mingaleva Z, Shpak N. Possibilities of solar energy application in Russian cities. Thermal Science. 2015;**19**(2):S457-S466. DOI: 10.2298/TSCI150330087M

[67] Ramkumar S, Mueller M, Pyka A, Squazzoni F. Diffusion of eco-innovation through inter-firm network targeting: An agent-based model. Journal of Cleaner Production. 2022;**335**:130298. DOI: 10.1016/j.jclepro.2021.130298

[68] Bofinger Y, Heyden KJ, Rock B. Corporate social responsibility and market efficiency: Evidence from ESG and misvaluation measures. Journal of Banking and Finance. 2022;**134**:106322

[69] Chen L, Zhang L, Huang J, Xiao H, Zhou Z. Social responsibility portfolio optimization incorporating ESG criteria. Journal of Management Science and Engineering. 2021;**6**(1):75-85

[70] Chouaibi Y, Zouari G. The effect of corporate social responsibility practices on real earnings management: Evidence from a European ESG data. International Journal of Disclosure and Governance. 2022;**19**(1):11-30

[71] Diaye MA, Ho SH, Oueghlissi R. ESG performance and economic growth: A panel co-integration analysis. Empirica. 2022;**49**(1):99-122

[72] Ferrero-Ferrero I, Fernández-Izquierdo MÁ, Muñoz-Torres MJ. Can board diversity enhance the integration of ESG aspects in management system? Lecture Notes in Business Information Processing. 2013;**145**:1-9

[73] Giese G, Lee L-E, Melas D, Nagy Z, Nishikawa L. Consistent ESG integration through ESG benchmarks. Journal of Index Investing. 2019;**10**:24-42

[74] Kaiser L. ESG integration: Value, growth and momentum. Journal of Asset Management. 2020;**21**(1):32-51

[75] Karwowski M, Raulinajtys-Grzybek M. The application of corporate social responsibility (CSR) actions

for mitigation of environmental, social, corporate governance (ESG) and reputational risk in integrated reports. Corporate Social Responsibility and Environmental Management. 2021;**28**(4):1270-1284

[76] Mingaleva Z. Ethical principles in consulting. Procedia-Social and Behavioral Sciences. 2013;**84**:1740-1744. DOI: 10.1016/j.sbspro.2013.07.024

[77] Parfitt C. ESG integration treats ethics as risk, but whose ethics and whose risk? Responsible Investment in the Context of Precarity and risk-shifting. Critical Sociology. 2020;**46**(4-5):573-587

[78] van Duuren E, Plantinga A, Scholtens B. ESG integration and the investment management process: Fundamental investing reinvented. Journal of Business Ethics. 2016;**138**(3):525-533

[79] Zaccone MC, Pedrini M. ESG factor integration into private equity. Sustainability (Switzerland). 2020;**12**(14) 5725:1-15

[80] Docherty M. Primer on 'open innovation': Principles and practice. Vision. 2006;**30**(2):13-17

[81] Gassmann O, Enkel E, Chesbrough H. The future of open innovation. Research-Technology Management. 2010;**40**:213-221. DOI: 10.1111/j.1467-9310.2010.00605.x

[82] Hajrizi E, Nagy K. Transformative research driven innovation - the artistry of innovation management in the age of spiritual machines. In: GBRS2018 International Conference, St. John's University, Roma, Italy, 13-15 June 2018. 2018

[83] Lopes APVBV, de Carvalho MM. Evolution of the open innovation paradigm: Towards a contingent conceptual model. Technological Forecasting and Social Change. 2018;**132**(C):284-298. DOI: 10.1016/j.techfore.2018.02.014

[84] Marullo C, Ahn JM, Martelli I. Open for innovation: An improved measurement approach using item response theory. Technovation. 2022;**109**:102338. DOI: 10.1016/j.technovation.2021.102338

[85] Oh D-S, Phillips F, Park S, Lee E. Innovation ecosystems: A critical examination. Technovation. 2016;**54**:1-6. DOI: 10.1016/j.technovation.2016.02.004

[86] Fulmer SI. Editor's comments: The craft of writing theory articles—Variety and similarity. Academi of Management Review. 2012;**37**:327-331. DOI: 10.5465/amr.2012.0026

[87] Gilson LL, Goldberg CB. Editors' comment: So, what is a conceptual paper? Group and Organization Management. 2015;**40**:127-130. DOI: 10.1177/1059601115576425

[88] Hirschheim R. Some guidelines for the critical reviewing of conceptual papers. Journal of the Association for Information Systems. 2008;**9**:432-441

[89] Lukka K, Vinnari E. Domain theory and method theory in management accounting research. Accounting, Auditing and Accountability Journal. 2014;**27**:1308-1338

[90] Travaglioni M, Ferazzoli A, Petrillo A, Cioffi R, De Felice F, Piscitelli G. Digital manufacturing challenges through open innovation perspective. Procedia Manufacturing. 2020;**42**:165-172

[91] Jaakkola E. Designing conceptual articles: Four approaches. AMS Review. 2020;**10**:18-26. DOI: 10.1007/s13162-020-00161-0

[92] Petticrew M, Roberts H. Systematic Reviews in the Social Sciences: A Practical Guide. New York: John Wiley and Sons; 2008

[93] Seuring S, Müller M. From a literature review to a conceptual framework for sustainable supply chain management. Journal of Cleaner Production. 2008;**16**:1699-1710. DOI: 10.1016/J.JCLEPRO.2008.04.020

[94] Baldwin C, von Hippel E. Modeling a paradigm shift: From producer innovation to user and open collaborative innovation. Organization Science, INFORMS. 2011;**22**(6):1399-1417. DOI: 10.1287/orsc.1100.0618

[95] Esposito De Falco S, Renzi A, Orlando B, Cucari N. Open collaborative innovation and digital platforms. Production Planning and Control. 2017;**28**:1344-1353. DOI: 10.1080/09537287.2017.1375143

[96] Hekkert MP, Suurs RA, Negro SO, Kuhlmann S, Smits R. Functions of innovation systems: A new approach for analysing technological change. Technological Forecasting and Social Change. 2007;**74**:413-432. DOI: 10.1016/j.techfore.2006.03.002

[97] Van Geenhuizen M, Ye Q. Responsible innovators: Open networks on the way to sustainability transitions. Technological Forecasting and Social Change. 2014;**87**:28-40. DOI: 10.1016/j.techfore.2014.06.001

[98] Boudreau K. Open platform strategies and innovation: Granting access vs. devolving control. Management Science, INFORMS. 2010;**56**(10):1849-1872. DOI: 10.1287/mnsc.1100.1215

[99] Carayannis EG, Campbell DFJ. "Mode 3"and "quadruple helix": Toward a 21st century fractal innovation ecosystem. International Journal of Technology Management. 2009;**46**(3-4):201-234. DOI: 10.1504/ijtm.2009.023374

[100] Gambardella A, Panico C. On the management of open innovation. Research Policy. 2014;**43**(5):903-913. DOI: 10.1016/j.respol.2013.12.002

[101] Matschoss K, Repo P. Forward-looking network analysis of ongoing sustainability transitions. Technological Forecasting and Social Change. 2020;**161**:120288. DOI: 10.1016/j.techfore.2020.120288

[102] Parker G, Van Alstyne M. Innovation, openness and platform control. Management Science. 2018;**64**:3015-3032. DOI: 10.1287/mnsc.2017.2757

[103] Tidd J, Thuriaux-Alemán B. Innovation management practices: Cross sectorial adoption variation and effectiveness. R & D Management. 2016;**46**(3):1024-1043. DOI: 10.1111/radm.12199

[104] Fukuda K, Watanabe C. Japanese and US perspectives on the national innovation ecosystem. Technology in Society. 2008;**30**(1):49-63. DOI: 10.1016/j.techsoc.2007.10.008

[105] Gawer A, Cusumano MA. Industry platforms and ecosystem innovation. Journal of Product Innovation Management. 2013;**31**:417-433. DOI: 10.1111/jpim.12105

[106] Siedschlag I, Meneto S, Tong KM. Determinants of Green Innovations: Firm-Level Evidence. ESRI WP643. Economic and Social Research Institute (ESRI), Dublin. Working Paper; 2019

[107] Tidd J, Bessant J. Innovation management challenges: From fads

to fundamentals. International Journal of Innovation Management. 2018;**22**(5):1840007. DOI: 10.1142/s1363919618400078

[108] Aquilani B, Piccarozzi M, Abbate T, Codini A. The role of open innovation and value co-creation in the challenging transition from industry 4.0 to society 5.0: Toward a theoretical framework. Sustainability. 2020;**12**(21):1-21. DOI: 10.3390/su12218943

[109] Fukuda K. Science, technology and innovation ecosystem transformation toward society 5.0. International Journal of Production Economics. 2020;**220**:107460. DOI: 10.1016/j.ijpe.2019.07.033

[110] Holroyd C. Technological innovation and building a 'super smart' society: Japan's vision of society 5.0. Journal of Asian Public Policy. 2022;**15**(1):18-31. DOI: 10.1080/17516234.2020.1749340

[111] Argyres N, Rios LA, Silverman BS. Organizational change and the dynamics of innovation: Formal R&D structure and intrafirm inventor networks. Strategic Management Journal. 2020;**41**(11):2015-2049. DOI: 10.1002/smj.3217

[112] Brown JR, Martinsson G, Petersen BC. Do financing constraints matter for R&D? European Economic Review. 2012;**56**(8):1512-1529. DOI: 10.1016/j.euroecorev.2012.07.007

[113] Cassiman B, Veugelers R. In search of complementarity in innovation strategy: Internal R & D and external knowledge acquisition. Management Science, INFORMS. 2006;**52**(1):68-82. DOI: 10.1287/mnsc.1050.0470

[114] Denicolai S, Ramirez M, Tidd J. Overcoming the false dichotomy between internal R & D and external knowledge acquisition: Absorptive capacity dynamics over time. Technological Forecasting and Social Change. 2016;**104**:57-65. DOI: 10.1016/j.techfore.2015.11.025

[115] Ketata I, Sofka W, Grimpe C. The role of internal capabilities and firms' environment for sustainable innovation: Evidence for Germany. R & D Management. 2015;**45**(1):60-75. DOI: 10.1111/radm.12052

[116] Teece DJ. Firm organization, industrial structure, and technological innovation. Journal of Economic Behavior and Organization. 1996;**31**(2):193-224. DOI: 10.1016/S0167-2681(96)00895-5

[117] Ankrah S, AL-Tabbaa O. Universities–industry collaboration: A systematic review. Scandinavian Journal of Management. 2015;**31**(3):387-408. DOI: 10.1016/j.scaman.2015.02.003

[118] Du J, Leten B, Vanhaverbeke W. Managing open innovation projects with science-based and market-based partners. Research Policy. 2014;**43**(5):828-840. DOI: 10.1016/j.respol.2013.12.008

[119] Miozzo M, Desyllas P, H-fen L, Miles I. Innovation collaboration and appropriability by knowledge-intensive business services firms. Research Policy. 2016;**45**(7):1337-1351. DOI: 10.1016/j.respol.2016.03.018

[120] Berrutti F, Bianchi C. Effects of public funding on firm innovation: Transforming or reinforcing a weak innovation pattern? Economics of Innovation and New Technology. 2020;**29**(5):522-539. DOI: 10.1080/10438599.2019.1636452

[121] Cecere G, Corrocher N, Mancusi ML. Financial constraints and public funding

of eco-innovation: Empirical evidence from European SMEs. Small Business Economics. 2020;**54**(1):285-302. DOI: 10.1007/s11187-018-0090-9

[122] Miethling B. The evolution of interactivity-new insights into innovation system change and the role of the state. International Journal of Innovation Science. 2014;**6**(4):213-234. DOI: 10.1260/1757-2223.6.4.213

[123] Reznik N, Palchevich G, Popov V, Petrenko L. Strategic Vectors of the State Financial and Credit Incentives for Innovation. Lecture Notes in Networks and Systems, Springer, Cham.; 2021. p. 194. DOI: 10.1007/978-3-030-69221-6_17

[124] Rukanova B, Post S, Tan YH, Migeotte J, Slegt M, Wong S, et al. The role of public funding in the initiation and upscaling of collective innovation trajectories. In: ACM International Conference Proceeding Series. Association for Computing Machinery (ACM), Seoul, Republic of Korea; 2020. pp. 336-337. DOI: 10.1145/3396956.3397007

[125] Bocken NMP, Geradts THJ. Barriers and drivers to sustainable business model innovation: Organization design and dynamic capabilities. Long Range Planning. 2020;**53**:101950. DOI: 10.1016/j.lrp.2019.101950

[126] Crespi F, Ghisetti C, Quatraro F. Environmental and innovation policies for the evolution of green technologies: A survey and a test. Eurasian Business Review. 2015;**5**(2):343-370. DOI: 10.1007/s40821-015-0027-z

[127] De Marchi V, Grandinetti R, Cainelli G. Does the development of environmental innovation require different resources? Evidence from Spanish manufacturing firms. Journal of Cleaner Production. 2015;**94**:211-221. DOI: 10.1016/j.jclepro.2015.02.008

[128] Mingaleva Z, Mirskikh I. The problems of legal regulation and protection of intellectual property. Procedia Social and Behavioral Sciences. 2013;**81**:329-333. DOI: 10.1016/j.sbspro.2013.06.437

[129] Wu B, Miao Y-N, Peng X-Q, Lin G-M, Deng S-J. Patent protection strategy of technical standards in medical innovation. Chinese Journal of New Drugs. 2018;**27**(5):494-497

[130] Awate S, Larsen MM, Mudambi R. Accessing vs. sourcing knowledge: A comparative study of R&D internationalization between emerging and advanced economy firms. Journal of International Business Studies. 2015;**46**(1):63-86. DOI: 10.1057/jibs.2014.46

[131] Cassiman B, Giovanni V. Open innovation: Are inbound and outbound knowledge flows really complementary? Strategic Management Journal. 2016;**37**(6):1034-1046. DOI: 10.1002/smj.2375

[132] Feller I. Industry-University R&D partnerships in the United States. In: 21st Century Innovation Systems for Japan and the United States. National Academies press. Washington, DC, USA; 2009. pp. 169-185

[133] Franke N, Shah S. How communities support innovative activities: An exploration of assistance and sharing among end-users. Research Policy. 2003;**32**(1):157-178. DOI: 10.1016/S0048-7333(02)00006-9

[134] Katz ML, Shapiro C. Systems competition and network effects. Journal of Economic Perspectives. American Economic Association. 1994;**8**(2):93-115. DOI: 10.1257/jep.8.2.93

[135] Mingaleva Z, Mingaleva A. Assessing innovation susceptibility

of regions and municipal districts. Procedia-Social and Behavioral Sciences. 2013;**81**:595-599. DOI: 10.1016/j.sbspro.2013.06.482

[136] Wagner M. Entrepreneurship, Innovation and Sustainability. Sheffield: Greenleaf Publishing, 2012

[137] Antonioli D, Borghesi S, Mazzanti M. Are regional systems greening the economy? Local spillovers, green innovations and firms' economic performances. Economics of Innovation and New Technology. 2016;**25**(7):692-713. DOI: 10.1080/10438599.2015.1127557

[138] Bahemia H, Squire B. A contingent perspective of open innovation in new product development projects. International Journal of Innovation Management. 2010;**14**(4):603-627. DOI: 10.1142/S1363919610002799

[139] Claisse F, Delvenne P. As above, so below? Narrative salience and side effects of national innovation systems. Critical Policy Studies. 2017;**11**(3):255-271. DOI: 10.1080/19460171.2015.1119051

[140] Khessina OM, Goncalo JA, Krause V. It's time to sober up: The direct costs, side effects and long-term consequences of creativity and innovation. Research in Organizational Behavior. 2018;**38**:107-135. DOI: 10.1016/j.riob.2018.11.003

[141] Todt G, Weiss M, Hoegl M. Mitigating negative side effects of innovation project terminations: The role of resilience and social support. Journal of Product Innovation Management. 2018;**35**(4):518-542. DOI: 10.1111/jpim.12426

[142] Antonioli D, Mancinelli S, Mazzanti M. Is environmental innovation embedded within high-performance organisational changes? The role of human resource management and complementarity in green business strategies. Research Policy. 2013;**42**(4):975-988. DOI: 10.1016/j.respol.2012.12.005

[143] Macher JT. Technological development and the boundaries of the firm: A knowledge-based examination in semiconductor manufacturing. Management Science. 2006;**52**(6):826-843. DOI: 10.1287/mnsc.1060.0511

[144] Sanchez P, Ricart JE. Business model innovation and sources of value creation in low income markets. European Management Review. 2010;**7**(3):138-154. DOI: 10.1057/emr.2010.16

[145] Amitrano CC, Tregua M, Russo Spena T, Bifulco F. On technology in innovation systems and innovation-ecosystem perspectives: A cross-linking analysis. Sustainability. 2018;**10**(10):3744. DOI: 10.3390/su10103744

[146] Busch L, Ransom E, Mckee T, Middendorf G, Chesebro JE. Paradoxes of innovation: Standards and technical change in the transformation of the US soybean industry. International Library of Environmental, Agricultural and Food Ethics. 2006;**6**:137-155. DOI: 10.1007/1-4020-3984-0_8

[147] Friedrich D. Normative market regulation by means of early standardization: A descriptive policy analysis for the biobased industry. Journal of Cleaner Production. 2019;**232**:1282-1296. DOI: 10.1016/j.jclepro.2019.05.362

[148] Hu J, Guan Y, Zhou L, Wang Y. Influence mechanism of ambidextrous innovation on technological catch-up in latecomer enterprises of technical standards alliance. Journal of Advanced Computational Intelligence and Intelligent Informatics. 2020;**24**(3):251-259. DOI: 10.20965/jaciii.2020.p0251

[149] Konwin K, Gravitz P, Oates W, Gustavson P. Igniting Innovation in the Creation of Future Technical Capabilities: A Standards Profile for Use of Modeling & Simulation across the Acquisition Life Cycle. SIW: Workshop; 2015

[150] Kováč E, Žigić K. International competition in vertically differentiated markets with innovation and imitation: Trade policy versus free trade. Economica. 2014;**81**(323):491-521. DOI: 10.1111/ecca.12093

[151] Morita H, Nguyen X. FDI and quality-enhancing technology spillovers. International Journal of Industrial Organization. 2021;**79**:102787. DOI: 10.1016/j.ijindorg.2021.102787

[152] Peñasco C, del Río P, Romero-Jordán D. Analysing the role of international drivers for eco-innovators. Journal of International Management. 2017;**23**(1):56-71. DOI: 10.1016/j.intman.2016.09.001

[153] Adner R, Kapoor R. Value creation in innovation ecosystems: How the structure of technological interdependence affects firm performance in new technology generations. Strategic Management Journal. 2010;**31**(3):306-333. DOI: 10.1002/smj.821

[154] Amit R, Zott C. Creating value through business model innovation. MIT Sloan Management Review. 2012;**53**(3):41-49

[155] Baden-Fuller C, Haefliger S. Business models and technological innovation. Long Range Planning. 2013;**46**(6):419-426. DOI: 10.1016/j.lrp.2013.08.023

[156] Bolton R, Hannon M. Governing sustainability transitions through business model innovation: Towards a systems understanding. Research Policy. 2016;**45**:1731-1742. DOI: 10.1016/j.respol.2016.05.003

[157] Boons F, Montalvo C, Quist J, Wagner M. Sustainable innovation, business models and economic performance: An overview. Journal of Cleaner Production. 2013;**45**:1-8. DOI: 10.1016/j.jclepro.2012.08.013

[158] Dietl H, Royer S, Stratmann U. Value creation architectures and competitive advantage. California Management Review. 2009;**51**:24-39. DOI: 10.2307/41166492

[159] Osorno R, Koria M. Delia Del Carmen Ramírez-Vázquez open innovation with value Co-creation from university-industry collaboration. Journal of Open Innovation Technology Market and Complexity. 2022;**8**(1):32. DOI: 10.3390/joitmc8010032

[160] Snihur Y, Bocken N. A call for action: The impact of business model innovation on business ecosystems, society and planet. Long Range Planning. 2022:102182. In Press. DOI: 10.1016/j.lrp.2022.102182

[161] Chouaibi S, Chouaibi J. Social and ethical practices and firm value: The moderating effect of green innovation: Evidence from international ESG data. International Journal of Ethics and Systems. 2021;**37**(3):442-465. DOI: 10.1108/IJOES-12-2020-0203

[162] De Marchi V. Environmental innovation and R & D cooperation: Empirical evidence from Spanish manufacturing firms. Research Policy. 2012;**41**:614-623. DOI: 10.1016/j.respol.2011.10.002

[163] Di Simone L, Petracci B, Piva M. Economic sustainability, innovation,

and the ESG factors: An empirical investigation. Sustainability. 2022;**14**(4):2270. DOI: 10.3390/su14042270

[164] Horbach J. Determinants of environmental innovation-new evidence from German panel data sources. Research Policy. 2008;**37**(1):163-173. DOI: 10.1016/j.respol.2007.08.006

[165] Katsamakas E, Miliaresis K, Pavlov OV. Digital platforms for the common good: Social innovation for active citizenship and ESG. Sustainability. 2022;**14**(2):639. DOI: 10.3390/su14020639

[166] Xu J, Liu F, Shang Y. R&D investment, ESG performance and green innovation performance: Evidence from China. Kybernetes. 2021;**50**(3):737-756. DOI: 10.1108/K-12-2019-0793

[167] Gambardella A, McGahan AM. Business-model innovation: General purpose technologies and their implications for industry structure. Long Range Planning. 2010;**43**:262-271. DOI: 10.1016/j.lrp.2009.07.009

[168] Lupova-Henry E, Dotti NF. Governance of sustainable innovation: Moving beyond the hierarchy market-network trichotomy? A systematic literature review using the 'who-how-what' framework. Journal of Cleaner Production. 2019;**210**:738-748

[169] Antonioli D, Mazzanti M. Towards a green economy through innovations: The role of trade union involvement. Ecological Economics. 2016;**131**:286-299

[170] Nagy K, Hajrizi E, Palkovics L. Responsible innovation in support of society 5.0 - aspects of audit and control. IFAC-Papers Online. 2020;**53**(2):17469-17474. DOI: 10.1016/j.ifacol.2020.12.2123

[171] Dahlander L, Gann DM. How open is innovation? Research Policy. 2010;**39**(6):699-709. DOI: 10.1016/j.respol.2010.01.013

[172] Fatemi A, Glaum M, Kaiser S. ESG performance and firm value: The moderating role of disclosure. Global Finance Journal. 2018;**38**:45-64. DOI: 10.1016/j.gfj.2017.03.001

[173] Fu X. How does openness affect the importance of incentives for innovation? Research Policy. 2012;**41**(3):512-523. DOI: 10.1016/j.respol.2011.12.011

[174] Henkel J, Schöberl S, Oliver A. The emergence of openness: How and why firms adopt selective revealing in open innovation. Research Policy. 2014;**43**(5):879-890. DOI: 10.1016/j.respol.2013.08.014

[175] Schneider S, Spieth P. Business model innovation: Towards an integrated future research agenda. International Journal of Innovation Management. 2013;**17**(1):1302001:1-1302001:130200134. DOI: 10.1142/S136391961340001X

[176] Cenamor J, Frishammar J. Openness in platform ecosystems: Innovation strategies for complementary products. Research Policy. 2021;**50**:104148. DOI: 10.1016/j.respol.2020.104148

[177] Colombo MG, Foss NJ, Lyngsie J, Lamastra CR. What drives the delegation of innovation decisions? The roles of firm innovation strategy and the nature of external knowledge. Research Policy. 2021;**50**(1):104134. DOI: 10.1016/j.respol.2020.104134

[178] Osorno R, Medrano N. Open innovation platforms: A conceptual design framework. IEEE Transactions on Engineering Management. 2022;**69**(2):438-450. DOI: 10.1109/TEM.2020.2973227

[179] Mingaleva Z, Mirskikh I. Psychological aspects of intellectual property protection. Procedia-Social and Behavioral Sciences. 2015;**190**:220-226. DOI: 10.1016/j.sbspro.2015.04.938

[180] Wang BL. Artificial intelligence technology simulation university three whole education moral education model research. Advances in Intelligent Systems Computing. 2021;**1303**:844-850

[181] Ahn MJ, Chen Y-C. Digital transformation toward AI-augmented public administration: The perception of government employees and the willingness to use AI in government. Government Information Quarterly. 2022; **39**(2):art.no.101664. DOI: 10.1016/j.giq.2021.101664

[182] Keating SJ, Leland JC, Cai L, Oxman N. Toward site-specific and self-sufficient robotic fabrication on architectural scales science. Robotics. 2017;**2**(5):art.no.eaan8986. DOI: 10.1126/scirobotics.aam8986

[183] Motomura Y. Interdisciplinary open innovation through activities in AIST artificial intelligence technology consortium: The scenario towards society 5.0 by artificial intelligence (AI) technologies that enable mutual understanding between AI and humans. Synthesiology. 2021;**13**(1):1-16. DOI: 10.5571/synth.13.1_1

[184] Takaoka K, Yamazaki K, Sakurai E, Yamashita K, Motomura Y. Development of an integrated AI platform and an ecosystem for daily life, business and social problems. Advances in Intelligent Systems and Computing. 2019;**787**:300-309. DOI: 10.1007/978-3-319-94229-2_29

[185] Yang G-Z, Bellingham J, Dupont PE, Wang ZL, Wood R. The grand challenges of science robotics. Science Robotics. 2018;**3**(14):eaar7650

Chapter 8

Digital Transformation: The Age of Innovations in Business and Society

Iryna Kovshova

Abstract

This chapter considers main factors of digital transformation in business and society. The latest studies of digital ad spend in Europe and a number of marketing technology solutions all over the world within the period 2011–2020 have confirmed a rapid development of digital technologies in business and society. It was justified that due to digitalization process companies have to revise their priorities and modify their main strategic goals for simultaneous achievement of commercial efficiency and a social effect. These goals need some adjustment to specific requirements and wishes of main process participants that form five levels of approval. Proposed marketing management model in digital transformation of business and society contains basic components, which lie in the digital contour. Responses of millennials (the people born at the turn of the century) on the use of digital technologies in different spheres of life are analyzed. The pilot research allowed to distinguish three groups of millennials depending on how actively they use digital technologies in different spheres of life. Main directions of innovative marketing management development are defined. The opportunities of implementing functionality of artificial intelligence, neuromarketing, augmented and virtual reality, marketing technologies MarTech in company business-processes are studied.

Keywords: digital transformation, marketing management, a millennial, a business-process, a society, a digital technology, neuromarketing, MarTech, augmented and virtual reality, artificial intelligence

1. Introduction

Nowadays technologies and innovations actively have effect on all spheres of human life triggering digital transformation in business and society. For the last two decades, digital technologies have rapidly developed and scaled. Wide spread of the Internet, the availability of various types of devices, the development of digital platforms, launching of social media and applications caused the emergence of generation of millennials, that is, those who were born at the turn of the century and have been growing within this period. These young people do not almost represent their lives without digital technologies, actively use them in their everyday lives and are mastering new functionalities and adjusting to new realities of a society. Unlike the senior generation, the youth aged from 18 to 25 can freely orient in the digital space and have a little different rational, emotional and behavioral responses when interacting with a society and environment. Millennials have become the main driving force of digital transformation in business and society due to their skills of mixing online and offline communication, rapid gaining digital skills, dexterity of working with databases and a desire to integrate technologies, products and systems in all spheres of life.

This young generation represents new requirements for goods, services or ideas and wishes more and more innovative products. By monitoring and analyzing customer needs and expectations, global technological corporations significantly contribute to the research and development of new products and digital solutions, which are gradually filling all spheres of life. Adjustment to society digital transformation factors and replacement of existing business models by more innovative ones have a significant impact on the development of digital skills of the senior generation and stimulate their use at work and everyday life for communication or doing certain actions.

Results of studying the status of digital marketing technologies in the world within the last 10 years witness that a number of only marketing technology solutions are growing in average at 995 items per year and at the end of 2020, there were 8000 items. However, for the development of successful business in digital transformation of society, it is not enough whether a company has only innovative technologies and products. A company has to focus on real human values and better understand its customers, employees, business partners, etc. In this connection, managerial staff has to modify traditional approaches to company management taking into account new trends and find innovative solutions to improve lives of people and society as a whole. An innovative approach to company administration in the new realities is implementation of a complex marketing management system containing a dual strategic goal—simultaneous achievement of maximum economic efficiency and a social effect.

Marketing management development depends on available digital technologies affecting people's lifestyle and transforms a whole society. Among innovative technologies used in the administration of company business processes by managerial staff, it is possible to distinguish the most experimental ones, such as artificial intelligence, neuromarketing, augmented or virtual reality and marketing technology MarTech. These four technologies grounding on the knowledge of different sciences combine variable methods and tools and actively develop integrating one to another and acquiring new functionality.

The problem to be solved in this chapter is to define factors of digital transformation impact on business and society to modify the existing approaches in management in accordance with the modern trends. To solve this comprehensive problem, the research was carried out in five stages: At the first stage, the main factors of digital transformation in business and society were defined; at the second stage, the basic hypotheses of marketing management in modern conditions were formulated; at the third stage, the up-to-date marketing management model in digital transformation of business and society was developed; at the fourth stage, the use of digital technologies by millennials in their everyday lives was studied; and at the fifth stage, the main directions of marketing management innovation development were defined.

2. Digital transformation: an age of innovations in business and society

2.1 Main factors of digital transformation in business and society

The COVID-19 pandemic has become a real challenge for business and society all over the world. The development trends of the period 2019–2021 have demonstrated that for survival at the market and for successful realization of its activity, the company needs the following: flexibility of managerial staff's thinking, adaptation to digital transformation of society and replacement of the existing business models by more innovative.

Since the beginning of pandemic technologies have developed rapidly and for many countries (especially for the countries of Europe and Northern America) have become the main way of connection between people (Human-to-Human, H2H), business partners (Business-to-Business, B2B), companies and consumers (Business-to-Consumer, B2C). Let us analyze the main factors of digital transformation in business and society, which are structured on **Figure 1**.

The up-to-date realities of society digitalization have determined the spiral development of companies as a result of effects of the following external factors: customer requirements and needs in communication and innovative products; business interests of global technological corporations; significant investments in scientific research and development and creation of innovative technologies and products.

Customer needs and requirements in communication and innovative products trigger the spiral of society digital transformation development. However, the locomotive of the up-to-date stage of development is global technological corporations in big batches producing personal computers, laptops, netbooks, tablets, smartphones and other devices having features to connect to global networks and systems. Marketing tools of global technological corporations are aimed, on the one side, to popularize new innovative products and involve partners in rising functionality of equipment and devices, and, on the other side, to increase a number of potential and existing customers and provide maximum product sales volumes.

The main factors of digital transformation in business and society are as follows: competition at the market and mixing of online and offline formats, up-to-date digital skills of humans, the availability of huge databases containing data on different

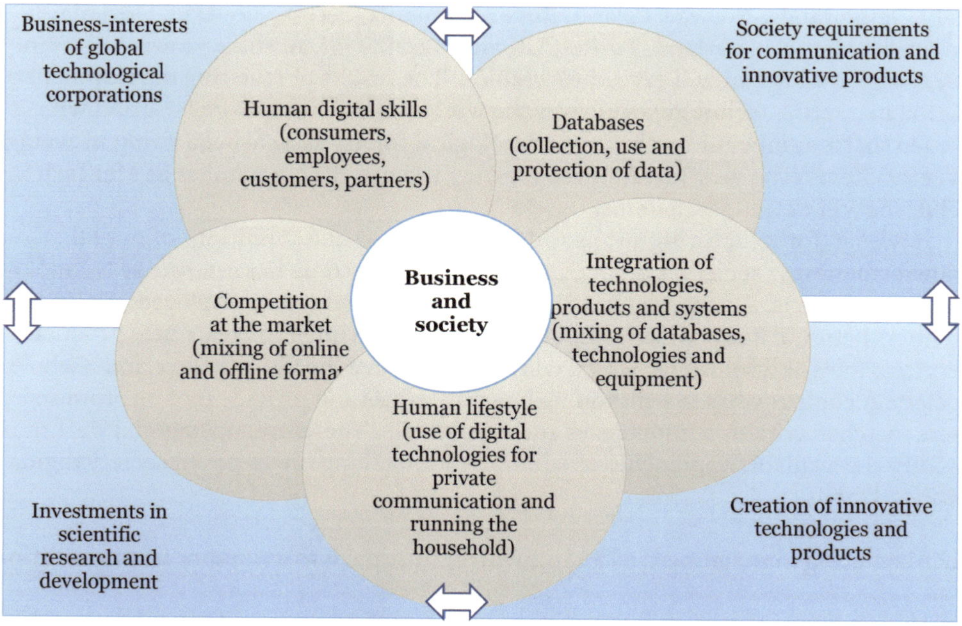

Figure 1.
Main factors of digital transformation in business and society.

aspects of society and business development, the use of digital technologies by people in various life spheres, integration processes of mixing technologies and devices, access to databases.

Competition at the market stimulates companies to active development of their online business [1]. At the same time, traditional offline business is transformed remaining the basis of digital superstructure. The companies, which have been working at the market for a long period, are afraid to lose their positions under the pressure of new ambitious players. Analyzing significant benefits from the use of digital technologies and products, these companies suppose that investment into this field is a precondition of their success and an opportunity of strengthening their own positions at the market [2–4]. It was what determined the popularity of creating new technological platforms, especially those providing automation of company's business processes, the efficient use of databases for making optimal management decisions, monitoring needs of individual consumers and a whole society.

Accumulation of vast data scopes by companies has determined the necessity of developed technologies for collecting, using and protection of information. Big Data help managerial staff to make balanced administrative decisions and develop effective innovative strategies mixing business interests, needs and wishes of a society. Besides, operational decisions of company employees often require approval at different levels that increase time for their acceptance and implementation. Integration of digital technologies, devices and systems of a company allows its employees to get the needed information quickly, increase overall performance and response to changes fast.

Digital technologies in business and society are actively developing (**Figure 2**). For example, total digital ad spend in Europe for the last 10 years (2011–2020) has been rising in average over €5 billion annually. The data have been received grounding on the analysis of 28 European countries: Austria, Belarus, Belgium, Bulgaria, Czech Republic, Croatia, Denmark, Finland, France, Germany, Greece, Hungary, Ireland, Italy, Netherlands, Norway, Poland, Russia, Romania, Serbia, Slovakia, Slovenia, Spain, Sweden, Switzerland, Turkey, UK and Ukraine [5]. At these growing rates in 2022, digital ad spend will exceed €79 billion. The results of studying development of digital marketing technologies all over the world within the analogous period witnessed that a number of marketing technological solutions have been rising in average over 995 items each year [6]. At these growing rates in 2022, a number of MarTech solutions will exceed 9900 items.

However, for structuring successful business under the conditions of digital transformation of society it is not enough if a company only has innovative technologies and products. A company has to understand its customers, employees, business partners better to know what is important for them, helping to create new products, services, tools and solutions, which will really improve the life of people and a whole society. A company has to focus on real human values and provide that its promises were matched with its competences and capabilities. Therefore, managerial staff must modify the available approaches to administration taking into account society digitalization trends.

2.2 Marketing management as an innovative approach to company administration

Marketing management is an innovative approach to company administration in conditions of changeable environment for achieving key objectives. At the same time,

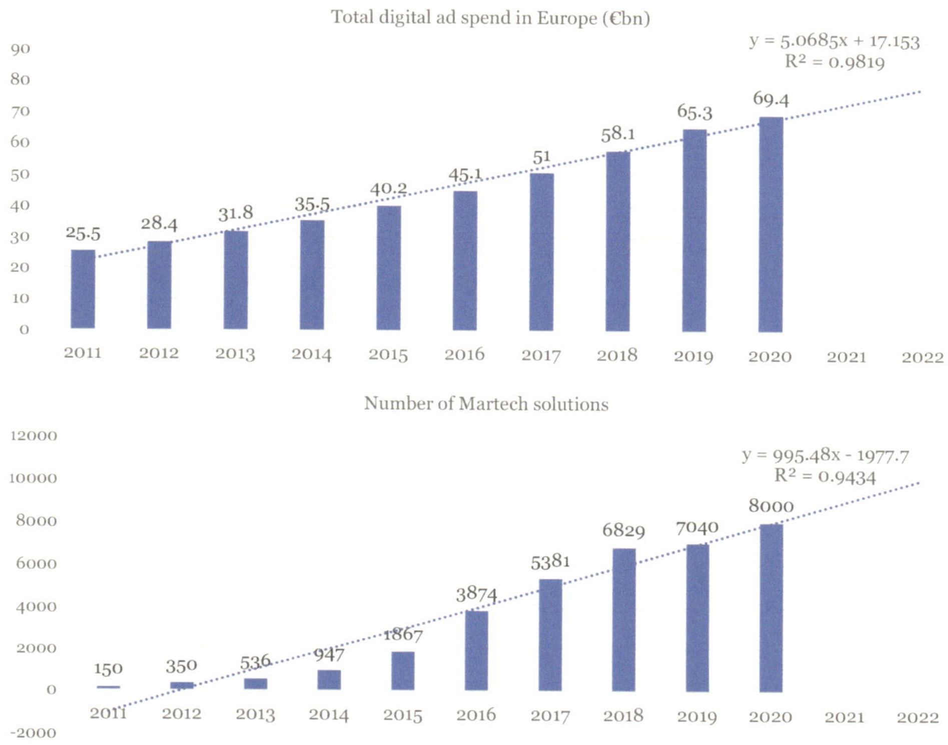

Figure 2.
Development of digital technologies in business and society [5, 6].

key objectives have to be harmonized with strategic goals and ethical codes acceptable in a society and must help to receive maximum economic and social effects.

Basic hypotheses of marketing management are as follows:

- A company functions within the environment having limited resources that stimulates its permanent struggle for survival. (According to survival theory, a company continuously adjusts and changes its fighting methods, but the essence is left unchangeable [7]).

- Marketing management contains a large number of elements bounded to each other and creating a definite integrity. (According to system theory, it characterizes patterns of creation, functioning and development [8]).

- A company functions within a society where people try to get a definite benefit from their lives. (According to Adam Smith's theory, private interests of people stimulate the level of their performance and individual development and also define the overall well-being [9]).

- Marketing management contains a complex of dynamic objectives, and to achieve strategic goals, optimal distribution of resources by each of them is required. (According to Pareto optimality theory, this is the achievement of such a condition when it is impossible to improve one business process without worsening of another one [10]).

- Marketing management best achieves established goals by arrangement of free and competitive exchange between all participants based on individual freedom principle. (According to individual choice theory, people are responsible for their own actions and are able to find the best way of interaction that can be reached if there are benefits for both parties [11]).

- Strategic decisions in marketing management are made by subjects entrusted with governing authorities after a collective discussion. (According to Arrow's impossibility theorem, it is impossible to participate in making a collective decision based on the common priorities without taking into account individual priorities [12]).

Consequently, the mathematical function of possibility to implement marketing management within a company is complex, dynamic, pluralistic and tolerant to the diversity of economic and social regulations.

Any business activity is realized to achieve a result. In marketing management, the main results are the achievement of commercial effectiveness and receiving a social effect. Implementation of the first goal allows a company to maintain balanced development, to provide an optimal level of profitability and income from its business activity, and to increase the volumes of selling goods, services or ideas at a definite level. At the same time, implementation of the second goal helps a company to achieve a certain social effect, namely to create a definite need or destroy it, to teach customers how to use products in all possible cases and in optimal volumes, to assign a definite status or fashion to products [13]. The mentioned company marketing management goals need a significant adjustment to specific requirements of main process participants that form five levels of approval (**Table 1**).

Therefore, major company marketing management goals have a certain hierarchy and structure. Economic goals more refer to company's commodity, distribution and price policies. Social goals are focused on achieving a definite effect by psychological impact of marketing events on consumer mentality and behavior, a general impression from a product. When implementing marketing management within a company, all goals approved at the mentioned five levels shall be optimally bounded to each other.

2.3 Up-to-date marketing management model in digital transformation of business and society

Digital transformation had an impact on companies' business processes. Transparent, clear and consequent communication allowed flexible interacting with a wide circle of customers and partners attracting the new and maintaining the current ones. To a certain extent, the modern marketing cannot exist without innovative technologies and products. This area is actively developing, and by now, there have been hundreds of digital tools for reducing the risks of making inefficient managerial decisions and increasing performance of employees. Technologies are becoming a much more significant component of marketing management, and there appear new digital tools to control the task fulfillment, employee motivation, arrangement and coordination of business processes. Correspondingly, managerial staff have to create such a marketing management model in digital transformation, which will become a competitive advantage of a company and enable to respond the market needs rapidly and flexibly. Nowadays, it is not enough to choose any innovative tool and test it. It is necessary to comprehensively implement a carefully chosen technology into a

Levels of approval		Major company marketing management goals	
		Commercial effectiveness	**Social effect**
1	Goals of company owners or managerial staff	• Profitability • Efficiency • Increase of a market share • Financial stability • Economic activity development	• Formation of consumer priorities • Positioning at the market • Awareness of goods, services and ideas • A product or a company status
2	Partner goals	• Maintenance of commercial effectiveness • Achievement of joint commercial goals • Mutual support • Joint project financing	• Creation or support of a definite need or a social effect • Maintenance of a product awareness • Conducting joint social events
3	Consumer goals	• Product quality and design • Less expenses on buying and servicing • Optimal balance "price/quality" • Comfort of buying and using	• Product manufacturing or safe use • Prestige or fashion • Esthetics and environment friendliness
4	Employee goals	• Increase of the wages and salaries fund • Optimal loading • Bonuses for improved results • Carrier development	• Work satisfaction • Social protection • Personal development • Social integration
5	Society goals	• Increased number of jobs • Preventing receipt of super profits • Social project financing	• Formation of definite perception • Attitude to the political climate • Social recognition

Table 1.
Major company marketing management goals by levels of approval.

company's activity and integrate technologies, products and systems at all levels. The up-to-date marketing management model in digital transformation of business and society is schematically presented on **Figure 3**.

The first block "Mission, vision, strategy of a company" is a key component of justifying the marketing management model. The strategy has to cover all business processes of a company, to set up internal and external communication channels and help to receive maximum economic and social effects. Strategic level of marketing management characterizes the process of long-term planning (for 1 year or more) and is focused on the development of strategies or scenarios for provision of company competitiveness and performance in the future. Tactic level of marketing management defines the process of short-term planning (for the period from a month to 1 year). At this stage, a strategy is detailed in compliance with modern realities, the current marketing conditions and business processes are analyzed, the planned indicators are established to provide the certain level of income and the order of actions is regulated to achieve company's strategic goals. Operational level of marketing management is realized by making a plenty of administrative decisions in all business areas in the real time.

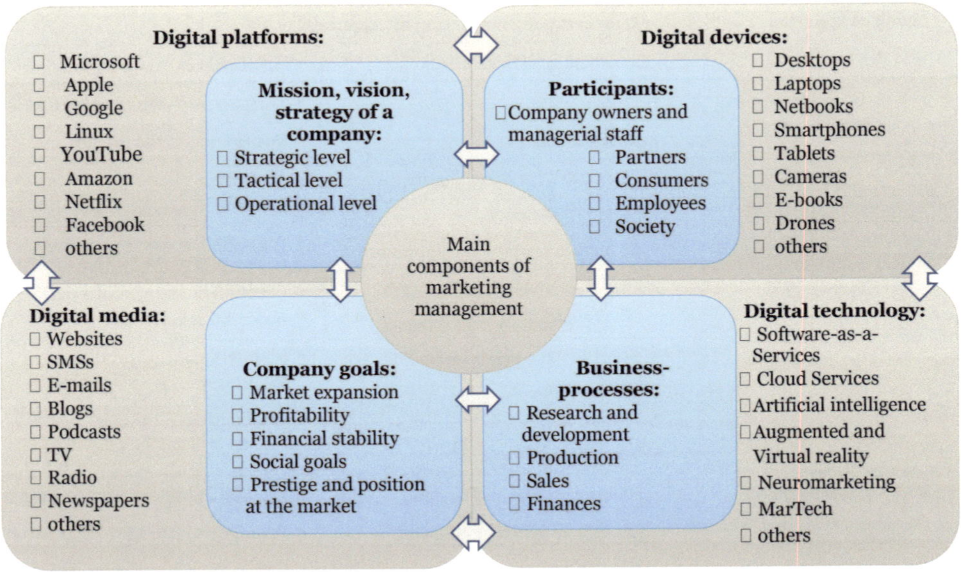

Figure 3.
The marketing management model in digital transformation of business and society.

The second block "Participants" covers the subjects of marketing management. For successful realization of a company's strategy, it is necessary to have a team of professionals who help to implement new digital tools into activities of all employees. Having received required skills, managerial staff and employees develop an innovative management system and stimulate digital communication with partners, customers and a society. This block is closely connected with the major marketing management goals at a company by levels of approval (**Table 1**). The first level is characterized by a dilemma of company owners and managerial staff regarding the effectiveness. At the next levels, marketing management goals are harmonized with partner agreements, customer requirements and wishes, company employee goals, society requirements and expectations [14–16]. Therefore, major marketing management goals have a definite hierarchy and structure.

The third block "Company goals" contains the following major marketing management goals: market expansion, profitability, financial stability, social goals, prestige and position at the market. They can be conditionally divided into two components—economic and social goals. Economic goals more refer to commodity, distributive and price policies of a company. The key market expansion indicators are a market share, a turnover, a role and significance of goods or services, new market volumes. To evaluate the profitability level, managerial staff analyzes profitability, reverse profitability, return on equity and return on total capital. To the key, financial stability indicators belong the following ones: creditworthiness, liquidity, self-financing structure, capital structure. Social goals are focused on gaining a certain effect through a psychological impact of marketing events on customer mentality and behavior, a general impression from a product. When defining a social effect, managers analyze employees' satisfaction with their work, wages, carrier development, social protection and social integration. At the same time, key indicators used to evaluate the prestige and position at the market are independence, image, political climate and social recognition. When marketing management is implemented within a company, all goals shall be optimally harmonized with each other.

The fourth block "Business-processes" contains the following main components: research and development, production, sales and finances. On the one hand, these are processes of planning, implementation, realization, correction and cancelation of fulfillment of managerial staff's decisions by company employees. On the other hand, these are the processes of interaction between technologies and systems, which provide digital optimization, operation of different devices, equipment operation speed, usability of interfaces, etc.

The mentioned four blocks of marketing management lie in the digital contour: digital devices ⇔ digital platforms ⇔ digital media ⇔ digital technologies. Nowadays, it is really difficult to separate decisions in business made by a human from technological solutions. Most decisions made by managerial staff are grounded on the analysis of databases and preventive digital models with the use of certain platforms and devices. Realization of business processes by company employees is impossible without digital media and technologies. The company's capability to propose a more personalized approach to each participant is a unique key to the use of innovative technologies and products. Accumulation of databases helps a company to better understand requirements and wishes of employees, partners, customers and a society in different regions. Quality analysis of available data performed by managerial staff allows to form a clearer mission, vision, strategy and goals. Effective realization of goals and tasks by employees creates more personalized suggestions of new technologies and products.

2.4 The use of digital technologies by millennials in their everyday lives

Unlike the senior consumers, millennials—the youth aged from 18 to 25 years old, who were born at the turn of the century (from 1997 up to 2003)—have different rational, emotional and behavioral responses to buying goods or services. Spread of the Internet, availability of devices, development of digital platforms, launching social media and applications were favorable for emergence of the audience with specific expectations for products according to their lifestyle. As a result of society digitalization, millennials are interested in the basic function of goods and services; however, they have specific emotional expectations for similar products.

To analyze emotional, rational and behavioral responses of the youth when buying goods or services, a pilot research was carried out among 350 respondents who gave answers to 100 questions divided into five blocks: (1) the use of digital technologies in everyday life; (2) areas of using augmented and virtual reality technologies; (3) buying goods and services online; (4) advantages and disadvantages of using devices, software and platforms and (5) responses to the use of digital technologies in everyday life. Summarized data on millennial responses to the use of digital technologies in different spheres of life are represented on **Figure 4**.

The answers of each respondent were summarized by each question and ranked in descending order. It enabled to distinguish three groups of millennials depending on a level of using digital technologies in different spheres of life: the first group (25%, 88 people)—the youth actively using digital technologies in all spheres of life; the second group (50%, 174 people)—the respondents using digital technologies for work, communication and buying certain goods and services; and the third group (25%, 88 people)—the millennials using digital technologies in certain spheres of their lives only if applicable.

The research results have demonstrated that young people (93%) understand the idea of augmented and virtual reality technologies. For the respondents who did not

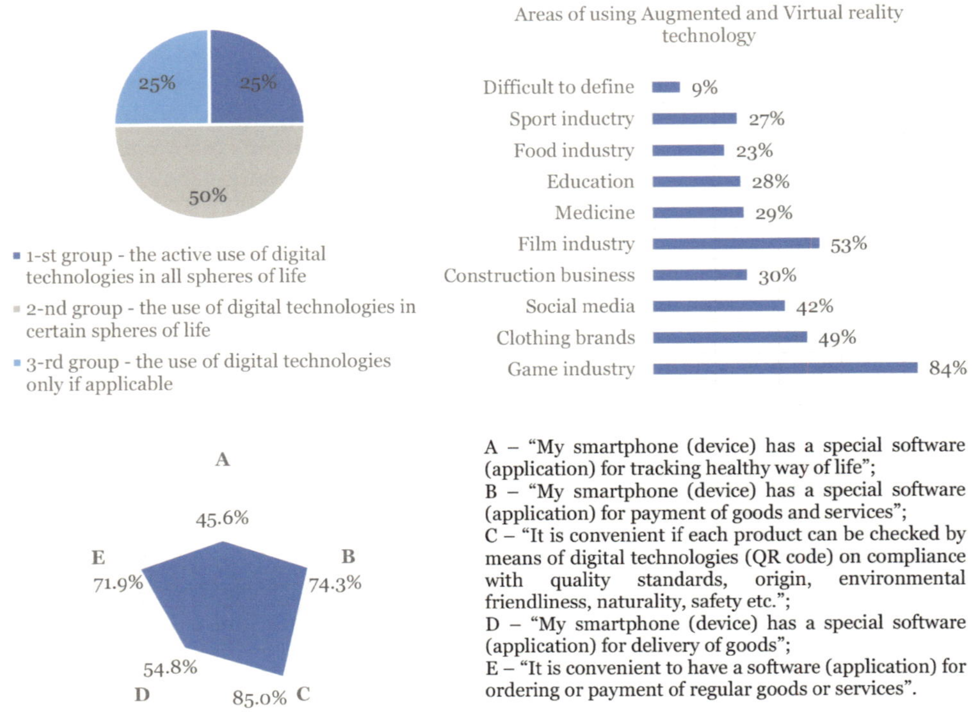

Figure 4.
Millennial responses to the use of digital technologies in different spheres of life (pilot research data).

know these technologies, the researches clarified the idea and demonstrated the variants of their application on definite examples. As for possible sphere of application of AR/VR technologies, it was established that most of respondents associate augmented and virtual reality with the game industry (84%), film industry (53%), clothing brands (49%) and social media (42%). Simultaneously, millennials less perceive the above-mentioned technologies in the food industry (23%), sport industry (27.5%), education (28%), medicine (29%) and construction business (30%). Only 9% of respondents could not define the place of AR/VR technologies in their everyday lives.

During the research, the respondents also evaluated statements characterizing their perception according to the scale: 0 points—strongly disagree with the statement; 2.5 points—rather disagree; 5 points—difficult to define (neutral position); 7.5 points—rather agree with the statement; 10 points—strongly agree. It helped to find out that most millennials (85%) wish to have an opportunity to check goods and services using digital technologies (QR code) on compliance with quality standards, origin, environmental friendliness, naturality, safety, etc. Most respondents (over 70%) have a special software for the payment of goods and services in their smartphones and wish to install an application for ordering and payment of regular goods and services. A half of young people (54%) use a special software for delivery of goods and only 45% of respondents use special applications for tracking healthy way of life.

According to the results of the survey, it was found out that all respondents visited online marketplaces, and 95% of them bought goods or services online. One-third of millennials (34%) buy goods on marketplaces monthly. An additional research allowed to reveal that 95% of young people agree to buy a product if it has a confirmation of authenticity from a brand manufacturer. Therefore, a negative stereotype about sales of fake products on marketplaces can be corrected by placement of detailed product characteristics and establishment of trustful open relationships with customers and partners.

2.5 Directions of marketing management innovation development

Marketing management innovation depends on the development of digital technologies, as they form a new lifestyle and change a view of a society creating competitive benefits for companies. Globalization and technologies have become two main factors, which define relations inside a society nowadays [17]. Correspondingly, the up-to-date marketing management strategy is grounded on multivariate choice of solutions regarding the use of definite innovative developments. That is, for realization of successful activity in digital transformation of business and society, a company permanently has to monitor the market and new tools, analyze customer needs and wishes, and maintain efficient communication with its partners.

Among the main marketing management innovation technologies can be distinguished: (1) artificial intelligence; (2) augmented and virtual reality; (3) neuromarketing and (4) MarTech. Further, we will consider them in detail.

The first innovative technology is the formation of artificial intelligence that is favorable for a company's uninterrupted interaction with customers, partners, employees and a society as a whole and helps to foresee peoples' intentions in different spheres of their lives and in different conditions. Artificial intelligence analyzes data and profiles, forms algorithms for better interaction and communication, systematizes required data providing maximum effectiveness and speed of making managerial solutions. In their activities, companies can use different variants, such as:

- voice processing technologies (e.g., virtual assistants for employees, partners and customers, which accompany the fulfillment of established tasks, handle orders, invite to joint events, recommend certain goods or services, evaluate effectiveness and loyalty);

- text processing technologies (e.g., virtual assistants, which reveal conflict situations and form algorithms of their solutions, develop marketing campaigns or different modifications of products basing on analysis of texts in social media, develop, analyze and reply to requests of customers, employees or partners);

- image recognition and processing technologies (e.g., recognition of faces to run certain business processes, definition of a health status grounding on mixing analysis of personal data with environment status data, analysis of images for a search and proposals of analogous goods, services or ideas);

- solutions making technologies (e.g., comparison of different alternatives for choosing a more efficient managerial decision, drawing up of an individual plan for personal development, career development, achievement of certain goals, motivation or rest).

The second innovative technology is augmented and virtual reality. Virtual reality is based on computer modeling of a three-dimensional image or environment where a human can interact with it if put on a special equipment (glasses, liens or helmet with a screen, a costume equipped with sensors). Augmented reality is a technology applying a computer reflection of imaginary additional product, idea or environment on a real image of a user, object or locality. Companies apply augmented and virtual reality technologies to design a customized product packaging (story living), and demonstrate test products under the real conditions of use (try before buy, location-based integration) [18–20]. To evaluate the effectiveness of implementing AR/VR technologies in marketing management, the following indicators are used: time of use, a number of actions, interaction with a content, a heat map, behavioral style, data of surveillance cameras, motility, quality of actions, voice timbre and modulation, tracking of eyes and body movements, understanding of further actions (preventions).

The third innovative technology is neuromarketing, which grounding on neurophysiological human behavior correlates and allows measuring human physiological and neuron signals to receive more clear representations about their motivation, wishes, decisions, etc. [21]. A neuromarketing technology combines a set of ways and methods of neuroscience and psychophysiology, namely, study of a brain, psychophysical reactions and behavioral features of a human. The mentioned researches are used in marketing management to analyze behavior of employees, partners, customers in different situations and conditions. The main neuromarketing tools can be conditionally divided into three groups [22–26]: (1) study of metabolic activities in brain (positron emission tomography and functional magnetic resonance imaging); (2) study of electrical activities in brain (transcranial magnetic stimulation, electroencephalography, magnetoencephalography, steady-state topography) and (3) study of physiological reactions (fixing of galvanic skin response, cardiovascular system, eye movement, contractions of facial muscles). Characteristics, advantages and disadvantages are given in **Table 2**.

The fourth innovative technology is MarTech combining marketing and technologies for gathering data on internal and external environment of a company. The choice of MarTech tools is an important component of development and realization of a company's successful strategy that permits to provide the optimal use of resources and harmonization of business processes. However, a tool must not substitute a strategy and implementation of digital technologies must not be just to pursuit technologies. The main MarTech tools can be conditionally divided into four groups [6]:

1. the management of data and digital assets of a company—the technologies, which store, control and maximally use digital data of a company to trace effectiveness of all business processes of marketing management and key performance indicators (KPI);

2. the management of relationships with customers—the technologies, which allow to control required structured data to maintain relationships with customers and partners;

3. the management of company's resources in separate spheres (marketing, financial, industrial, logistic, etc.)—the technologies, which are used for digital planning, administration, coordination and control of certain resources and combine data, procedures, tools and employees;

4. the management of social media and content—the technologies, which accumulate and analyze data of social media platforms to improve communication processes and increase recognizability of a company, a brand, a product, a service or an idea in a society.

Neuromarketing tools	Characteristics	Advantages and disadvantages
(1) Study of metabolic activities in brain		
Positron emission tomography	A method of medical radioisotope diagnostics grounding on application of radiopharmaceuticals being isotope-labeled and positron radiating. Using special equipment, decay of radionuclides is traced and metabolic activities in human brain are studied.	Advantages: a wide research spectrum; significant detailing of results, high-resolution anatomical images Disadvantages: high cost, a need in highly qualified specialists, psychological stress for an object of research, insignificant radiation effect
Functional magnetic resonance imaging	A method of medical diagnostics grounding on measuring hemodynamic responses caused by neuron activities in human brain. Using special equipment, correlation of cerebral blood flow and neuronal activity is traced	
(2) Study of electrical activities in brain		
Electroencephalography	A method of medical diagnostics grounding on graphical registration of biopotentials of human brain that permits to analyze physical maturity and state, general cerebral activity and its character. Using special equipment summarized, bioelectrical activity in human brain is fixed and analyzed	Advantages: a wide research spectrum; significant detailing of results, equipment mobility Disadvantages: limited resolution images, a need in highly qualified specialists, psychological stress for an object of research
Magnetoencephalography	A method of medical diagnostics grounding on measurement and visualization of magnet fields emerging as a result of electrical activity in human brain. Using special equipment helps to localize neuronal activity sources in time and space	
(3) Study of physiological reactions		
Fixing galvanic skin response	A method of diagnostics grounding on a human peculiarity to sweat while anxiety or experiencing other strong emotions. Using special equipment, the data on electrical conductivity of skin are fixed and interpreted into a conclusion about an emotional state of a human	Advantages: equipment mobility, low cost, significant detailing of results, a possibility of mixing with other tools Disadvantages: limited resolution research, a need in highly qualified specialists, psychological stress for an object of research
Fixing cardiovascular system response	A method of diagnostics grounding on monitoring of changes in heart rate, blood pressure and vascular tone. Using special equipment, the data on cardiovascular system are fixed and interpreted into a conclusion about a change of attention and emotional state of a human.	
Fixing eye movement response	A method of diagnostics grounding on video fixation of gaze direction, size of a pupil, duration of gaze delay. Using special equipment, the data on eye movement are fixed and interpreted into a conclusion about concentration of attention on the object, the order of data revision.	
Fixing contractions of facial muscles	A method of diagnostics grounding on monitoring of contractions of facial muscles. Using special equipment, the data on individual movements of facial mimic are fixed and interpreted into a conclusion about certain emotions or feelings of a human.	

Table 2.
Main neuromarketing tools [21–26].

Lately, the tools for the management of social media and content have been developing most actively. At the market, there are a large number of social platforms having a great many users, especially among millennials. Some of media platforms are universal and are spread all over the world, such as Facebook, Instagram, Twitter, TikTok, Pinterest, LinkedIn. But most of them have a certain specific and are popular among different target audiences or in definite regions and countries.

Among the most spread MarTech tools for the management of social media and content can be distinguished as follows:

- Google Analytics, which enables to verify the effectiveness of a marketing strategy at different levels of interaction with customers, partners and different audiences to accumulate and analyze databases;

- Sprinklr and Kontentino, which make it easier to work with social media and help a company to minimize staff loading in this sphere;

- Buffer, which permits to manage posts in different social networks to keep several online profiles from one information panel, to plan posts in advance and trace statistical databases;

- ManageFlitter, which administrates the management of Twitter subscribers and finds influencers, allows to cover more followers and plan posts, defines frequency of posts and analyzes statistical databases;

- Buzzsumo, which helps to monitor new tendencies, demonstrates most popular materials and trends, searches for influencers, recommends up-to-date social media platforms and materials for a target audience, defines an average number of posts by certain topics and forms detailed analysis;

- Canva, which permits to create a visual content for social networks and graphical design based on professionally developed templates and availability of various convenient tools;

- Bitly, which generates URL addresses with a limited number of signs and measures links and URL clicking indicators;

- Brandmaker, which helps to develop marketing campaigns of a company, calculate budgets, measure results;

- Contentpepper, which uses automated processes to generate company content by means of Content Management System (CMS), and send materials to a target audience to different websites and communication platforms.

When planning implementation of any digital technology, managerial staff's first steps are queries in search engines, comparison of sets of functions and prices, discussing advantages and disadvantages of a certain technology with professionals, testing a free demo version for checking the compliance with goals and specific of a company [27].

Different packages of software and platforms can be compared by their features, but a real value of software for marketing management lies in a strategy and approach to the achievement of key goals of a company or desirable end results. Before implementing a definite digital technology in company's activity, it must be harmonized with a mission, vision and strategy. Tools, equipment and systems cannot be in conflict with each other or double certain spheres and business functions. Managerial staff has to carefully study all details, evaluate advantages and disadvantages of implementing a new technology, define opportunities and threats and only after that they must make an optimal managerial decision, which will concern company's business processes, employees, partners, customers and even a society.

3. Conclusions

Considering a rapid progress of digital technologies, needs and wishes of a society are permanently changing. It determines the importance of implementing innovative marketing management tools in company's business processes to solve a wide spectrum of tasks connected with a necessity of maintaining successful activity at the market. For complex evaluation of a company development status, now it is not enough for managerial staff to have the key economic quantitative indicators enabling to calculate expenses, revenues, incomes by separate operations, products, business units or processes. They have to be completed by qualitative indicators, which will help to define consumer priorities, staff loyalty, partner reliability, product positioning, uniqueness of goods or services, social recognition, etc. Consequently, the main goals of innovative marketing management conquering positions at the markets, which have not been developed yet, and increase of presence at already existing ones based on intellectual property, investments in research and development, innovative management methods, digital technologies in the care of employees, consumers, partners and a society as a whole.

Nowadays, the main marketing management innovations are connected with implementation of artificial intelligence, neuromarketing, augmented and virtual reality, marketing technologies MarTech in business processes of functionality. These technologies can be combined and applied in different spectrums of company's activity or various spheres of human life. Particularly, it can refer to millennials. The use of digital tools allows to analyze huge databases, detail results, develop preventive actions, predict future trends, test products, equipment or software, foresee consequences of decisions, find optimal variants of problem solutions, etc. Besides, innovative technologies help to study real requirements and wishes of people, reveal deep-seated needs and motives, balance different life spheres, test new ones, change habits, gain knowledge and skills, etc.

Therefore, marketing management and technologies are a certain symbiosis of people's decisions and digital data. That is why correct choice of digital tools in marketing management is impossible without clear understanding of a vision, mission, strategy and corporate values by managerial staff and employees. All these determine a choice of technologies and successful implementation due to consequent passing through five main stages. At the first stage, managerial staff accumulates the available actual information on different technological tools and solutions, analyzes their compliance with a mission, vision and strategies of a company, studies parameters of integration with other systems. At the second stage, an optimal technology is chosen that best meets business goals and tools start being implemented at strategic level. Implementation of new technologies at this level allows a company to evaluate an innovation focus, if it is necessary to correct, and define skills and competences required for staff's work. At the third stage, gradual implementation of innovative technologies in business processes of a company and active cooperation with IT specialists at each operation takes place. The main goal of technological marketing management at this stage is reduction of staff's time spends on training or advanced training due to creation of intuitively understood interfaces for users and digital materials to help in solving standard task algorithms. At the fourth stage equipment, devices, platforms and tools are integrated into one system. A new system has to cover all actual business processes and contains required functionality for perspective directions. At the fifth stage, managerial staff monitors and evaluates effectiveness of business processes, analyzes advantages and disadvantages, develops improvements and recommends new solutions to increase marketing management effectiveness. Thus, implementation of digital technologies in business processes of a company significantly depends on a team's motivation and belief in success of innovations.

Establishment of factors of digital transformation impact on business and society to form innovative approaches in management in accordance with the modern realities is a complex comprehensive problem. To solve this problem, we carried out a research, which can conditionally be divided into five stages: At the first stage, the main factors of digital transformation in business and society were established; at the second stage, the basic hypotheses of innovative marketing management were formulated; at the third stage, up-to-date marketing management concept in digital transformation of business and society was developed; at the fourth stage, the use of digital technologies by millennials in their everyday lives was analyzed; at the last fifth stage, the main four directions of marketing management innovation development were defined. The conducted research enabled to reveal that fast and active implementation of innovative tools by certain companies can lead to the occurrence of covert and open conflicts between millennials and the older generation that will have a negative impact on corporate culture and psychological climate in company staff. Therefore, innovation technologies and management model in digital transformation of business and society have to be implemented gradually in compliance with strategic priorities defined by a company.

Author details

Iryna Kovshova
National University of Kyiv-Mohyla Academy, Kyiv, Ukraine

*Address all correspondence to: iryna.kovshova@ukma.edu.ua

References

[1] Zubko T, Hanechko I, Trubei O, Afanasyev K. Determining the impact of digitalization on the economic security of trade [Internet]. 2021. Available from: http://journals.uran.ua/eejet/article/view/248230/247009. [Accessed: 19 January 2022]

[2] Fisher L. US Programmatic Ad Spending Forecast 2018 [Internet]. 2019. Available from: https://www.emarketer.com/content/us-programmatic-ad-spending-forecast-2018. [Accessed: 19 January 2022]

[3] Rinaldi J. Where is Video Marketing Going in 2019 and Beyond? [Internet]. 2019. Available from: https://www.impactplus.com/blog/video-marketing-in-2019-infographic. [Accessed: 19 January 2022]

[4] Wyzowl. Video Marketing Statistics 2021 [Internet]. 2021. Available from: https://www.wyzowl.com/video-marketing-statistics/. [Accessed: 19 January 2022]

[5] IAB Europe's AdEx Benchmark Report is the Definitive Guide to the State of the European Digital Advertising Market [Internet]. 2021. Available from: https://iabeurope.eu/all-news/iab-europe-releases-full-2020-adex-benchmark-report-to-reveal-digital-advertising-market-size/. [Accessed: 10 January 2022]

[6] Martech Market Size and Growth [Internet]. 2021. Available from: https://www.martechalliance.com/stories/what-is-martech. [Accessed: 10 January 2022]

[7] Daft R. Organization Theory & Design. 12th ed. Cambridge, MA: Cengage Learning; 2016. p. 736

[8] Bertalanffy L. Obshchaia teoriya sistem [General systems theory: Foundations, development, applications], Translated from English, System research. Yearbook, "Science," Moscow, Russia. 1969. p. 153

[9] Lambin J-J. Menedzhment, oriyentirovannyy na rynok [MARKET-DRIVEN MANAGEMENT Strategic & Operational Marketing], Translated from English V.B. Kolchanov, St.-Petersburg, Russia. 2007. p. 800

[10] Positselskaya L. Ravnovesiye i optimalnost po Pareto v shumnykh diskretnykh dueliakh s proizvolnym kolichestvom deystviy [Equilibrium and Pareto optimality in noisy discrete duels with an arbitrary number of actions] [Internet]. 2002. Available from: http://www.mathnet.ru/links/2d712883b22bedd3dd5cab2905e5029a/fpm700.pdf. [Accessed: 10 January 2022]

[11] Brodskiy B. Informatsionnaya teoriya individualnogo vybora [Information theory of individual choice] [Internet]. 2007. Available from: http://data.cemi.rssi.ru/GRAF/center/methodology/organization/download/infochoice1.pdf. [Accessed: 10 January 2022]

[12] Arrow Kenneth J. Kollektivnyu vybor i individualnye tsennosti [Social Choice and Individual Values], Translated from English, GU BSHE, Moscow, Russia. 2004. p. 202

[13] Kovshova I. Orhanizatsiya marketynhovoho menedzhmentu na pidpryyemstvi [Organization of marketing management at the enterprise]. 2017. Available from: https://economyandsociety.in.ua/journals/11_ukr/41.pdf. [Accessed: 10 January 2022]

[14] Laibson D, List J. Principles of (Behavioral) Economics [Internet]. 2015. Available from: https://www.aeaweb.org/articles?id=10.1257/aer.p20151047. [Accessed: 19 January 2022]

[15] Bordalo P, Coffman K, Gennaioli N, Shleifer A. Stereotypes [Internet]. 2016. Available from: https://scholar.harvard.edu/files/shleifer/files/stereotypes.qje_.october2016.pdf. [Accessed: 19 January 2022]

[16] Kapinus L, Labins'ka N, Skrigun N. Marketing Behavior of Buyers of Goods in the Marketplace [Internet]. 2020. Available from: https://doi.org/10.32782/2520-2200/2020-2-23. [Accessed: 19 January 2022]

[17] Levitt T. The Globalization of Markets, Harvard Business Review [Internet]. 1983. Available from: https://hbr.org/1983/05/the-globalization-of-markets. [Accessed: 10 January 2022]

[18] Hobbs R. Gucci Partners with Snapchat for AR Try-On [Internet]. 2020. Available from: https://www.stylus.com/gucci-partners-with-snapchat-for-ar-tryon. [Accessed: 19 January 2022]

[19] Bhattacharyta S. Lowe's is Using VR and AR to Get People into Stores [Internet]. 2018. Available from: https://digiday.com/?p=296460. [Accessed: 19 January 2022]

[20] Sharma R. SK Telecom Launches Augmented Reality (AR) Service Based on 5G Edge Cloud. [Internet]. 2021. Available from: https://www.thefastmode.com/services-and-innovations/17727-sk-telecom-launches-augmented-reality-ar-service-based-on-%20 5g-edge-cloud

[21] McClure S, Li J, Tomlin D. Neural correlates of behavioral preference for culturally familiar drinks. Neuron. 2004;**520**:379-387

[22] Zurawicki L. Neuromarketing: Exploring the Brain of the Consumer [Internet]. 2010. Available from: https://books.google.com.ua/books?hl=uk&lr=&id=gy45SfmuxK4C&oi=fnd&pg=PR3&dq=Exploring+The+Brain+For+Measuring+Consumer+Behavior&ots=1tTsP0gJd-&sig=Jo4CVjb8qU3vw6tSyXN1SjDFS-Zo&redir_esc=y#v=onepage&q=Exploring%20The%20Brain%20For%20Measuring%20Consumer%20Behavior&f=false. [Accessed: 10 January 2022]

[23] Ariely D, Berns G. Neuromarketing: The hope and hype of neuroimaging in business. Nature Reviews Neuroscience. 2010;**11**(4):284-292

[24] Banks S, Bellerose J, Douglas D, Jones-Gotman M. Bilateral skin conductance responses to emotional faces. Applied Psychophysiology and Biofeedback. 2012;**37**(3):145-152

[25] Fortunato V, Giraldi J, de Oliveira J. A review of studies on neuromarketing: Practical results, techniques. contributions and limitations. Journal of Consumer Marketing. 2014;**6**(2):201

[26] Zubko T, Kovshova I, Sydorenko O. Prospective Trends in Neuromarketing Tools of the Food Industry in View of Ukrainian Society Digitalization [Internet]. 2019. Available from: http://ekmair.ukma.edu.ua/bitstream/handle/123456789/17814/Zubko_Prospective_Trends_in_Neuromarketing_Tools.pdf?sequence=5. [Accessed: 19 January 2022]

[27] Kotler P, Kartajaya H, Setiawan I. Marketing 5.0: Technology for Humanity. John Wiley & Sons; 2021. p. 204

Chapter 9

Perspective Chapter: Data as Currency - On the Impact of ICTs and Data on the Saudi Economy and Industrial Sector

Kinda R. Dahlan, Ahmed A. Badawi and Ali Megahed

Abstract

In delineating successful digital application models in Saudi Arabia, this chapter explores the country's digital readiness to further expound its industrial strategic goals. We argue that a gap exists between the availability of data and technology and the availability of human capabilities that can facilitate the meaningful processing of industrial data. Data deluge brings substantial challenges in the collection and management of massive amounts of unstructured data towards decision making. Likewise, unprecedented production of information exceeds the ability of authoritative bodies to create regulations and policies that can keep up with these transformations in the nature of work. We explicate the impact of well-timed policies (fiscal and monetary), prediction of long-term structural changes in the industrial sector, industrial strategy formulation practices, and examine the economic studies and analysis of sustainable development in these areas.

Keywords: digital transformation strategy, Industry 4.0, data governance, digital readiness, Saudi Arabia

1. Introduction

The industrial sector plays a critical role in solving society's most pressing issues—from resource preservation, to climate change, to social stability. The adoption of industry 4.0 technologies and practices utilize data and favour circular production models that allow for better decision making, optimized resource usage and energy consumption. This requires round-the-clock data collection and adapted analytical frameworks managed under well-timed policies, both fiscal and monetary. To this effect, Saudi Arabia began turning its attention towards a sustainable model of economic growth aimed at propelling the Kingdom towards a new development trajectory guided by its national strategic vision—*Vision 2030*. This trajectory seeks to diversify national economy and promote industrial innovation, social well-being, and progress. With new modernization strategies in place, attention has been placed on developing a model of intricate economic systems, equipped with the latest technologies, for the industrial sector to reduce its dependency on oil and petrochemicals, and where data access and sharing is at the heart of innovation and successful digital transformation.

In delineating such digital application models in Saudi Arabia, this chapter explores the country's digital readiness to further expound the potential to achieve its industrial strategic goals. We argue that although the Kingdom has invested heavily in ICTs and telecoms infrastructure, a gap exists between the availability of data and technology and the availability of human capabilities that facilitate meaningful processing of industrial data. That is, there are two main hypotheses driving the research outlined in this chapter: (1) data deluge brings substantial challenges in the timely collection and processing of massive amounts of information and unstructured data towards decision making; (2) the unprecedented production of information exceeds available human capabilities and the ability of authoritative bodies to create regulations and policies that can keep up with these transformations.

This chapter explicates the impact of well-timed policies (fiscal and monetary), prediction of long-term structural changes in the industrial sector, industrial strategy formulation practices, and examine the economic studies and analysis of sustainable development in these areas to address these challenges. It begins with a description of the research methodology (Section 2), followed by an analysis of the Saudi national strategy detailing its aspirations for the industrial sector, the state of digital readiness in the country, and the availability of human capabilities to match these aspirations (Section 3). The following section, Section 4, provides an overview of how the COVID19 pandemic catalysed Saudi digital transformation efforts, and discusses the economic impact of data on the industrial sector given the global crisis. Section 5, highlights the successful utilization of ICTs in Saudi Arabia in light of further potential for development, and explores the alignment of these applications with the Saudi industrial strategic Vision 2030. Finally, we conclude with the potential of applying such technologies to the industrial sector by reviewing the macroeconomics of well-timed policies in this scope.

Our findings reveal that there are limitations in educational initiatives targeting digital upskilling to meet the needs of the aspirations of the national strategy. We have found that there are innovative efforts to address this gap within the Kingdom through various government-backed programs. We also observed that though foreign investment is gaining traction, knowledge transfer and exchange remains limited via these investments. Research also shows that traditional formal education remains the dominant national model in the Kingdom, limiting opportunities that arise from other educational streams. In conducting this research, the hope for this work is to highlight successful achievements to then draw attention to strategic areas of improvement over the next period, such as the production of globally competitive ICT products and services, alternative educational models, and directions to enhance the utilization of available data across different sectors and economic activities.

2. Method

The methodological goals of this research are to examine how aligned Saudi's strategic objectives are with its reported digital readiness and to shed light on its digital transformation journey in order to make recommendations for further development. The research methods adopted thus follow a *content analysis* framework whereby it is defined as "a careful, detailed, systematic examination and interpretation of a particular body of material in an effort to identify patters, themes, biases, and meanings"

[1]. As such, the axiology informing this normative methodology is based on a *critical hermeneutic* approach that establishes media resources (such as websites) as displays of society's most pressing concerns, interests, and values [2]. Within this scope, reasoning behind this research is *inductive*, whereby it moves from specific observations in data and information practices towards broader generalizations and theories. That is, we utilize a *purposive sampling* strategy of data [3] to analyse our findings *inductively* vis-à-vis a content analysis [1]. A methodology designed in this way establishes a regulatory framework that facilitates the extrapolation and assessment of extant information for the purpose of arriving at, and validating, new knowledge [4].

Given that this is a country-specific study, the body of material utilized is based on a non-probability sampling method of data sourced from two main resources: official Saudi Government databases and digital readiness indices published by not-for-profit (NFP) organizations. This is then supplemented by peer-reviewed research accessed through several databases. Saudi official sources include resources available through websites that end with *.gov.sa* in their URLs, while NFP resources include the UN Public Administration Network's (UNPAN) e-Government Readiness Index [5], the FitchSolutions Industry 4.0 Market Maturity Index [6], and the International Telecommunications Union's (ITU) Digital Opportunity Index (DOI) and the ICT Opportunity Index (ICT-OI) [7]. This allows for a comparative analysis between globally-available assessments of the Kingdom and its reported national objectives and achievements.

Because websites are media outlets, the researchers opted to use communication research methods in the research design. That is, communication research methodology provided a blueprint to examine *messages* that are transmitted through one or several components of the traditional model of communication: messages, people, channels, and contexts [1]. This includes "studying how new technologies affect the flow of information" where data is certainly a by-product of this process and thus central to the research at hand [1].

Further research was consulted in the literature review to include studies on Saudi Arabia. Because the sampling method is a non-probability purposive sampling, only materials that mention, discuss, or reference Saudi Arabia and related fields in ICTs, economy, data, and industrial manufacturing were selected; and because the corpus of this research is country-specific, the research discourse scheme is based on a discourse of "Saudi Arabia," "Industry 4.0," "technology," and "digital readiness." This includes word variations including *Saudi, Saudi Arabia, KSA, the Kingdom of Saudi Arabia, The Kingdom, Arabia, technology, ICT, ICTs, digital, data, Industry 4.0, industrial economy*. To better frame this research to fit the parameters of our research problem, a complimenting precedent-setting criterion was applied. Terms and sentences that denote national development, strategic objectives, public opportunity and achievements were taken into consideration in the selection process of journal articles. This non-probability purposive sampling scheme provides a reliable and reproducible method to examine other country-specific material in a similar fashion [8].

3. Saudi Arabia digital readiness and development

It is important to point out that there is no one-size-fits-all method to measure data and ICT readiness—let alone a means to determine the value of data as currency in general. Digital readiness for Saudi Arabia is determined from data accessed through several indices. Alongside these indices, this section examines the strategic national

Vision, popularized as *Vision 2030*, key strategic partnerships with tech-relevant companies, telecommunication infrastructure, data governance and accessibility, and available human capabilities. The following sub-sections delineate these key areas further.

3.1 The Saudi national strategy: vision 2030

Saudi Vision 2030 is a set of reforms categorized under 3 pillars, with 6 objectives that are translated into 11 vision-realization programs. Each objective under each pillar has a set of sub-objectives totalling to 27, which are then further divided into 96 strategic objectives. There are two key objectives outlined under each of the 3 pillars. The first pillar, *a vibrant society*, aims to (1) improve Saudi standard of living, through world-class healthcare and education systems, and (2) preserve and celebrate cultural heritage, and national identity. Some of its goals include increasing Umrah capacity, enhance entertainment avenues and increase spending in this sector, improve Saudi's ranking in the Social Capital Index, and increase average life expectancy. The second pillar, a *thriving economy*, has two more objectives: (1) to grow and diversify the economy, and (2) to increase employment and unlock business opportunities. The final pillar, an *ambitious nation*, seeks to (1) create a high-performing government to empower citizens, private sector, and not-for-profit organizations, and (2) to enable social responsibility. Goals under this pillar include raising Saudi's rank in the e-Government Survey Index from 36 to the top 5, raising Saudi's ranking in the Government Effectives index from 80 to 20, and increasing non-oil government revenue [9].

Digital transformation reforms and objectives are at the core of the second pillar, a *thriving economy*. According to the vision [10]:

> *"A sophisticated digital infrastructure is integral to today's advanced industrial activities. It attracts investors and enhances the fundamental competitiveness of the Saudi economy.*
>
> *We will partner with the private sector to develop the telecommunications and information technology infrastructure, especially high-speed broadband, expanding its coverage and capacity within and around cities and improving its quality.*
> *Our specific goal is to exceed 90% housing coverage in densely populated cities and 66% in other urban zones. We will also develop building standards to facilitate the extension of broadband networks.*
>
> *We will strengthen the governance of digital transformation through a national council. Additionally, we will improve our regulations and establish an effective partnership with telecom operators to better develop this critical infrastructure.*
> *We will also support local investments in the telecommunications and information technology sectors."*

Through its 11 vision realization programs, which include the Human Capability Development Program (CDP), the Public Investment Fund Program (PIF) the National Transformation Program (NTP), and the National Industrial Development and Logistics Program (NIDLP), Saudi has outlined key objectives relating to ICTs, technology, data accessibility, and industrial development. This includes, localizing technology and knowledge, building human capabilities, developing technological infrastructure, and facilitating e-services.

NIDLP for example, aims to transform the Kingdom into a leading industrial powerhouse as well as an international logistics platform in several sectors with a focus on applied internet technologies (a.k.a. Industry 4.0). This is meant to create more jobs, enhance trade balance, and maximize local content. NIDLP covers 4 sectors: industry, mining, energy, and logistics. PIF promotes local and international investment, fostering economic partnerships to deepen its impact beyond Saudi-borders, and bolstering various existing sectors with the latest technologies, including: healthcare, manufacturing, energy, and smart cities.

Another key component of the Saudi Arabian Vision 2030 strategy for digital transformation is to "realize a smart government" through the Digital Government Authority. The Saudi government recognizes the value of data for a knowledge-hungry economy and a growing immersive e-commerce ecosystem that is charged by its, predominantly, young population. As of 2020, and summarized in **Figure 1**, the largest age group of the 35+ million Saudi population is the 35 to 39 group [11]. Of the total population, 69% are younger than 40. This age group is technologically literate and make up the bulk of users targeted by e-government programs. In response, the government has developed a national strategy for digital transformation [12] and has been investing heavily in telecommunication systems and Information and Communication Technologies (ICTs) over the past decade.

For Saudi Arabia to achieve such ambitious goals, outlined in Vision 2030 [9], to improve public services, diversify its economy, and identify societal needs, it must also incorporate processes that leverage on data access and analytics. In line with this new direction to modernize and grow its industrial sector, Saudi Arabia has established the Saudi Authority for Industrial Cities and Technology Zones (MODON), funded several mega projects in the form of industrial cities (e.g., Oxagon), smart cities (e.g., NEOM), and programs (e.g., NIDLP). Technology is central to these new initiatives, shaped by unprecedented capabilities and applications of Industry 4.0 and Artificial intelligence (AI) technologies such as machine learning,

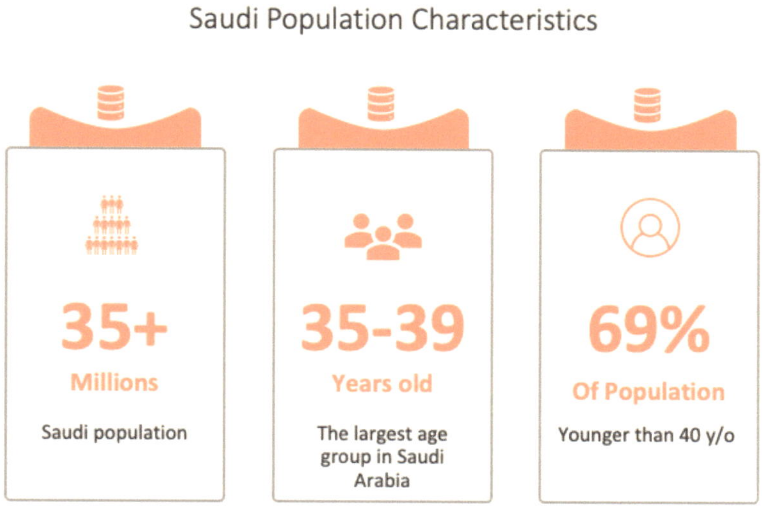

Figure 1.
Saudi Arabia Demographics. The figure depicts highlights the total population, largest age group, and percent of youth within population in 2020. Copyrights: Ali Megahed 2021.

internet of things (IoT), and Big Data analysis. Immediately, this offers growth opportunities for less data-intensive fields such as manufacturing and construction [13]. This trajectory also emphasizes sectoral digital transformation strategies reliant on data that are valid, reliable, and sustainable.

As process, digital transformation creates disruption that triggers strategic responses to value-creation paths in industry and manufacturing operations. It also impacts structural changes and surfaces new organizational barriers affecting process outcomes. The industrial sector in Saudi Arabia for instance, through MODON, is increasingly adopting disruptive technologies to utilize the abundance of available data as part of its strategic aspirations to compete in a data-driven global market. Overall, Saudi industry is a key driver in regional economic and social transitions currently taking place. Alongside its digital transformation strategy, the Kingdom has announced plans for its green renewable energy initiative as of 2021 [14].

In order to remain an engine of prosperity, the Kingdom is investing massively in these areas and in moving toward Industry 5.0 technologies with a vision that aims beyond efficiency and productivity. Compared to Industry 4.0 (i4.0), Industry 5.0 (i5.0) emphasizes research and innovation towards human-centric and sustainable industry. Multiple Saudi entities have been looking at educational partnership through signed agreements with academic institutions to transition from i4.0 to i5.0. King Abdullah University of Science and Technology (KAUST) and King Abdulaziz University are at the forefront with active agreements with international academic institutions and with a variety of government research entities to support and implement research projects that serve the industrial sector and contribute to creating a knowledge-based economy through scientific research. The Saudi government has also signed an agreement with the World Economic Forum (WEF) to establish an in-Kingdom branch of WEF's Centre for the Fourth Industrial Revolution, the fifth of its kind worldwide [15]. This involves cooperation between WEF and King Abdulaziz City for Science and Technology (KACST) to manage the center, which aims to develop mechanisms, plans, and applications for Industry 4.0 nationally. This includes awareness and governance plans that support the adoption of technology and best practices regionally and globally, positioning Saudi well within the global 4th Industrial Revolution network, along with countries such as India and China. The center also acts as a platform for further cooperation opportunities with other government agencies and institutions to develop solutions and support capacity building, skill advancement and other competencies as they relate to Industry 4.0 [16].

3.2 On Saudi data governance and accessibility

The successful implementation of the Saudi national strategy and its programs relies heavily on data and information. This section describes critical issues surrounding data governance and accessibility in Saudi Arabia.

Ostensibly, data are critical for production. Unlike labour and capital—or oil, in the context of Saudi Arabia—data are a non-depletable resource that can be reused again and again for different purposes, in different contexts. The value of data, arguably, increases the more it is used [17]. For Saudi Arabia, the use of its public social data, and the integration between different applications, has resulted in the creation of an array of government services. Even so, despite being non-depletable, data can become less relevant with time, thereby reducing its value. Data characteristics have a direct corelation to their value. Data that cannot be used, are inaccessible, or otherwise cannot be parsed or processed have little value.

Understanding these characteristics and employing the right human capabilities can turn a single data point, with little value, into a repurposed value-multiplying commodity that has meaning and context when "aggregated and analysed with other relevant data" [18]. Accumulating data enhances productivity and enhances decision making. Opening it up for greater access has the promise of greater innovation when more firms are able to use it and compete in generating knowledge.

In the industrial sector, the high-capital intensity and necessary control over operating costs stands to benefit from automation in remote areas through the utilization of sophisticated technological solutions that produce reliable and unbiased information. As it stands, and given the harsh desert climate and inaccessible remote terrain in Saudi Arabia, such remote areas are typically manageable by "powerful companies" that are capable of bearing the risks of carrying these projects out—financially and technically. More data can cut down cost, opening up further opportunities for small and medium sized entities (SMEs) to compete [17].

Needless to say, companies that generate large datasets have incentive to hold on to their assets, stifling the potential of open access data for fair competition and innovation. This not only reduces the social benefits of data access, but also threatens privacy and ethical usage of data. As there are types of data, utilized for different purposes, there are different types of disadvantages. For personal information, generated through social data, an individual is at a disadvantage when her/his/their information is transacted in an unsafe way or without their knowledge. Protecting such information is expensive and complicated, and for the most part, the law has not caught up with the complexities surrounding data. Governments, in turn, should work towards deploying policies that encourage data sharing to promote competition and innovation, and to protect privacy.

Big Data for instance, is rapidly becoming a common approach as the range of variables for industrial indicators are expanded. However, access to such data depends on (a) access to sizable data, and, of course, (b) data that is optimized through cloud computing and services. This means that cooperation between various entities, especially across borders becomes essential. Although countries are moving towards centralizing information to make use of "the cloud" (e.g., European Union Cohesion Policy [19, 20]) Saudi has chosen to adopt an edge model by imposing strict localization regulations for government and public data [19].

This comes in light of several strategic steps that were taken to ensure the privacy and protection of personal data as the country competes to become a contender in efficient implementation of Industry 4.0, AI, and in growing its data assets. In 2020, SDAIA announced its National Strategy for Data and Artificial Intelligence (NSDAI), and in 2021, the National Data Management Office (NDMO), promising a strategic roadmap for disruptive technology integration into the healthcare, energy, logistic, and government sectors, and regulations for the management and digitization of data as a national asset[1]. this enables the protection of personal and sensitive data, by developing required strategies, laws, policies and regulations to ensure their application and compliance. Such an integration brings into focus major issues of privacy, competition, and stability.

That is, traditionally, these issues have been handled by separate ministries, and only recently subject to integrated approaches to effective data policy that manage complex trade-offs. The NDMO [21], established in 2019 as a sub-entity of SDAIA,

---

[1] Find out more about the NDMO at https://sdaia.gov.sa/ndmo/?Lang=en.

released a variety of regulations to oversee and regulate data management across all government and semi-government entities. Similarly, the personal data protection law (PDPL), issued in September 2021, is the first of its kind [22] in the country. It is proceeded by the 2020 Communication and Information Technology Commission (CITC) regulations surrounding user data privacy within the telecoms sector [23]. Through a royal decree No. (M/19) and cabinet resolution No. (98), the PDPL is designed to protect the privacy of personal data and regulate data sharing practices to prevent privacy breaches and abuse of information given how quickly data sharing happens, how opaque data market are, and the more digital literate the country becomes. The law outlines obligations, limitation, accountability, and penalization policies surrounding data use. It also draws out the roles and responsibilities for data collectors and users to register, update, and maintain data processing records and rights. This also applies to non-Saudi companies operating within Kingdom or those processing Saudi data.

Saudi also applied restrictions on cross-border data transfers that require approval for data processing by designated government authorities. Any data controller must register with SDAIA through a paid membership plan. As mentioned earlier, Saudi has one of the strictest localization laws globally. It requires foreign companies without local presence to appoint a local representative that is licensed to process its data within Kingdom by 2023. This new law encompasses the processing of personal data which includes financial, genetic, credit, health, and otherwise private information as set forth by the local Shari'ah law.

According to SDAIA, further regulations are to be set as the Kingdom completes its inventory of data needs and requirements. What is of interest here is that the law requires companies to inform SDAIA of any breaches or data leakage, which then notifies concerned subjects. When it comes to the associated penalization framework, the law outlines up to 2 years of imprisonment coupled with fines of up to SR3 million Saudi Riyals (Approx. $ 800K USD) [22].

3.3 On Saudi strategic tech-partnerships

When it comes to partnerships, Saudi Arabia boasts several strategic partnerships regionally, globally, as well as across various national governmental and private entities as touched upon in Section 3.1. It began with the country's National Center for Artificial Intelligence (NCAI) signing agreements with China's Huawei and Alibaba Cloud to design AI-related Arabic-language systems. Saudi Arabia also has an agreement with IBM to implement blockchain applications for government and commercial services [5]. The Saudi Data and Artificial Intelligence Authority (SDAIA) also secured key strategic partnerships with The World Bank to help countries create "policies and initiatives that use AI to support national development and growth" [24]. These efforts focus on identifying gaps in readiness to accelerate the creation of AI policies and innovation that support sustainable development goals as well as newly-established governance frameworks. SDAIA also partnered with the International Telecommunication Union (ITU) to collaborate on designing AI applications for the sustainable development of new projects, initiatives, and activities to facilitate international cooperation and knowledge sharing that meet UN goals. In 2020, the Saudi Telecoms Company (STC) announced its partnership with US-based tech company Nvidia to build the Kingdom's first AI and deep learning cloud infrastructure, becoming the first cloud service provider in the region to offer AI-capabilities in the country [6, 24].

3.4 On Saudi telecommunication infrastructure

In terms of its infrastructural readiness, Saudi Arabia is ranked amongst the top. Currently, it boasts a strong telecoms infrastructure that is imperative for the successful implementation of an Industry 4.0 ecosystem. According to a FitchSolutions report, the Kingdom has a robust 5G coverage as of Q2-21 [24]. All network operators offer 4G LTE services, while STC and Zain have launched 5G services in 2019. Opportunities that arise from a stable 5G network include long-term industrial growth prospects, especially in major connected and smart-cities initiatives. According to the report, "[n]ew investment in 'smart-cities' may bolster telecommunications connectivity in the country if implemented and lead to a faster uptake of advanced technologies in the kingdom" supporting the growth and development of AI in the country. At a glance, Saudi Arabia ranks second, after China, in terms of its investment in AI technology [5].

Partnering up with the private sector, the government succeeded in the provision of fibreoptic network coverage to more than 3.5 million homes in 2020, and overall telecom services to 100% of households [12], 99% of which are covered by at least 3G mobile network, and 98% covered by 4G network [7]. This includes broadband for 576k homes in rural and remote areas [12]. Worthy of note here is that Saudi "is one of only two GCC countries in which nationals outnumber foreigners, accounting for 69% of the population" [25]. The data comparing mobile and fixed telephone subscriptions is telling in that more and more individuals have access to smartphone technology, thereby access to the Internet [7] at 98% of the total population with Internet access. Saudi Arabia also boasts a youthful population that is expected to contribute to the uptake of new technologies and best practices, where the age range between 15-24 make up the majority of internet users since 2017 (99% [7], 93% for 25-75 years old; 92% for age group <15; no information is available about data access for the age group 75+). **Figure 2** summarizes the main strengthens of the Saudi telecom infrastructure as of 2021 in relation to its population.

Another Fitch report also highlighted the significance of access allocation by the Saudi Communications and Information Technology Commission (CITC) to approximately 23GHz of spectrum; "CITC will allow license-exempt access to the entirety of

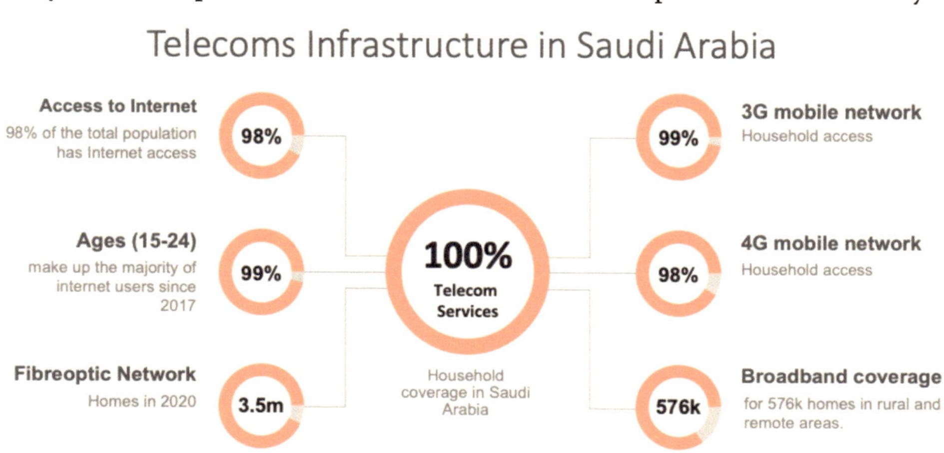

Figure 2.
Saudi Arabia Telecommunication Infrastructure at a Glance. The figure summarizes the main advancement in telecoms in Saudi Arabia as of 2021 where it boasts 100% coverage for all households. Copyrights: Ali Megahed 2021.

the 6GHz band, a move which is expected to facilitate the wider deployment of broadband services" [6]. This allocation of additional spectrum demonstrates the Kingdom's awareness of the importance of, and the intense demand for, data, which has escalated over recent years with the growth of Industry 4.0 technologies. This technological proliferation is expected to continue—especially in light of the pandemic, and facilitated by Saudi's digitization programs [6]. Operators such as STC will benefit from the development of new use cases for Internet-based technologies, bolstered by government support. This push for digital transformation will in turn raise the profile of diverse sector-led industries.

Another key achievement in developing the Industry 4.0 ecosystem is the development of technological regulations. CITC has successfully developed regulations for cloud computing, with guidelines that will extend to IoT and AI [6]. According to the FitchSolutions Industry 4.0 Market Maturity Index, Saudi Arabia comes in second regionally, "with a total score of 40.6 points out of a potential 100" [6]. The Kingdom also does relatively well in terms of "readiness to realize Industry 4.0." Analysis from the report shows that Saudi already leads regionally in the *demand* pillar of the index, showcasing its strong commitment to investing in disruptive technologies.

Saudi Arabia's technological and telecoms infrastructure enhances its appeal to tech investors globally through its readiness to deploy WIFI 6 [6]. This is significant because it has risen from a bandwidth-deficient market in only 5 years (since 2016), achieving a remarkable spectrum increase of 226% (from 340MHz to 1,110MHz) according to a MENA Telecoms Risk/Reward Index [6]. Saudi Arabia has paved the way as a pioneer and as the first country in the EMEA region "to designate 6GHz band completely for license-exempt use [6]. This also sets the stage for lucrative partnerships with operators and other entities to improve high-speed broadband coverage in unserved areas, allowing services to reach more factory and industrial sites: an "infrastructure development pipeline will bode well for national technological uptake over the coming decade" [24], whereby the number of enterprises and foreign investment will grow rapidly in the coming years.

The robust infrastructure is no surprise, given that Saudi is one of a handful of countries that mandates the localization of data to ensure data security and domestic digital infrastructure [19]. In fact, the more advanced data-oriented technologies become, the higher the expectations are for stringent data transfer restrictions to be embedded in cybersecurity laws and policies in order to safeguard data [19]. During the COVID19 pandemic, and as a result of infrastructural readiness, internet traffic rose by 30% in Saudi Arabia—doubling traffic through the Saudi Arabian Internet Exchange (SAIX). Internet speed in the Kingdom also increased to 109 Mbps in 2020 from 9Mbps in 2017. Likewise, Saudi successfully completed the expansion of network coverage at the Holy Mosque in Makkah to support annual pilgrimage and Umrah [12]—an annual religious event with high-intensity network usage, within a relatively small geographic space, during a narrow timeframe.

3.5 On Saudi digital index rankings

Different indices and reports exist for an array of data categories. While they diverge, there are common elements between them. The international community, through UN membership, recognizes the importance of the availability of proper indicators for the design and implementation of ICT and data policies that are efficient and effective in bridging the digital divide and aiding countries in utilizing technology to develop their industrial sectors better. According to the Tunis Agenda of the World

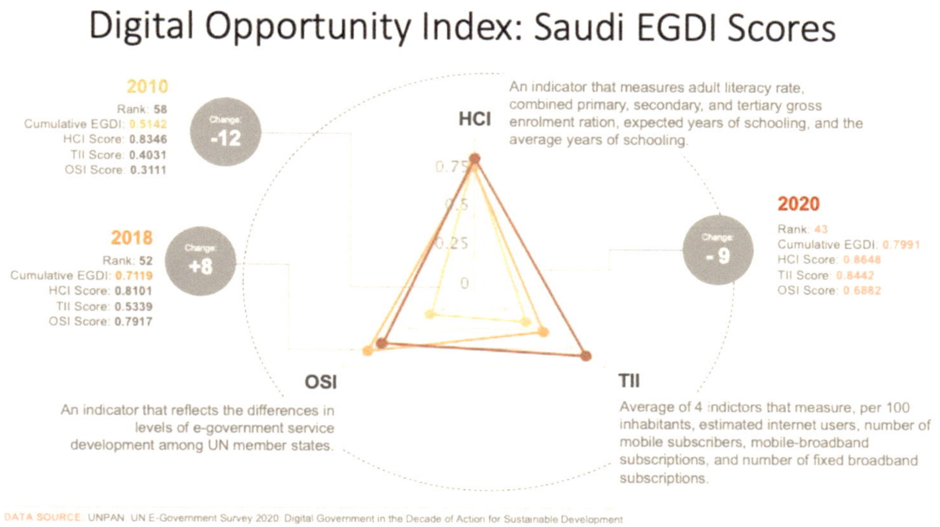

Figure 3.
E-government development (EGDI): Saudi ranking. The figure summarizes Saudi Arabia's e-government development scores for three indicators in 2020, out of 193 assessed countries, as per UNPAN data. Copyrights: Kinda Dahlan 2021.

Summit on Information Society, "[t]he development of ICT indicators is important for measuring the digital divide." [26]. Some of the key indices used in this analysis include the UN Public Administration Network's (UNPAN) e-Government Readiness Index [5], the FitchSolutions Industry 4.0 Market Maturity Index [6], and the International Telecommunications Union's (ITU) Digital Opportunity Index (DOI) and the ICT Opportunity Index (ICT-OI) [7].

In terms of e-government development (EGDI), summarized in **Figure 3**, Saudi ranked as *very high* in the latest cumulative EDGI report by the UNPAN Digital Opportunity Index [5], moving from *high* to *very high* rankings between 2018-2020 for the first time. Saudi is accompanied by 6 other countries (china, Kuwait, Malaysia, Oman, Turkey, and Thailand) in this ranking. Cumulatively, it ranks 43 at an EDGI score of 0.7991 as of 2020, compared to 0.7119 in 2018. Overall, the average EDGI in Asia is 0.5779, and in the Americas 0.5898 [5]. Saudi Arabia is joined by six other gulf countries in the very high EGDI group. At the top of the GCC countries, the UAE ranks highest as part of the V3 class, while Saudi sits at the top of the V2 class as of 2020. What is noteworthy is that the Kingdom secured its V2 placement under the *very high* classification rank, skipping V1, suggesting a rapid increase in development. This is also in light of the drop in the number of countries that were classified under the *high* category compared to previous reports [5].

Likewise, Saudi Arabia scored 0.8648 in the Human Capital Index (HCI), and 0.8442 in terms of the Telecommunication Infrastructure Index (TII). The HCI is an indicator that measures adult literacy rate, combined primary, secondary, and tertiary gross enrolment ration, expected years of schooling, and the average years of schooling. However, it does not measure digital literacy due to insufficient data. TII is an average of four indictors that measure, per 100 inhabitants, estimated internet users (KSA: 93.3%, compared to data from [7, 12]), number of mobile subscribers (KSA: 120), mobile-broadband subscriptions (KSA: 111.1), and the number of fixed broadband subscriptions (KSA: 20.24) [5]. As described earlier, due to its proactive response during the pandemic, the TII score for Saudi Arabia is anticipated to grow by the next report. Additionally, Saudi Arabia scored 0.6882 in the Online Service Index (OSI), following Kuwait, Albania, Portugal, and Armenia, and followed by Costa Rica, Ukraine, and Indonesia. The OSI reflects the differences in levels of e-government service development among UN member states.

3.6 On Saudi human capabilities

Reiterating from the previous section, Saudi scored 0.8648 in the Human Capital Index (HCI), a score higher than its OSI. This indicates that there is potential for further development in terms of its OSI ranking—should its HCI score be indicative of available human resources [5]. However, given that the HCI does not measure digital literacy, as indicated by the UNPAN methodology [5], there may as well be restraints in gaging the actual digital divide happening within the Kingdom, contributing to ostensible limitations.

Through a different index however, the ITU World Telecommunication/ICT Indicators Database [7], further insight on digital literacy can be assessed. This is summarized in **Figure 4**. According to the database, 21% of the Saudi population have advanced ICT skills, while 65% are armed with standard skills as of 2020. This is compared to 14% and 56% in 2019, respectively [14]. Advanced skills imply capabilities in computer program authoring using specialized programming languages, compared to standard skills, which refer to the use of basic arithmetic formulas and the use of computer applications (spreadsheets, presentations ... etc.), connecting and installing devices, and installing and configuring software. Notwithstanding, as of 2020, 61% of the population (compared to 68% in 2019) are said to have basic computing skills that involve the ability to send emails, copy-paste, and otherwise general information access and sharing practices [7].

Emphasising Vision 2030 objective, "[d]igital inclusion and leaving no one behind are high on the Kingdom's Government agenda" [27]. According to the Global Competitiveness Report published by the World Economic Forum in 2020 [27], Saudi Arabia has successfully implemented programs and initiatives that allowed it to compete in the top 10 countries in digital skills. The goal is to increase basic digital literacy from its current 61% to 90% by 2024. On par with these objectives, Saudi Arabia has

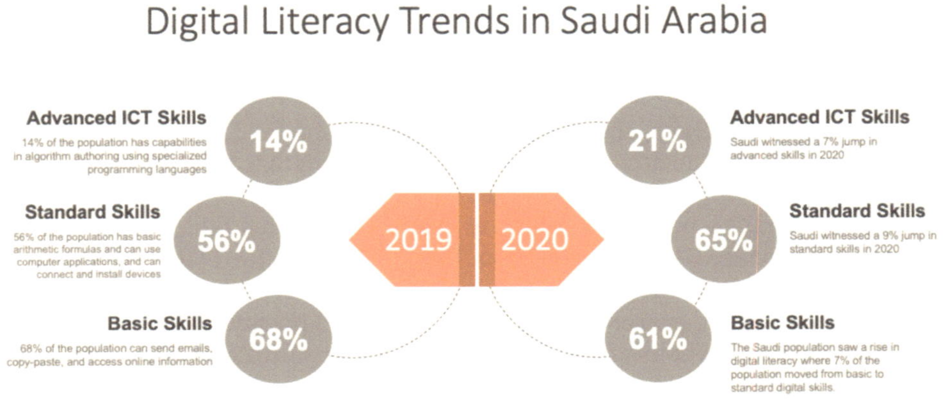

Figure 4.
Digital literacy in Saudi Arabia. The figure compares digital literacy development as it pertains to ICT skills within the general population between 2019 and 2020. Copyrights: Ali Megahed 2021.

also emphasized women empowerment through various programs that aims to enable women in both private and public sectors. The Kingdom has won the 2020 ITU Women Empowerment in Technology award [27]. This program is amongst several launched by the Ministry of Communication and Information Technology.

Despite this, data access and sharing practices remain well below potential within the population but is on a steady path of growth, and in contrast to the rapid advancements in e-government services [13]. This highlights the importance of raising digital literacy as a critical objective for the government to mitigate digital security and privacy risks. Although the Kingdom does impose strict data localization regulations to counteract this, without proper efforts to enhance digital literacy, data breaches and intellectual property rights violations pose an imminent risk. Some governments entities and private sector actors established various initiatives to counteract these possible risks. But according to the OECD [13], these efforts remain uneven across borders and sectors. One key challenge to these efforts has been in the utilization of Linked Data[2] [28] to implement interoperability between different governance frameworks. The gap between such frameworks (local, regional, national, and transnational) is stark. But Linked Data holds much promise in making it easier to locate information using ICT by creating connections between, and interlinking, data using web technologies, standards, and protocols as delineated in the next section.

Another challenge the exacerbates the need for advanced human capabilities, beyond the challenges of linking differing governance frameworks, is that new disruptive internet technologies such as cloud computing, social networking, GPS, sensors, satellites and smartphones facilitate unprecedented generation of large volumes of data—both simple and complex [29]. The biggest challenge here is in processing and making use of exorbitant quantities of data—namely Big Data— due to limitations in the capacity of conventional tools and processes to manage, store, and make meaningful connections from these data in reasonable time. Big Data in essence cannot exist without the "small 'complex' data" that validate them [28]. That is, the problem is in finding the connections between data types rather than the policies surrounding them; turning unstructured data to structured data. So, although automation holds the potential promise to simplify the management of large quantities of information—whereby, automation is a process that involves utilizing information and communication technologies (ICTs) to mechanize what traditionally requires manual labour [30]—it is not, yet, a tangible goal, given the current available human capabilities and the strict localization laws.

Automation requires the proper use of data in order for processing to occur seamlessly. Skilled data practitioners are required to verify and validate such processes to enable machine learning towards a knowledge-based economy. According to one research, this will require "that citizens are equipped with analytical skills and other key abilities that are demanded by the private sector and are needed to function in a globalized market" [25], and hence a substantial reassessment, diversification, and upgrade of the quality and availability of Saudi education and research.

The importance of such skills is tied to the nuances associated with complex data. Complex data require proper presentation and representation that is intuitive and dynamic. Not an easy feat given that data are often contextual, originate from different sources, and more often than not, unstructured. Combining datasets can and often

---

[2] Visit www.linkeddata.org and www.w3.org/standards/semanticweb/ for more information, and consult Franklin, Stam & Clayton (2009) and Ruiz-Calleja et al. (2012).

do result in new datasets, unique and, arguably, independent of its provenance due to its unpredictable structure [29]. Most complex datasets are volatile and useful within a timeframe and can cause chaotic behaviour when not managed properly and sustainably. Because of this, tools and human capabilities surrounding data management must evolve to keep up with this complex growth. This includes emergent techniques in computing research, data mining, and visual analytics [29].

Research shows that Saudi Arabia still has a long way towards realizing such a labour force. Efforts are being made towards modernizing the Saudi educational system, with special emphasis on higher education and entrepreneurship to meet the demands of this job market [25]. This is especially true in the private sector, which falls short in contrast to the public sector. According to Al-Naimi [25], "the large population, together with the underdeveloped Saudi economy, has resulted in falling GDP in Saudi Arabia, even though it is one of the largest exporters of oil. The majority of the population are currently equipped with a traditional education, which has led to problems such as high youth unemployment, a concentration of jobs offered in the public sector, and an increase in rates of poverty." Youth unemployment is forecasted to increase, in light of automation, especially among females, and despite empowerment efforts. In one research [30], automation accounts for half of labour share decline posing another threat to the growth of human capabilities in Saudi Arabia and the lauded benefits of automation—given that most technologies are transferred or imported rather than sourced locally.

4. Successful ICT applications in the Kingdom

4.1 On the economic impact of the pandemic

There is no doubt that COVID19 has had an impact on the industrial sector in Saudi Arabia, on its economy, as well as on the international economy. There are three dimensions that reflect the ramification of the pandemic on Saudi industry [31]: (1) supply chain, (2) global demand, and (3) oil market prices. For the first, supply chains across the Kingdom witnessed a decline in production of imported goods, leading to higher input prices that prompted a need for new sources of supply. Global demand also suffered a decline that led to a decrease in Kingdom exports.

According to the Saudi General Authority for Statistics (GASTAT), the "total commodity exports decreased by 33.5% in 2020 compared to 2019" as a result of the 40.5% decrease in oil exports. Oil export decline caused a marked decline in oil prices by march 2020 at 35% compared to 2019 [31]. Likewise, the industrial sector labour market witnessed a massive decline by the end of 2020, where unemployment saw a loss of more than 5000 non-Saudi employees [31]. Even so, total unemployment rate among Saudi nationals reached 12.6% [31] in the last quarter of 2020, but was steadily improving by the end of the first quarter of 2021 at 11.7% (**Figure 5**) [32].

The success the Kingdom has achieved in managing the pandemic within its borders can be corelated to the successes of Vision 2030. According to the Bloomberg COVID Resilience Ranking [33], Saudi Arabia ranks second following the UAE, having risen 18 rungs to this position, taking into account 12 indicators. The two most significant are measured in terms of its positive response to the aftermath of the first 100 confirmed cases and successful nation-wide vaccination provision of 154.9 doses per 100 individuals. Its GDP is forecasted to grow at about 5.9% in 2022 [33]. Overall, managing the logistics in relation to the virus has been accomplished in several ways,

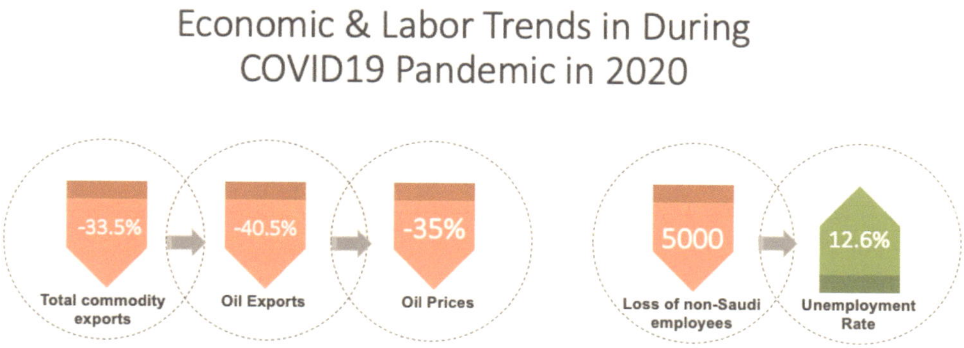

Figure 5.
Economic and labor market trends in the aftermath of COVID19. The figure summarizes the impact of the pandemic on the Saudi economy during 2020. Copyrights: Kinda Dahlan 2021.

critical to which has been the use of ICTs and the establishment of a unified national digital platform that is supported by the country's robust infrastructure.

When it comes to national economy, the government offered several e-facilitated support packages within the first and second quarter of 2020. Most packages were designed to provide liquidity for the needs of the private sector [31]. The value of packages in 2020 reached SR 70 billion Saudi Riyals (Approx. $ 18.6B USD). It entailed suspending tax payments, fees, and other dues to increase National Development Fund funding [31]. Likewise, the government also launched a program worth SR 670 million Saudi Riyals (Approx. $ +178M USD) that permitted loan repayment postponement.

Other measures included the provision of temporary electricity subsidies for the commercial, agricultural, and industrial sectors valued at nearly SR 1 billion Saudi Riyals (Approx. $ +266M USD). The Saudi government also authorized insurance-scheme packages for the private sector to counteract unemployment to promote retention of Saudi employees, whilst the Saudi Central Bank (SAMA) mandated banks to postpone loans repayment for Saudi employees for a period of three months without interest [31]. At the monetary level, SAMA launched a package worth SR 50 billion (Approx. $ 13.3B USD)—or nearly 2% of the GDP—to support the private sector. It provided financing to banks to facilitate the postponement of loan repayment and increase corporate lending [31].

Following the strategic Vision 2030, the government also implemented its localization policies to the industrial sector and supply chains as a response to the pandemic and other possible global shocks. This has resulted in a positive rise in local demand in certain sectors such as in the health supply industry (e.g., masks, sanitizers). Despite the opportunities, some industries were negatively impacted due to a high dependency on imported goods and global demand [31].

4.2 On the use of ICTs during the pandemic

During the COVID19 pandemic, which roughly began with the announcement of a nation-wide lockdown in March 2020, Saudi Arabia forged governmental policies and regulations to counter the spread of the virus by leveraging on ICTs and facilitating mass-public-health services.

Of note is the integrated unified national platform GOV.SA [34], which is in fulfilment of the digital aspirations of Vision 2030. This platform offers more 2500 government services, with more than 130 applications for 70 government agencies [35]. This unified digital platform offers an omni-channel user experience and can be accessed through a variety of central applications centralized around *Absher* [36], which provides government services to individuals, businesses, and government entities online. During the pandemic, two new apps were developed: *Tawakkalna*[3], a Saudi Data and Artificial Intelligence Authority (SDAIA) application that issues mobility permits for both government and private sector employees during curfew [37], and *Sehhaty*, a Ministry of Health application that facilitates access to accurate health information and the latest COVID19-related services [38].

Tawakkalna's 28 services are integrated with the public health awareness campaign "Cautiously We Return[4]". The remaining 15 are activitated during public lockdown. Tawakkalna also relies on near-real time social network data that can help detect possible contagion hot zones, alerting users and public officials of possible outspread. This has helped curb the *Delta* strain and limit the *Omicron* strain tremendously in the aftermath of the global pandemic. Both applications were developed and linked to the national platform GOV.SA. Other apps were also developed to provide national and international services such as *Eatamarna*, to facilitate Hajj and Umrah logistics and services.

In 2021, the apps, given the intricacies of the unified platform, were integrated such that users are able to access services from within these key applications, including nationally-sponsored entertainment ticketing services, traffic violations, and civil services. This was precedented by pandemic precautions that necessitated a means to organize mass-polymerase chain reaction (PCR) tests and vaccinations. These services are enabled due to structured citizen and resident data that has been captured and designed relationally to promote seamless logistics across the Kingdom. Other tangible benefits included the government's ability to support small and medium businesses (SMEs) in establishing their online presence during this time, postponing loan repayments, and developing new policies and regulations, along with multiple logistics processes that bolstered the existing infrastructure in support efforts for social distancing.

5. Discussion

5.1 Enabling Industry 4.0 in Saudi Arabia

Research shows that the ICT sector in Saudi Arabia will grow by 50% and the level of this sector's "Saudization"—or the promotion of Saudi national employment to alleviate heavy dependency on foreign workers—will increase to 50% by 2023 [39]. The Saudi government aims to transform the Kingdom into one of the world's leading countries in the field of ICTs "by building a digital economy based on the principles of the fourth industrial revolution and digital society management" [39]. The fourth industrial revolution, or Industry 4.0, is a paradigm shift [40]. This shift "requires the participation and commitment of different stakeholder groups [so that] industry can completely redesign supply chains, aiming at resource efficiency and circularity" [40].

[3] For more on Tawakkalna visit: https://ta.sdaia.gov.sa/en/index.

[4] Visit https://ta.sdaia.gov.sa/en/index to learn more about the awareness campaign.

Industry 4.0 is characterized by a set of enabling technologies that aggregate through the Internet and, as mentioned previously, Industry 5.0 complements 4.0 by centralizing innovation and sustainability. This trend is widely adopted as seen in the growing investment and rise in industrial engineering in the Kingdom [41]. If implemented properly, Industry 4.0 can produce real-time information on the locations and state of people and equipment involved in a process (IoT), it can provide measurement of connections and interactions (Big Data), and can produce predictive diagnostics and forecasts of system dynamics (ML and predictive analytics). To reach this state, data must first be converted into value. The popularized, almost cliched, *4 Vs of Big Data* hold true here when it comes to measuring the value of data: *volume* (the amount of data), *velocity* (the flow of data), *variety* (the type and characteristics of data), and *veracity* (the validity and reliability of data).

Lessons learned and research in data management suggests integrating policy, sharing practices and data characteristics into data architecture [42]. Key to these endeavours are mechanisms that verify the validity and reliability of the data stream because produced data and the way in which they are structured change from one use case to the other. Understanding when data are duplicated or missing is critical to the successful implementation of regulations that can transfer data into currency in a reusable and sustainable manner that supports innovation and market competition. Providing context, provenance, and other metadata helps mitigate unanticipated anomalies in data models.

It is important to note that the relationship between information technology (IT) infrastructure and data science is based on the utilization of datasets. Where one builds the infrastructure in the form of systems and platforms (IT), the other trades in its currency (data science)—namely data. For IT, the main role is to create platforms, storage and backup solutions, sustainability plans, and other mechanisms for organizing and maintaining data. For data scientists, the focus is to utilize available datasets in meaningful ways using machine learning and computation to aggregate, extract, clean, and validate data. In essence, data scientists *design* and *build* new processes for data extraction, modeling, and production. They use algorithms, prescriptive and predictive models, and custom analysis using prototypes to facilitate analysis. To develop a robust national Industry 4.0 infrastructure, both IT and data science expertise are needed to enhance manufacturing processes and to optimize the use of resources that bring about cost reduction and the elimination of wasted time. Saudi Arabia utilizes Industry 4.0 to optimize the use and manufacturing of non-oil-based resources, focusing on efficiency and upskilling. However, as we have delineated so far, concentration has been placed on securing ICTs and developing the IT components of this ecosystem rather than on data science and the development of human capabilities. This can be attributed to several reasons.

According to research by SAMA [43], there were several key points that were considered in creating a Saudi industrial development plan. First, it is essential to account for the differences between current and past structures, locally, regionally, and transnationally for any joint ventures to prosper. This is because of the unprecedented changes and developments in technology and shifting local and global demands (*volume* and *velocity*). Second, manufacturing has varying strategic definitions that are neither universal nor consistent—especially across borders—which necessitates an understanding of competitive advantage for each industry (*veracity* and *variety*). The application of internet technologies does not occur in equilibrium across business functions, industries, sectors, or even economies making a comparative analysis of digital transformation difficult to pinpoint.

For Saudi Arabia, there is an immediate planned adoption of Industry 4.0 technologies. This refers to Artificial Intelligence (AI), a subset of which is machine learning (ML), and the Internet of Things (IoT), which includes Linked Data and the linkage of devices and systems via the web. Other technologies include "robots, smart cities, the governance and future shaping of technology and data policy, automated mobility, unmanned aerial vehicles (UAVs), and the future of airspace" [16]. The biggest challenges facing Saudi Arabian industrial development and activity is the lack of demand—especially for SMEs—and the quality of natural resources, and shortage of skilled workers and expertise.

Further to this point, other challenges facing Saudi Arabia in the adoption of Industry 4.0 technologies and developing skills around it include: (1) "[l]ack of interest on the part of major industrial companies stemming from either a lack of awareness with respect to the existence of such technologies or reservations with regards to its effectiveness;" (2) "[l]ack of funding encountered by some firms to upgrade their production equipment, especially considering that equipment at the levels needed for Industry 4.0 are more expensive than conventional counterparts;" (3) a shortage in "human capital as qualified workers are needed to properly utilize these technologies," and finally (4) "[t]he strength of the Kingdom's communication structure and the information security infrastructure needed to utilize these technologies reliably and with enough protections" [44].

As mentioned earlier, these challenges can be counteracted through proper strategic planning and enabling supply-chain integration with machinery and databases. The adoption of new work models and implementation mechanisms are central to the realization of the Kingdom's Vision 2030 in that they necessitate a move away from relying on natural resources towards utilizing data as currency [45]. These challenges, and also opportunities and benefits, are summed up and illustrated in (**Figure 6**).

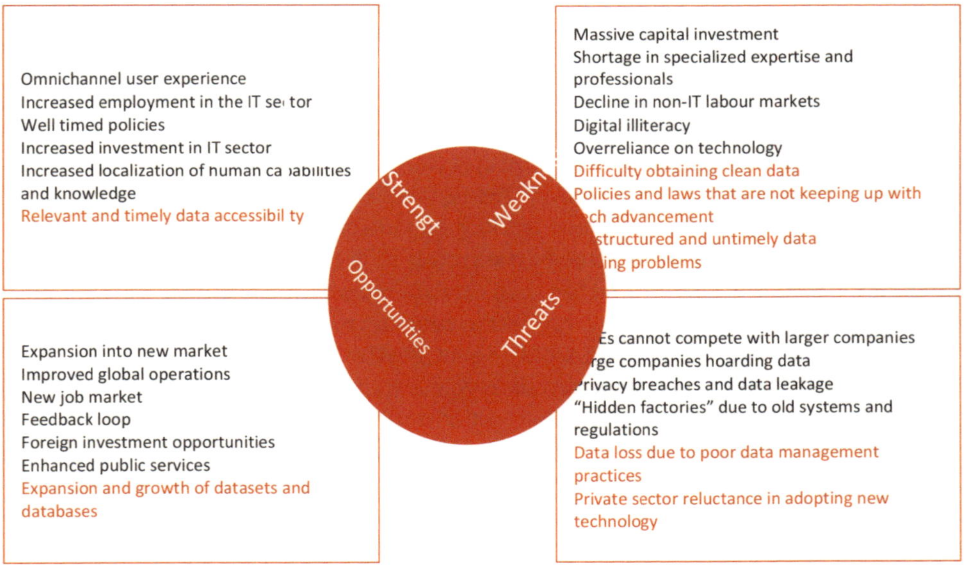

Figure 6.
The strengths and weaknesses of disruptive technologies in enabling Industry 4.0 in Saudi Arabia. The figure depicts the key advantages and disadvantages of utilizing ICTs and other web technologies. It also highlights the key issues facing data accessibility and management. Copyrights: Kinda Dahlan and Ali Megahed 2021.

Economic theory establishes that good economic data are a precondition to effective macroeconomic management: of GDP growth (oil and non-oil), of inflation rate, and of unemployment rates. This is particularly true in times of crisis for several reasons. First, due to macroeconomic policy timing, including monetary policies and fiscal policies, and second because of corrective policies that depend on well-timed availability of data. To be successful in offsetting the economic effects of crises, policy makers need to recognize these effects using real-time data. When there is a discontinuity between policy response and crisis impact, existing policies may not be effective enough to offset threats. Typically, this lag exists in the implementation of economic policies that are long and variable for monetary policies. However, we argue that the availability of clean and timely data can play a significant role in reducing this gap.

5.2 On the value of data and the limitations of data policies

For example, during the COVID19 pandemic, which began in December 2019, and taking into account the extensive time needed for the production of economic statistics to be collected (or published) by statistical authorities, regulatory responses (whether by government or businesses) were often late in interacting with accelerated changes for a given situation [42]. Untimely and messy data led to some poor decisions. This refers to incomplete, inaccurate, and insufficient data that impacted the manufacturing sector. To understand this further, it is important to visualize the degree of complexity in manufacturing data.

The Saudi manufacturing sector is composed of thousands upon thousands of units that belong to a wide spectrum of sectors as captured in the strategic vision. These sectors are interrelated through forward and backward links along the supply chain. These units are also interrelated with different nonmanufacturing sectors. Compounding this are interrelations with different cross-border manufacturing and nonmanufacturing sectors through international trade. We know that the COVID crisis caused many bottlenecks in the Saudi production processes, but also beyond it, due to supply chain disruptions as well as the accumulation of inventories as a result of shortage in product local and global demand.

As so, accessibility to robust and reliable datasets offer several benefits. First, they help identify bottleneck points and analysis of the possible different production paths. Second, they facilitate analysis of market supply and demand capacities in a way that enables predictions of market trends and potential action plans to minimize losses. Finally, reliable data helps government policy formulation in supporting sectors, subsectors, and/or units that are impacted most by a crisis. Economies usually keep track of sectorial interrelationships through what is known as input-output tables or Social Accounting Matrices (SAM). Such detailed data employ the use of advanced sophisticated mathematical models that accurately measure the impact of different economic shocks and hence the setting of appropriate policies.

Likewise, high quality effective data helps reduce uncertainty surrounding a country's economic conditions. This is a key interest for foreign investors, considering that one objective of Vision 2030 is precisely that: attracting foreign investment into the Kingdom. In practice, the quality of data housed in databases quickly degenerates over time, where estimates suggest that "2% of records in a customer file become obsolete in one month" [46]. The problem here is that data quickly becomes obsolete—a critical problem to data quality and value. Research shows that this not only has an impact on decision making, but that "dirty" redundant data cost "businesses 600 billion USD each year [... and that] stale data accounts for a large part of the losses" [46].

This highlights the importance of treating data as currency. Examining data as currency establishes the current values of entities within databases and datasets. This would not be a challenge if data values carried timestamp and provenance information. In reality, this metadata is often inconsistent, missing, or inaccurate. Likewise, the processing, and overprocessing, of data often results in incomplete, inaccurately-contextualized, and otherwise inadequate datasets. For Saudi Arabia, language is another challenge, keeping in mind that the language of the internet and web technologies is vastly English. The majority of data is either bilingual, or translated from Arabic into English for processing, increasing the odds of duplication, errors, and redundancy.

With low quality data in mind, and during the COVID crisis, there was a sharp decline in the flow of foreign direct investments (FDIs). According to the UN Conference on Trade and Development (UNCTAD) [47], global FDI flows in 2020 dropped by about 35% of what it was in 2019, reaching its lowest since 2005. This has had dire ramifications on economic development, and recovery from this situation required policymakers to position their countries as attractively as possible for FDIs.

When it comes to the manufacturing sector in Saudi Arabia at the time of the Corona virus outbreak, the government responded to the economic crisis, as many countries around the world have: by announcing stimulus packages to support its economy. Reiterating from earlier, at the monetary level, SAMA unveiled an economic stimulus package worth 2% of its GDP to support the private sector, especially small and medium enterprises (SMEs) [31]. At the fiscal level, the government allocated SR 70 billion Saudi Riyals (Approx. $ 18.6B USD) to help businesses through exemptions and postponement of government taxes, fees, and customs and to provide liquidity for private sector enterprises.

Both fiscal and monetary policies should be coordinated in such circumstances to boost support for impacted households and firms. To promote this, the availability of real-time valid and reliable data and, most importantly, forecasted data, is crucial to the successful management of the crises. This includes data on national public debt, its relation to GDP, and detailed sectorial data that enable policy makers to determine the most affected sectors. Under this category, there should be clear and up-to-date data on sectors that have high economic multipliers. These are the sectors that are deeply interrelated with other economic sectors through backward and forward links. Likewise, datasets of value should include sectors that depend heavily on imported raw material, sectors that are export-oriented, and sectors that are labour-intensive in order to evade severe impact on labour share and unemployment rates.

In turn, since the impact of policies ranges from short term to medium and long terms, relevant data should include solid predictions of economic variables that are based on reliable models. For example, although debt can push economic problems from the present to the future, doing so can aggravate the problem given that policies are often only as accurate as the input that delivered them initially are. It is important to observe here that the COVID crisis is related to real economy (supply and demand) not to financial problems; a distinction that highlights the lengthiness of recovery.

The policy taken by the Saudi government is ever so critical, but requires a serious consideration of policy timeframes to maximize its impact: is it a one-quarter shock? A two-quarter shock? Or perhaps more? The success of economic policies in offsetting the effects of a possible recession depend substantially on quick detection of the length of the recession. Such a policy should be consistent with the recessionary effects of the nature of the pandemic. This means that estimates are required for the starting and recovery time of the recession to distribute the policy tools accordingly. In this sense, access to raw data.

Well-structured, extensive, time-sensitive data is also an apparatus for post-policy measurements. In the case of the Corona crisis, access to adequate data facilitate the evaluation of stimulus packages effectiveness. This is done by measuring policy impact on real GDP and employment, whilst holding all other factors that affect real GDP and employment constant, as for example, other monetary policy tools, or business cycle changes. The mechanism behind such estimation is complex in nature and is affected by several factors that change supply and demand and, in effect, equilibrium GDP. In such a crisis, the success of policy is not as certain as regular times, leading to a wide variance in the estimation of the impact of stimulus packages.

Data used for such estimation are a significant factor in getting accurate results. For example, theoretically, the policy aims at shifting money-supply curve to the right, but the effect depends mainly on the behaviour of firms and households as a response to this shift. This response needs further examination using massive data (Big Data) extracted from surveys and other data sources that thoroughly address the behavioural motivations and decisions of households and businesses.

With this in mind, and given the limited data sources currently available for the Saudi economy, we recommend strengthening the quality of micro-level data, mainly through surveys at subsector or firm level, to expound the impacts of COVID19. This includes data beyond social data; on firm cost structures, consumer expenditures, and firm production and revenue. Similarly, improving data organization and structure, and enhancing national data lifecycle through proper database design, management, and archiving is elemental. This includes having more disaggregated data at the manufacturing level.

Data need to be collected at a higher frequency than currently is, and disseminated at regular intervals for timely analysis. To be able to have a forward-looking perspective, regular forecasts for many macroeconomic variables using solid and sophisticated modelling techniques such as advanced timeseries forecasting and regression models are necessary. Additionally, data should be tested frequently for accuracy, validity, and reliability as a means to improve quality. Likewise, accessibility is essential for conducting research studies that support policy makers.

As one research points out, "[a]mong the lessons learned are that data on the same variables are gathered by multiple means, that data exist in many states and in many places" and that "[d]ata sharing is embraced in principle but little sharing actually occurs, due to interrelated factors such as lack of demand, lack of standards, and concerns about [...] ownership, data quality, and ethics" [42]. To assess data quality, and begin evaluating data as currency, Saudi Arabia must pay attention to data quality, accessibility, and provenance. This includes understanding the characteristics of data being generated; its frequency, flow, and reliability; for what certain and potential purpose(s); for whom, and with what access rights and regulations.

Further research needs to look into how data criteria vary in different contexts, what policy frameworks need to be applied, with what measures, controls and limitations. And while Saudi has made massive strides in utilizing ICTs in the public health and e-government sectors, we also recommend assessing the value of data, where several models exist to measure data as currency (e.g. [46]), and applying appropriate standards and practices towards maintenance and sustainability.

6. Conclusion

So far, we have described the Saudi national strategy, Vision 2030, in the context of utilizing technology and data to diversify national economy. We described the various localization efforts by government to strengthen the Saudi economy, improve human capabilities, and leverage on local content to reduce oil dependency. Likewise, we assessed Saudi digital readiness using several indices to examine e-government services, digital literacy, and to gage the realization of strategic objectives. We have also reviewed Saudi Arabia's response to the COVID19 crisis, detailing its utilization of ICTs, development of support packages, and regulation implementation. We conclude our chapter by addressing how our hypothesis levels against our findings, summarizing research results and implications, limitations, work advances, contribution to knowledge, and further avenues for research.

Reiterating from the introduction, there are two main hypothesis driving our research: 1) Data deluge brings substantial challenges in the timely collection and processing of massive amounts of information towards decision making, and that 2) the unprecedented production of information exceeds available human capabilities and the ability of authoritative bodies to create regulations and policies that can keep up with these transformations. Our findings reveal that there is a scarcity in research that looks into these concerns in Saudi Arabia. Our contribution to knowledge here is thus expanding on this body of work by providing insight into the successes and challenges facing the country as it journeys into its digital transformation and move towards realizing its strategic objectives. Our work has shown that there are limitations in educational initiatives targeting the development of human capabilities to meet the needs and aspirations of the national strategy. We have found that there are innovative efforts to address this gap within the Kingdom through various government-backed programs. However, our research also shows that traditional formal education remains the dominant national model in the Kingdom, limiting opportunities that can arise from the diversification of educational systems.

We also observed that while foreign investment is on the rise, knowledge transfer via these investments remains limited due to a heavy emphasis on ICT acquisition rather than on promoting knowledge transfer and exchange. Here we recommend further examination and research on the Saudization model to take advantage of foreign investment as a means for diversifying education, improving technical skill, and digital literacy.

Ostensibly, Saudi Arabia is a developing country that seeks to increase its potential economic growth through a number of policies and programs that include, among others, leveraging on digitization, capturing the value of data availability, ICTs, foreign investment, and industrialization. Economic growth studies suggest that capital, as an important input in the production function, could be classified into two categories: ICT capital and non-ICT capital. We have focused on the first whereby ICT capital includes spending on information, computing, and technology. Economic growth theories further reveal how this type of capital spending have been a crucial key driver of growth realized in developed countries over the last decade. Hence, ICT investment share trends in GDP is a very important measure of economic growth potential.

As so, and in terms of accurate data availability and accessibility, we showed that one of the most important causes of economic failures in the market is lack of data. Be they in the form of government setting policies that address economic issues, businesses that seek to maximize profitability, research bodies that try to analyse different economic or social phenomenon, or even on an individual scale to optimize better-informed decision-making processes. In all cases, data are invaluable currency. Linking the two points above is thus ever so critical in the formulation of information policy in Saudi Arabia. The work done in this chapter confirms the strong relation between economic growth and data availability and accessibility, and highlights the importance of investment in human capital and digital literacy alongside ICT capital. Using the Saudi case, where there has been an ambitious plan to converge the nation with developed economies, digitization and availability of accurate data remain key assets in this process. We studied the challenges associated with government responses to the COVID19 crisis. This included how data played a major role in counteracting the pandemic and helping in the formulation of government corrective policies. Studies to quantify the relationship between quality and availability of data and achieving economic targets for developing countries that have long term vision plans is a field for further studies.

Acknowledgements

I would like to thank Dr. Ahmed Badawi, my co-author, for his contribution in analysing the economic impact of data on the industrial sector in Saudi Arabia. Without his invaluable expertise in MENA industrial economics, this work would not have been possible. I would also like to thank Mr. Ali Megahed for his editorial feedback, excellent visualization skills, and SWOT analysis contribution, and for the endless discussions that brought Dr. Badawi and myself together in writing this piece. His assistance in developing the conceptualization and structure of this work is invaluable.

We also thank Mr. Omar Al-Zouman, Mr. Ahmed Al-Baqawi, and Mr. Mohammed S. Al-Harbi for their endless support and encouragement. Last but never least, we thank our families for their patience, support, and care through this writing, and through the many COVID19 challenges and PCR-scares that stood in the way of collaboration and remote work.

Author details

Kinda R. Dahlan*, Ahmed A. Badawi and Ali Megahed
Market Studies, Saudi Industrial Development Fund, Riyadh, Saudi Arabia

*Address all correspondence to: kinda.dahlan.14@ucl.ac.uk

References

[1] Frey LR, Botan CH, Kreps GL. Asking questions about communication. In: Eid M, Lagacé M, editors. Communication Research Methods: Quantitative and Qualitative Approaches. Boston: Pearson Publishing; 2007. pp. 561-592

[2] Baran SJ, Davis DK. Mass Communication Theory. Boston, MA: Wadsworth Cengage Learning; 2009

[3] Neuman WL. Qualitative and quantitative sampling. In: Eid M, Lagacé M, editors. Communication Research Methods: Quantitative and Qualitative Approaches. Boston: Pearson Publishing; 2007. pp. 345-370

[4] Berg BL. Qualitative Research Methods for the Social Sciences. Boston: Pearson; 2007

[5] UNPAN. UN E-Government Survey 2020: Digital Government in the Decade of Action for Sustainable Development. New York, USA: Department of Economic and Social Affairs; 2020

[6] FitchSolutions. Quick View: Saudi Spectrum Release to Support Industry 4.0 Ambitions. 2021

[7] ITU. World telecommunication/ICT indicators database. In: Digital Development Dashboard: An Overview of the State of Digital Development Around the World Based on ITU Data: International Telecommunication Union (ITU); 2021

[8] Neuman WL. Qualitative and quantitative measurement. In: Eid M, Lagacé M, editors. Communication Research Methods: Quantitative and Qualitative Approaches. Boston: Pearson Publishing; 2007. pp. 205-244

[9] Kingdom of Saudi Arabia (2020) Vision 2030. Available from: https://www.vision2030.gov.sa/en

[10] Saudi Vision 2030 Document. Available from: https://www.vision2030.gov.sa/media/rc0b5oy1/saudi_vision203.pdf

[11] GASTAT. Saudi Population by Age Groups and Gender. Saudi Arabia; 2020

[12] Saudi Digital Government Authority. Digital Transformation. Available from: https://www.my.gov.sa/wps/portal/snp/aboutksa/digitaltransformation

[13] OECD. Data Governance: Enhancing Access to and Sharing of Data 2021. Available from: https://www.oecd.org/sti/ieconomy/enhanced-data-access.htm

[14] Saudi Green Initiative. Available from: https://www.saudigreeninitiative.org/about-saudi-green-initiative/

[15] SPA-WAS. Modon Presents the Digital Transformation Plans Towards the 4th Industrial Revolution in Front of the Saudi-German Business Forum [Translated from Arabic]. Riyadh, KSA: Saudi Press Agency; 2019. Available from: https://www.spa.gov.sa/2012965

[16] United National Platform. Saudi Arabia Signs Agreement with the World Economic Forum to Establish a Branch in the Kingdom of the Centre for the Fourth Industrial Revolution. Saudi Press Agency; 2020. Available from: https://www.my.gov.sa/wps/portal/snp/content/news/newsDetails/CONT-news-07112019%201

[17] Litvinenko V. Digital economy as a factor in the technological development

of the mineral sector. Natural Resources Research. 2020;**29**(3):1521-1541

[18] United Nations. Data economy: Radical transformation or dystopia? Frontier Technology Quarterly. 2019. Available from: https://www.un.org/development/desa/dpad/wp-content/uploads/sites/45/publication/FTQ_1_Jan_2019.pdf

[19] UNCTAD. Digital Economy Report 2021 Cross-Border Data Flows and Development: For Whom the Data Flow. New York, NY, USA: United Nations Publications; 2021

[20] European Commission. EU Cohesion Policy 2014–2020: Targeting Investments on Key Growth Priorities. 2020. Available from: https://ec.europa.eu/regional_policy/sources/docgener/informat/2014/fiche_ict_en.pdf

[21] SDAIA. The National Data Management Office. 2021. Available from: https://sdaia.gov.sa/ndmo/?Lang=en

[22] Personal Data Protection System [Translated from Arabic]. 2021. Available from: https://laws.boe.gov.sa/BoeLaws/Laws/LawDetails/b7cfae89-828e-4994-b167-adaa00e37188/1

[23] CITC. General Rules for Maintaining the Privacy of Personal Data of Users [Translated from Arabic]. 2020. Available from: https://www.citc.gov.sa/ar/RulesandSystems/privacy/Documents/Data_Privacy_Principles_For_ICT.pdf

[24] FitchSolutions. Saudi Arabia Telecommunications Report Q3 2021. Fitch Solutions Country Risk & Industry Research. 2021. Available from: https://libguides.babson.edu/fitchconnect/searchtips

[25] Al Naimi SM. Economic diversification trends in the gulf: The case of Saudi Arabia. Circular Economy and Sustainability. 2021;**2**

[26] World Bank. ICT Indicators and Implications for Methods for Assessing Socioeconomic Impact of IC. 2012. Available from: https://openknowledge.worldbank.org/handle/10986/18370

[27] Saudi Digital Government Authority. Digital Inclusion. 2021. Available from: https://www.my.gov.sa/wps/portal/snp/careaboutyou/digitalinclusion

[28] Dahlan KR. Digital Waters: An Assessment of Information and Communication Practices in Oceanography and Multidisciplinary Science. London, UK: UCL (University College London); 2019

[29] Alvarado-Pérez JC, Peluffo-Ordónez DH, Therón-Sánchez R. Bridging the Gap between Human Knowledge and Machine Learning. Advances in Distributed Computing and Artificial Intelligence Journal, Ediciones Universidad de Salamanca / CC BY_NC_ND. 2015

[30] Eden M, Gaggl P. On the welfare implications of automation. Review of Economic Dynamics. 2018;**29**:15-43

[31] SIDF Annual Report. Saudi Arabia: Saudi Industrial Development Fund. Statistical Studies Unit. 2020;**2021**:72

[32] GASTAT. Labor market statistics Q1 2021. 2021. Available from: https://www.stats.gov.sa/sites/default/files/LM_Q1%202021%20%28Press%20release_EN%29_0.pdf

[33] Chang R, Varley K, Tam F, Lung N, Munoz M. The Covid resilience ranking: The best and worst places to be as we learn to live with Covid. In: O'Brien E, editor. Bloomberg; 2022. Available from: https://www.bloomberg.com/graphics/covid-resilience-ranking/#data-reference

[34] Saudi Digital Government Authority. About National

Platform GOV.SA. 2021. Available from: https://www.my.gov.sa/wps/portal/snp/aboutPortal/!ut/p/z0/04_Sj9CPykssy0xPLMnMz0vMAfIjo8zivQIsTAwdDQz9_d29TAwCnQ1DjUy9wgwMLEz1g1Pz9AuyHRUBI89e_A!!/

[35] Muzafar S, Jhanjhi N. Success Stories of ICT Implementation in Saudi Arabia. Employing Recent Technologies for Improved Digital Governance: IGI Global; 2020. pp. 151-163

[36] Absher. Absher Platform. 2022. Available from: https://www.absher.sa/wps/portal/individuals/static/footer/about/!ut/p/z1/jY_BCoJAFEW_xq3vzYgm7UariRIqo7LZhMY4FeqImf5-VivBore7l3MuPBAQgSji5qri-qqLOOvyUTgnhwY-mbt0iXtngpspXbv2jFBcWnB4A5wQNqccA85DihufEWvEPOISG8Q__g_g5eOXY9j5YgBh6IXUsxD5ig4CvY0FCJXp5PMuKxLLVSAqmcpKVuaj6upLXZf3sYEGtm1rKq1VJs2zzg0cUi76XkPUJ2ErCyjzXYQ3O2uClD 0B84zzrg!!/dz/d5/L2dBISEvZ0FBIS9nQSEh/

[37] SDAIA. About Tawakkalna Application. 2021. Available from: https://ta.sdaia.gov.sa/en/index

[38] Saudi Ministry of Health. COVID-19 E-Services. 2021. Available from: https://www.moh.gov.sa/en/eServices/Pages/Vaccine-date.aspx

[39] Rogozhin A. ICT as a direction for diversifying the economy of saudi arabia. Outlines of Global Transformations: Politics, Economics, Law. 2021;**4**:122-141

[40] Garcia-Muiña FE, González-Sánchez R, Ferrari AM, Settembre-Blundo D. The paradigms of Industry 4.0 and circular economy as enabling drivers for the competitiveness of businesses and territories: The case of an Italian ceramic tiles manufacturing company. Social Sciences. 2018;**7**(12):255

[41] Alkahtani MS, El-Sherbeeny AM, Noman MA, Abdullah FM, Choudhary A, editors. Trends in industrial engineering and the Saudi vision 2030. In: IIE Annual Conference Proceedings. Orlando, Florida: Institute of Industrial and Systems Engineers (IISE); 2018

[42] Borgman CL, Wallis JC, Enyedy N. Little science confronts the data deluge: habitat ecology, embedded sensor networks, and digital libraries. International Journal on Digital Libraries. 2007;7(1):17-30. p. 14

[43] Al-Nuwaisr S. Measuring the productivity of manufacturing activity in the Kingdom of Saudi Arabia. In: Agency SAM, editor. Economic Research Department—Saudi Arabian Monetary Agency [Translated from Arabic]. 2020 Available from: https://www.sama.gov.sa/ar-sa/EconomicResearch/WorkingPapers/%D9%82%D9%8A%D8%A7%D8%B3%20%D8%A5%D9%86%D8%AA%D8%A7%D8%AC%D9%8A%D8%A9%20%D9%86%D8%B4%D8%A7%D8%B7%20%D8%A7%D9%84%D8%B5%D9%86%D8%A7%D8%B9%D8%A7%D8%AA%20%D8%A7%D9%84%D8%AA%D8%AD%D9%88%D9%8A%D9%84%D9%8A%D8%A9%20%D9%81%D9%8A%20%D8%A7%D9%84%D9%85%D9%85%D9%84%D9%83%D8%A9%20%D8%A7%D9%84%D8%B9%D8%B1%D8%A8%D9%8A%D8%A9%20%D8%A7%D9%84%D8%B3%D8%B9%D9%88%D8%AF%D9%8A%D8%A9.pdf

[44] US-Saudi Business Council. Overview of the National Industrial Development and Logistics Program: Industry 4.0. 2019. Available from: https://ussaudi.org/overview-of-the-national-industrial-development-and-logistics-program-industry-4-0/

[45] United National Platform. Minister of Communications and Information

Technology: The Fourth Industrial Revolution is Essential to Achieve the Vision of the Kingdom 2030. Riyadh, KSA: Saudi Press Agency; 2021. Available from: https://www.my.gov.sa/wps/portal/snp/content/news/newsDetails/CONT-news-113032018

[46] Fan W, Geerts F, Wijsen J. Determining the currency of data. ACM Transactions on Database Systems (TODS). 2012;**37**(4):1-46

[47] UNCTAD. World 2021 Investment Report: Investing in Sustainable Recovery. New York: United Nations Publications; 2021

Chapter 10

Yacht Digital Design: Technologies toward a Computational Morphology System

Arianna Bionda and Andrea Ratti

Abstract

The huge transformation fostered by the current industrial revolution is changing each side of our society. In the design field, the use of digital and connected technologies improves not only the representation but also the formal references and the creative process itself. The research investigates the role of the digitally enabled technologies in modifying the disciplinary approaches to yacht design, a particular field of industrial design in which engineering and design approaches are mixed and overlapped. Through case studies and forecasting workshops, the research proposes a journey toward a more digitally conscious and virtually collaborative environment, highlighting as the traditional process of the yacht design discipline is no more valid. The research results, presented in the form of three roadmaps, show as 4.0 digital technologies are deeply transforming not only the representation of a design project but also its formal references and tools. For this reason, the three possible shifts in the yacht design practices are highlighted—input data are moving from analogic to digital reframing the focus from the measuring to inferring, the use of parametric and generative tools is shifting the "digital doing" from drafting to logic, digital twins are modifying the approach to communication media toward more collaborative strategies.

Keywords: digital technologies, forecasting framework, yacht design, design practices, digital design

1. Introduction

The present paper presents the final results of a three years research process that explores the topic of the digitally enabled technologies of Industry 4.0 with the purpose of understanding its role in yacht manufacturing transformation and then introducing its challenges into the field of yacht design practices. The choice of focusing on this research topic does not derive from a recognized field of study—the Yachting 4.0 topic is almost absent in the literature review—but rather from an intuition about the need to foresight the role of the new digital technologies and new manufacturing models in the transformation of the yacht design sector to understand and guide the undergoing digital transformation.

Since 2011, when it was first conceptualized, Industry 4.0 has been at the center of increasing attention from organizations, governments, and the scientific community [1][1]. As described by Herman et al. [2], the fascination for Industry 4.0 is two-fold. First, for the first time, an industrial revolution is predicted a-priori, not observed ex-post providing opportunities for both researchers and companies to shape the future actively. Second, the economic impact of this industrial revolution encompasses the entire design system, on new business models, product-service systems, and human behaviors [3].

The yacht design sector seems not aware and influenced by the disrupting transformations of digital production technologies and the new manufacturing models. The discussion on new technology impacts on the yacht design discipline struggles in considering the transition to a digital representation and digital manufacturing as a paradigmatic change of practices. Besides the few applications of smart materials and virtual technologies on board, the research is often limited to listing opportunities and challenges and in terms of technological availability, without really asking the question of whether and how the yacht design process itself will have to change to drive the digital (r)evolution. Despite the central role of the design discipline in a yacht design project, in the literature, this field of study is generally explored with an engineering approach[2]. The yacht design process is overall described as an iterative trial-and-error procedure aiming at satisfying predefined requirements; a sequence of operation represented as a spiral involving incremental optimization from the yacht's requested capability to the final design evaluation [5].

In this research, a reflection on novel yacht design practices driven by the digitally enabled technologies of Industry 4.0 is fostered. The explorations of future alternatives pointed at answering the two main research questions: *How could these technologies be better implemented in the yacht digital product-service ecosystem scenario? How do these scenarios modify the disciplinary approaches to the yacht design project and its practices?*

In the field of design, the Internet of Things, robotics, collaborative technologies, and intelligent products are profoundly transforming not only the representation of a design project but also the formal references, the input data, the communication strategy, and the design process itself. Digitally enabled technologies of Industry 4.0 revolutions—Industrial Internet of things (IIOT), Cloud Manufacturing, Additive Manufacturing (AM), Co-robots, Big Data Analytics, Simulation and system integration, Virtual and Augmented reality (VR/AR), and Advanced Human Machine Interfaces (AHMI)—are broadly considered the main drivers of the ongoing transformation. According to the main European Industrial plan,[3] the digital technologies could be divided into four families—connecting (IIoT and Cloud Manufacturing), manufacturing (AM and Co-robots), intelligence (Big Data Analysis and Simulation and System Integration), and digitalizing (VR/AR and AHMI). Furthermore, they come together with the six 4.0 Design principles [2, 6]—virtualization, self-configuration, real-time capability, service

[1] A bibliometric study identified an exponential growth in the number of publications per year on the topic, from only three papers in 2012 to more than 500 in 2015, and roughly 5,800 articles in 2018 [1].

[2] The large quantity of scientific articles is focused on naval architecture (the study of resistance to the movement of the hull), aero-dynamics (efficiency of the appendages and sails), structural engineering, construction, and material technology [4].

[3] Industrie 4.0 (Germany), Piano Nazionale Impresa 4.0 (Italy), Danish MADE, Made in Sweden 2030, Industrie du Future (France), Digital revolution in Industry (The Netherlands).

orientation, decentralization, and flexibility—to strengthen the relationship between product-service systems and the manufacturing process.

The literature highlights two behaves of design principles (consciousness and interoperability) and two different levels of integration in the manufacturing and design processes as schematized here in a graphical representation. As shown in **Figure 1**, the principles make possible the development of Industry 4.0 at two levels of integration—a horizontal level—peer-to-peer and over the business value networks—and a vertical level through the manufacturing system, value chain, and customer services. Horizontal integration refers to the integration of the systems for and across the various product, production, or business planning processes. In other words, horizontal integration is about digitization across the whole value chain, whereby data exchanges and connected information systems are centralized managed. Whereas horizontal integration is about systems and flows in the value chain and the various processes happening across it, vertical integration has a hierarchical level component. These hierarchical levels are, respectively, the field level (interfacing with the production process via sensors and actuators), the control level (regulation of both machines and systems), the process line-level (that needs to be monitored and controlled), the operations level (production planning, quality management and so forth), and the enterprise planning level (order management and processing, the overall production planning, etc.). In this integration, a digital execution platform plays a central role in transforming the manufacturing headquarter into a hub of information and connectivity [4].

Trying to connect the digitally enabled technologies of Industry 4.0 and the six 4.0 Design principles, the authors presented in 2020 a radar diagram analysis, based on case studies, that resulted in a clear understanding of the technology strategic strengths in relation to their vertical and horizontal integration in the yachting industry digital framework (for methodological approach see Bionda [7]).

As shown in **Figure 2** "4.0 Design principles—digital technologies radar diagrams", AM and co-robot are employed in the horizontal integration in

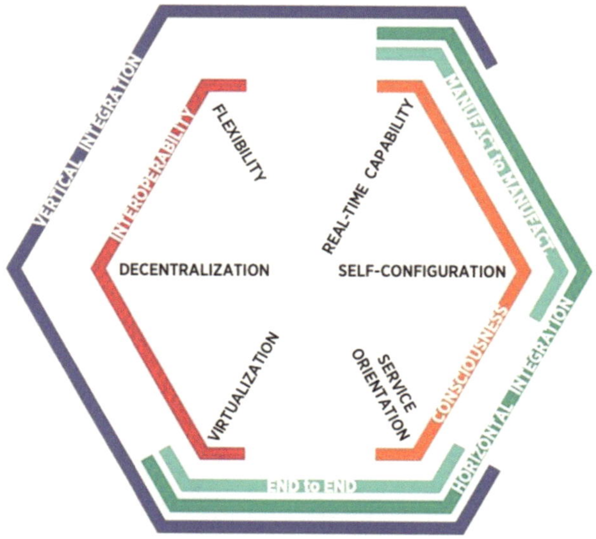

Figure 1.
Graphical interpretation of the design principles according to the different dimensions of digital integration.

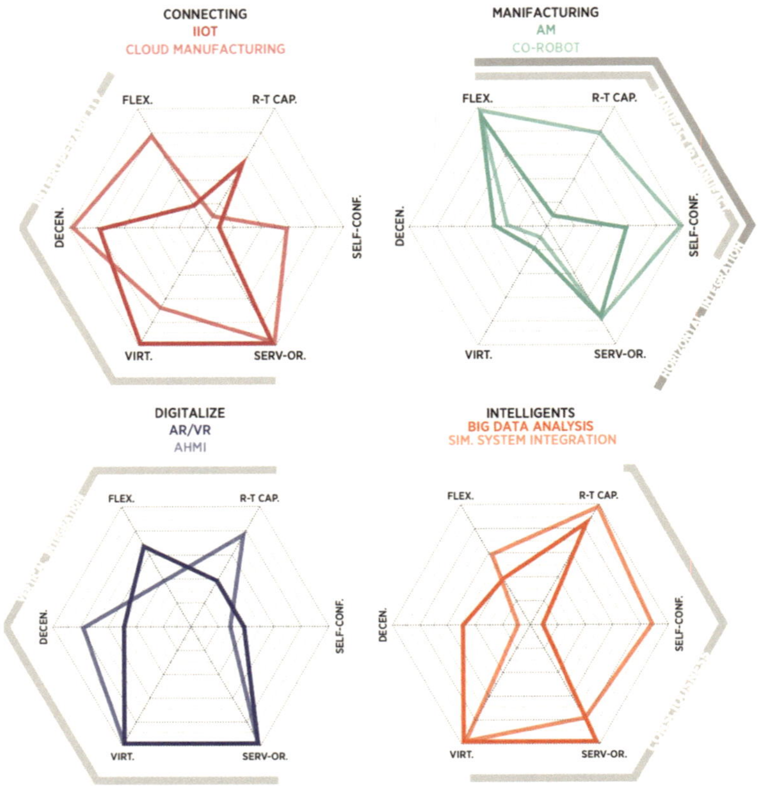

Figure 2.
4.0 Design principles—digital technologies radar diagrams.

manufacturing processes (manufacturing to manufacturing or design studio to manufacturing) with the main characteristics of enabling a more flexible production and, therefore, higher customization. The 4.0 technologies of the connecting family allow interoperability, the ability of a system to exchange and make use of information [6], and are applied in vertical integration processes. Close to the manufacturing family are the technologies big data and simulation and system integration allowing awareness of and responsive actions. These technologies share with IoT a high level in virtualization and service orientation and are able to respond in real-time for horizontal integration of manufacturing and design processes. Looking at the radar chart, the two families connecting and intelligence have complementary behaviors. At last, as the technologies of the digitalize group are mostly digital and virtual communication media, they could be implemented in vertical integration processes, not only at the two extremity of costumer journey sections—communication user-company and communication product-company—but also in each phase of design and manufacturing processes. The digitalized family technologies rely, furthermore, on the design principles of flexibility (i.e., higher customization) and real-time capability, collecting data, analyzing it, and making decisions straight away according to the new findings.

The enabling technologies of the fourth industrial revolution have overlapping areas of application and their implementation is based on digital design and simulation, highly automated manufacturing processes, production data management, and networking. The two main characteristics that describe the evolving system of digital manufacturing-plus-design are "information-driven"—referring to the consciousness principles—and "cyber-physical" with the connection of digital and real word and the ability of a system to exchange and make use of information through and across the value chain (interoperability).

The information-driven system is triggered by IoT and the idea of tagging and tracking "things" with low-cost sensor technologies. In this context, some authors also refer to the Internet of Services, which is based on the idea that services are becoming easily available through web technologies, allowing companies and private users to combine, create, and offer new kinds of value-added services [8]. On the other hand, cyber-physical systems can be defined as "a new generation of systems that integrate physical assets and computational capabilities and are able to interact with humans" [9]. In general, it consists of two main functional components—(1) the advanced connectivity that ensures real-time data acquisition from the physical world and information feedback from cyberspace; and (2) intelligent data management, analytics, and computational capability that constructs cyberspace [10].

Connecting the information-driven capacity with the cyber-physical system, the Industry 4.0 scenario will result in an increased capability of self-organization of manufacturing and other systems, which requires their digital modeling (i.e., virtual factory) and the use of advanced artificial intelligence for process control. As argued by Rodič [11], in this panorama, the product-manufacturing-service system has a unique digital representation, called Digital Twin, consisting of a digital shadow of the real product or manufacturing that alters its properties, condition, and behavior by means of models, information, and data.

It is clear as, in the contemporary panorama, a designer needs to face up design requirements strongly influenced by these advanced technological systems characterized by connected, computational, and open-sourced digital manufacturing. However, the discussion on Industry 4.0 impacts on design discipline is still immature, with few papers discussing the arguments since 2016, only [12].

In the next paragraph, the research methodological approach is presented together with methods and tools adopted. Then, the findings of the analysis of case studies are depicted and discussed as key drivers in the Yachting 4.0 forecasting framework. At last, the research results are collected in three scenarios and three roadmaps toward a yachting computational morphology system. The implications on yacht design processes of these roadmaps were then analyzed in the final paragraph of the chapter, showing the possible future shifting in the design practices on data input, design process and tools, and communication media.

2. The methodological approach: design for the future

If future scenarios and challenges cannot be predicted with an unquestionable level of uncertainty, they can be foresighted and understood to inform present acting. Due to the freshness and the "unexplored complexity" [13] of the Industry 4.0 topic and the lack of reference in literature, strategic thinking to explore alternative futures—Future Studies [14]—is prioritized. The beginning of all industrial revolutions took place in the industry and caused a massive change in society. The current industrial revolution is the opposite. The beginning of the transformation process is not driven directly by the industry itself [15] but is triggered by a hyper-connected society. For the first time in history, the industrial revolution is predicted, providing opportunities to shape the future actively.

For this reason, the methodological framework of the research is placed in the broader area between the Discipline of Anticipation [16] and Design, aiming to push the boundaries of yacht design practices. Furthermore, this context of investigation compels the research to continuously shift from field exploration and interpretation (surveys and case studies) and forecasting activity (participatory scenario-building workshop), opening up to several tangents or critical matters that position the study at a conceptual level to be verified with on-site practices.

Even though there are no data about the future, companies, designers, and policymakers currently use many strategies, methods, and tools to gather data for future investigation. Among them, the present study refers to the six-ing steps of activities depicted by Hines and Bishop in the book *Thinking About the Future, Guidelines for Strategic Foresight* [17] to answer the research questions. These steps were identified by the Association of Professional Futurists' Development Team as fundamental for a comprehensive foresight strategy. The six activities—Framing, Scanning, Forecasting, Visioning, Planning, and Acting—aimed at getting a systemic understanding of expected, alternative, and preferable changes in introducing the digitally enabled technologies of industry 4.0 in yacht design and construction practices. The concept of "system" implies that drivers of changes affect the behaviors in a network of interaction and feedback loops between input and outcomes. With this perspective, the present study, while aiming at investigating the changes in yacht design processes and tools, includes the broader sector of the yacht industry at the core of strategic forecasting research. The whole system embraces the design and production process as well as the user interaction, that is, sailing and maintenance stages.

The research strategy mirrors the six -ing steps of strategic forecasting, dividing the activities into likewise steps to drive the study from the initial literature review to the future study agenda, as following described.

The phases *Framing* and *Scanning* aimed at building a robust forecasting framework through desk research and case studies highlighting drivers in the digital yacht ecosystem, challenges, and uncertainties. The identification of the good practices for the case studies analysis was undertaken, thanks to the consultation with stakeholders—academics, naval and nautical shipyards, and suppliers, yacht designers, nautical industrial associations—while the case studies data sourcing was performed in two steps—primary source semi-structured observation (during the main nautical trades 2017–2019) and second data document review (online data). Then, the features of each case study were analyzed on the following four parameters—enabling technologies and sub-technologies for UX implementation, relevant 4.0 design principles, impact on YD process, and impact on the customer journey. The collective and parallel analysis of the multiple cases was executed, thanks to a card-sorting activity where the cases were gathered in overlapping clusters. This activity results in the Yachting 4.0 forecasting framework, described in detail in the next chapter.

Then, scenario-building workshop (*Forecasting* and *Visioning* phases) was selected as a forecasting method based on the nature of the uncertainty involved in the activity and referring to the Future Studies framework proposed by Courtney [18]. While case studies analysis was conducted with an expert mindset, the forecasting phase had a participatory mindset, involving stakeholders as co-researchers. To foster the participation and the interaction among stakeholders a proper set of activities and tools were designed following the Future Technology workshop method (FTW) [19], a method specifically suited to involve people with everyday knowledge or experience in a specific industrial process in an envisioning activity to design the interactions between current and future technology in a specific sector. The scenario-building workshop was divided into the four main FTW phases—a general introduction on purpose and forecasting framework, a structured brainstorming, a free envisioning session, and a scenario model building exploring the gap between current and future technology. The fourth step of the workshop involved, also, listing requirements and outlining critic aspects for future technology applications. This activity was the link with the next -ing phases—*Planning* and *Acting*—where a retrospective analysis to ground the workshop results in an understanding of novel yacht design approaches, processes, and tools driven by the Yachting 4.0 forecasting framework takes place.

The research results were then presented in the form of roadmaps, as the bridge between the forecast and the present situation [20], taking the scenarios developed in the participatory research at the destination. The method here adopted comes from Phaal et al. [21], where the roadmaps are conceived as the strategic plan that defines the digital scenarios connecting the different dimensions of the innovation strategy, the significant technologies and tools needed, and the plotted timeline.

3. Technology drivers for the digitalization of the yachting industry

As previously shown in the 4.0 design principles-technologies diagrams (**Figure 2**), the enabling technologies of the fourth industrial revolution have common behaviors and overlapping areas of applications that set the conditions on which to build a forecasting framework for the 4.0 development in the yachting sector. With the aim of further investigating that relation and revealing opportunities and trends for the scenario-building phase, a Case Studies analysis on digitally enabled technologies applied in the yachting industry was carried out. A card-sorting activity with an expert mindset was performed to grouped cases with the same behaviors without clustering them merely according to technologies adopted. After desk research, case studies were divided into three macro areas—design, manufacturing, and sailing. Some samples were placed across two groups representing a link between them. Looking at these links, two different groups were identified—the cases in which 4.0 technologies allow collaboration within multiple actors and the cases in which the virtualization and decentralization of communication media are predominate. The second stage of clustering involved the parallel investigation of the already labeled cluster to identify common grounds. The cases were, then, sub gathered according to the levels of consciousness in Industry 4.0 integration and to the influence on the disciplinary approach on the yacht design project in its processes and tools.

A graphic map to collect all the card-sorting clusters is here proposed to highlight the respecting relation between them (**Figure 3**). The map shows, at the central line, the depicted five levels of consciousness in Industry 4.0 integration—digital data gathering, simulation, optimization, system integration, and generative design. These five levels are put in relation to the two dimensions of communication and collaboration identified in the first step of cluster analysis. The resulting case studies groups are following labeled and described.

Digital data gathering: Projects integrating IoT and AHMI with the primary purpose of monitoring yacht assets. This group collects all the cases based on digital gateways, onboard electronic logs, and digital platforms for vessel system control and automation. Plus, it includes the environmental digital data analysis with the main purpose of gathering and analyzing field data to (in perspective) inform the design

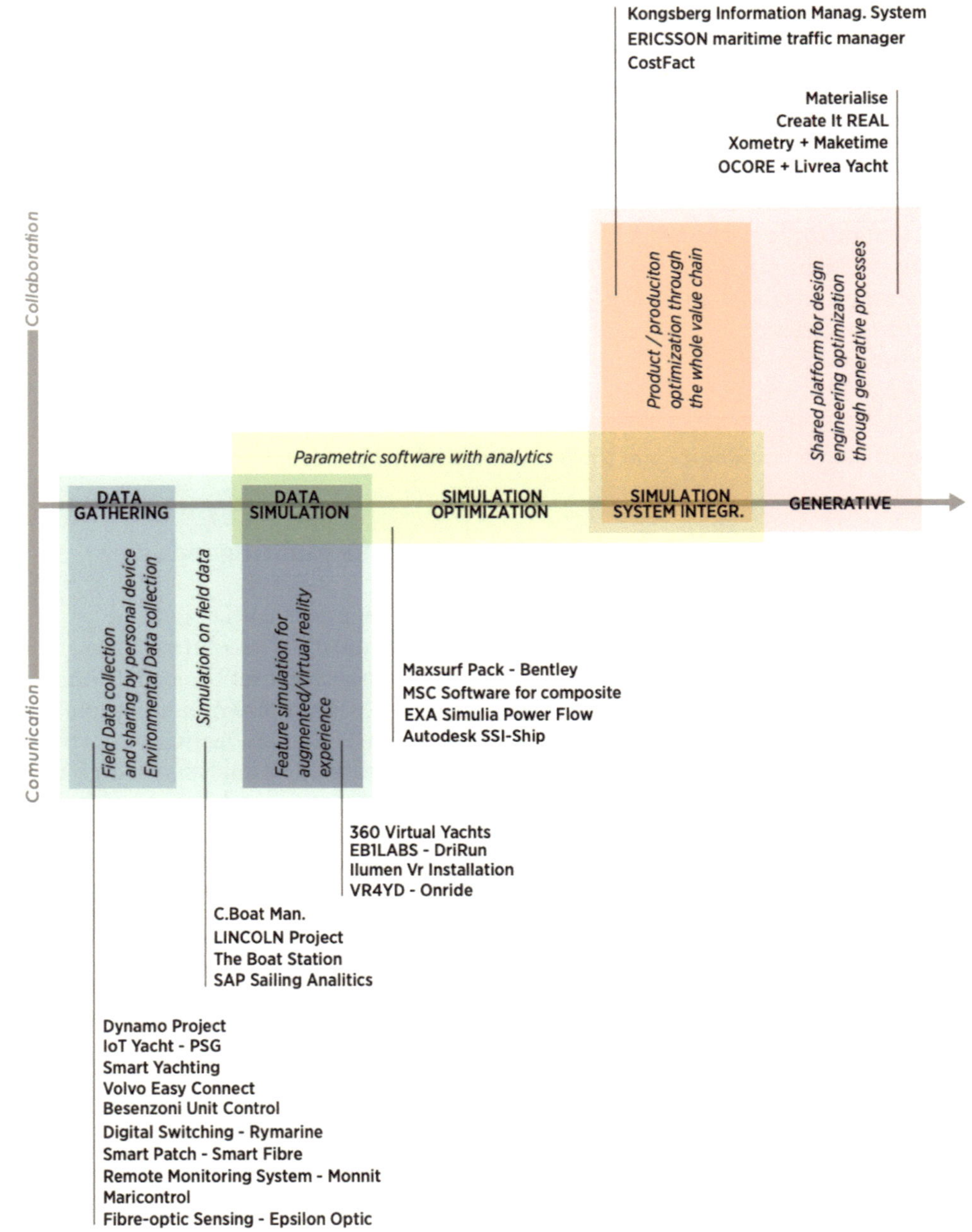

Figure 3.
Case studies map.

process. Vessel and marine environmental data gathering from IoT structures are mainly used in this cluster for maintenance purposes. Only one case experiments the possibility of confronting field data with design data.

Data simulation for communication purposes: Projects not informed (or partially informed) by field data integrating big data, simulation, VR, and AHMI. The main examples are a virtual reality in marketing strategic communication and virtual sailing testers.

Simulation analysis and optimization: Projects not informed by field data in a not-integrated ecosystem. This group encompasses simulation software to predict real-world performance and tools for manufacturing process optimization.

Optimization through system integration: Projects with a collaborative nature aiming at the optimization of both product and process through the whole value chain. This group collects all the collaborative platforms developed for the marine and yachting industry to manage the design phases, the value chain, or the offshore and sailing operation.

Optimization through generative: Projects involving generative design tools to optimize and self-configuring product shape according to the manufacturing process. This cluster encompasses the collaborative platforms currently used for managing the manufacturing process with the aid of digital assisted tools as additive manufacturing and collaborative robots. These case studies have a collaborative nature aiming at self-configuring product shapes according to the manufacturing process by the use of generative design tools. A few cases, including cloud manufacturing as the key technology, are gathered in this group.

We can observe in the map, a clear separation between the two categories, which are communication and collaboration. Communication strategies are more implemented with low consciousness projects, while collaborative strategies lead projects with a higher level of systemic integration and self-configuring processes. The technologies adopted on the left side of the map refer to the design principles virtualization, service orientation, and decentralization. On the other hand, cases that implement the use of collaborative platforms for generative design do not make use of field data through the entire value chain, as well as the optimization processes. We can observe that the technology adopted here leads directly to flexibility, self-configuration, and real-time capability as design principles crossing the two areas of horizontal integration in manufacturing and design. In particular, new media of communication are emerging in the relation within companies and the yacht final user to allow (i) a more immersive experience, and (ii) faster and easier access to information through digital platforms and self-devices.

4. The Yachting 4.0 forecasting framework

To build the forecasting framework for the scenario-building phase, the results of case studies analysis are observed through the lens of the ecosystem approach for Industry 4.0 scenarios by PWC [22]. The PWC Industry 4.0 scenario framework identifies four steps in moving from a product-oriented to a platform-focused approach—(i) Core Product, the traditional base offering, which can be "digitized" by adding digital layers around it; (ii) Digital Augmentation, digital customer interfaces, visualization, touchpoints, and channels augment the experience and allow a variety of interaction models; (iii) Digital Service in which digitally enabled services are added to the physical core product providing an end-to-end solution to a broader customer need; and (iv) Digital ecosystem with interfaces to suppliers, partners, and customers, the product is embedded in an ecosystem for co-creation and additional value capture.

In the present study, the PWC Industry 4.0 scenario is expanded to include the manufacturing process in the systemic approach and the "after launch" stage. As we can observe in **Figure 4**, the scheme becomes a group of four concentric circles divided into four sectors by the vertical and the horizontal axes.

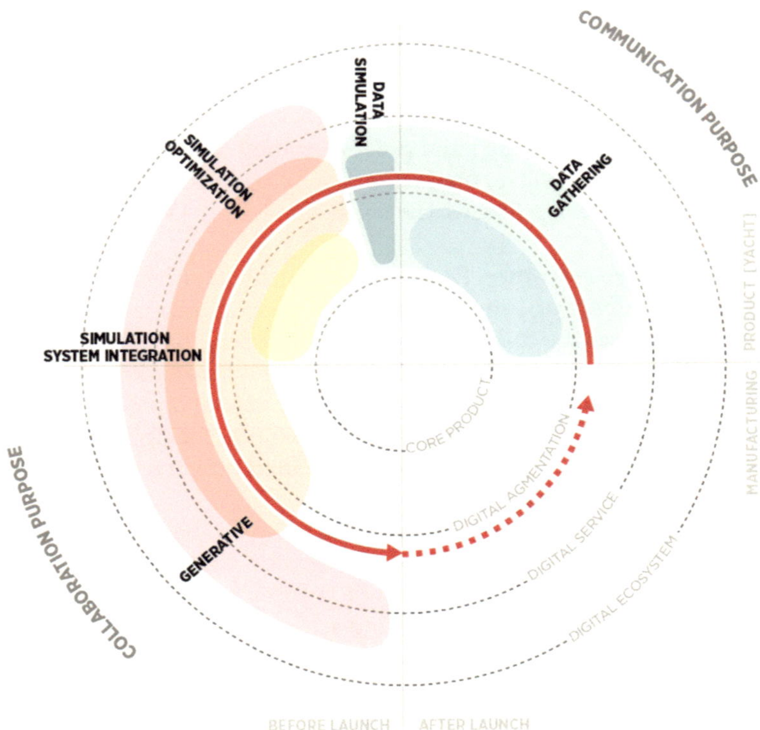

Figure 4.
Yachting 4.0 forecasting framework.

The horizontal axis separates the focus on product from the focus on production, while the vertical axis marks the temporal division between before launch and after launch phases. The four sectors of the circles result in design (focus on the product before launch), manufacturing (focus on production before launch), sailing (focus on the product before launch), and maintenance (focus on production after launch). The Yachting 4.0 forecasting framework is built by overlapping the groups of the Case studies map to the scenario framework scheme with the purpose of giving fundament in answering the first research question—How could these technologies be better implemented in the yacht digital product-service ecosystem scenario?

A clear barrier between the "before launch" and the "after launch" sections is observed. This evidence refers to the previously depicted separation between collaboration and communication. The digital data coming from field and user engagement are not yet employed in the design phase and maintenance stage. This results in a disconnection between the after launch and before launch phases at the expense of input data design quality and quantity.

On the design and manufacturing side, horizontal integration of digital data for simulation, optimization, and self-configuration (generative) process is arising. While communication strategies are more implemented with interoperability projects, collaborative strategies lead projects with a higher level of consciousness and of systemic horizontal integration. In these cases, the implementation in the use of collaborative platforms for optimization and generative design process does not make use of field data through the entire value chain. At last, the visual representation of the Yachting 4.0 forecasting framework shows a lack of experiences in the last circle, the digital ecosystem, and an insufficient connection between the four sectors of the graph. This fact is a further confirmation of the general immaturity of the yachting sector on the theme of Industry 4.0 and a need for systemic visions, leading the research activity into the scenario-building workshop.

5. Three scenarios for the yacht digital design

The workshop activity, conceived as a co-research phase, had three objectives—(i) discuss and validate the scenario framework; (ii) explore and build alternative scenarios on Yacht Design 4.0, outlining drivers and criticalities; and (iii) involving and making aware of the specific industrial community on digital technologies opportunities. To achieve the intended research objectives, the workshop involved experts in the yacht design field—yacht designers and draftsmen in the yard, shipyards project and production managers, yacht industrial association managers, and experts in digital transformation and policymakers. The workshop took the FTW scheme as a reference aiming at reaching an informed understanding of a grid of four boxes—everyday technology and activities (core product), an everyday activity supported by new technology (digital augmentation), a new activity supported by current technology (digital services), and new activities with new technologies (digital ecosystem). Moving inside the grid, the workshop partakers are guided in the scenario visioning activity.

The workshop was focused on yacht design practices, but a systemic view on the whole yachting sector was fostered. For this reason, even if the whole scenario-building workshop was divided into the four main phases described in the methodology, parallel and circular activities were performed in an iterative conversation among challenges and opportunities, especially in the free envisioning and scenario exploration phases. As a workshop result, three visions symbolized by the three Roadmaps were created.

The definition of the Yacht Design 4.0 Roadmaps was, in itself, a design matter. Sustained by all the qualitative data and knowledge, collected by case studies and by the co-design visioning activity, the roadmaps represent the synthesis of the collaborative activities, and the grounding of the workshop results in an understanding of novel yacht design approaches, processes, and tools driven by the Yachting 4.0 forecasting framework.

The multiple scenarios developed in the workshop were grouped up based on common ground identification looking at (i) the four steps of digitalization of the Yachting 4.0 forecasting framework; (ii) the insight coming from the workshop scenario exploration phase and shared by the workshop partakers; and (iii) the three cluster of yacht product and production, which are [23] top of the line, model-based, and semi-custom. The timeline for a roadmap toward a computational morphology system was defined according to the workshop results discussed with the partakers:

- current: digital augmentation, within five years;
- near future: digital services, within 10 years;
- and futures: digital ecosystem, from 10 to 20 years.

In the next sub-paragraphs, the three roadmaps are presented and depicted together with their implications on designer work and their critic aspects, as discussed with the scenario-building workshop partakers. The implications on yacht design processes were then analyzed on the primary levels already set in the previous research activity (case studies)—data input, design process and tools, and communication media.

5.1 Top of the line roadmap to digital product-service ecosystem

The top of the line cluster encompasses companies dealing with a high level of product customization and looking toward the larger segment of super- and mega-yachts. This type of boat is part of what is called luxury design, where the project is highly influenced by the specific culture and personality of the client [24], where the request for a craftmanship tailor-made product is continuously increasing, and the focus of the market is shifting on rare and personalized experiences [25]. The roadmap takes the peculiarity of this cluster into account, proposing a journey toward a digital product-service ecosystem in which personalized service and yacht components are designed on real data gathered in a digital experience platform.

Current: The first step is the digital augmentation of both the design project, that is, 3D model of the yacht, and the product, that is, the yacht itself. The yacht design modeling becomes parametric. The designer interacts with a digital structure that was generated by a mechanism according to a set of predefined relations between shapes and components. In this way, the first phase of preliminary concept design embeds the design engineering steps allowing rapid change of design dimension and structure in the project representation. On the other hand, sensors and remote-control networks are placed on-board, transforming the vessel into a connected object. The first level of services proposed is (i) the electronic log for sailing automated data recording, (ii) the gateway of the universal system, and (iii) the social media integration. The user experience data are recorded in a knowledge management platform.

Near future: The second step is the connection of the knowledge management platform, featured with big data real-time analysis, to the design project. Knowledge management platform examines large and varied field data sets to unveil hidden patterns represented by formal, computer-interpretable rules. The design project makes use of the data resulting from the iterative process of data analysis and simulation to verify the yacht premises. Furthermore, the yacht 3D model becomes a non-living digital twin—a digital replica of all the physical and IoT assets of the vessel, allowing direct communication with both the production site and the whole supply chain. Virtual/augmented reality and AHMI tools could be used as communication media for a preliminary customer immersive experience. For what concern novel digital services, the use of big data analysis allows the development of on-board personalized service including optimized and automated routing according to sailing analytics, to environmental and forecast data, maintenance and marina service feed by real-time field data, and legal insurance services.

Future: The digital product-service ecosystem encompasses the physical and the virtual world, and data are transmitted seamlessly (and in two ways) between the yacht and the living digital twin. The knowledge management platform examines not only the field data sets but also the design project information, allowing interoperability and vertical system integration between yacht components. At the same time, the parametric digital twin is conceived as a living project providing insight on both the elements and the dynamics of how digital devices operate and live throughout the yacht life cycle. The yearly maintenance or refitting stage benefits from the field data gathering and analysis of the digital experience platform, allowing a yacht optimization on real customer needs.

Implication on yacht design process and tools: In this scenario, the yacht design processes maintain its character of an iterative cycle of refinement steps. Due to the use of a parametric design tool,[4] the sequence of steps of simulation and optimization are integrated into a unique analytical process on geometrical models.

In this contest, the living digital twin is managed by parametric design technologies and optimized by the result of the digital experience platform analysis. Moreover, the design platform could allow multiple evaluative analyses and support the collaboration among the different design and engineering teams involved in the yacht design process. At last, the living digital twin embedded in the digital experience platform could be visualized through virtual reality digital devices both for augmented customer experience and manufacturing/maintenance purposes. The representation highlights not only the yacht feature and the control gateways but also the information on how the yacht, the systems, and the components operate throughout the whole life cycle.

Critic aspects: The scenario shares with the broader Industry 4.0 development the challenge in data and privacy protection. Even if the ethical challenges created by mass data gathering through online interactions are scientifically reported [27], there is not a clear policy ethical framework on digital technologies due to the rapid and disruptive changes in the information technology environment. On the other hand, maritime sector suffers from cybersecurity as well. According to the EU report on cyber security challenges in the maritime sector [28] and the findings of the collaborative scenario-building workshop, maritime cybersecurity awareness is currently low to nonexistent.

5.2 Semi-custom model-based roadmap to generative-integrated ecosystem

The second group represents the companies with a model-based production with a high level of flexibility and customization of the core product, of digital integration in design and production processes, and experience in 4.0 enabling technologies. The roadmap to a generative-integrated ecosystem takes the current advancement of the cluster into account, proposing a journey in which the virtual data coming from user experience and field measurements could inform the design phase in generative processes for higher optimization and personalization in project development. The roadmap from optimization to generative consists of three steps, which are as follows:

Current: To support the present design process (from concept to design engineering), a knowledge management platform is placed across the sailing and the production stages. Data coming from the digital augmentation of the yacht and the vessel production tools are recorded and analyzed. The process data outputs are formal, computer-interpretable rules that are considered in the parametric yacht design modeling. Knowledge-based methods have been intensively studied and applied in other transportation industrial sectors, such as maritime; however, it has not been studied or adopted in the yachting industry, dominated by low volume production and small or medium-sized companies, so far. Despite that, the large amount of already formalized engineering knowledge in codes and regulations could be implemented in the yacht design as well.

[4] The relations between the project dimensions are no more directly drafted on a digital continuum space (as in a cad direct modeling tool) but are dependent upon various parameters. This process is generally described as predictive models, as opposed to direct modeling, in which the descriptive modeling process brings together with manufacturing logic and material proprieties [26].

Near future: The second phase represents the knowledge integration into the yacht digital twin. The refinement optimization steps are directly managed by the digital replica of all the physical and IoT assets of the yacht. The integration in a unified platform allows direct communication with both the production site and the whole supply chain. The communication media becomes a digital interface on personal devices, and production work teams could interact with the digital replica sending feedback to the knowledge management tool. Virtual reality and augmented reality could be used to verify the features and the assembly operation of onboard optimized components.

Future: A generative design tool is integrated into the knowledge management platform to transform the data coming from user experience and field measurements into alternative shapes. This process allows the generation of different solutions by changing the parameters of design constraints (from knowledge management platform) and design requirements (from direct design modeling). Consequently, the quantitative analysis of computational techniques based on the finite-element method is translated into qualitative alternatives of complexity. The use of parametric and generative design tools is driven by the possibility of applying advanced manufacturing processes to yacht production. In particular, additive manufacturing and cloud manufacturing could represent a turning point in the customizability of yacht components.

Implication on yacht design process and tools: In the generative-integrated ecosystem, the current parametric design process is shifting toward a computational process model of digital design under the impact of a new generation of associative algorithms. The linked and iterative cycles of design, analysis, simulation, and optimization of the yacht design spiral are no more valid in describing the new paradigm of the yacht design process. The two platforms of knowledge-generative design and integrated management have unified the process of simulation, evaluation, and fabrication within designer-scripted morphogenesis processes. Furthermore, the integration of the 4.0 enabling technology of additive manufacturing and collaborative robotics in the roadmap led to including the "making level" in the design process.

Critic aspects: Besides the previously mentioned ethical issues on data confidence and privacy and cybersecurity, a discussion on the shifting role of designers emerged. Although the parametric approach has increased the interoperability of systems and the flexibility among geometry relations, the exploration of yacht design alternatives is still limited by the manual operation of designers in varying individual parameters. Whereas, what a generative approach does is asking artificial intelligence to explore the design space semi-autonomously, revealing options that would otherwise be hidden. The designer role is shifting at the beginning and final stage of the process interacting with the generative structures of the yacht model, defining the project requirements and the grammar of shapes, and finally evaluating the generative results. New digital skills are requested for designers and a new way of thinking. These challenges are also arising in academic research around the concept of digital design thinking [26].

5.3 Model-based roadmap to co-modular digital ecosystem

The third cluster encompasses the companies that have a lower value in customization and an engineered production process. The cluster is mainly represented by shipyards dealing with low series and mass assembly core products even if a request for higher personalization is rising in the market, which are claiming for more flexible and integrated process in both the design and the production of yachts. Moving from mass production to mass personalization is challenging the worldwide industry from the early 90s and is extensively discussed in theory and applications [29, 30]. However, the integrated use of the enabling technologies of Industry 4.0 seems to offer a solution to the dilemma between the economies of scale and scope triggered by the concept of mass customization [31]. In this context, the model-based roadmap envisions a journey toward an integrated-modular digital ecosystem, where the yacht product, design, and production processes consist of integrated (design-production-product) subsystems with little interdependencies serving as modules links.

Current: As for the previous roadmaps, the first step in digitalization is the digital augmentation of the yacht design project and the model-based yacht. The parametric design tool for yacht 3D modeling is directly connected to a virtual configurator, able to manipulate the set of parameters according to the designer's work. In this phase, the customers interact through a personal smart device (AHMI) with a digital structure generated to link furniture finishing and components features. A knowledge management platform received and store the data coming from the onboard IoT system as component sensors and universal system gateways. The service offered to the final user is the ones described in the roadmap to the digital product-service ecosystem.

Near future: A yacht digital twin is optimized with the data coming from the onboard IoT systems. This digital replica of all the physical and IoT assets of the vessel represents the link between the production site and the customer virtual configurator. The yacht project is conceived as a flexible assembly of different modules regulated by interdependences in a virtual logic structure. In this vision, the boat could be highly customizable. The effectiveness of the modular yacht concept is already proven by several commercial proposals and academic research [32, 33]. The customer virtual configurator is conceived as a co-creation guiding tool to build customized solutions based on predefined design variables and limits. The opportunity offered by VR/AR on smart devices and AHMI allows to virtual test the finished product and provide end-user with product support.

Future: An integrated and modular digital platform is placed at the core of the design process involving not only the yacht conceptualization and engineering through digital twin modeling tools but also the production and supply chain assets managing. Both the design and the production process are divided into interconnected and integrated subsystems. An interdependence logic structure manages the modules relation based on configuration variables and yacht design constraints. Furthermore, the subsystems are optimized by the analysis of the digital field data coming from the connected vessel (i.e., connected subsystems of different vessels) and the digital-based production tools, such as co-robots and additive manufacturing. Although introduced on modular yacht design products, the concept of modularity is now applied to many different areas of the production system, production planning, and optimization processes.

Implication on yacht design process and tools: A sequence of four steps divides the design process of the co-modular digital ecosystem scenario. (i) Definition of a pre-set of general condition and parameters mirroring the first cycle of the yacht design spiral aiming at setting the interdependence logic structure of yacht based on the configuration variables and the yacht design principle and constraints; (ii) Variants generation of subsystems according to market and trend research. This step involves, furthermore, the module links definition and the logic correlation between subsystems; (iii) Variant optimization by field data from product performances (sailing and user experience), from the production process, and supply chain management;

and (iv) Variant selection, final product visualization, and evaluation by customers through virtual reality. The collaborative design process here involves the customers in flexible customization. In this scenario, the design process is supported by a parametric tool involving the generation and management of digital representations of physical, functional, and production properties of subsystems and their logic/construction links.

Critic aspects: In addition to the previous scenario criticalities that remain constant even in this third vision, a generally low level of digital experiences in the yachting sector could represent a crucial aspect in the development of the roadmap. Furthermore, the small and (sometimes) family dimension of the nautical supply chain could be a barrier to digital integration. To bridge this gap, specific design competencies in parametric and integrated design are needed across the whole value chain at different hierarchical levels.

6. Computational strategies in digital yacht design

At last, this paragraph discusses the research results presented through the roadmaps, putting them in a broader conversation with the recent debate on parametric morphologies, computational design engineering, and digital design thinking. As shown by the roadmaps, the journey toward a computational morphology system affects not only the design practice with the use of novel design tools but also the input data, the design process, and the communication media between designers-customers and designers-manufacturing. The roadmaps highlight that the yacht design process is progressively moving away from the linked and iterative cycles of design, analysis, simulation, and optimization of the yacht design spiral. The novel approach seems reflecting the level of 4.0 consciousness previously described in the framework—simulation, optimization, and generative design (**Figure 5**). The Yachting 4.0 forecasting framework also suggests that the digitally enabled technologies are driving the yacht design process toward a more digitally conscious and virtually collaborative environment. Three different approaches to the yacht design process driven by digital and computational modeling tools are depicted and named—digital yacht design spiral, digital yacht module optimization cycle, and generative yacht design tangle.

At first, in the roadmap toward a digital product-service ecosystem, the yacht design process maintains its characteristic of an iterative cycle of refinement steps feed by real-time data. The Digital yacht design spiral (**Figure 6a**) represents the first level of the 4.0 consciousness: simulation. The data analysis and the design process are still being separated, and the manual operation of designers drives the optimization process in varying individual parameters. In this process, the use of parametric design tools allows interoperability between different design and engineering teams as well as a direct connection with the digital twin (conceived as the communication medium between stakeholders and digital assets). However, the exploration of yacht design alternatives is still directly connected with the capability of designers in interpreting customer requirements, setting production and material constraints, and understanding simulation results to appropriately vary the individual parameters of 3D models.

The second level of 4.0 consciousness in yacht design processes—optimization—is represented by the roadmaps to the co-modular digital ecosystem and the process "Digital yacht module optimization cycle" (**Figure 6b**). In this roadmap, the yacht

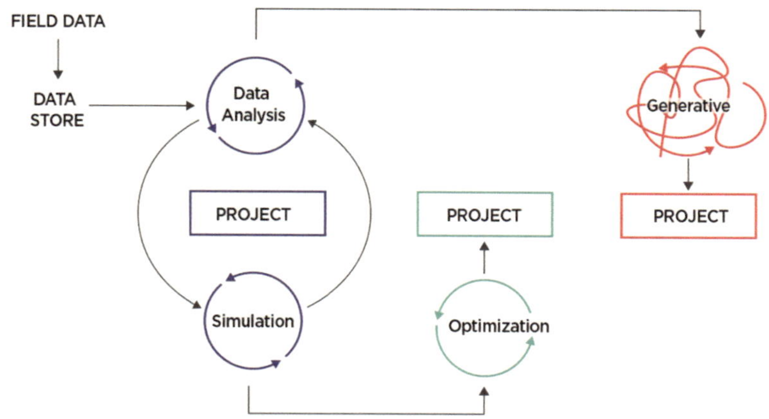

Figure 5.
Computational strategies in the Yacht design process.

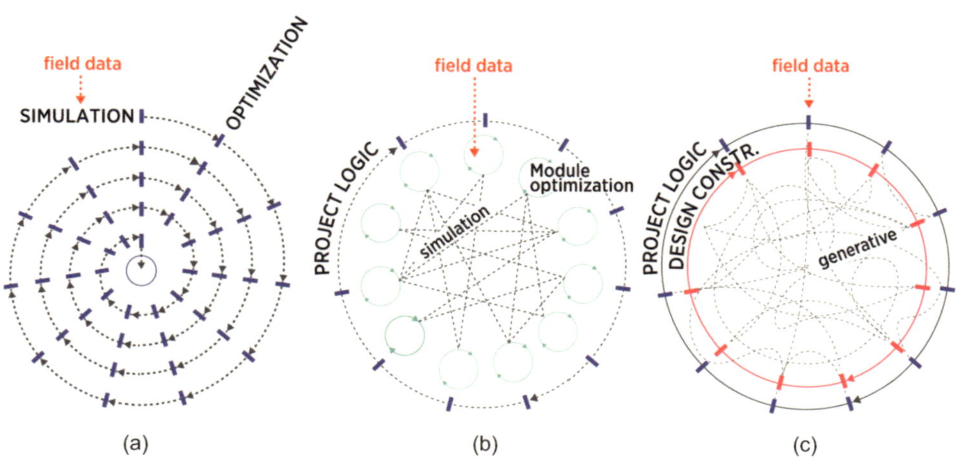

Figure 6.
Approaches to the yacht design process driven by digital and computational modeling tools: (a) Digital yacht design spiral; (b) Digital yacht module optimization cycle; and (c) Generative yacht design tangle.

design process is not entirely managed by the designer/team itself but is the result of a collaborative process of co-creation with customers. The sequence of refinement steps characteristic of the yacht design process is here moving from the entire product conceptualization to the design of the single subsystem. The exploration of yacht alternatives is directly managed by customers and mediated by a digital platform that embedded the logic of the project and the self-assembly optimization parameters. Working on the logic of vessel design, structure, and modules interconnection, the yacht design process is not opened to disrupting co-design results, even if novel assembly systems and unexpected results could be created by co-design interaction.

In the generative-integrated ecosystem, the current parametric design process is shifting toward a computational process model driven by associative algorithms, driving the reflection toward the Generative yacht design tangle (**Figure 6c**). Already experimented in a few yacht design cases and intensely explored in the literature review in the industrial design and architectural field, generative processes are disrupting the dichotomy between creative thinking and digital drafting. In the generative processes, the focus of artificial intelligence is not analyzing and simulating data but exploring alternatives and creating a solution. Within the different types of generative processes, a grammar-based approach emerged as the more suitable in the yacht design field. In this process, the designer interacts with the generative structures, their limits, and input, defining the grammar of shapes, and finally evaluates the generative results [34].

Contrarily from the previous two processes, here, the design results are multiple and interchangeable. The selection criteria of the proper design solution is still an open issue, not discussed in the present study, and weakly tackled in the literature review on the design engineering field. The research highlights three possible (future) shifts in yacht design practices.

Input data: Data are moving from analogic to digital and the opportunity to networking information distributed across many different sources shifts the focus of data input from measuring to inferred (i.e., big data analysis). Parallel to analogic data—marketing and customer insight, specific designer and engineering knowledge, and onboard experience—yacht designers could make use of a large quantity of direct data measured by sensors and smart devices. In the digital augmentation sphere, not only IoT design data are accessible everywhere, but information from many different devices can be combined in datasets. It is important to underline that digital data coming from production processes and intelligent vessels become the new oil for design empowering and customer involvement only if they can be fully understood within a qualitative context framework of previous analogic yacht design knowledge.

Design processes and tools: The use of parametric and generative design tools is shifting the "digital doing" from digital drafting to digital logic in which the digital focus is the creative process itself. In focusing on the design process, moving from direct modeling to parametric design and then, to generative yacht design, could fragment the dichotomy between the creative thinking and the digitally drafting of the vessel shapes. Here, artificial intelligence is asked to explore the design space semi-autonomously to disclose options based on predefined generative rules, relations, and principles. An alternative way is presented through the roadmaps and identifies the journey toward a modularized system of optimization. Even in this process, the digital focus is moved to the logic structure. While in the generative design process the "logic" refers mainly to the design principles and the grammars of shapes, in modular-computational processes, it has to do with the relation between elements and junction constraints. This focus on the reasoning level of the design process is highlighted in the purposes of generative and computational design processes [35]: "creating responsive objects able to react to external stimuli by modifying the formal shapes while conserving the morphogenesis logic."

Communication media: The digital twin is modifying the approach to communication media toward a more collaborative media strategy. Parallel to the availability of field data and the shifting of digital focus in yacht design processes, the 4.0 enabling technologies and new manufacturing paradigms of Industry 4.0 could enable a novel approach to the communication, and therefore collaboration, tools for yacht design and engineering. In the journey depicted in the roadmaps, it acts as a medium virtually replacing the paper draft and drawing and project render. As a shadow of the projects embedding all the physical and digital assets, the digital twin could be furthermore used as a co-design tool between yacht designers and engineers as well to involve customers or manufacturing teams and supply chain in the project definition. Furthermore, the Digital Twin supports the visualization and management of the vessel throughout the whole life cycle, becoming a valuable tool in the maintenance stages.

7. Conclusion and further steps

The paper presents an explorative study of the topic of Industry 4.0 in the yachting field. The research focus raised from an intuition about the need to foresight the role of the new digital technologies and new manufacturing models in the transformation of the yacht design sector to understand and guide the undergoing digital transformation, filling the literature gap where no scientific publications consider the impact of Industry 4.0 in the yacht fields on its entirety.

Due to the freshness and the unexplored complexity of the Industry 4.0 topic in the yacht design practices, strategic thinking and collaborative research activities to explore alternative futures were prioritized, using case studies analysis and scenario-building participatory workshop as main research methods. With the purpose of building a robust forecasting framework, a card-sorting analysis on 4.0 enabling technologies applied in the yachting industry was carried out to ground the knowledge on relations between industry 4.0 design principles and digital technologies. This activity led to the discussion on opportunities and trends for the Yachting 4.0 forecasting framework. This first research result was used in the scenario-building participatory workshop as a guiding backdrop.

Then, three scenarios and three roadmaps toward a computational morphology system are presented. The definition of the Yacht Design 4.0 Roadmaps was, in itself, a design matter. Sustained by all the qualitative data and knowledge collected by case studies and by the co-design visioning activity of a scenario-building workshop, the roadmaps represent an unavoidable subjective synthesis of the research results, conceived as a guide in bridging the gap between the current situation and the visions developed. Furthermore, they contain a reflection on novel yacht design practices affected by the new manufacturing models and digital technologies of Industry 4.0 as the main contribution of the study in the yacht design field.

The research evidence highlights three central possible (future) shifts in the yacht design practices, which are as follows:

- the input data are moving from analogic to digital, reframing the focus of the designer practice from the measured data to the inferred data;
- the use of parametric and generative design tools is shifting the "digital doing" from digital drafting to digital logic driving the process toward a more digitally conscious and virtually collaborative environment;
- the digital twin is modifying the approach to communication media toward a more collaborative media strategy.

The research achievements resulted positioned on a conceptual level. The founding has numerous links and overlapping with the research on Computational design and morphogenesis logic design [35]. For this theoretical nature of the research, the results still need to be pragmatically tested and verified by applied research projects both the shipyards and in design studios. Plus, the workshop discussions point out numerous criticalities at different levels that should be considered for future study in the field—(i) the emerging role of digital yacht designers and the new skills necessary to face the digital transformation, (ii) the design of specific tools for yacht design co-creation, (iii) the issue of data using and data protection, and (iii) the challenges on cybersecurity in the maritime sectors.

Author details

Arianna Bionda* and Andrea Ratti
Politecnico di Milano, Design Department, Milan, Italy

*Address all correspondence to: arianna.bionda@polimi.it

References

[1] Muhuri PK, Shukla AK, Abraham A. Industry 4.0: A bibliometric analysis and detailed overview. Engineering Applications of Artificial Intelligence. 2019;**78**:218-235

[2] Herman M, Pentek T, Otto B. Design Principles for Industrie 4.0. Dortmund: Technische Universität Dortmund; 2015. p. 45

[3] Drath R, Horch A. Industrie 4.0: Hit or hype? [industry forum]. IEEE Industrial Electronics Magazine. 2014;**8**(2):56-58

[4] Industry 4.0 and the Fourth Industrial Revolution Explained [Internet]. i-SCOOP. 2022. Available from: https://www.i-scoop.eu/industry-4-0/

[5] Eliasson R, Larsson L, Orych M. Principles of Yacht Design. Vol.1. London: A&C Black; 2014. pp. 5-7

[6] Qin J, Liu Y, Grosvenor R. A categorical framework of manufacturing for industry 4.0 and beyond. Procedia Cirp. 2016;**52**:173-178

[7] Bionda A. Toward a Yacht Design 4.0 How the New Manufacturing Models and Digital Technologies [Could] Affect Yacht Design Practices. [dissertation]. Politecnico di Milano.: Milan, IT; 2020

[8] Barros A, Oberle D. Handbook of Service Description. USDL and Its Methods. New York: Springer; 2012

[9] Baheti R, Gill H. Cyber-physical systems. The Impact of Control Technology. 2011;**12**(1):161-166

[10] Lee J, Bagheri B, Kao HA. A cyber-physical systems architecture for industry 4.0-based manufacturing systems. Manufacturing Letters. 2015;**3**:18-23

[11] Rodič B. Industry 4.0 and the new simulation modelling paradigm. Organizacija. 2017;**50**(3):193-207

[12] Celaschi F, Di Lucchio L, Imbesi L. Design e phigital production: Progettare Nell'era Dell'industria 4.0. MD Journal. 2017;**4**:6-13

[13] Magruk A. Uncertainty in the sphere of the industry 4.0–potential areas to research. Business, Management and Education. 2016;**14**(2):275-291

[14] Bell W. Foundations of futures studies: Human science for a new era: Values, objectivity, and the good society. Piscataway, NJ: Transaction Publishers; 2011

[15] Schuh G, Potente T, Wesch-Potente C, Weber AR, Prote JP. Collaboration mechanisms to increase productivity in the context of industrie 4.0. Procedia Cirp. 2014;**19**:51-56

[16] Miller R. Anticipation: The discipline of uncertainty. In: Curry A, editor. The Future of Futures. Houston, TX: Association of Professional Futurists; 2012

[17] Hines A, Slaughter RA. In: Bishop PJ, editor. Thinking about the future: Guidelines for strategic foresight. Washington, DC: Social Technologies; 2006

[18] Courtney H. 20-20 foresight: Crafting strategy in an uncertain world. Financial Executive. 2001;**17**(8):16

[19] Vavoula GN, Sharples M. Future technology workshop: A collaborative

method for the design of new learning technologies and activities. International Journal of Computer-Supported Collaborative Learning. 2007;**2**(4):393-419

[20] Simonse L. Design Roadmapping: Guidebook for Future Foresight Techniques. 2018

[21] Phaal R, Simonse L, Den Ouden E. Next generation roadmapping for innovation planning. International Journal of Technology Intelligence and Planning. 2008;**4**(2):135-152

[22] Geissbauer R, Vedso J, Schrauf S. Industry 4.0: Building the digital enterprise. [Internet]. PWC. 2016; 1. Available from: https://www.pwc.com/gx/en/industries/industries-4.0/landing-page/industry-4.0-building-your-digital-enterprise-april-2016.pdf

[23] Pollicardo L. Dinamiche e prospettive della filiera nautical del diporto. CNA Produzione Nautica. IT; 2017

[24] Celaschi F, Cappellieri A, Vasile A. Lusso versus design. Italian Design, beni. 2005

[25] Camper & Nicholsons and Wealth-X. The state of wealth Luxury and Yachting. Camper & Nicholson International. London. UK. 2017

[26] Oxman R. Theory and design in the first digital age. Design Studies. 2006;**27**(3):229-265

[27] Royakkers L, Timmer J, Kool L, van Est R. Societal and ethical issues of digitization. Ethics and Information Technology. 2018;**20**(2):127-142

[28] Maritime, Critical Infrastructure and Services. [Internet]. Enisa. 2017. Available from: https://www.enisa.europa.eu/topics/critical-information-infrastructures-and-services/dependencies-of-maritime-transport-to-icts

[29] Gilmore JH, Pine BJ. The four faces of mass customization. Harvard Business Review. 1997;**75**(1):91-102

[30] Piller FT. Mass customization: Reflections on the state of the concept. International Journal of Flexible Manufacturing Systems. 2004;**16**(4):313-334

[31] Brettel M, Friederichsen N, Keller M, Rosenberg M. How virtualization, decentralization and network building change the manufacturing landscape: An industry 4.0 perspective. FormaMente. 2017;**12**(8)

[32] McCartan S, McDonagh D, Moody L. Luxification and Design-Driven Innovation in Superyacht Design. London: The Royal Institution of Naval Architects; 2011. pp. 125-133

[33] Vallicelli A, Di Nicolantonio M, Lagatta J, Biagi A. "Just in Time" product design: Case study of a high-customizable chase boat. In: International Conference on Applied Human Factors and Ergonomics. Cham: Springer; 2018. pp. 254-263

[34] Kolarevic B. Architecture in the Digital Age: Design and Manufacturing. Milton Park, Abingdon-on-Thames: Taylor & Francis; 2004

[35] Rossi M, Buratti G, editors. Computational Morphologies: Design Rules Between Organic Models and Responsive Architecture. Berlin, Germany: Springer; 2017

Chapter 11

Applied Mathematics Tools in Digital Transformation

Francesco Calabrò, Maurizio Ceseri and Roberto Natalini

Abstract

Digital transformation is a process that companies start with different purposes. Once an enterprise embarks on a digital transformation process it translates all its business processes (or, at least, part of them) into a digital replica. Such a digital replica, the so-called digital twin, can be described by Mathematical Science tools allowing cost reduction on industrial processes, faster time-to-market of new products and, in general, an increase of competitive advantage for the company. Digital twin is a descriptive or predictive model of a given industrial process or product that is a valuable tool for business management, both in planning—because it can give different scenario analysis—and in managing the daily operations; moreover, it permits optimization of product and process operations. We present widespread applied mathematics tools that can help this modeling process, along with some successful cases.

Keywords: data mining, digital twin, modeling simulation optimization (MSO), numerical linear algebra, scientific machine learning

1. Introduction

What is digital transformation? According to Ebert and Duarte [1], Digital Transformation (DX) is "about adopting disruptive technologies to increase productivity, value creation, and the social welfare". The above definition is quite general meaning that DX can be adopted in many circumstances and by many actors: governments (from local to national level), multilateral organizations, industries. Digitalization, and in particular the concept of Digital Twin, has applications in many different fields [2]: Health, Meteorology, Manufacturing, Education, Cities and Transportation, and Energy.

Indeed, DX is having a huge impact on society at large. For instance, concerning labour force, a report from the World Economic Forum [3] states that by 2025, as a consequence of digitalization, 85 million jobs will be destroyed, while 97 million new jobs will be created worldwide. Thus, new competencies and skills will be necessary in a digitally transformed world. Among the top skills listed in the WEF report are the following: Critical thinking and analysis, Active learning and learning strategies,

 IntechOpen

Analytical thinking and innovation, Complex problem-solving, Systems analysis and evaluation. We can observe that a person with a background in mathematics possesses the above skills. More generally, STEM education will offer great opportunities in DX. A recent study [4] shows that in the US the automation and the use of robots in the productive environment has increased the enrolment at Universities and higher education levels in the field like Computer Science and Engineering. This shows an increasing awareness of the workforce of the importance of updating labour competencies.

This paper focuses in particular on the digital transformation of Industry. Throughout this paper, the term "Industry" means business and commerce, public and private research, development, and production facilities; in practice, all the activities that lie outside the field of academic research and education. For the industrial sector, DX leads to huge changes in how a company is managed and can also significantly affect customer satisfaction and product quality. The effects of digital transformation can be seen at many levels of an organization: the way employees work, how business processes operate, and how to collect, analyze, and use data. All the above considerations imply that DX does not mean simply the digitization of information. This is just a first indispensable step of a bigger transformation of the way a company is managed: in short, DX requires a digital culture within an enterprise [5].

Digitalization is enabled by a series of technologies:

- **IoT**: different objects in a system (a product or a manufacturing environment) are connected by sensing devices to the Internet and can interact with one another; this allows the control of the system throughout its life cycle.

- **Big Data**: the huge amount of data collected every moment on the system are a powerful tool to understand the process, and extract information.

- **Cloud**: the data collected has to be stored properly and safely and made available to the users; the user, in turn, may operate on the data through, for instance, simulations to understand what is happening on the system under control.

But one of the most important technologies enabling the Digital Transformation is Mathematics. Modeling, Simulation, and Optimization methods (MSO) have demonstrated their usefulness for solving problems in real life: forecast of air pollution, image processing, filtration processes, cultural heritage conservation, just to mention a few. MSO are becoming very important in a digitalized world, since they make it possible to extract information and knowledge from the data collected. In fact, in the last years research have developed new mathematical tools to be applied, for example, in Digital Twins [6, 7]. And some authors have talked explicitly of an "Era of Mathematics" [8].

This paper will give an overview of the mathematical tools that can be applied in a digitally transformed enterprise. It is organized as follows. Section (2) will describe the two main approaches of applied mathematics to digitalization: Physics-Based and Data-Driven. We will depict the main differences and how they can be combined to increase their effectiveness, with an example from an Industrial case. Section 3 will introduce some tools from linear algebra that can be applied to process collected data. Finally, in a concluding section, we will summarize our points and stress the importance of promoting Mathematics towards Industry.

2. Physics-based versus data-driven approach: competition or collaboration?

The Digital Transformation implies the use of mathematical models and methods to take advantage from the (possibly huge) amount of data collected by an enterprise about its own processes. When an enterprise wants to digitalize its processes it may apply a physics-based approach or a data-driven approach. The above approaches imply different methods to deal with a problem, each one with its pros and cons [9]. In recent years, however, Hybrid methods have been developed building on the two approaches. The hybrids have been developed in such a way to sum up the advantages of both model-based and data-driven approaches while reducing the disadvantages.

2.1 Physics-based

With the Physics-Based (PB) approach, we mean a description of the process or device based on first principles. Thus, the digital counterpart of the process is a mathematical model that describes the physics of the system taking into account all the relevant scales. Such an approach is also named Model-Based to emphasize the role of mathematical modeling.

Thus given a system to be digitized, the enterprise has to translate it in a mathematical model with a variable degree of complexity. The complexity of the model depends on the problem at hand and on the business objectives. The model can be used to monitor the performances of the system and then decide how to manage possible anomalies. How possible anomalies can be detected? Sensors are positioned on the system to collect data about its functions. The data are then compared with model output evaluating the residual, *i.e.*

$$r_i = |u_i - d_i|, \quad \text{for} \ \ i = 1, \dots, N \tag{1}$$

where u_i is the outcome of the mathematical model, d_i is the data collected by the sensors, and N is the number of data collected. If the residual exceeds a given threshold, then the system does not "behave properly" and some countermeasure has to be implemented.

Physics-based models can be powerful tools to create a Digital Twin. They can give great support in the first design of the digital system; in fact, they can give useful information on the processes to be described without great moles of data. As an example, physics-based modeling can give a first idea on what variables shall be monitored.

Physics-based models are characterized by transparency: this makes straightforward the interpretation of results.

Generalization is another important characteristic of PB models. The underline assumptions, as well as the approximations due to the development of the model determine the extent to which a model, can be generalized to other cases not previously considered. In general, in a PB approach, the limits of applications of a model are known in advance and this makes clear the range of problems it can describe.

One of the main problems of such an approach is the complexity of the resulting system of equations; in the presence of multiple processes interacting with one another (multi-physics systems) and at multiple spatial and/or temporal scales (multiscale systems), the difficulty in solving the equations will increase very rapidly. Some techniques have been developed, such as Reduced Order Modeling, to diminish model and computational complexity and end up with a more manageable system of equations, while maintaining the accuracy of results [10].

Nevertheless, such an approach is the one that permits a automotive industry to do crash test only via numerical simulations and new applications of the PB are growing up. For example, we are now able to simulate the whole heartbeat where all the physical parts (electrophysiology, the passive and active mechanics of the cardiac muscle, the microscopic force generation in sarcomeres, the blood flow in the heart chambers, and the valve dynamic) concur to the final simulation, see [11].

PB approaches have been applied also in the field of building automation: in [12] the authors focused on predictive maintenance of biomass boilers trying to minimize user discomfort.

2.2 Data-Driven

Data-Driven (DD) approach implies the use of methods from Machine Learning or even Deep Learning to exploit directly the data collected by sensors on system performance. Artificial Intelligence tools are suitable when very high amounts of data are available and can be used to find hidden patterns in the sample that cannot be discovered otherwise. Such a pattern can be refined whenever new data are collected. In such a way, we can say that the tool "learns from experiences".

The methods applied are diverse and comprises the following:

- Support Vector Machines
- Artificial Neural Network
- Convolutional Neural Network
- Recurrent Neural Network
- Generative Adversarial Network

The main advantage of the DD approach is the ease with which the solutions can be found, compared with the first principle approach. They have proven to be a very good alternative to PB models. If enough data are available, tools like neural networks can find hidden structures in very complex problems, where it is difficult to describe exactly the underlined physical structure. To give an example in the field of Material Sciences, in [13] the authors developed a Neural Network to simulate a Cellular Mechanical Metamaterial (CMM) and compared the performances with Direct Numerical Simulations (DNS), usually applied in this kind of problem. While the DNS needs about 10^5 Degrees of Freedom and $5 \cdot 10^2$ s to describe the mechanical properties of CMM, the Neural Network scheme needs only 290 DoF and about 6 to 8 s to provide a solution.

The ability to generalize a DD model is very limited. A DD model can describe circumstances only spanned by the data already available. It will need a large number of new data to take into account a more general setting. The need for (possibly large) amount of information is an overall limit to the development of the DD approach; sometimes, one does not have sufficient data to describe properly a given process.

Another problem is the lack of transparency. DD model builds in general so-called *black-boxes* that do not permit a clear interpretation of results. This led to the development of explainable AI [14].

According to Gartner [15], thirty-seven percent of companies have implemented AI in some form, translating to a 270 percent increase over the last four years. Customers are accustomed to bots and AI mechanisms that provide, among others, recommendations on services such as Netflix or Spotify. Not surprisingly, 31 percent of companies plan to increase the share of artificial intelligence in their business.

2.3 Hybrid approach

Recently, some researchers attempted to compare the two approaches in order to understand the advantages and the disadvantages of both. For example, in [16] the authors compared PB and DD approaches to the problem of fault detection and isolation in an automotive application. They found the same performances for both approaches in terms of detection and robustness and described the main shortcomings of both. However, Moallemi and coauthors [17] applied both Model Based and DD models to the problem of Structural Monitoring of a building; they found that Model Based approach results in best performances and point out that scarcity of data limits the behavior of DD algorithms. Thus, the debate is still open on what is the best approach for digitalisation.

The recent tendency, however, is to take advantage of the benefits of both by building hybrid methods that mix together. First principles with data-intensive modeling [18–20]. In [21] the authors survey the research literature on this topic and propose a taxonomy of the developed methods. The integration of PB and DD approaches has several applications. PB models of complex processes require approximations to have a usable set of equations. Approximations are necessary whenever the process is not completely understood in all of its elements. This will introduce bias in model results. Another issue is due to the presence of physical parameters that have to be estimated some time with a small amount of data. On the other hand, Machine learning tools need a large amount of data to reproduce with precision a given process and have limited generalization capabilities. The use of DD techniques in combination with first principle modeling may help to overcome such limitations and this has been shown to be very useful in practice.

One attempt is the so-called *Physics-Informed Neural Networks* (PINN) [22]: a deep learning framework for the resolution of PDE in several application (fluid dynamics, quantum physics, reaction–diffusion systems, etc.). Neural networks are defined by minimizing a loss function incorporating physical constraints. If one wish to solve an equation of the type $\mathcal{A}(u) = 0$, the solution is given by the minimum of the following function

$$\frac{1}{N}\sum_{i=1}^{N}|\mathcal{A}(u(x_i))|^2 + \frac{1}{M}\sum_{j=1}^{M}\left|u\left(x_j\right) - u_j\right|^2 \tag{2}$$

where $\left(x_j, u_j\right)$ for $j = 1, \dots, M$ are training data (including initial and boundary conditions), and (x_i) for $i = 1, \dots, N$ are points where the solution is defined.

The interplay of Pb and DD approaches has been employed in Unmanned Aerial Vehicle (UAV) management; in [23], the authors present a Component Based

Reduced Order Model coupled with Baysian state estimation to allow a small aircraft to adjust dynamically its trajectory.

Hybrid methods have been applied to describe a spring-mass system subjected to damping that evolves according to multiple time scales [24]; such an application is relevant for many industrial settings and is generally very difficult to solve numerically.

2.4 An example in predictive maintenance

Through the technologies described it is possible to solve usual problems of engineering and computational mechanics but also to explore new fields in which up to now mathematical modeling had not been able to replace the experience or the direct control of the mechanism. One of the most interesting areas is that of predictive maintenance [25], already mentioned above. In some sectors, such as in aircraft maintenance, the benefits of having guidelines available to ensure the correct functioning of circulating machines are well known: in civil aeronautics, periodic checks and periodic replacements, for example, of bolts or panels subjected to greater stress is an established practice, but this practice comes from the combination of experience and modeling. On the other hand, it is well known that it is not at all easy in a complex system to keep all the components under control to have guarantees on correct functioning and to prevent possible failures and/or breakages. Machines are often equipped with many sensors that monitor correct operation, signaling anomalies on what each sensor is capable of measuring. Unfortunately, it is often only from the combination of information that the general picture is obtained, and therefore if only the single sensor is monitored, this information collected is not really helpful in decisions. Some industrial sectors, such as boating or highly automated production, would greatly benefit from the possibility of preventing critical situations before failures occur that can put in danger the correct functioning of the machinery. The modeling available to complex tools—which work on different scales and interact with each other—often has to overlook some effects and does not allow predictive models so accurate as to be able to help decision makers determine if or when to intervene with substitutions or repairs. Most of the time one can notice a problem when it is already too late.

The recent literature on predictive maintenance foresees the possibility of combining the effect of a control on the physics of phenomena, possibly linked to the information of the sensors, and of an experience given by the analysis of the available data processed through artificial intelligence. For example, in [26] the authors describe the use of hybrid techniques for controlling the operation of Computer Numerical Control (CNC) machines. These are fundamental briks in modern industries (from Wikipedia): "CNC is the automated control of machining tools (such as drills, lathes, mills and 3D printers) by means of a computer. A CNC machine processes a piece of material (metal, plastic, wood, ceramic, or composite) to meet specifications by following coded programmed instructions and without a manual operator directly controlling the machining operation." Authors in [26] present how it is possible to build a digital twin that provides information on the expected behavior of the machine and at the same time, through the data collected by the sensors inside the machine, the on-situ behavior of the machine. Then, by taking a comparison of the two, this reveals a good ability to highlight anomalies, based on the physical modeling. At the same time, however, the acquisition of a large amount of data through sensors allows the elaboration of a database that also includes a sort of forecasting model: this increases the knowledge of the ongoing process and helps in prediction.

The use of hybrid approach helps to meet the targets of predictive maintenance:

- Fault diagnosis
- Fault forecast
- Intelligent decision
- Intelligent maintenance.

3. Applied linear algebra tools

Now we consider how the tools coming from linear algebra can manage to solve the problems considered in the previous section. We consider both problems, namely the search of a model that can justify some available data and the case where the model is given and some prediction is done via numerical computations. What we present next is inspired by [27, 28], where readers can find full details of the topics introduced in this section.

3.1 Modeling with linear functions

First, we consider that a dataset is given; instances $\left(x^{(i)}, y^{(i)}\right)$ are known $\forall i = 1, \dots, M$. As previously discussed, such dataset is described with numbers, and we identify it as input x and y is the output. Each of the inputs is vectors of numbers $x^{(i)} \in \mathbf{R}^d$ while we consider the output to be a number $y^{(i)} \in \mathbf{R}$. The dataset then can be described as an input matrix $D \in \mathbf{R}^{M \times d}$ whose rows are the instances and the columns are the features, and a column vector Y that stores the output.

Our modeling problem is to describe the dependence of the output from the input, so to identify a mathematical law $F : \mathbf{R}^d \to \mathbf{R}$ in good agreement with the available dataset $F\left(x^{(i)}\right) \approx y^{(i)}$. The most simple mathematical law that we can introduce would be the linear function. This is completely described by the coefficients $w \in \mathbf{R}^d$: $F(x) = \sum_{j=1}^{d} w_j x_j$. If we impose the agreement with the data, we have that the unknown coefficients solve the problem:

$$\text{Find } w \in \mathbf{R}^d \text{ such that } Dw - Y \approx 0 \qquad \text{(Linear System PB)}$$

Such a problem, if settled out in the square ($d = M$) and exact framework, is the well-known resolution of linear systems. We prefer to write the search problem in an approximate way, so we use the $\approx$ symbol, because usually we consider inexact data or non-square datasets, so that existence of the solution is not guaranteed. In the next section we discuss the resolution of the linear (approximate) problem. Finally, when the w are calculated, for a new instance $\bar{x} \in \mathbf{R}^d$ the model would predict $\bar{y} = \sum_{j=1}^{d} w_j \bar{x}_j$.

3.2 Model approximation

When a model is given, this is used to predict the behavior of the quantity of interest for forecasting, i.e., in unseen cases. Mathematical models are relations involving, in many cases, operations that are not tabled or easily computable. In order to understand how the tools of applied mathematics apply in such cases, we can start from a general formulation where the quantity of interest is a u^* (an unknown function in the general case or a vector/scalar) that is the solution of a problem: $\mathcal{P}(u^*, \delta) = 0$ where δ are the given data.

$$\text{Find } \alpha \in \mathbf{R}^{\mathrm{N}} \text{such that } \quad u(x_i) \equiv \sum_{j=1}^{N} \alpha_j f_j\left(x^{(i)}\right) - y^{(i)} \approx 0 \;\; \forall i = 1 \ldots M$$

To begin with a simple example, consider the approximation/extrapolation of data. As in the previous section, the inputs are made of vectors of numbers $x^{(i)} \in \mathbf{R}^d$ while we consider the output to be a number $y^{(i)} \in \mathbf{R}$ so that the known data are $\delta = \left(x^{(i)}, y^{(i)}\right)_i \; \forall i = 1, \ldots, M$. Eventually, the outputs $y^{(i)}$ are evaluations of a "black box" function that we want to describe in a different way. In the previous section, we considered the resolution of a liner problem in order to look for a linear model that could justify the dependence of the output by the input data. In this case, we start from different knowledge and look for a non-linear model that gives "exactly" the dependence of y from x. The approximate solution will be a function $u \approx u^*$ that can be described by a finite set of coefficients. We look for u such that $u\left(x^{(i)}\right) \approx y^{(i)}$, where $u(x) = \sum_{j=1}^{N} \alpha_j f_j(x)$, i.e., u is a linear combination of N fixed functions $f_j(x)$. The coefficients of the linear combination, $\alpha \in \mathbf{R}^N$ determinate the solution of our approximated problem u. One way to fix such coefficients is to impose accordance with the available data:$\sum_{j=1}^{N} \alpha_j f_j\left(x^{(i)}\right) = y^{(i)}$.

This problem is exactly in the same framework as the ones seen in the previous section: a matrix problem where the matrix is the so-called collocation matrix $\Phi \in \mathbf{R}^{M \times N}, \;\; \Phi_{j,i} = f_j\left(x^{(i)}\right)$.

Remark. The choice of the functions f_j strongly affects both the quality of the solution and the ability to solve the discrete problem easily. Usual choices are polynomials or piece-wise polynomial functions. Nevertheless many systems of functions can be used instead and the results on the capability to approximate general functions, known as the Universal Approximation Theorem (UAT), are available. One of the reasons why the Neural Network (NN) functions are widely used in numerical approximations is due to the fact that there are available UAT results in this case. We remark that in the general case of NN also some parameters inside the functions can be tuned so that the overall determination of the network is a nonlinear optimization problem.

Moving from the approximation of a given function to different scientific models, we encounter the case of equilibrium laws based on first principles, as described in the previous section on Physics-Based approach. Also in this case the unknown is a function but in this case, the model is written as a solution to a mathematical problem $\mathcal{P}(u^*, \delta) = 0$ that involves some operators applied to the unknown function: derivatives and/or integrals (that are linear operators) and eventually nonlinear transformations. (The problem of interpolations described at the beginning of this section can be sought as the resolution of a mathematical problem that involves only evaluation of functions on sites, which is a linear functional.) Also in the case where only linear operators are considered, approximated problems for integration and derivation are needed because both operations are intrinsically infinite-dimensional [29, 30]. In general, two main roads—or combinations of these two—can be taken for the numerical resolutions of problems that involve the use of operators:

- instead of considering general functions, look for a solution written as a linear combination of simple functions where the operation can be done simply $\Rightarrow u = \sum \alpha_i \phi_i \approx u^*$;
- instead of considering exact modeling approximate the operators and look for solutions in particular cases, ad example in fixed sites $\Rightarrow \mathcal{P}_N \approx \mathcal{P}$.

Applied mathematics tools aim to introduce methods that translate the original model in some approximation that is consistent with the original formulation and gives an accurate approximation of the unknowns. The initial problem $\mathcal{P}(u^*, \delta) = 0$ is then reformulated in an approximate way ($\mathcal{P}_N \approx \mathcal{P}$) and the sought solution is an approximation of the mathematical solution ($u \approx u^*$). The final resolution step, in most cases revels in the resolution of a linear problem as the ones seen before.

3.3 Numerical resolution of linear systems

Because many problems seen in this excursus are finally modeled via linear systems, we aim to present some of the ingredients that can be used for the resolution of linear systems. The problem written in (Linear System PB) is the one that we aim to solve.

As commented, the unknown vector w has to solve the problem of interpolating the available data with a linear function, i.e., if $D_i^{(j)}$, $j = 1, \dots, d$ are the features of the $i-$th individual and Y_i is the output, then w_j are such that $\sum_j w_j D_i^{(j)}$ should be close to Y_i $\forall i = 1, \dots, M$. The first case that we consider, is the one where we have more parameter to fix than available information, so that the number of features d is greater of the number of individuals M; the problem is also referred as overparametrized.

First of all we introduce the rank $r \leq d$ of the matrix D: this is the number of columns of the matrix that are linearly independent, i.e., columns that cannot be written as a linear combination of the other ones. Thinking of the matrix as a collection of features from individuals, the rank would be the number of information that we collect that are linearly independent. Because our aim is to find the coefficients w_j that solve the linear system, if we call $D^{(j)}$ the $j-$th column of D, the linear system can be written as $\left[\sum w_j D^{(j)}\right] - Y \approx 0$ thus only columns that are linearly independent give useful information for the determination of the w. The real dimensionality of the problem, the number of degrees of freedom that can be sought, is then the rank of the matrix.

An important feature when data are collected with some error—or "noise"—is that the rank of the matrix could be affected by this error: some columns can be linearly independent only for effect of the randomness of the noise. Then, a different preliminary analysis—the so-called feature selection—that reduces the dimension of the columns could be necessary. One possible way to proceed is by exploring the Singular

Value Decompostion of the matrix and, in particular, the order of magnitude of the singular values. All these procedures that avoid the presence of redundancy on the feature collection, end up with the so-called active features. When this preprocessing of the data is done, we need to solve the problem of the determination of $d^* \leq d$ coefficients w^* to be fixed from the M linear equations: a linear problem of the type $D^* w^* - Y \approx 0$. If d^* is still greater or equal to M, the problem—which is referred as square if $d^* = M$ or underdeterminated if $d^* > M$- has always an optimal solution, i.e., a solution to the matrix problem $D^* w^* - Y = 0$. If the problem is square, the solution is unique. It has more solutions when $d^* > M$: to select between these solutions we can introduce the square problem $(D^*)^T D^* \tilde{w} = (D^*)^T Y$, where $(\cdot)^T$ stands for the transposed matrix. Such equations are referred as "normal equations" for the non-squared linear problem. The solution $\tilde{w}$ solves a square linear system and is one of the possible vectors w^*.

Overdetermined linear problems are the ones where the number of features (or active features as described above) are less than the number of individuals, that is, the number of rows of the matrix M; the problem is also referred as overfitted. To focus on such an overdeterminated case, we can focus on the scalar case, where $d = 1$. The coefficient $w \in \mathbf{R}$ is, then, the slope of the straight line that we want to construct in order to give a law of direct-proportionality between x and y: $wx_i = y_i$. This problem admits a solution only if $M = 1$ or if the points (x_i, y_i) are aligned (and aligned to $(0, 0)$).

In the general cases, in order to solve the linear problem $D^* w^* - Y \approx 0$ one has to introduce an optimality condition and try to solve the problem of "best fit". After some computation, what turns out to be a good solution is the solution of the normal equations as introduced in the underdeterminated case.

4. Conclusions

What about the need for companies of such technologies? What we experience every day is that new technologies are deeply changing markets, as if this is "second wave of digital transformation". In fact, Robotics, Machine Learning, Big Data and Artificial Intelligence are becoming more and more common.

Using properly DX, companies have the opportunity to optimize operating costs and thus increase process efficiency via new services. Additionally, the digitalization of company data produces the so-called "digital capital" made of huge amounts of information from various sources, which increases the possibility to settle out predictive models. This allows companies to better meet customers' needs. DX is the present for companies that aim to remain competitive, and the use of simple mathematical tools opens up great opportunities in unexpected fields.

However, Enterprises are not completely aware of this point and how they would benefit from the application of Mathematical research in their daily operations. In the last few years, a new professional figure emerged world wide to promote:

- MSO towards enterpises, and
- Industry-Academic Collaborations.

The above role is played by the *Technology Translator*. A Technology Translator has strong competencies of Mathematical research and on the other hand good knowledge of industrial processes; thus, he/she is the right person to talk both with mathematicians and enterprises. Since Academics and Industrialists have different languages,[1] the need has emerged for a professional figure that can translate Industrial problems in mathematical terms enabling the cooperation among the two world. There are several Institutions in Europe employing Technology Translators. In Italy, the National Research Council of Italy promotes the project *Sportello Matematico per l'Innovazione e le Imprese*.[2] The main objectives of Sportello Matematico are: Promoting Mathematical Technologies as source of Industrial Innovation; Activating cooperations between Enterprises and Research Centers; Facilitating the employment of Mathematicians in Industry [31]. The work of Technology Translators contributes to the change of perspective required by the complex challenges of Digital Transformation.

[1] This is also related to the fact that Industry and Academia have different objectives and timescales.
[2] www.sportellomatematico.it.

Author details

Francesco Calabrò[1*†], Maurizio Ceseri[2†] and Roberto Natalini[2]

1 Università di Napoli "Federico II", Naples, Italy

2 Istituto per le Applicazioni del Calcolo "Mauro Picone", Consiglio Nazionale delle Ricerche, Rome, Italy

*Address all correspondence to: calabro@unina.it

† These authors contributed equally.

References

[1] Ebert C, Duarte CH. Digital transformation. IEEE Software. 2018; **35**(4):16-21

[2] Rasheed A, San O, Kvamsdal T. Digital twin: Values, challenges and enablers from a modeling perspective. Ieee Access. 2020;**8**:21980-22012

[3] World Economic Forum. The Future of Jobs Report. Geneva, Switzerland: World Economic Forum; 2020

[4] Di Giacomo G, Lerch B. Automation and Human Capital Adjustment: The Effect of Robots on College Enrollment. 2021. Available from: SSRN 3920935

[5] Ivančić L, Vukšić VB, Spremić M. Mastering the digital transformation process: Business practices and lessons learned. Technology Innovation Management Review. 2019;**9**(2):36-50

[6] Hartmann D, Van der Auweraer H. Digital twins. In: Progress in Industrial Mathematics: Success Stories. Berlin, Germany: Springer, Springer, Champions; 2021. pp. 3-17

[7] Hauret P. At the crossroads of simulation and data analytics. European Mathematical Society Magazine. 2021; **16**(121):9-18

[8] Bond P. The Era of Mathematics; An Independent Review of Knowledge Exchange in the Mathematics Sciences. 2018. Available from: epsrc.ukri.org/newsevents/pubs/era-of-maths/ [Accessed: February 9, 2022]

[9] Rueckert D, Schnabel JA. Model-based and data-driven strategies in medical image computing. Proceedings of the IEEE. 2019;**108**(1):110-124

[10] Magargle R, Johnson L, Mandloi P, Davoudabadi P, Kesarkar O, Krishnaswamy S, et al. A simulation-based digital twin for model-driven health monitoring and predictive maintenance of an automotive braking system. In: Proceedings of the 12th International Modelica Conference, Prague, Czech Republic, May 15-17, 2017. Vol. 132. Linköping: Linköping University Electronic Press; 2017. pp. 35-46

[11] Quarteroni A, editor. Modeling the Heart and the Circulatory System. Berlin, Germany: Springer; 2015

[12] Cauchi N, Macek K, Abate A. Model-based predictive maintenance in building automation systems with user discomfort. Energy. 2017;**138**:306-315

[13] Xue T, Beatson A, Chiaramonte M, Roeder G, Ash JT, Menguc Y, et al. A data-driven computational scheme for the nonlinear mechanical properties of cellular mechanical metamaterials under large deformation. Soft Matter. 2020; **16**(32):7524-7534

[14] Longo L, Goebel R, Lecue F, Kieseberg P, Holzinger A. Explainable artificial intelligence: Concepts, applications, research challenges and visions. In: International Cross-domain Conference for Machine Learning and Knowledge Extraction. Berlin, Germany: Springer, Champions; 2020. pp. 1-16

[15] GARTNER. What Is Artificial Intelligence? Avaiable from: https://www.gartner.com/en/topics/artificial-intelligence

[16] Yang R, Rizzoni G. Comparison of model-based vs. data-driven methods for fault detection and isolation in engine idle speed control system. Annual Conference of the PHM Society 2016 8 1 PHM Society San Diego, California

[17] Moallemi A, Burrello A, Brunelli D, Benini L. Model-based vs. data-driven approaches for anomaly detection in structural health monitoring: A case study. In 2021 IEEE International Instrumentation and Measurement Technology Conference (I2MTC) 2021 May 17 1 6 IEEEManhattan, New York, US

[18] Liu Z, Meyendorf N, Mrad N. The role of data fusion in predictive maintenance using digital twin. In: AIP Conference Proceedings. Vol. 1. Melville, NY: AIP Publishing LLC; 1949. p. 020023

[19] Shetty P, Mylaraswamy D, Ekambaram T. A hybrid prognostic model formulation system identification and health estimation of auxiliary power units. In: 2006 IEEE Aerospace Conference. Manhattan, New York, US: IEEE; 2006. p. 10

[20] Slimani A, Ribot P, Chanthery E, Rachedi N. Fusion of model-based and data-based fault diagnosis approaches. IFAC-PapersOnLine. 2018;**51**(24): 1205-1211

[21] Willard J, Jia X, Xu S, Steinbach M, Kumar V. Integrating physics-based modeling with machine learning: A survey. arXiv preprint arXiv: 2003.04919. 2020;**1**(1):1-34

[22] Raissi M, Perdikaris P, Karniadakis GE. Physics-informed neural networks: A deep learning framework for solving forward and inverse problems involving nonlinear partial differential equations. Journal of Computational Physics. 2019;**378**:686-707

[23] Kapteyn MG, Knezevic DJ, Huynh DB, Tran M, Willcox KE. Data-driven physics-based digital twins via a library of component-based reduced-order models. International Journal for Numerical Methods in Engineering. 2020: 1-18

[24] Chakraborty S, Adhikari S. Machine learning based digital twin for dynamical systems with multiple time-scales. Computers Structures. 2021;**243**:106410

[25] Ran Y, Zhou X, Lin P, Wen Y, Deng RA Survey of Predictive Maintenance: Systems, Purposes and Approaches. arXiv preprint arXiv:1912.07383. 2019

[26] Luo W, Hu T, Ye Y, Zhang C, Wei Y. A hybrid predictive maintenance approach for CNC machine tool driven by digital twin. Robotics and Computer-Integrated Manufacturing. 2020;**65**: 101974

[27] Deisenroth MP, Faisal AA, Ong CS. Mathematics for Machine Learning. Cambridge: Cambridge University Press; 2020. Available from: https://mml-book.github.io/

[28] Strang G. Linear Algebra and Learning from Data. Cambridge: Wellesley-Cambridge Press; 2019

[29] Calabrò F, Manni C, Pitolli F. Computation of quadrature rules for integration with respect to refinable functions on assigned nodes. Applied Numerical Mathematics. 2015;**90**: 168-189

[30] Calabrò F et al. Null rules for the detection of lower regularity of functions. Journal of Computational and Applied Mathematics. 2019;**361**:547-553

[31] Bertsch M, Ceseri M, Natalini R, Santoro M, Sgalambro A, Visconti F. On the Italian network of industrial mathematics and its future developments: Sportello Matematico per l'industria italiana. In: European Consortium for Mathematics in Industry. Berlin, Germany: Springer, Champions; 2014. pp. 173-178

Chapter 12

Perspective Chapter: The Sovereign Way - How Diversity in Construction Is Key of Success in the Digital Age

Bianca Christina Weber-Lewerenz

Abstract

It is true that women no longer have to be looked for with a magnifying glass in the executive floors of German businesses; however, their share is still small. The digital age holds great potential for increased inclusion and closure of the "Gender Leadership Gap," especially in the construction industry. Industry standards, including global ones, are being examined to achieve more inclusive corporate governance models. The construction industry, which is regarded as one of the most traditional and conservative, male-dominated industries, serves as the best example for a long-overdue need for dynamic restructuring and action related to women's leadership. This research is an approach to outline the framework answering the need to redefine, recalibrate and reshape this industry by increasing women's role in the social, digital and business transformation processes. This approach is the most important finding as it bridges the current divide and facilitates movement from discussion and advocacy toward application and practice.

Keywords: women leadership, responsible leadership, digital innovation, digital transformation, digitization, AI, construction industry, diversity mandate, ethics, inclusion, diversity, blockchain

1. Introduction

Despite the good order situation, construction companies are exposed to persistent cost pressure and a shortage of skilled workers. New digital technologies and artificial intelligence (AI) improve operational efficiency, offer new business models and provide training for new qualification requirements that correspond to new job profiles. The construction industry is the key industry in Germany; it plays an important economic role. For example, construction investments by the German economy added more than EUR 387 billion in 2020—the highest level since the 2008 recession as per the statistics by the Main Association of the German Construction Industry [1]. Around 10% of the German gross domestic product is used for construction work. In 2020, the share of gross value added in the construction industry in Germany was around 6.1% of Germany's total economic gross value added. With almost 2 million

IntechOpen

employees, the construction industry supports the overall economy in the COVID-19 crisis but is responsible for 38% of all global energy-related CO2 emissions. Energy and climate, digitization and the need for skilled workers directly affect the construction industry. The industry could benefit significantly by implementing the strategic decision-making processes, planning and operating phases more efficiently by standardizing both digital technologies and methods of AI in more diverse environments, pushed by legal regulations. In short, diversity and a new culture of thought are essential for the future-oriented portfolio in the construction industry to make the digital transformation holistic, successful and sustainable. Nevertheless, there is a lack of recognition of the potential of new technologies, there is a lack of courage and willingness to use them, and there is a lack of diversity.

The digital age holds great potential for increased inclusion and closure of the "Gender Leadership Gap" [2]. The construction industry, which is regarded as one of the most traditional and conservative, male-dominated industries, serves as the best example for a long-overdue need for dynamic restructuring and action related to women's leadership [3, 4]. The Status Quo listed below is evidence of the strong need to redefine, recalibrate and reshape this industry by increasing women's role in the social, digital and business transformation processes. By assessing why diversity is the key factor, this approach bridges the current divide and facilitates movement from discussion and advocacy toward application and practice. The evaluation of such assessment comes with two theses. Dealing with these goes hand in hand with significant calls for action on both legal and an overall societal level. They lay the ground for implementing diversity and follow the sovereign way to set value accents for Construction 4.0.

2. Status quo of diversity

The 25th-anniversary celebration of buildingSMART Germany on October 27, 2021, in Berlin spurred the diversity discourse on-site and around the globe with the author's keynote speech and a panel discussion on the "Success factor diversity in the construction industry" [5]. It offered approaches on how diversity in corporate culture and knowledge can help avoid discrimination and gender bias, optimize inclusion and further improve crucial aspects of digital ethics in data-driven technologies—such as fairness and transparency in AI.

Women strengthen public trust in AI, their communication skills, transparency and network breadth speak as independent characteristics for the success of female leadership potential. This is all the more important in an industry like construction, which has a very high share of the economy but lags behind digitization and AI, diversity and inclusion. The construction industry is traditionally conservative, a male-dominated industry with the attitude "Let's do it as always," "It works" and "We need a strong man on-site." The "good old boys" network and gatekeeping have a long tradition. In recent years, the industry has had to accept a significant decline in the number of skilled workers. The digital transformation creates the conditions for disruptive reforms and changes to include women, win them over to STEM and offer new career paths. Virtual reality (VR) and blockchain technology for example show a great development from the technical perspective but especially from the innovation factor's perspective carried by inclusion and diversity [6]. When it comes to global crises such as economic and pandemic crises, it is crucial to secure human and social rights. Furthermore, it is even more important to strengthen diversity, gender parity and inclusion and maintain democratic values to successfully master historical crises [7].

Nevertheless, there are prejudices and a lack of role models, although the construction industry cannot do without the qualifications, know-how and socially communicative digital high potential of women. To fundamentally rethink the technological progress that enables new business models and to keep pace with digitization in the long term, all those involved are required to promote best skills, diversity and inclusion. Thus, the digital change is also accelerating the merging of these previously separately working units. Evidence of hard facts such as increased profitability (ROI) and overall excellence in digital corporate culture rationalize the gender discussion. The need for action is high: increasing the far too low proportion of women in the construction industry in general (**Figure 1**), enthusiasm for more female students in civil engineering (**Figure 2**), toward more female mandates and

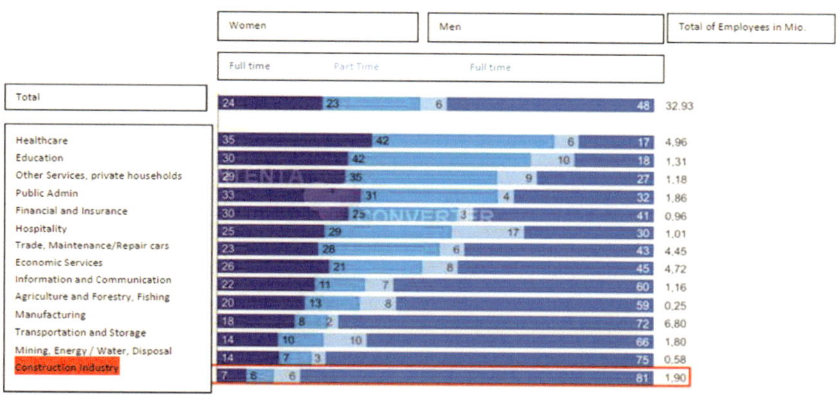

Figure 1.
Women in construction in Germany source: statistics in construction 2021, main association of the German construction industry (German HDB).

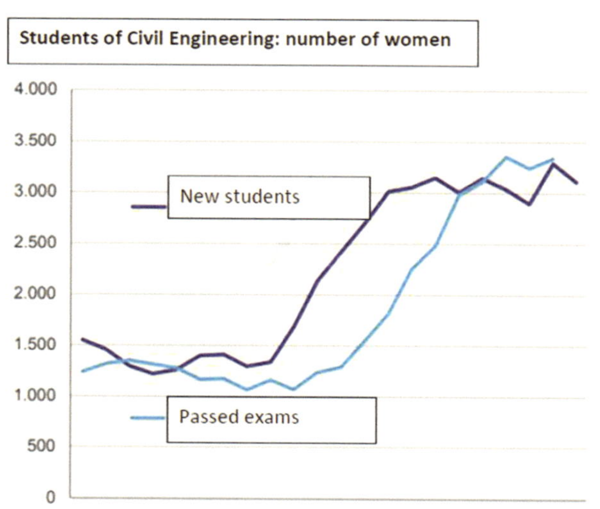

Figure 2.
Female civil engineer students in Germany source: statistics in construction 2021, main association of the German construction industry (German HDB).

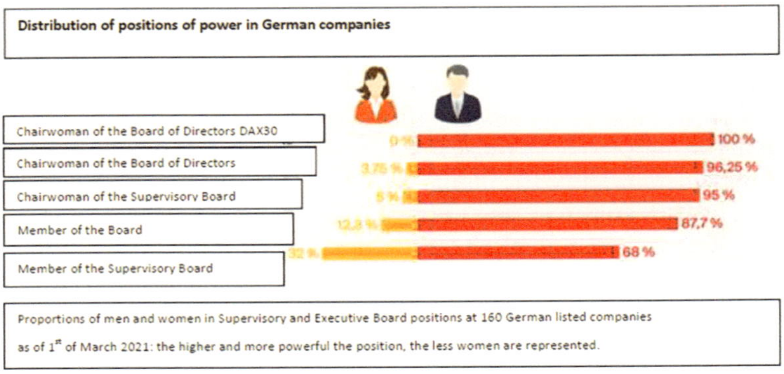

Figure 3.
Distribution of positions of power in German companies source: allbright report as of 05th march 2021 [8].

Figure 4.
Gender proportions in machine learning (ML) research source: EQUALS report 2019 [9].

board members (**Figure 3**) and closing the still serious gender gaps in AI occupational fields (**Figure 4**).

Companies that prioritize gender equality in their hiring practices and workforce also generate 41% more revenue than those that do not. Recently, McKinsey & Company found that companies with different leadership teams were 21% more likely than their counterparts to outperform their peers. Plus, they were 27% more likely to create and deliver value [10]. According to a McKinsey and Company study in 2015, AI-controlled talent intelligence immediately triples the diversity of the talent pool and at the same time lowers recruiting costs by up to 60%; diverse teams are 35% more profitable and 1.7 times more innovative; interview pools with a diversity of at least 40% tend to optimize the hiring processes.

AI is the result of human intelligence, enabled by their enormous talents and also prone to their limits. Hence, it is imperative that all teams working in technology and AI be as diverse as possible. Diversity of people does not only mean the obvious in terms of demographics such as race, ethnicity, gender and age, but also people with different skills, experiences, educational backgrounds, cultural and geographical perspectives, opinions, ways of thinking and working. The digital transformation has great potential to make the life cycle of construction projects economical and efficient and to enable the greatest possible social benefit, economic prosperity and the protection of our natural foundations of life. However, the digital age requires strengthening strategic values for a more inclusive environment and the common good. Gender mainstreaming is the answer, as this concept of gender equality at all social and political levels fundamentally and systematically takes into account the interests of women and men.

Courage and the will to innovate-this courage is expected, especially from the German building trade. Here is a lot of strength, self-confidence and potential for innovation, as well as in other parts of the world [11]. Diverse knowledge, skills and strengths are necessary to tackle the challenges. They are key for success, weighing up decisions and exploiting the potential. Where technical feasibility and social responsibility meet, a field of tension arises. The particularly high shortage of skilled workers, the loss of attractiveness of entrepreneurs for applicants, the increasing pressure in global competition and the more necessary interdisciplinary dialog strongly clarify the need for action. With diversity in technical and interdisciplinary know-how, through diverse backgrounds, communication that "takes people with you," a good mix of personal and social strengths, human and technical transformation is filled with life and the digital era is shaped sustainably. The digital era means both opportunities and risks. Diversity leads to success.

The step-by-step implementation of various gender and equality strategies initiated by UN, EU, UNESCO, UNICEF and World Economic Forum are reason to celebrate but always combined with the task of responsibly dealing with high-tech, building, traditions and our society as a whole—and its transparency and control [12, 13]. It requires full attention to find out which technology helps the human, how and where it supports human work best, makes human work more efficient, much easier and safer, and how the human can (and must) make full use of the potential and lay new paths in the digital era. To date, there has been no lack of technical development, especially in construction. We all know where the dowel should fit. We all know where the nail on the head needs to be hit. But do we always have our compass ready for internal alignment and meaningful changes of direction and decision-making?

We live and work in complex surroundings with increasing data, more technology, faster, more tasks, more interfaces and more specialist knowledge. We devote ourselves passionately to our daily work topics, but also to shaping our future together. It is us, humans, we shape the environment in which we live and work. We daily operate in multi-complex areas of tension: between what is technically feasible and in ethical compliance, digital change and humane change, innovative technologies and social expectations.

3. Why diversity is key for success

Here are two theses: Digitization does not automatically lead to more diversity. Technology does not solve our social problems either.

We want to create value, we want useful technology that supports us, humans, we want complete data of the highest quality to make AI non-discriminatory. At the same time, we are surrounded by a complex world of data, constantly new requirements, in a less agile environment. There is a lack of knowledge, not only in construction but also across disciplines: "Think outside the box" with qualified and diverse specialists. In 33.5% of companies in building construction, in civil engineering even 37.9% lack skilled workforce according to construction industry statistics as of September 2021. Demographic change shows in October 2021: There are more retirees than trainees and students.

Many of us are not equally familiar with digitization and AI or are aware of their potentials or their unwanted effects. To unravel the aforementioned areas of tension, there is a key factor: DIVERSITY and a change in the culture of thinking. The pressure is already there:

1. Companies need to provide evidence of their social commitment and how they are fulfilling their responsibilities and inclusion.

2. Only as an attractive employer is it possible to attract new skilled workers with new knowledge.

3. It is important to reaffirm the trust of stakeholders, employees and customers, in particular by showing intangible values in annual reports.

Recent examples of successful interdisciplinary and diverse cooperation for technical innovation in construction are the German pavilion at Dubai EXPO2021: All strengths are bundled, and diverse and talented teams laid the foundation for the integrative multidisciplinary environment for sharing knowledge and strengths leading to this outstanding construction project. Same with the world's first adaptive skyscraper at the University of Stuttgart, which is used for research purposes: this project brings together interdisciplinary knowledge, for example, from engineering and mechanical engineering: Hydraulic cylinders are integrated into supports and are part of 128 measuring points, to, for example, make environmental influences on the building measurable.

These strategies are vivid samples of the Berlin Declaration at the 68th Assembly of the Federal Chamber of Engineers in October 2021 states: "*Engineering competence is an indispensable value for the design of our environment ... sustainability .... a must: to consider the entire life cycle of buildings ... .*"

"*City, Country, Construction - We can do more than just build!*" Everything at the Construction Industry Day 2021 revolved around innovation, added value, such as "Construction sites become new models" and other value strategies embedded in the European Green Deal [14] to minimize CO2 and become first climate-neutral continent.

Diversity is a topic that stimulates, touches and sets vibrations. So how does diversity define success in construction?

- Diversity ensures balance and creates values

- Diversity means allowing many aspects, listening, and requires mindfulness, empathy, respect

- Diversity facilitates well-balanced decisions (strengths complementing each other)

- Knowledge from many subjects, professional diversity that comes together

- The complexity of know-how, data, people, requirements, expectations, constantly new technology and possibilities, changing environmental conditions

- Diversity of interfaces enables the exchange of knowledge in times of digitization and AI; diversity is indispensable to design this technological support for people regardless of gender

- New job profiles, new areas of responsibility, new professional and personal qualifications, an adaptation of curricula and teacher qualifications

- Adaptation of training: teaching qualifications, access to education, access to media and digital working media, information
- Interface skills (well beyond specialist boundaries), broad-based networks, cooperation in various teams (complement each other, change of perspective)
- Role models, role models, best practices are in abundance (successful companies/research/innovations led by women = statistics show where and how women are the engine and key factors for technical innovations and entrepreneurial success.)
- Country and culture, specialist discipline, skills and knowledge, strengths, experience, perspectives and ways of looking at things
- Diversity brings together skills and strengths. Joint search for concrete approaches.

Diversity connects us, humans, strengthens trust, creates mutual professional benefits and supports lifelong learning. Trust, security, awareness and education are key elements for understanding and applying new technologies. buildingSMART Germany, as part of the global construction-wide competency network buildingSMART International, copes with the challenges of the digital era by sharing user practice and up-to-date research findings with its innovative members. The author contributed keynotes and scientific presentations during their events.

With a view to the two previously raised theses: Digitization does not automatically lead to more diversity. Technology does not solve our social problems either.

Isn't diversity rather an engine, one of the most important success factors in the digital age?

By paving new paths for your success as a competitive company, you are building the foundation for diversity in your children's professional lives and their career opportunities! Let us make full use of this historical opportunity, which this technical and human change offers—well thought out, and with full speed.

The German building craftsmanship, our engineering skills and our values are considered as a role model in the world. A seal of quality shines on our partners all over the world. For example in China one says, the Germans build for eternity, German products are extremely reliable, and German engineering craftsmanship deserves the highest recognition. This awareness of how German engineering and engineering ethics are valued from outside of the country, knowing, which expectations are equally directed toward us, and how we repeatedly challenge ourselves is a great motivator and inherits large responsibility. Because such responsibility means to maintain and strengthen values and constantly develop our skills. New technologies offer a historic opportunity! It is important to prove the reputation of the construction industry.

4. Calls for action

Strategies on the national, European and global levels drive diversity, gender issues and inclusion toward more innovation in AI and digital change (**Table 1**). Statistics from the AllBright Foundation 2021 show that corporate governance codes or ethical codes are not half as effective as corporate management that exemplifies these values in a diverse corporate culture.

• The 17 Sustainability Goals of the United Nations (2016)—UN SDGs
• United Nations Convention on Women's Rights (1981)
• The Pontifical Academy for Life in Rome (2020)—Rome Call for AI Ethics Guideline [15]
• Digital inclusion strategies from UNESCO, UNICEF, World Economic Forum [16]
• EU Gender Equality Strategy 2020–2025 (Union of Equality) [17]
• European Commission (2020) White Paper on Artificial Intelligence—A European Approach to Excellence and Trust (world's first proposal for a legal framework for AI) [18]
• European Commission (2021) Proposal for a regulation of the European Parliament and of the Council: Harmonized rules on AI (Artificial Intelligence Act) and amending certain Union acts
• European digital strategy 2030
• Enquête Commission of the German Bundestag "Artificial Intelligence—Social Responsibility and Economic, Social and Ecological Potential" [19]
• Data Ethics Commission of the Federal Government (2019) Report on data ethics
• AI strategy of the Federal Government
• Federal Ministry of Transport and Digital Infrastructure BMVI (2017). Implementation of the step-by-step digital planning and construction
• Curriculum: in preparation (2021) by the German Chamber of Architects: "BIM in academic teaching"
• T20 Policy Briefs for G20 summit Italy 2021

Table 1.
Calls for action source: Bianca Weber-Lewerenz.

The construction industry, which is considered to be one of the most conservative, male-dominated industries, is the best example of a long-overdue dynamic need for restructuring and action in relation to a more diverse environment. The most important catalyst is diversity in all social, digital and business transformation processes.

5. The sovereign way: new approaches to implementing diversity

Success in the digital age requires a strong push, disruptive innovations in an interdisciplinary environment with an open corporate culture exemplified by the management. Well-balanced decision-making and the full exploitation of potential are possible when advantages and disadvantages, chances and risks of digital methods and AI are thoroughly thought out, and where diversity enabling new innovations is seen as an opportunity, particularly, when it comes to creating the corporate unique selling point with innovative digital business models. In companies, long-term personnel development is one of the main focuses and is one of the approaches for the practical implementation of diversity (**Table 2**).

One of the core tasks in the digital age for decision-makers in the societal, political, social and business environment is to recognize the benefits of AI and to operationalize it in a responsible and morally justifiable manner. The ethical components of diversity are essential for the non-discriminatory design of AI. Progress helps to develop creativity and improve the quality of life. Because technical decision-making processes are about evaluating and weighing up advantages and disadvantages, opportunities and harm, freedom from discrimination and equality are top priorities. For buildingSMART, it is both mandatory and encouraging to pursue the key factor diversity more closely.

New approaches to implementing diversity
• The role model role of women in the social, digital and business transformation processes
• Enable new data-driven technologies and AI
• Diverse, integrative environments = the basis for successful, sustainable paths
• Bridging the current gap between discussion and practical implementation
• Responsible leadership, diversity mandate, ethics council
• Diverse corporate culture and management that exemplifies diversity
• Legal regulations (in addition to entrepreneurial personal responsibility)
• Key competencies, qualified staff, adapted curricula
• Increase the share in the value chain
• Aligned to the common good and sustainability goals
• Renown abroad: "A transparent and ethical AI - Made in Germany."

Table 2.
New approaches to implementing diversity source: Bianca Weber-Lewerenz.

6. Conclusion and value accents for construction 4.0

Diverse, integrative working groups ensure a variety of perspectives and thus a quality boost for research and development. The fundamentally necessary discussion about diversity and humane change in the construction industry could not be better embedded than in the digital transformation process. New technological feasibility creates new opportunities for the design, visualization, realization, use and recycling of a building. It is important to localize, implement, control, maintain and protect the sensible use of AI. It is critical to implement and enforce a framework of rules and best practices that, when organizations adopt AI tools, they are well allocated and trained, and that there is a clear strategy to demonstrate transparency about how the algorithms are designed and identify who is involved, how the software applies and data need to be fed and updated. It will be necessary to adopt a number of principles of digital ethics to guarantee diversity and equality of the sexes, guarantee data protection and data security—going well beyond the general provisions of the General Data Protection Regulation (GDPR), and also making the adoption more transparent promote measures (e.g. the IEEE Standard P7003 adopted in 2021 to avoid algorithm bias, algorithmic testing of fair, gender-independent treatment).

Ethically justifiable products are regularly more competitive, and the responsible use of digitization and AI can only be achieved through diversity. The people who fill civil engineering with life are challenged to re-think radically, face innovative technologies openly, align professional personal skills with them and build them up anew. The discourse on the design of corporate responsibility in the digital society requires a new quality of discussion. The implementation of these requirements is the key competence in Germany. The author fills this scientific niche with her research project on CDR in construction [20].

How does technology support us, humans, sustainably and in our value-based decisions in the construction industry? [21] How do we design a digital transformation in construction that makes sense, makes work safer, and processes more efficient? [22] Old questions that are more modern than ever—in the course of the digital transformation—especially under the focus of the humane transformation [23]. This debate is completely absent in the construction industry [24]; the author introduces it for the first time in the course of her research. It goes beyond the dominant financial focus by deriving signposts for meaningful and value-based digitization and AI. These offer orientation in thinking and acting, enabling them to act as a role model in Germany and to become a seal of quality for the German construction industry at home and abroad.

Nevertheless, a radical rethinking is required: the traditionally conservative attitude, hesitations and the lack of legal regulations on the mandatory use of digital methods, which are still strongly anchored in the construction industry, worry [25, 26]. These are still the greatest obstacles to more efficient building life cycles, progress and the acquisition of skilled workers. The time is long-overdue to restore society's trust, to show that construction projects can be performed professionally, successfully and sustainably. More courage and willingness to innovate would help the construction industry as a whole to regain a positive reputation.

Such a holistic approach as tackled by this research is new and builds on the previously outlined calls for action. CDR in construction enables companies to implement and live up to their responsibility for diversity, technological innovations and shaping a sustainable digital age. This field of research is still completely new in the construction industry, and there is only comparative literature in other specialist disciplines. Unfortunately, diversity in a traditional, conservative industry, such as construction still, is promoted very little, even though it is one of the most important drivers of digital change for the construction sector.

Diversity in construction is an essential element of building trust, involving various perspectives and strengths, enhancing innovation and moving technological development forward. It is key for a successful digital transformation.

Acknowledgments/other declarations

This chapter is to encourage everyone to use the full potential of women in the Digital Era—in their thoughts and actions. The unexploited reservoir of women's potential is to increase the share in the value chain for more sustainability and success at all levels.

I would like to thank all of the experts interviewed in this research. They not only shared valuable insights but contributed to the founding of the "*Excellence Initiative for Sustainable, human-led AI in Construction*." I would like to thank the European Association for REsearch on SERVices (RESER) and the buildingSMART Network for the great cooperation and support in addressing the ethics and diversity debate for moving digital innovations forward.

In particular I would like to thank my supervisor, Prof. Dr.-Ing. Marzia Traverso, Head of Chair of the Institute of Sustainability in Civil Engineering, Faculty of Civil Engineering at RWTH Aachen University, Germany.

Statistics and reports were of great support with data and facts to underlay the statements and recommendations made in this chapter. The huge interest in this chapter by experts, companies, decision-makers and activists in the Digital Era demonstrates the key role of women leadership.

This research received no specific grant from any funding agency in the public, commercial or not-for-profit sectors.

Conflict of interest

The author has no relevant financial or non-financial interests to disclose. There is no conflict of interest/competing interest.

Publication permission was given by all respondents. Some public statements, which come from the Internet, literature and archive research, also underline the quality and statistical values of the expertise and survey values obtained, as well as limitations and urgently necessary measures.

The author of this study conducts external research, is company-independent and is not financially supported by third-party funds, companies or other institutions. She is free in her research and shares her findings at the interface of "application practice - applied technical research - economic and social transfer." In this way, the author is researching the responsible use of digitization and AI—neutrally, critically and inclusive—and promoting the ethical debate about AI technologies.

Author details

Bianca Christina Weber-Lewerenz
Excellence Initiative for Sustainable Human-Led AI in Construction, Bianca Weber-Lewerenz Engineering, Aichtal, Germany

*Address all correspondence to: bianca.christina@gmx.de

References

[1] HDB Hauptverband der Deutschen Bauindustrie. Women in construction 2021. In: Statistic Report Women in Construction 2021. Berlin: HDB Printing; 2021

[2] Deloitte. Data-driven change: Women in the boardroom – A global perspective. Global Center for Corporate Governance. In: Study by Deloitte Research Center for Energy & Industrials 2019. 6th ed. Munich: Publishing Company Deloitte; 2019

[3] Weber-Lewerenz B. Gender innovation in construction in digital era. In: Bienzeisler B, Peters K, Schletz A, editors. Conference Proceedings and Oral Presentation; 14 October 2021; Reser Conference 14-15 October 2021 Heilbronn, the Disruptive Role of Data, AI and Ecosystems in Services. Conference Proceedings of the 31st RESER Conference. Munich: Fraunhofer Publishing; 2021. p. 29 et sqq. URN: urn:nbn:de:0011-n-6429286 [Accessed: December 10, 2021]. Available from: http://publica.fraunhofer.de/dokumente/N-642928.html

[4] Weber-Lewerenz B. Corporate Digital Responsibility in Construction Engineering – Construction 4.0; Ethical Guidelines for Digitization and Artificial Intelligence (AI). Conference Proceedings and oral presentation at ICACE 2021 Artificial Consciousness and Ethics Conference in Rome, Italy, 18-19oct2021. World Academy of Science, Engineering and Technology (WASET). In: International Journal of Cognitive and Language Sciences. Vol.15, No.10, 2021. [Internet]. Available from: https://publications.waset.org/abstracts/138222/corporate-digital-responsibility-in-construction-engineering-construction-40-ethical-guidelines-for-digitization-and-artificial-intelligence. [Accessed: December 10, 2021]. International Scholarly and Scientific Research & Innovation 15(10) 2021

[5] Weber-Lewerenz B. More success by diversity in construction. Key note with discussion; 27 October 2021; Berlin. In: 25th buildingSMART Forum. Dresden, Germany: buildingSMART. Available from: https://youtu.be/cid7zP7bXY4. 2021 [Accessed: October 27, 2021]

[6] Georgiadou A. Equality inclusion and diversity through virtual reality. In: Park SH, Gonzalez-Perez MA, Floriani DE, editors. The Palgrave Handbook of Corporate Sustainability in the Digital Era. Cham: Palgrave Macmillan; 2021. DOI: 10.1007/978-3-030-42412-1_10

[7] Vassilopoulou J, Kyriakidou O, Da Rocha J, Georgiadou A, Mor Barak M. International perspectives on securing human and social rights and diversity gains at work in the aftermath of the global economic crisis and in times of austerity. European Management Review. 2018;**16**(4):837-845. DOI: 10.1111/emre.12333

[8] AllBright Foundation. The proportion of women on DAX boards has recovered. In: Interim Status March 2021. Edition as of 5th of March 2021. Berlin: AllBright Foundation Printing; 2021

[9] EQUALS & UNESCO. Closing Gender Divides in Digital Skills through Education United Nations: The 17 SDGs Sustainable Development Goals, No. 5 Gender Equality. Geneva: United Nations Publishing; 2019. Available from: https://www.un.org/sustainabledevelopment/gender-equality/ [Accessed: October 8, 2021]

[10] McKinsey & Company. How inclusion matters. In: Diversity Wins Report 2020. Munich: Publishing Company McKinsey & Company; 2020

[11] National Association of Women in Construction NAWIC. Statistics in 2019. New York: NAWIC Publishing; 2019. Available from: https://www.nawic.org/nawic/Statistics.asp [Accessed: October 8, 2021]

[12] Weber-Lewerenz B. KI im Kontext zur Ethik und gesellschaftlichen Werten und Grundsätzen. In: BIM und KI in Wissenschaft und Unternehmenspraxis. Dresden, Germany: BuildingSMART Publishing (bSD); July 2021. Available from: www.buildingsmart.de/buildingsmart/aktuelles/jetzt-neu-bim-und-ki-wissenschaft-unternehmenspraxis [Accessed: October 8, 2021]

[13] Weber-Lewerenz B. "Ethik in der KI im Bauwesen in Deutschland" und "KI Methoden und Erfahrungswerte" im Rahmen der Studie von Giannakidis, Alexandros; Weber-Lewerenz, Bianca; Stolze Denis „KI im Bauwesen in Deutschland" des Fraunhofer Instituts Stuttgart IAO im Auftrag des Cyber Valley Stuttgart – Tübingen. 2021. http://publica.fraunhofer.de/eprints/urn_nbn_de_0011-n-6306697.pdf [Accessed: April 28, 2021]

[14] Patel A, Robinson T. The European Green Deal Explained. Brussels: Norton Rose Fulbright; 2021. Available from: www.nortonrosefulbright.com/en/knowledge/publications/c50c4cd9 [Accessed: November 25, 2021]

[15] The Pontifical Academy for Life in Rome. Rome call for AI ethics guideline. In: Rome Call for AI Ethics; Rome. 1. Edition. Rome: Pontifical Academy for Life in Rome Publishing; 2020. Available from: https://www.academyforlife.va/content/pav/en/news/2021/rome-call-for-ai-ethics-one-year-later.html/ [Accessed: February 28, 2020]

[16] World Economic Forum. The Reskilling Revolution Can Transform the Future of Work for Women. Geneva: WEF Publishing; 2020. Available from: https://www.weforum.org/agenda/2020/01/women-reskilling-revolution-future-of-work/ [Accessed: November 25, 2021]

[17] European Commission. A union of equality: Gender equality strategy 2020-25. In: Proceedings of the Gender Equality Strategy. 1st ed. Brussels: European Commission Publishing; 2020

[18] European Commission. White paper on artificial intelligence - a European approach to excellence and trust. In: White Paper of European Commission Brussels. 1st ed. Brussels: European Commission Publishing; 2020 [Accessed: February 19, 2020]

[19] Enquête-Commission of the German Bundestag. Künstliche Intelligenz – Gesellschaftliche Verantwortung und wirtschaftliche, soziale und ökologische Potenziale. In: Final Report of the Enquête-Commission. Berlin: German Bundestag Publishing; 28 October 2020. 2020 Document No. 19/23800

[20] Weber-Lewerenz B. Corporate Digital Responsibility (CDR) in construction engineering - ethical guidelines for the application of digital transformation and artificial intelligence (AI) in user practice. Springer Nature SN Applied Sciences. 2021;**3**(10):801 et sqq. DOI: 10.1007/s42452-021-04776-1

[21] Schallmo D et al. Digital transformation of business models—Best practice, enablers, and roadmap. International Journal of Innovation Management. In: Digital Disruptive

Innovation. Munich: World Scientific Publishing; 2020. pp. 119-138

[22] Gfrerer AE et al. Digital needs diversity: Innovation and digital leadership from a female managers' perspective. In: Schallmo DRA, Tidd J, editors. Digitalization. Management for Professionals. Cham: Springer; 2021. DOI: 10.1007/978-3-030-69380-0_19

[23] Wilson EJ III et al. Leadership in the digital age. Encyclopedia of leadership. 2004;**4**:858-861

[24] Hermansson H et al. Exploring Digital Innovation in the Construction Industry: The Case of Consultancy Firms. Stockholm, Sweden: KTH Royal Institute of Technology Publishing; 2020. Available from: https://www.diva-portal.org/smash/get/diva2:1460868/FULLTEXT01.pdf [Accessed: January 11, 2022]

[25] Sandi R. Environmental impact on digital era by architectural production. Journal of Environmental Science and Sustainable Development. 2019;**2**(1): 26-47. DOI: 10.7454/jessd.v2i1.28

[26] Haugsten Hansen H. et al. Learning Mechanisms from Digital Innovation Projects: A Case Study of the Swedish Construction Industry. Stockholm, Sweden: KTH Royal Institute of Technology Publishing; 2018. Available from: http://kth.diva-portal.org/smash/get/diva2:1253037/FULLTEXT01.pdf [Accessed: January 1, 2022]

Chapter 13

Education and Training in the Digital Era: A Compass for "Building Forward Better"

Bianca Christina Weber-Lewerenz

Abstract

Knowledge is the greatest raw material. To build a secure future, you need knowledge, skills, to network and get involved in the new. Digitization with the technological and social challenges requires a rethinking and adjustment of professional qualifications at the same time. More than half of 70% of the open AI positions in companies are currently unfilled. This high number describes the dilemma and the challenges for the teaching and training of tomorrow. Are we ready for the technological challenges of tomorrow? This research found that there is significantly high potential for diverse teams, staffing the STEM fields with more female specialists and fully using specialist knowledge and personal qualifications of men and women. Last but not least, this research contributes setting up compass for building forward better by ensuring gender-independent decision-making structures in human-technology interaction and use diversity as key for reaching sustainable goals and set milestones in the digital era. The main research results consist that the foundation for diversity, inclusion and sustainable digital innovations can only be ensured by adjusted education and academic training. To achieve sustainable digital transformation with a strategy foundation, education and academic training are most essential. This research fills the gap by highlighting the importance of these two essential areas that call for immediate action: Diversity, education, and training represent the drivers for the sustainable success in the Digital Age.

Keywords: education, academic training, curricula, STEM, digital innovation, digital transformation diversity, inclusion

1. Introduction

The Italian Presidency decided at the Digital Economy Ministers' Meeting in Trieste on the 5th of August 2021 to place digitization at the core of G20 discussions. Participation in education and training for all to eliminate digital gender gaps and challenge stereotypes are, thus, not just buzzwords anymore but lived engagement. The diversity of existing regulatory approaches and technologies within the G20 means that many questions are yet to be answered: how to make digitization an opportunity for all? Fostering diversity and inclusion in the digital era is essential to protect and enlarge global value chains, create a trustworthy Artificial Intelligence (AI) ecosystem, enhance the digital to achieve sustainable growth. In other words,

IntechOpen

when using the term "sustainability of digital innovations" in this article, it refers to securing the necessary basis for the solid ground for innovations: education and training. It lays the foundation in digital era and guides as compass for "Building Forward Better."

As a Senior Civil Engineer with a background of international experience in Europe and China, the author deals with all aspects of new technologies in Construction Engineering in multidisciplinary, intercultural environments, arising with Industry 4.0. The author's field of expertise in the Construction Industry covers her own engineering company in multinational environments since 2007—after filling various management and leadership positions—and mentoring female apprentices and academics in STEM disciplines. In 2019, she took a pioneering role by starting as the Representative for *"Sustainable, Human-led AI in Construction Industry"* by investigating human-technic interaction. Therefore, in 2020, she founded the Excellence Initiative under the same name [1]. Her research examines ethical, social, and economic impacts of digitization and AI on human, societal, and technological development [2].

By assessing how and why education and learning lay the essential foundation of the digital age, the research also found out that knowledge and AI not only automatize learning processes but strengthen Corporate Digital Responsibility (CDR), diversity, and inclusion in Construction 4.0.

Pioneers are role models equally to develop and implement technical innovations. They shape the digital age as they share their experiences as Best Practices.

The research includes political strategies, but also makes new demands and work out specifically, where the advantages and disadvantages of the current curricula lie in order to provide the future educational foundation as broad as possible. With that, the acquisition of both the appropriate professional and personal social skills could succeed in the best possible way.

2. Knowledge and AI automatize learning processes

The tension between the new qualification requirements through digitization and AI and existing resources for teaching and curricula with an adequate academic infrastructure could not be greater. New job profile descriptions clearly speak of holistically thinking experts and system-integrating specialists. The learning curve for everyone involved is steep, and the demands in construction are equally high: Climate and environmental protection, sustainability with resource efficiency, thinking through the entire construction life cycle—from the project idea to dismantling and recycling, budget compliance, and efficient timeline as well as a building project of highest quality. New technologies not only may ensure, but perform such processes in a much more structured, efficient, safer, successful, and profitable way. Teaching and training carry responsible roles in order to explain these powerful technological tools, to practice first approaches and to allow making mistakes. The safe and efficient use of emerging technologies and knowing its positive and negative effects require targeted instruction within this innovative interaction between human and technology.

Why is it important to specifically integrate digital methods and AI into teaching in Civil Engineering? Because only construction experts are able to localize obstacles and weak points in construction projects, name improvements, and define potential fields of application for digital methods and AI. They know the processes, interfaces, and hurdles exactly and know "where things get stuck."

The digital transformation and the latest technologies require a rethinking of previous teaching methods, teaching aids, teaching environment (laboratories, equipment, IT), knowledge in theory and practice, practical samples of application, the relationship between theory and practice, the qualifications of the teaching staff and their openness, and networks across disciplines [3–6].

3. The path forward: education and training in digital era

The basis for diversity, inclusion, and sustainable digital innovations can only be ensured through appropriate training and further education [7, 8]. The Action Plan for digital education is an essential prerequisite for creating a European education area by 2025. It contributes to the realization of the goals of the *European Skills Agenda* [9], the *Action Plan* on the European Pillar of Social Rights and the *"Digital Compass 2030: The European Path to the Digital Decade."*

The dependencies and weaknesses of European digital capacities, competencies, and technologies are becoming increasingly clear. They see a need for action particularly in the area of AI [10].

Numerous studies and forecasts on digital transformation provide information about the extensive effects on jobs. New professional fields and task profiles are emerging; they require new knowledge and skills. Some professional fields will no longer exist in the course of digital change, but new ones emerge. They accelerate the development, use and further improvement of new digital technologies and AI, and facilitate imparting the necessary knowledge to others.

AI will not only change people over the next few decades, but society as a whole. Companies that want to forego 50% of their talent face a massive problem in the medium term. Digital twins, self-learning construction sites, automation and robotics on construction sites, VR, Smart Design, Smart Construction, Smart Operation, Smart Cities, Blockchain, AI, Next Generation Computing, 5G and 6G, IoT, AIoT, AR, VR, and XR strongly influence corporate business models and daily construction site organization, construction operations, building informatics, and technical building automatization.

Analyzing the content of curricula of selected universities and colleges, crystallize out, that terms such as BIM (Building Information Modeling) and AI are mostly not or rarely listed in the overview of lectures—both for Bachelor and Master. At the same time, it can be seen that more and more new curricula modules are being set up in construction, such as Computational Engineering or Data Engineering. The aspects of human responsibility that engineers, designers, and developers bear by the nature of profession cannot be adequately taught, e.g., with the modules for Ethics: it is taught on the sidelines, and—as interviewed experts share—is usually still an optional subject on a voluntary basis. Some teachers fear that they will have to forego their own learning content and therefore see no point. These aspects are part of an even larger package of influencing factors in education and teaching, why—at this stage—education and teaching cannot do justice to the expectations and requirements of the economy and society.

In addition, there are innovative research initiatives at universities and emerging AI hubs, digital campus locations, AI labs, increasing digital transformation competence networks, endowed professorships and chairs sponsored by corporates, high-tech offensives launched by individual federal states, and AI centers as well as completely newly created modules: "Applied AI" and "Digital Ethics," "Digital Transformation,"

"Human-Computer Interaction," "Digital and Data Science Engineering," "AI-based Technical Building Automatization," "Digital Process Management of Construction Projects."

4. Shared experience from user practice

It now depends on the answers we humans give, how we can fill these gaps, and the new professional fields. For the analysis and evaluation in this research work, experts were interviewed based on the qualitative method: representatives from universities, colleges, newly created chairs and professorships, professional associations, new corporate departments, and institutes. They share their opinion and tendencies they assess. Statistics and job profile descriptions in national and international newspapers and professional journals were evaluated for obtaining a picture as accurate as possible of where we "stand" in the Construction Industry. What are the concrete measures to be taken to set up adequate curricula? And what distinguishes the skilled workers and "engineers of tomorrow"?

Teizer [11], partner and head of the management of technology and innovations at VOLLACK, is active in academic teaching himself. "*AI is rarely or rarely promoted and taught in teaching. For example, architecture students at many colleges and universities still have to create and present analog designs and models. BIM is often not used. The day-to-day work that follows looks different. Perhaps one of the reasons is that decades of standards are reluctant to go crazy. And with civil engineers, the purely technical discipline way of thinking is a hindrance. In order to master the digital transformation successfully and together, however, interdisciplinary cooperation, openness with an innovative flair and the integration of new technologies are required.*"

Kiefer [12] refers to the results of the study carried out by the VDI in 2017/18 on "Engineering training for digital transformation." "*Professors, students, representatives from business environment and executives were interviewed. The feedback was sobering, as in parts of the professorships, among other things, results brought to light about insufficient knowledge, less open attitude to innovations, lack of willingness to participate, underestimated importance of the influence on engineering training and the necessary measures. The discussions have high priority, especially at universities.*" Kiefer offers further important insights: "*Engineering training has already changed fundamentally: it has been opened up, via modularized design and internationalization. Highly recommended for considering the university's commitment: the umbrella organization '4ING', the Faculty Days for Engineering and Computer Science at Universities. The German Federation of European National Engineering Associations FEANI (in German "Föderation Europäischer Nationaler Ingenieurverbände") tries to influence engineering training on the european level, to agree on the necessary qualification profiles across national borders, to level the differences between the countries, to facilitate the professional entrance for the engineers, to be armed with knowledge and skills successfully. In fact, to be fully committed designing the digital transformation process in Construction. Indeed, there are major discussions about the engineering profile at FEANI. The process of opening up to realignment and adjustments is ongoing. In addition, it is the current generation, which defines the different attitudes and attitudes toward the topic.*"

Digital transformation bears high potential to aid both economical and efficient building project life cycle and greatest possible social benefit, economic prosperity, and protection of our natural resources of life.

But at the same time, the economy is lagging behind digitization and AI, diversity, and inclusion. 60% believe that the lack of diversity in the tech workplace is a serious issue [13]. Strong support for change comes from national and international networks and associations promoting the fields of STEM, construction, and digitization. In the 2020, *Digital Education Action Plan* and the *European Skills Agenda*, the Commission announced a range of actions to ensure and develop digital skills. In the next few years, the need for skilled workers will continue to increase and corporate personnel planning will have to adopt. Digital transformation changes job profiles and creates new ones. Universities, colleges, and training centers feel this change and start expanding their curricula to accommodate the subjects of digitization and AI so that the next generation of engineers and specialists provide ethical and interdisciplinary skills in digitization and AI. This is a key competence in Germany for "AI—Made in Germany", which is recognized worldwide as a seal of quality.

The decisive factor is leadership behavior, the example of top management and clear communication of the culture of values [14]. It is the responsibility of every corporate management to promote diversity at all levels, inclusion, best qualifications, and personal competence, to maintain, to ensure sustainable and—in the interests of the common good—to increase its contribution to the value chain. Corporate environments with agile, dynamic management style, and female leadership should be a matter of course to generate high performance.

Profound insights, openness, and recommendations of the interviewed experts enabled this research to reveal these new findings and set constructive approaches as a Call for Action into the ongoing debate. The wide variety of specialist knowledge and areas of responsibility illuminated the challenges and innumerable chances of diversity from different angles.

Furthermore, the holistic, inclusive, interdisciplinary approach of the author not only empowers to educate, raise awareness, and provide orientation in dealing with digital transformation but adds value to this new field of scientific research.

Algorithms, which make AI possible, are daily routine for computer scientists, but only a negligibly small proportion of society is familiar with AI and speaks this expert language. Trust in this new technology therefore is imperative but can only be established and built where it is explained and awareness is formed. In total, 125 million girls of primary and secondary age in the developing world are out of school. Girls' exclusion from education begins early and increases over their lifetime (**Figure 1**). While the vast majority of adolescent girls of upper secondary age begin primary education, fewer than half make it to the upper secondary level where STEM skills can be further solidified.

It is essential to give access to girls and women around the globe to learn and utilize these technologies; they possess high communicative, social skills as well as significant high human-driven decision-making process dynamics and are catalysts for highly dynamic and efficient learning processes, which is the real core of this innovation.

The young generation has high expectations of teaching and training in handling and transferring knowledge about both future key technologies and offer constructive solutions and gain required professional and personal skills. The best indicator for job seekers is companies that are already actively shaping the digital transformation, using methods such as BIM, helping to develop the first AI technologies, defining potential fields of application, and developing new business models as a result. The opportunities are significant and diverse for young skilled workers and engineers to prove their qualifications and enlarge the value chain by their contribution to success.

It takes people, fully participating to reach these goals, platforms, visionaries, and men of action from fields of teaching, education, business, politics, and society. *We see a strong need for the discourse, this is the only way to constructively investigate the question of*

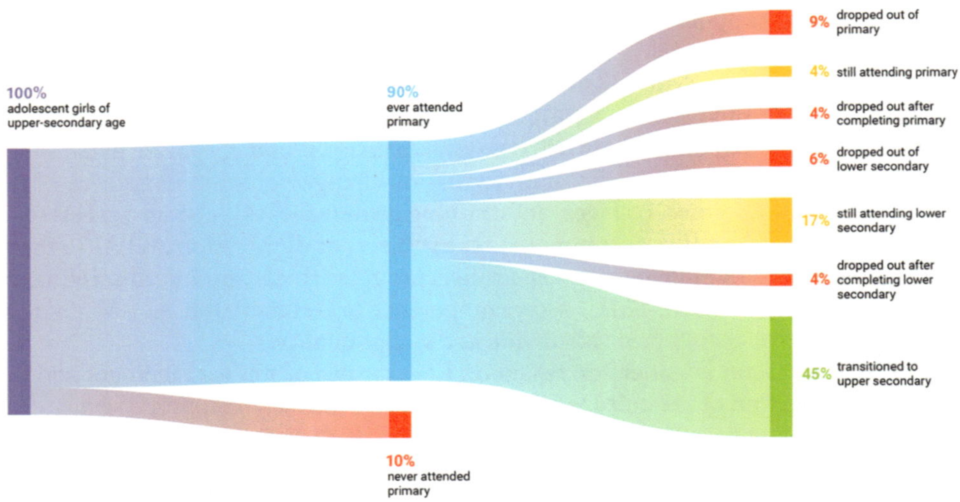

Figure 1.
Education pathways of girls in: the story of disparities in STEM, mapping gender equality in STEM from school to work source: UNICEF 2020 [15].

the qualification profile ... of the "engineers of tomorrow", which digitization and AI require. Decision-makers have a responsibility. Certain things taken for granted from the past will no longer apply in the future ... Innovative technologies—hand in hand with ethical questions—must generally be included in teaching. That has not happened yet. Mistake and problematic: it is a process in which everyone, and not just individual, has to deal with the effects of digitization and AI. Reservations, an attitude of rejection, waiting, or the attitude "we don't need" have no chance in this process that affects all of them," state Lautwein and Fox [16].

5. Algorithm complexity and gender bias

Digital transformation sets flag for disruptive reforms in the educational landscape. Best Practices are evidence for best results in increasing both personal social and expert skills. Axel Wallrabenstein sets impulses: "*Diversity in management bodies is not only important, but essential for the success of companies and for our society.*" His counterpart Rainer Esser follows, "*Companies that want to fore-go 50 percent of their talent will face a massive problem in the medium term*" [17].

New approaches offer the historical chance to break boundaries, move forward global digital competition, add value to the system of computer algorithms, and increase its share in the value chain. Women are underrepresented, so there is less data, data of lower quality, not free of bias. Thus, the results are unpredictable and unexpected. There are serious concerns regarding the scalability of taking automatically biased decisions that can affect large sectors of the population, particularly minorities and more vulnerable communities. A growing body of evidence is indicating that algorithms are increasingly affecting decisions by replicating unequal or unfair treatments [18].

In line with the European Commission' priority to strive for a "Union of Equality" by its *Gender Equality Strategy 2020–2025*, the author's Memorandum (**Table 1**), shared with the *T20* Task Force Digital Transformation in preparation of the *G20 Summit* in October 2021, focus on:

• Develop technologies and algorithms to evaluate and address bias in AI-based systems. These methods will help addressing gender in AI-based systems and support the deployment of such bias-free AI-based solutions.
• Develop standardized processes to assess and quantify the trustworthiness of the developed AI systems, in particular assessment of bias, diversity, non-discrimination, and intersectionality—based on different types of bias measures. Consider diversity and representativeness of data, ensure the reliability, traceability, and explain ability of the AI systems. Include mechanisms to flag and remove risks of biases and discrimination.
• Develop recommender and algorithmic decision-making systems, which reduce bias in the selected use case.
• Conduct trainings and awareness rising on preventing gender and intersectional bias for AI researchers, students, and practitioners in line with the Digital Education Action Plan 2021–2027.
• Cooperate with relevant partnerships across industrial and digital sectors, including digital professional associations (e.g., IEEE), computing industry, hi-tech start-ups/SMEs etc., to further promote the use and uptake of the developed tools.

Table 1.
The memorandum, shared with the T20 task force digital transformation in preparation of decision papers at G20-summit in oct 2021. July 2021 source: Bianca Weber-Lewerenz and Ingrid Vasiliu-Feltes.

6. Disruptive changes in curricula

Digitization abolishes traditional structures and boundaries. Thus, it is necessary to highlight the digital era's opportunities for society and new fields of activity that have so far been largely ignored.

Digital teaching itself becomes an aspect of teaching: having access to digital equipment is not a matter of course, because there is no fundamental right and universities and educational institutions need to apply for funding. It is about the acquisition of devices such as laptops, tablets, or whiteboards and the integration of these devices into lessons. Not every university is financially that well positioned to have extensive digital teaching equipment and facilities. Here, new challenges require new strategies.

Pure knowledge transfer can succeed very well, if not better than with previous teaching, by fully using digital possibilities. Digitization offers a way to open up the access to education to a larger extent.

The engineering training sets most important basis. It requires an open-minded, interdisciplinary, collaborative mentality of all those involved. The engineer of tomorrow will no longer just plan, construct, maintain a building, but bring people together that are involved in the construction project. The engineer networks knowledge, uses interfaces and interdisciplinary perspectives, shares technical engineering knowledge, leads a project, is part of a large team with a common goal: to use skills and knowledge in a goal-oriented and efficient manner toward a successful, sustainable project. It is about a building that is realized by help of a lot of emerging technologies. The engineer of tomorrow is a visionary, a dedicated one. He tackles work with foresight, works on solutions that are compatible with the common good; the engineer takes a stand on social issues, prevents violations, helps to shape the dynamic field of work preventively, to curb possible negative developments. The engineer promotes an open dialog between the construction and society in order to protect the culture of values in construction industry. His interdisciplinary approach is the most essential requirement. Thus, the curricula need to be thoroughly adapted; the reality of life must be made the subject of engineering training.

Furthermore, from the beginning of studying and training, the engineer needs to work interdisciplinary: with other faculties such as Architecture, Design, Computer Science, Law, Philosophy, Media, and Cultural studies. As the sustainable, value-based design of the living and urban worlds of tomorrow, future-proof urban infrastructures, space, and society are enabled by the necessary ethical principles in dealing with digital technologies and AI, the more technically oriented engineer can supplement his knowledge.

In higher education across the world, the progress of digitization is deeply influenced by government policies and institutional development strategies, both of which play a key role in shaping the digitization landscape of higher education [19].

The following dilemmas require deeper research: Nowadays, university research and teaching have to look for funds and, therefore, choose topics according to demand. Students are confronted with the omnipresent situation of the labor market; lecturers are already part of the academic precariat. The structure and organization of teaching are determined less by a belief in the educational ideal than by the learning of competencies that are intended to increase the individual's chances of competition. Not every excellence strategy and funded chair—often financially supported by companies—means excellent teaching and training. Digitization of teaching hand in hand with a more humane education allows contemporary teaching. Content and structure of academic training require concrete revisions, balancing theory, and practical application with case studies. Transferred to practice this means, e.g., the integration and application of BIM, digital twins, applying simulation methods, getting first contact with AI-based forecasting methods, self-experiencing virtual reality tools. Training personal skills include social, communication skills, network-oriented thinking, critical reflection based on holistic approaches, and interdisciplinary environments.

Digital teaching and training increase the flexibility of study and working hours as much as possible. It demands from each individual a high level of responsible behavior and planning. Such freedom offers high potential: gender-independent access for each and every one.

From November 2019 and February 2021, the author carried out primary studies with expert and interview surveys for winning more information on the recent status of corporate and training policy discussions and implementation of digital technologies and AI, as well as receiving more insights on how companies respond to and handle new needs in terms of specialist knowledge and new job profiles in the digital era. In addition, multipliers were interviewed for interdisciplinary holistic approach—including industry associations and chambers of crafts, foundations, representatives of various specialist disciplines at universities and colleges, educational and teaching institutions.

Fraunhofer Institute IAO and Cyber Valley Stuttgart-Tübingen published the common study with the author [20]. New findings were shared at presentations and conferences with a multidisciplinary, international audience [21]. The reason for choosing the qualitative research method was that the research field is a fringe area, the topic is new, and only the intensive expert interviews offer deep insights into the status and use of technologies, needs, tendencies, critical reflections, social problems, and recommendations for constructive solutions. The evaluation shows a practical implementation of education, knowledge, and awareness building, still bearing a lot of ignorance, business planning performance "on sight," attitude of rejection, and reservations about scientific interdisciplinary work. These conditions that prevent success have to be named. They not only hinder the exchange between specialist disciplines and the search for holistic solutions in the design of the digital transformation process, but also the innovative progress and digital change in construction in

Germany. "*In the technical sciences, it is still a long way off those values and principles are used and that ethics training has to be anchored in training,*" Loh knows [22].

7. Strengthen social and professional skills

Technical experts confirm that progress and reforms in digital change can only be achieved through critical questioning and new food for thought. Responding to corporate responsibility in the digital society requires a new quality of discussion.

The study considers both UN sustainability goals and requirements of the EU Commission in its "*White Paper on AI*" as guide for designing value-based, sustainable digitization and AI. These guidelines offer orientation to strengthen the responsible role of the construction industry. Ethical values and codes of conduct have to be further developed in order to strengthen trust in new technologies. New job profiles tailored to digital competence, automation, robotics, AI and related sustainability issues, are steadily reflected in increasing numbers of start-ups, tailor-made specialist and managerial positions, and new job advertisements. The professional and personal requirements are diverse and extensive (**Tables 2** and **3**).

In addition, new university research initiatives, endowed professorships and chairs are founded, sponsored by industry and companies, and new areas of lesson created. They have in common the formation of technical, interdisciplinary project cooperation—as early as the training phase. For a holistic view, faculties increasingly work cross-disciplines in intercultural teams. Train such forms of cooperation, team structures, processes, and methods from the earliest stage enable to keep pace with technological, economic, and societal changes. The most precious foundation is: reflecting, thinking ahead, and thinking outside the box. Values and ethics, digitization, and AI can no longer only be assigned to other specialist disciplines such as philosophy, law, IT. They must be embedded in the teaching and education of tomorrow's engineers, the engineering sciences.

• Self-learning competence.
• Decision-making ability: In the future, it will be crucial to be able to differentiate between the essential and the insignificant and to be able to assess alternatives.
• Cooperation competence: Engineers should be able to work together, find consensus, and be able to accept each other. In addition to being able to work in a team, this also requires the ability to enter into non-organizational collaborations.
• Cognitive skills.
• Empathy.
• Thinking and acting with foresight, far-sighted leadership.
• Working in partnership with employees, suppliers, and customers (Covid-19 crisis clearly shows: the human factor and good management is the highest selection factor and criterion for quality).
• Think first, then act.
• Creativity.
• Interdisciplinary, network-oriented thinking
• Foreign language opens up for thinking along, empathizing with other people and situations, and empathizing with others.
• Value—and common good—oriented.

Table 2.
Social skills. Source: Bianca Weber-Lewerenz.

• Hybrid competencies: In addition to knowledge and skills of the respective subject area, the engineers of tomorrow also have knowledge of the digital disciplines.
• Interdisciplinary competencies: digital transformation will succeed through interdisciplinary and trans-disciplinary cooperation.
• Simulation technologies: Understanding simulation technologies is the basis for developing systems and scenarios in the digital world.
• Big Data: Engineers know how to obtain information using sensors and how to implement it using actuators. In addition, they should be able to filter large amounts of data and have knowledge of agile process methods in software development.
• Technology assessment: Questions such as data protection and misuse as well as data security and falsification, but also decision parameters of autonomous systems are part of engineering developments. In addition, engineers help shape normative processes.
• Understanding of quality: Engineers must balance well security measures on the software side and the limits of the underlying model approaches.
• Acquisition of skills in the context of digital work and business processes designed as an interdisciplinary cross-sectional task.
• Strategic knowledge and working style
• Intelligent weighing for the use of AI.
• Predictive analytics.
• Safe handling of data, data protection (basic knowledge on legal regulations).
• Being able to explain technologies and thus gain confidence.

Table 3.
Professional skills source: Bianca Weber-Lewerenz.

That is, the Faculty of Applied Computer Science offers a wide range of courses: classic computer science topics and teaching the latest advances in technology. The course is intended to offer future skilled workers a wide range of opportunities on the job market, i.e., to contain potential dangers that arise through the use of digital processes ("Cyber Security") or to develop learning systems ("Artificial Intelligence"). Whether courses such as Applied Computer Science, Business Informatics, or the Internet of Things (IoT), one can choose between countless job offers and be part of shaping digital change. Applied AI, Digital Ethics, Digital Transformation, Digital and Data Science Engineering, Technical Building Automatization, Chief Digital Officer, Digital Ethic Boards, Digital Process Management of Construction Projects, Learning Transport Infrastructure are some of the new job portfolios. In the area of Technical Building Automatization—as part of the climate protection programs—the latest digital methods and AI are applied. In corporate trainings, teaching of hybrid competencies is in full swing.

Daily digital work assumes not only teaching and training digitally but, thus, re-orientation and adaption of qualifications of the teachers. New chances for women arise as to fill in these positions, promote digital innovations, and represent role model for other women. The inclusion of underrepresented and marginalized groups in the design development, and training of the AI systems, and a transdisciplinary approach, involving multidisciplinary and intersectoral partners in the consortium will be essential.

The path of understanding and dealing with AI, understanding opportunities and risks only is paved by an adequate education and rigorous academic training. Education is the core element required to build a legacy of gender equality.

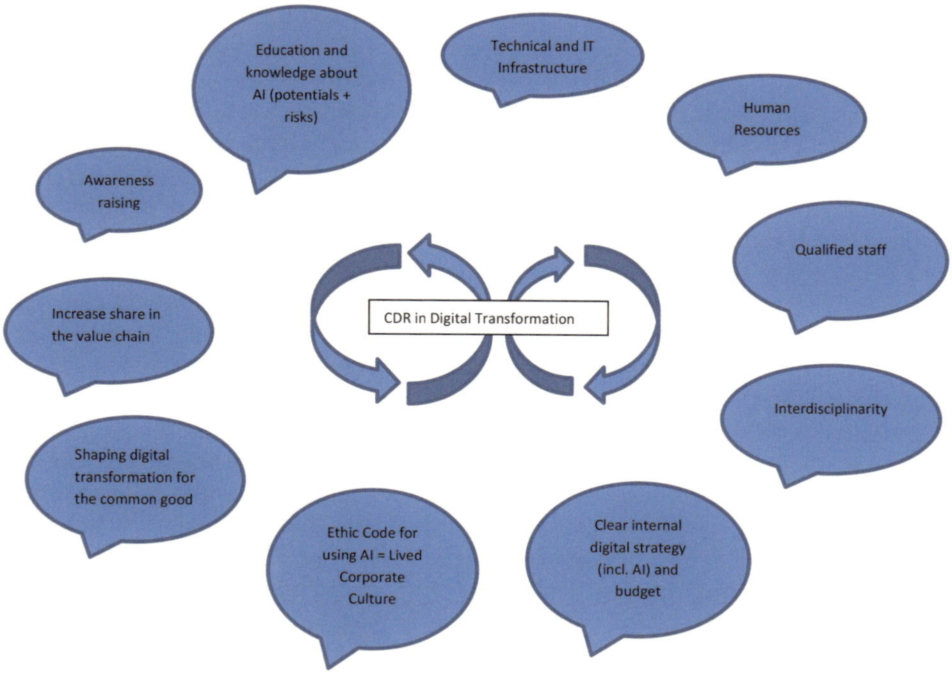

Figure 2.
Mind map "The interrelationship among the key elements of CDR" source: Bianca Weber-Lewerenz.

However, there are several complex issues we need to address. How do we define an optimal "future-proof" curriculum? Who is qualified to teach young children skills that will be beneficial for their future life and careers? How should we deliver this new curriculum? How and should we even score their performance of this revised future-oriented curriculum? The *UNESCO* presented its key findings in the *Global Dialog on AI* and *Gender Equality Report 2020*. The digital era takes diversity, inclusion, and integration into account. What is long overdue must now be pushed faster: adjusted teaching and training regulations, adjusted training and qualification of teachers, creation of new digital learning methods. Innovative, agile university, college, and training locations are in the focus when it comes to the choice of teachers and students determining new work places and study locations.

In times of crisis—such as the corona pandemic—it also became clear who was ahead of the pack when it came to dealing with these tasks. In the digital transformation, they are the key factors for successful implementation in construction (**Figure 2**), which must be sustainably anchored in research, teaching, and training.

8. "German engineering": construction in the focus

New job profiles clearly speak of holistically thinking experts and system-integrating specialists. The learning curve is steep for everyone involved, and the demands in daily construction industry business are equally high: Climate and environmental protection, sustainability with resource efficiency, thinking through the overall construction cycle—from the project idea to dismantling and recycling, keeping within budget and time, as well as realizing the highest quality. New technologies not only ensure but make such processes significantly more efficient, safe, and successful. Teaching and training represent responsible roles for explaining these powerful technological tools and practicing initial approaches. The safe, efficient use of this technology and its effects require targeted instruction in this innovative interaction between human and technology. Why is it important to specifically integrate digital methods and AI into teaching in civil engineering? Because only construction experts are able to localize obstacles and weak points in construction projects, name improvements, and define potential fields of application for digital methods and AI. The sensible use of this technology with the help of an AI strategy tailored to the company and highly qualified staff require a joint rethinking, process and communication improvement, awareness raising with the help of comprehensive education, and orientation through a lot of knowledge. It offers orientation and security for users and employees at all times. Digital growth strategies require digital skills. This is the only way to completely redesign new business models in the construction industry in the digital world of work 4.0. According to experts, the planning and construction industry must redefine itself with reference to its own business models in its own task and job profiles. Close corporate contacts with universities and colleges support the development of professional skills. By communication and technology exchange—via guest lectures and the supervision of bachelor and master theses of students—skilled engineers can be trained. Another perspective is that universities and colleges should be attractive for students and stand out innovatively in the educational landscape. Working in the Construction Industry has lost its attractiveness, maybe it will be possible to revive it with new, exciting technologies?

To women this digital era offers enormous potential in construction in fields of work, research, networking, building trust in new technologies, widen application areas, and set up innovative business models.

In the future, the technical competence increases mutual benefit between young and experienced employees. Because lacking experts in digital technologies and AI, teaching and training make a significant contribution to building on existing skills with the help of additional digital knowledge and to promoting the use of innovation technologies. This increased awareness of the need to create appropriate teaching and lecturing digitization and AI. Following the opinion of university experts, according to interview evaluation, these fields should not just lead to one new field of academic lesson in addition to existing subjects, but be holistically integrated, taught cross-disciplines, and be embedded in all modules and lessons.

In the opinion of economic experts, a general entrepreneurial rethinking and new approaches in corporate recruiting and personnel marketing are required. In terms of strategic personnel planning, companies should define task and job profiles and address them to universities, colleges, and training centers. New job profiles require the integration of new specialist skills.

Universities and colleges should stand out innovatively in the educational landscape when training architects and engineers. Digitization with BIM and AI are opening up new opportunities that could revive the lack of attractiveness of the entire construction industry for years. The use of new technologies and production methods such as the three-dimensional printing of entire components or even houses will be able to counteract the now noticeable shortage of skilled workers.

The Construction Industry has an extraordinarily high reputation: "German engineering" and "German craft ship" stand for the highest quality and sustainability worldwide.

Teaching and training are no longer just training, but to think holistically and in networks, shaping and paving the way for successful digital change.

9. Conclusion and outlook

There are *four main pillars* of disruptive and transformative change our society needs to undergo as to fully ensure diversity and gender equality: education, profession, culture, and governance. It is important to address all levels of education from preschool to executive level [23, 24]. Furthermore, skills that are expected to be in highest demand in the digital era need to be embedded into the classical curriculum [25].

WEF highlights that some of the top skills in demand by 2025 will be creativity, analytical and innovative thinking, active learning, complex problem-solving, as well as technology design, use, monitoring and control to only, name a few [26].

By offering full access to quality education and equal employment opportunities, societies around the globe ensure to not leave any girl's and women's rights neglected [27].

To be clear: education and training represent the strategic basis for both sustainable digital and human transformation. However, to bring it to the next level, the adaptation of higher education and training will almost certainly need to be accelerated to keep up with the already high dynamics of the digital ecosystem and the emerging technologies. Some of the latest emerging technologies (such as Blockchain, Quantum Computing, Metaverse, AI, IoAI, Next-Generation Computing, 5G and 6G, 3D, IoT, AR, VR and XR etc.) can serve as catalysts or gateways to enhance inclusion and diversity when deployed mindfully [28].

Curricula is far from satisfying the needs of companies and fulfilling the requirements of economy and society. Strategies and white papers are seen too much of theory, there is a gap between the media hype of talking about digital ideas, dreams, and visions, what we can, what we should do, could do, what would be good, what would be great. The gap goes deep right into the daily practice, the practical ways of highly interested companies in implementing such tools and methods, and modern digital working environments, daily routine utilizing digital methods and AI.

Only a minority of universities, universities of applied sciences and schools offer adequate digital infrastructure and learning environment [29]. But innovation requires qualified experts and skilled workforce with diverse and inclusive backgrounds—on both sides: teaching and students. Best practice, user experiences help interested and new users at the start.

How can it be that only a handful of the 100 advertised AI professorships are filled [30], the course content is still not adapted to the requirements of the digital transformation, and companies are desperately facing the shortage of skilled workers, which is still growing?

This research is a direct approach to calls made by the various national and international strategies with focus on the Construction sector—a branch that is being studied scientifically for the first time with this research.

It represents a significant path forward that some Best Practices already walk. For the holistic understanding, algorithm complexity and gender bias are shortly introduced and social and professional skills stressed. Thus, clear definitions of the concrete disruptive changes in curricula can be provided, eventually leading to the German Engineering seal of quality.

This chapter is intended to be a plea for more disruptive thinking and acting in teaching and training. The digital and human transformation begins in the head—where education lays the foundation.

Acknowledgments/other declarations

Education is the foundation for progress. Knowledge is the door to the world.

I thank my mentors and all supporters who share this vision.

I thank all the experts interviewed in this research. I thank all who strengthen education and training in digital transformation process.

In particular I would like to thank my supervisor, Prof. Dr.-Ing. Marzia Traverso, Head of Chair of the Institute of Sustainability in Civil Engineering, Faculty of Civil Engineering at RWTH Aachen University, Germany.

Statistics and reports were of great support with data and facts to underlay the statements and recommendations made in this paper.

This research received no specific grant from any funding agency in the public, commercial, or not-for-profit sectors.

Conflict of interest

The author has no relevant financial or non-financial interests to disclose. There is no Conflict of interest/Competing interest.

Publication permission was given by all respondents. Some public statements, which come from internet, literature, and archive research, also underline the quality and statistical values of the expertise and survey values obtained, as well as limitations and urgently necessary measures.

The author of this study conducts external research, is company-independent, and is not financially supported by third-party funds, companies, or other institutions. She is free in her research and shares her findings at the interface of "application practice—applied technical research—economic and social transfer." In this way, the author is researching the responsible use of digitization and AI—neutrally, critically, and inclusive—and promoting the ethical debate about the AI technologies.

Key Terms

AI	Artificial Intelligence is a branch of computer science that deals with the automation of intelligent behavior and machine learning. It is an attempt to reproduce certain decision-making structures in humans, e.g., B. a computer is built and programmed in such a way that it can deal with problems relatively independently. Often, however, it is also used to designate an imitation intelligence, whereby an "intelligent behavior" is to be simulated using mostly simple algorithms.
BIM	Building Information Modeling describes a working method for networked planning, construction, and management of buildings and other structures using software. All relevant building data are digitally modeled, combined, and recorded.
Diversity	Diversity is the range of human differences, including but not limited to race, ethnicity, gender, gender identity, sexual orientation, age, social class, physical ability or attributes, religious or ethical values system, national origin, and political beliefs. Diversity of people does not mean just the obvious in terms of demographics such as race, ethnicity, gender, and age. Diversity means people

	with different skill sets, experiences, educational backgrounds, cultural and geographic perspectives, ways of thinking and working. Diversity is part of social, corporate, and political responsibility.
STEMs	These fields include Science, Technology, Engineering, and Mathematics.

Author details

Bianca Christina Weber-Lewerenz
Excellence Initiative for Sustainable Human-Led AI in Construction,
Bianca Weber-Lewerenz Engineering, Aichtal, Germany

*Address all correspondence to: bianca.christina@gmx.de

References

[1] Weber-Lewerenz B. Excellence Initiative for Sustainable, Human-Led AI in Construction. 2020. Available from: https://www.bwl-engineering.com/iethics

[2] Weber-Lewerenz B. Corporate digital responsibility in construction engineering: Ethical principles in dealing with digitization and AI. International Journal of Responsible Leadership and Ethical Decision-Making (IJRLEDM). 2020;**2**(1):32-49. DOI: 10.4018/IJRLEDM.2020010103

[3] Burnett M. Doing inclusive design: From gender mag to inclusive mag. In: Human-computer Interaction Institute Seminar Series Paper [Paper Presentation]. Pittsburgh, PA: Carnegie Mellon University; 2020. Available from: https://scs.hosted.panopto.com/Panopto/Pages/Viewer.aspx?id=1fa67161-215d-45e8-b228-ab3e00f844ce [Accessed: December 14, 2021]

[4] AI Ethics Lab. A Guide to the Dynamics of AI Principles: Our Toolbox for Understanding & Using AI Principles. 2020. Available from: https://aiethicslab.com/big-picture [Accessed: December 14, 2021]

[5] World Economic Forum. These are the Top 10 Job Skills of Tomorrow—and How Long it takes to Learn Them. 2020. Available from: https://www.weforum.org/agenda/2020/10/top-10-work-skills-of-tomorrow-how-long-it-takes-to-learn-them [Accessed: December 14, 2021]

[6] UNESCO. New UNESCO Report on Artificial Intelligence and Gender Equality. Report 2020. 2020. Available from: https://en.unesco.org/AI-and-GE-2020 [Accessed: December 14, 2021]

[7] German Federal Ministery for Education and Research. Digital Future: Learning. Researching. Knowing—The Digital Strategy. 2019. Available from: https://www.bildung-forschung.digital/digitalezukunft/de/unsere-ueberzeugungen/digitalstrategie-des-bmbf/die-digitalstrategie-des-bmbf/die-digitalstrategie-des-bmbf.html [Accessed: December 14, 2021]

[8] European Commission. Action Plan for Digital Education (2021-2027). 2021. Available from https://ec.europa.eu/education/education-in-the-eu/digital-education-action-plan_de [Accessed: December 14, 2021]

[9] European Commission. European Competency Agenda. 2021. Available from https://ec.europa.eu/social/main.jsp?catId=1223&langId=en [Accessed: December 14, 2021]

[10] Merkel A, et al. 2021. Europe must see its Digital Sovereignty. Letter to the Head of the EU Commission. Available from: https://www.handelsblatt.com/meinung/gastbeitraege/digitalisierung-appell-von-vier-regierungschefinnen-an-die-eu-europa-muss-seine-digitale-souveraenitaet-staerken/26962398.html?share=mail&ticket=ST-12911066-YRfg5bjTdBqhfCVlySXD-ap6 [Accessed: December 14, 2021]

[11] Teizer K. Dealing with Digitization, AI and ethics in construction at Vollack Company. Telephone Interview with the author as of 21 December 2020. 2020

[12] Kiefer T. Dealing with Digitization, AI and ethics in construction at the German Association of Engineers: International Job Policy and Technical Education (German "VDI Verein Deutscher Ingenieure"). Telephone

Interview with the author as of 03 December 2020. 2020

[13] Agarwal P. Gender Bias in STEM: Women in Tech Still Facing Discrimination. 2020. Available from: https://financesonline.com/women-in-technology-statistics [Accessed: December 14, 2021]

[14] Wieland J. Founder of Governance Ethics, 1996 Founder of the Ethic Management in Construction Industry Association (Since 2007 renamed "EMB - Value Management Association of Construction Companies"). 1996. Available from: https://www.emb-werte.com

[15] UNICEF. Education Pathways of Girls. In: The Story of Disparities in STEM, Mapping Gender Equality in STEM from School to Work. 2020. Available from: https://www.unicef.org/globalinsight/stories/mapping-gender-equality-stem-school-work [Accessed: December 14, 2021]

[16] Lautwein M, Fox J. Dealing with Digitization, AI and ethics in construction at the Federal Institute for Building, urban and spatial research (BBSR), at the Federal Office for Building and Regional Planning (BBR). [Dealing with Digitization, AI and Ethics in Construction at the Federal Institute for Research of Building, City and Environment Planning]. Interview by the author as of 04 December 2020. 2020

[17] All Bright Foundation. Introduction of Board Members. 2021. Available from: https://www.allbright-stiftung.de/English [Accessed: December 14, 2021]

[18] Leavy S. et al. Mitigating gender bias in machine learning data sets. In: Boratto L, Faralli S, Marras M, Stilo G. Bias and Social Aspects in Search and Recommendation. BIAS 2020. Journal of Communications in Computer and Information Science. 2020;**1245**. DOI: 10.1007/978-3-030-52485-2_2

[19] Walker R, Jenkins M, Voce J. The rhetoric and reality of technology-enhanced learning developments in UK higher education: Reflections on recent UCISA research findings (2012-2016). Journal of Interactive Learning Environments. 2016;**26**(7):858-868. DOI: 10.1080/10494820.2017.1419497

[20] Weber-Lewerenz B. Ethik in der KI im Bauwesen in Deutschland" und KI Methoden und Erfahrungswerte im Rahmen der Studie von Giannakidis, Alexandros; Weber-Lewerenz, Bianca; Stolze Denis KI im Bauwesen in Deutschland" des Fraunhofer Instituts Stuttgart IAO im Auftrag des Cyber Valley Stuttgart - Tübingen 2021. 2021. Available from http://publica.fraunhofer.de/eprints/urn_nbn_de_0011-n-6306697.pdf [Accessed: April 28, 2021]

[21] Weber-Lewerenz B. Gender innovation in construction in digital era, Conference Proceedings and Oral Presentation; 14 October 2021; Reser Conference 14-15 October 2021 Heilbronn, The Disruptive Role of Data, AI and Ecosystems in Services. In: Bienzeisler B, Peters K, Schletz A, editors. Conference Proceedings of the 31st RESER Conference. 2021. p. 29 Available from http://publica.fraunhofer.de/dokumente/N-642928.html [Accessed: December 10, 2021]

[22] Loh J. Künstliche Intelligenz und Ethik: Alles gut, oder was? [AI and Ethics: Is All Good?]. Podium Discussion as of 05 December 2018. Bonn, Germany: Telekom Headquarter; 2018

[23] Lazareva M et al. Digital technologies in preschool education: Risks and prospect. In: Proceedings of the 2021 1st International Conference on Technology Enhanced Learning in Higher Education

(TELE). Piscataway, New Jersey, United States: IEEE; 2021. pp. 93-95. DOI: 10.1109/TELE52840.2021.9482538

[24] Zevenbergen R. Digital natives come to preschool: implications for early childhood practice. Contemporary Issues in Early Childhood. 2007;**8**(1):19-29. DOI: 10.2304/ciec.2007.8.1.19

[25] Grimus M. Emerging technologies: Impacting learning, pedagogy and curriculum development. In: Yu S, Ally M, Tsinakos A, editors. Emerging Technologies and Pedagogies in the Curriculum. Bridging Human and Machine: Future Education with Intelligence. Singapore: Springer; 2020. DOI: 10.1007/978-981-15-0618-5_8

[26] World Economic Forum. These are the Top 10 Job Skills of Tomorrow – and How Long it takes to Learn Them. 2020. Available from: https://www.weforum.org/agenda/2020/10/top-10-work-skills-of-tomorrow-how-long-it-takes-to-learn-them [Accessed: December 12, 2021]

[27] Krieger-Boden C et al. Labour market opportunities for women in the digital age. Journal of Economics. 2018;**12**(1):10567. DOI: 10.5018/economics-ejournal.ja.2018-28

[28] Tortoriello M et al. Being a catalyst of innovation: The role of knowledge diversity and network closure. Journal of Organization Science. 2015;**26**(2): 423-438. DOI: 10.1287/orsc.2014.0942

[29] Edler J et al. Technology sovereignty as an emerging frame for innovation policy: Defining rationales, ends and means (No. 70). In: Fraunhofer ISI Discussion Papers-Innovation Systems and Policy Analysis. 2021 Available from: https://www.econstor.eu/handle/10419/236194 [Accessed: January 01, 2022]

[30] Mah D et al. Künstliche Intelligenz in Studium und Lehre. Überblickstudie zu Professuren und Studiengängen der Künstlichen Intelligenz in Deutschland. Berlin: VDI/VDE Innovation+ Technik GmbH; 2019. Available from: https://www.plattform-lernende-systeme.de/files/Downloads/Diverses/Studie_KI_in_Studium_und_Lehre.pdf [Accessed: January 01, 2022]

Chapter 14

Virtual Internet of Things Laboratory Using Node-RED

Kalapatapu Venkata Sai Krishna Raja Shiva Kumar, Attaphongse Taparugssanagorn and Arunya Prasantha Senadeera Senadiri Dumunnage

Abstract

Due to the pandemic or any other tough situations, attending the student laboratory session physically is difficult or even impossible. To overcome this problem, a virtual laboratory can be introduced. In many universities, virtual teaching methodology is not implemented widely. While there are several existing visual programming languages developed for various applications, an open-source visual programming language named Node-RED, which is particularly used for Internet of Things (IoT)-based applications, is taken into consideration in the book chapter. A complete outlook of Node-RED, which can be applied for an IoT-based virtual laboratory, is described. Its simplicity providing many built-in entities makes it possible to evolve innovative platforms with less coding complexity. The configuration, the flow development, the requirements, and the usage of the Node-RED are explained with respect to handling all the various types of errors. A few experimental cloud-based services are implemented on an IoT platform using serial port and message queuing telemetry transport (MQTT) broker service as well as providing live camera capturing feature with artificial-intelligence-based object detection. The results show that real-time IoT sensor data can be efficiently measured and visualized in dashboard and live object detection can be done with good accuracy.

Keywords: node-RED, visual programming language, open-source, Arduino MQTT, amazon cloud

1. Introduction

In this modern era, there has been a lot of development and upgradation in the field of Internet of things (IoT). The development has been actively growing in various sectors, for instance, industries, healthcare, education, agriculture, just to name a few. Consequently, it creates more employment opportunities. Thus, IoT should come into intensive usages with very careful awareness. The development of IoT programs can be done in various ways into the society. Although there have been a plenty of IoT development and applications, only very few academic institutions throughout the world are fully IoT equipped in their laboratories.

Since 2019, the COVID-19 pandemic has resulted in shutdown of educational institutions across the world. Globally, over 1 billion children are out of the classroom. As a result, education has changed dramatically with the distinctive rise of e-learning, whereby teaching is undertaken remotely and on digital platforms. While lecture sessions have been quite well organized, the laboratory sessions might be still challenging and dependent on the types of laboratories. To overcome this problem for an IoT design class, a virtual laboratory can be implemented. With a virtual laboratory, a laboratory session can be launched with flexibility of time. Self-learning process can be achieved by becoming more self-determining. It also supports collaborative group works and helps us develop critical thinking skills while doing individual assignments. The most important advantage is that it can be accessed from any location through Internet. Thus, any materials from the Internet can also be used. Nevertheless, there are some challenges in the virtual laboratory, which includes setting up the virtual laboratory environment, lack of social interaction between students and instructors, accessibility to various laboratory required technologies, software requirement and software inconsistency, student's issues while teaching simultaneously, etc. A visual programming language (VPL) is any programming language that lets users create programs by manipulating program elements graphically rather than by specifying them textually. A VPL allows programming with visual expressions, spatial arrangements of text and graphic symbols used either as elements of syntax or secondary notation. Many VPLs known as dataflow programming are based on the idea of boxes and arrows, where boxes or screen objects are treated as entities connected by arrows, lines, or arcs representing relations. Different prototyping boards have its own programming language, such as C, Python, Java, and similar. To develop an IoT system, at least one of these programming languages is required. However, it is fortunate that during these days, several VPLs have been developed to help us start programming without knowing the programming language. These IoT visual programming tools have a user-friendly approach of programming. It has a graphical user interface (GUI), where the user can just drag and drop moving code blocks and execute a simple piece of logic.

Node-RED VPL is an open-source software, which is a flow-based development tool originally developed by International Business Machines (IBM) for wiring hardware devices together with application programming interface (API) and few online services as part of the IoT. Node-RED can be used flexibly under the Apache2 license. Some developed their own services based on Node-RED, while others changed to their own user interface (UI) and deployed it as built-in. It can be established as a platform where we can publish our own developed node so that anyone can use it. The open-source software is an alternative to interact with the class. Students can practice, study, and understand with basic engineering skills or even develop an IoT-based system with artificial intelligence (AI) capabilities, e.g., prediction, regression, clustering, and classification. It can be installed locally on a personal computer (PC) or a laptop. With its simplicity for learning and using as well as several built-in entities, it can be used in evolving innovative platforms providing ability to assign code to all interfaces with less coding complexity. In addition, it supports several IoT prototyping board such as Arduino, Raspberry, and Android as well as cloud-based platforms.

The objectives of the book chapter are as follows.

- To describe the environment and features of Node-RED software with its abilities of numerous functions.

- To deliver a complete outlook on each function of Node-RED that can be applied for an IoT-based virtual laboratory.
- To talk over the suitability and rightness of machine learning and deep learning centered explanations in numerous practical fields.
- To arrange for a broad opinion on machine learning algorithms, which can be put to build-up the abilities of a data-driven approach.
- To highlight and summarize the possible study for smart systems including cloud technology.
- To bring out the virtual awareness/importance of IoT including laboratory sessions.

The rest of the book chapter is organized as follows. Section 2 presents the past related existing works on VPL and NodeRED. In Section 3, the step-by-step methodology of the work is described in detail, which includes getting started, configuration, utilization, and machine learning (ML) package for Node-RED. The experimentational examples are provided along with the corresponding results in Section 4. Section 5 discusses about the results. Lastly, the conclusion is drawn in Section 6.

2. Related work

IoT has been playing an important role throughout the globe. It is a combination of both software and hardware tools. With the support of VPL, IoT can be applied into our day-to-day essential things. According to the survey by Ray in 2017, there were 13 VPLs for the usage and for the upgradation of IoT [1]. The VPL is classified into two types, namely open-source and proprietary-source with the four following main features, i.e., programming atmosphere, license, project source, and platform support [1]. Students can use open-source VPL such as Node-RED to learn and implement an IoT system or device with basic engineering skills and low-code programming. It helped many programmers to develop new software [2, 3]. Node-RED was initiated and was developed by IBM for connecting hardware devices with web-based editors [2, 3]. It was then applied further in the field of IoT. Rajalakshmi and Shahnasser came with a problem while making a cloud-system for IoT devices [4]. This is difficult to update the firmware by reinstalling the devices. To solve this issue, Node-RED was used without reinstalling the device and changing the programming code with quick setup [4]. In 2018, a model based on LoPy, which is a MicroPython triple-network development platform doubling up as a long-range (LoRa) Nano gateway, was connected to a system that uses Node-RED for interfacing with a local actuator and the external data with protocols [5, 6]. Their IoT development could be done in fog/clouds. The introduction of the IoT in education allows Internet-based communications to occur between things, sensors, and actuators. This has improved educational institutions [7–14]. In 2015, Giang et al. implemented a distributed Node-RED (D-NR) framework for building various types of IoT applications, which can work efficiently with simple designing process and less time [15]. Abdel-Basset et al. could make an efficient framework by new ideas with lower cost and greater security [16].

The advantages in maximizing IoT became more for the institutions, i.e., bringing out an affluent knowledge, better quality of working efficiency, and gaining real-time experiences [17]. In addition, they could keep track record of all the university resources with secured data accessibility. Using an open-source platform such as Node-RED, it helps for the creation of new ideas, i.e., linking up with many other specialized courses, for instance, information and communication technologies (ICTs), embedded system design, humanities, agricultural, just to name a few, yielding a good IoT program of study for students to learn and make research [16]. Another model was proposed by Marquez et al. as an IoT educational platform for virtual academic communities [17]. In 2020, Torres et al. used VPL with Node-RED to improve their IoT system by reducing the time taken for the development, i.e., reducing the number of failed attempts while deploying an IoT system [18]. Home automation consisting of water heater, cooling systems, electrical outlets was raised all over the IoT using cloud-platform where Node-RED is used to make fast setup for remote monitoring and control of data with a mutual communication [19]. In 2021, David et al. worked on indoor crop agriculture by monitoring parameters such as humidity, temperature, and light intensity with the help of IBM-Bluemix, which is the IBM open cloud platform providing mobile and web developers access to IBM software for integration security transaction and other key functions [20]. The data was transformed into Node-RED platform through a mobile application for tracking purpose of the farmers. Thuluva et al. made a solution for interoperability problem for IoT semantic web technologies in industrial field using semantic Node-RED models with feasibility and scalability approach [21]. A rapid and low-cost IoT prototype was developed by Ferencz and Domokos within less time on Node-RED using the combination of various cycle power plant dataset [22]. A low-power wide area network (LPWAN) technology called LoRa with its medium access control (MAC) layer protocol called LoRaWAN was deployed by Fox et al. in 2019, and these end devices interact with a gateway using Node-RED connection to an IBM-IoT platform [23]. Node-RED was applied and analyzed by Olsson and Eric in terms of modeling and security with misuse of API and providing security guarantees [24]. Clerissi et al. made a model for testing and developing IoT platforms using Node-RED with the functional behavior and the static view of the system. The class diagrams were used by testing, defining, and generating in java script using a Mocha test framework [25]. Proper regulations and rules for all the Node-RED developers were given by Clerissi et al. [26]. They are about the comprehensibility issues, which can be used to increase efficiency by reducing errors and time to complete tasks.

VPL is any programming language that lets users create program by manipulating program elements graphically rather than by specifying them textually [27, 28]. A VPL allows programming with visual expressions, spatial arrangements of text and graphic symbols used either as elements of syntax or secondary notation. For instance, many VPLs known as dataflow or diagrammatic programming are based on the idea of "boxes and arrows," where boxes or other screen objects are treated as entities, connected by arrows, lines, or arcs representing relations [29–31]. There are several different VPLs, which can be divided into different fields of applications, such as education (23 languages), multimedia (26 languages), video games (18 languages), systems (34 languages), automation (4 languages), data warehousing (8 languages), legacy (5 languages), and miscellaneous (10 languages) [29–31]. The difference between a regular programming and visual programming, in terms of type, nature, flexibility, speed, efficiency, interface, learning complication, space usage, and example, is shown in **Table 1**.

No	Context	Regular programming	Visual programming
1	Type	Use only text	Use only graphics
2	Nature	Not user-friendly	User-friendly
3	Customizable	Very high	Moderate
4	Flexibility	High	Low
5	Speed	Very high	Low
6	Efficiency	Very high	Moderate
7	Interface	Not good	Great
8	Learning Complication	Take time	Easy to learn
9	Space Usage	Less	High
10	Example	Python, Java, etc.	Drakon, Helix, etc.

Table 1.
Difference between regular programming and visual programming.

Node-RED is preinstalled in many devices, such as Raspberry Pi, Intel, Fujitsu, just to name a few. Moreover, there are several different cloud services including Cisco, Nokia, IBM, Hitachi, etc., using Node-RED as a VPL and a dataflow programming.

3. Methodology

This section describes the complete scenario of methodology process. As can be seen in **Figure 1**, the first stage is installation, which involves the three following types, i.e., local machine, Raspberry Pi, and cloud services. After the correct installation, the Node-RED is configured involving all the basic nodes required to make a workflow with deployment activities. Next, the utilization is the main stage in which the development of the flows, handling errors of all the core nodes are explained. Accordingly, when the utilization process is completed, any type of experiments can be implemented with the expected and accurate outcomes.

3.1 Getting started

Getting started by installing Node-RED can be done on various criteria, which are explained as follows.

1. Running on a local machine for Windows 7 and above

   Windows 7 and above versions have the capability of installing Node.js, Node-RED, and node package manager (npm) using command prompt (cmd) or Powershell. The procedure is described as follows.

   - Node.js (version 14.x long term support (LTS) or above) is installed.

   - All the local administrators are given their rights.

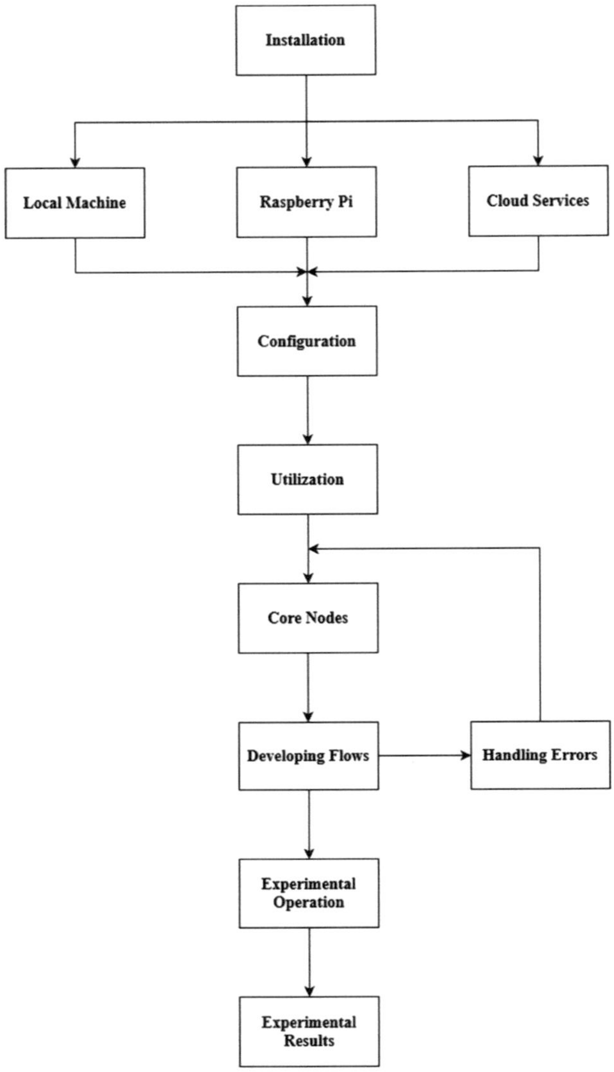

Figure 1.
Block diagram representing methodology workflow.

- Cmd or Powershell is opened and the following code is run to check if it is installed correctly or not installed.
- “node –version; npm –version” (Powershell),
- “node –version && npm –version” (cmd)
- Node-RED is installed by the command “npm install -g –unsafe-perm node-red.”
- As soon as installed, the cmd and type “node-red” is opened. As an output, a terminal log of Node-RED is displayed on the screen.

2. Running on a Raspberry Pi or any other IoT module

   Buster is the supported version for Node-RED at present for all the Raspberry Pi Operating Systems (OS).

   - The subsequent command is used to install node.js, npm and node-red on any Raspberry Pi.

   "bash < (curl-sLhttps://raw.githubusercontent.com/node-red/linuxinstallers/master/deb/update-nodejs-and-nodered)".

   (This command is used on any Debian-based OS like Ubuntu, DietPI.)

   "bash < (curl-sLhttps://raw.githubusercontent.com/node-red/linux-installers/master/rpm/update-nodejs-and-nodered)".

   (This command is used on any Red-Hat packet management (RPM) based OS like Red Hat, Fedora, CentOS, Oracle Linux.)

3. Running on different cloud services (IBM cloud, Amazon web services, Microsoft Azure)

   Node-RED is used on different cloud-based services with many features depending on the user or the client requirements.

   - For International Business Marketing (IBM) cloud: It is highly virtualized with high power, storage, networking, security, data management, analytics, developer tools, IoT, and integration and migration of virtual servers.

   - For Microsoft Azure: It is also having the same abilities like IBM cloud with some extra added features such as replacing as an supplement for many other on-premise virtual servers with best recovery support.

   - For Amazon web services (AWS): It has various new features when compared with many other cloud-services for developing new innovative smart devices, where it includes all the required API with less cost for the third-party usage.

3.2 Configuration

This section describes about various types of configurations that are needed for the deployment of each different application with default parameters in the default file directory.

- Normal application: Entire structure is loaded by default settings file, which is a built-in source.

- Embedded application: It is passed into property called RED.init(), where embedded.

- Run-time configuration: It defines the time-value of each node during the deployment.

- Logging configuration: Only console logging is supported in Node-RED.
- Node configuration: It is in the hierarchical format used for the application deployment.
- External module configuration: It defines about the run-time handling external npm modules and decides whether the editor allows new node modules to be installed such as the function node to have their own dynamic configured dependencies.
- Editor configuration: It is a set of files with different coding styles with various text editor plugins.

    1. adminAuth: It permits security for user in the editor and admin API.
    2. paletteCategories: It describes the sequence of types in the palette. By default, the pattern is subflow, common, function, network, sequence, parser, storage.

The run-time configuration is explained as follows.

- Flow file: It is used to store the flows.
- Userdir: It is used to store user data, credentials, and library data.
- Nodesdir: It is used to search additional installed nodes.
- Uihost: It is an interface to listen all connection on IPv4.
- Uiport: It is a port to serve ui editor.
- Httpadminroot: It is the root url, which contains both API and editor UI.
- httpAdminAuth: It allows HTTP validation on the editor UI.
- httpAdminMiddleware: It is an array of all functions, which is added to all admin routes.
- httpNodeRoot: It is the node root for all the urls that run HTTP at all endpoints.
- httpNodeAuth: It enables HTTP Basic Authentication
- httpRoot: It enables the root url to run on both admin and node endpoints through overriding httpAdminRoot and httpNodeRoot value.
- https: It permits https.
- httpStaticAuth: It supports basic confirmation and validation of HTTP with the static content.

- httpNodeCors: It is source distribution for the nodes, which are responsible for HTTP endpoints with cross-origin authentication.
- httpNodeMiddleware: It permits custom processing. For example, validation is required for the node.

Various stages of logging configuration used in Node-RED are described as follows.

- Fatal: Errors that make application unworkable are tracked.
- Error: Tracked errors for requests and fatal errors.
- Warn: Record of the problems about non-fatal and fatal errors.
- Info: Tracked information of application, warnings, error, and fatal errors.
- Debugging (Debug): Tracked information, which is more verbose than information, warnings, error, and fatal errors.
- Tracing (Trace): Tracks about all complete logging, debugging, info, warnings, error, and fatal errors.

The node configuration is explained as follows.

- Function Node: It is for gathering bits and pieces to attach into universal functions.
- functionExternalModules: It allows adding additional modules that are available to the function.
- Debug Node: Any message directed to the debug sidebar tab with maximum size and characters.
- MQTT Nodes: If the link is misplaced, how much time to pause in milliseconds before trying to connect.
- Serial Nodes: How much time to pause in milliseconds before making an effort to revive into serial port
- socketReconnectTime: How much time to pause in milliseconds before trying to connect again.
- socketTimeout: How much time to pause in milliseconds before scheduling out any port.

3.3 Utilization

3.3.1 Core nodes

The important nodes used for the basic functioning of the Node-RED are called "core nodes." The main six types of core nodes are explained as follows.

1. Inject: It starts any flow manually by clicking the inject button. It can be at required intervals or any time within the editor.

2. Debug: It is used to show messages in the Debug sidebar in the editor, and the control on the node can be used to permit or restrict its outcome.

3. Function: It permits JavaScript code to run beside the messages delivered from it.

4. Change: It is used to transform message properties and fix context properties without changing a Function node with multiple operations such as set, change, move, delete.

5. Switch: It permits messages to be routed into different divisions of a flow by means of calculating set of instructions compared with each message with rules values, sequence, expression, otherwise property.

6. Template: It is used to produce text by message properties to fill the template.

3.3.2 Developing flows

It is the section in which all the necessary placement and arrangement of the nodes are done for the successful execution on the Node-RED.

1. Flow structure: It helps us organize flows, approaches for splitting into smaller, reusable components, and how to modify them to make use in different platforms.

2. Message design: It helps how to design messages to create nodes and flows, which can work together with any number of nodes and are easier to maintain.

3. Documenting flows: It helps about making or providing documentation on what tools and techniques Node-RED provides.

3.3.3 Handling errors

It is described as tracing out the bug or an error, which helps to reduce the developing time and correct the errors easily. The different types of errors on Node-RED are explained as follows.

1. Logging error: It displays the error with the date and time of the error and the node, which is noted as an error.

2. Catchable error: It will not be logged, but it informs about run-time error. Then, the Catch node will be used to produce a flow which can handle it.

3. Sub-flow error: It will not be logged but it informs about run-time error. Then, the Catch node will be used to produce a flow, which can handle it.

4. Uncatchable errors: If the error is written in the log, then a message is seen in the Debug sidebar and log outcome. But creation of a flow is not possible to handle it.

5. Uncaught errors: It causes the Node-RED run-time to shut down and cannot be controlled in the flow as they are produced by bugs in nodes.

6. Status changing errors: It is used to control modifications in node position by including the position property which provides the data about the position with the node that caused the incident.

3.4 Machine learning (ML) package for node-RED

This node-red-contrib-machine learning module for Node-RED contains a set of nodes offering machine learning functionalities. Such nodes have a python core that takes advantage of common ML libraries such as SciKit-Learn and Tenserflow. Classification and outlier detection can be performed using this package.

3.4.1 Usage

These flows create a dataset, train a model, and then evaluate it. Models, after training, can be used in real scenarios to make predictions.

Flows and test datasets are available in the "test" folder. We need to make sure that the paths specified inside nodes' configurations are correct before trying to execute the program. "node-red" can be run from the folder ".node-red/node-modules/node-red-contrib-machine-learning" and the paths will be automatically correct. The flow shown in **Figure 2** loads a csv file, shuffles it, and creates a training and a test partition.

The flow shown in **Figure 3** loads a training partition and trains a "decision tree classifier" and then saves the model locally.

The flow shown in **Figure 4** loads a test partition and evaluates a previously trained model.

Figure 5 shows the flow of how to use a trained model during deployment. Data is received via mqtt, predictions are made and then sent back.

Figure 2.
Flow for loading a csv file, shuffling it, and creating a training and a test partition.

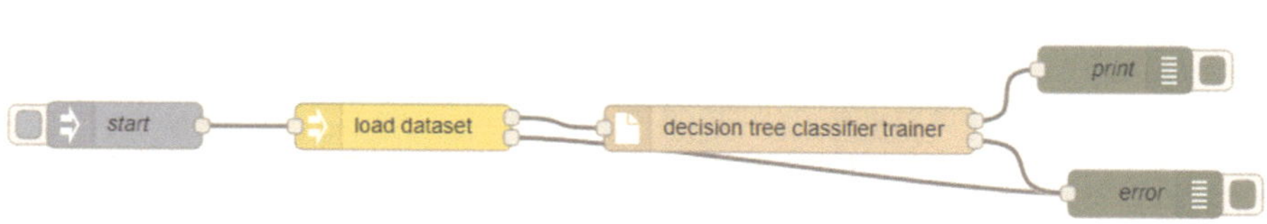

Figure 3.
Flow for loading a training partition and training a "decision tree classifier".

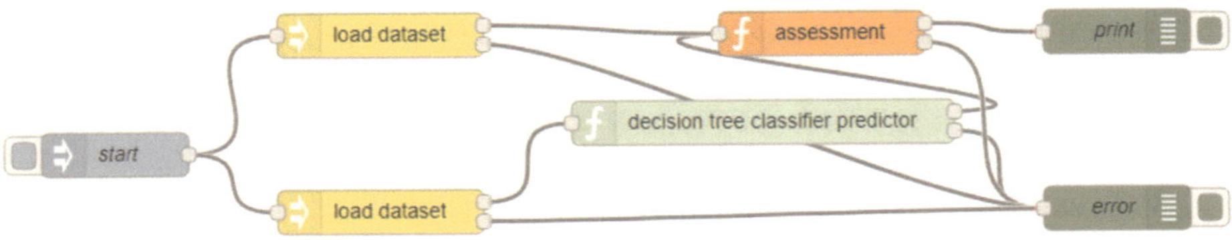

Figure 4.
Flow for loading a test partition and evaluating a trained model.

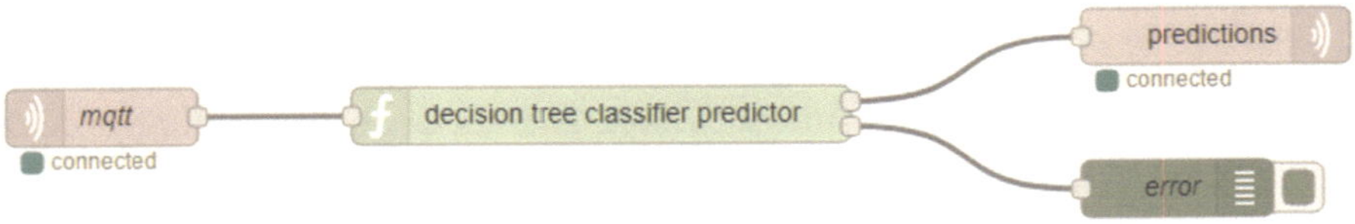

Figure 5.
Flow for showing how to use a trained model during deployment.

4. Experimentation

In this section, various types of experiments related to IoT are provided. ESP32, which is a microcontroller chip manufactured by Espressif Systems, is applied. It consists of a low-cost and a low-power chip with features such as Wi-Fi (IEEE802. 11 b/g/n), Bluetooth, and built-in antenna. The distributed hash table (DHT11) is a basic, ultralow-cost digital temperature and humidity sensor. It uses a capacitive humidity sensor and a thermistor to measure the surrounding air and spits out a digital signal (using an 8-bit microcontroller unit (MCU)) on the data pin. An Arduino integrated development environment (IDE) is used to write and upload programs to the Arduino compatible boards supporting the languages C and C++. Message queuing telemetry transport (MQTT), which is a lightweight messaging protocol, is used on such a small microcontroller that allows messaging between device to cloud and cloud to device with supporting several IoT devices. By using MQTT commands can be sent to control outputs, data can be read and published from sensors. Therefore, communications between multiple devices can be established. We can send a command with a client to control outputs, or we can read data from a sensor and publish it to a client.

4.1 Experimental examples

Example 4.1.1 DHT11 Sensor Data on Node-RED using a Serial Port (ESP32). The procedure of this task is described as follows.

1. The ESP32 is connected to the DHT11 sensor as shown in **Figure 6** (GND TO GND, 3.3 V TO VCC, GPIO4 TO DATA PIN).

2. If the connections are correct, then a light present on the DHT11 sensor is turned on.

Figure 6.
ESP32 connection with DHT11 temperature sensor (serial port).

3. The DHT11 sensor is programmed into the Arduino integrated development environment (IDE) and uploaded into the ESP32 to show the corresponding temperature and humidity.

4. If the required packages are absent, then the Arduino IDE shows an error while uploading the code.

5. After the code is successfully uploaded, we can click on the serial monitor to see the corresponding temperature and humidity readings of the DHT11 sensor.

6. The Node-RED software is installed into the system. Then, the local hosting address of the Node-RED is open. This can be run on any browsers.

7. The required nodes, i.e., dashboard and serial port, are installed.

8. A flow is created as shown in **Figure** 7.

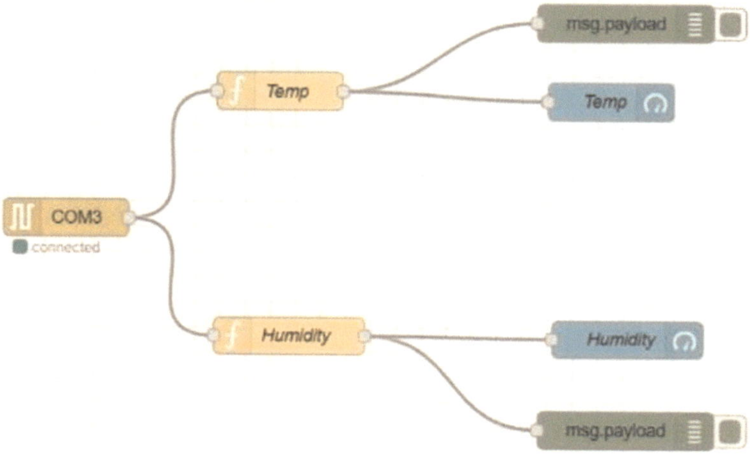

Figure 7.
Node-RED serial port connection for temperature and humidity.

9. A serial is inserted into the port node, one function node for temperature and another function node for humidity, which display the DHT11 sensor data.

10. To get the representation, two-gauge nodes for temperature and humidity are inserted and connected to their respective function nodes.

11. Finally, the overall workflow is deployed.

Example 4.1.2 MQTT Broker Service (ESP32) on Node-RED with DHT11 Sensor Data. The procedure of this task is described as follows.

1. The ESP32 is connected to the DHT11 sensor as shown in **Figure 8** (GND TO GND, 3.3 V TO VCC, GPIO4 TO DATA PIN).

2. If the connections are correct, then a light present on the DHT11 sensor will be turned on.

3. The DHT11 sensor is programmed into the Arduino (IDE) and uploaded into the ESP32 to show the temperature and humidity.

4. If the required packages are absent, then the Arduino IDE shows an error while uploading the code.

5. After the code is successfully uploaded, click on the serial monitor to see the temperature and humidity readings of the DHT11 sensor.

6. The Node-RED software is installed into the system. Then, the local hosting address of the Node-RED is open. This can be run on any browsers.

7. The required nodes, i.e., dashboard, MQTT-in, and MQTT-out nodes, are installed.

8. A flow is created as shown in **Figure 9**.

Figure 8.
ESP32 and DHT11 temperature sensor (MQTT broker service).

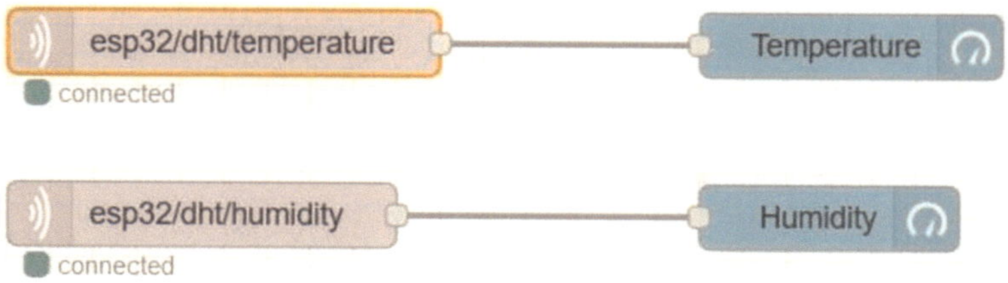

Figure 9.
MQTT broker service for temperature and humidity with node-RED.

9. Two MQTT-in nodes, one for temperature and another for humidity, are inserted.

10. This extracts the sensor data from the ESP32 through the MQTT broker service and gets into the Node-RED platform with the help of the local-host ip address.

11. To display this data, the one gauge is connected to the temperature node and the other is connected to the humidity node.

12. Finally, the overall workflow is deployed.

Example 4.1.3 Live Camera Capture and Object Detection using Machine Learning (ML).

In this example, a user interface (UI) has a major role for making an interface between the user and the Node-RED dashboard by the means of a system camera and a UI-table. **Figure 10** shows the procedure of this task, which is described as follows.

1. The Node-RED software is installed into the system. The local hosting address of the Node-RED is opened. This can be run on any browser.

2. The required nodes, i.e., random, dashboard, UI-table, UI-webcam, tfjs-coco-ssd, tf-model, tfjs-node (tf = tensorflow), are installed.

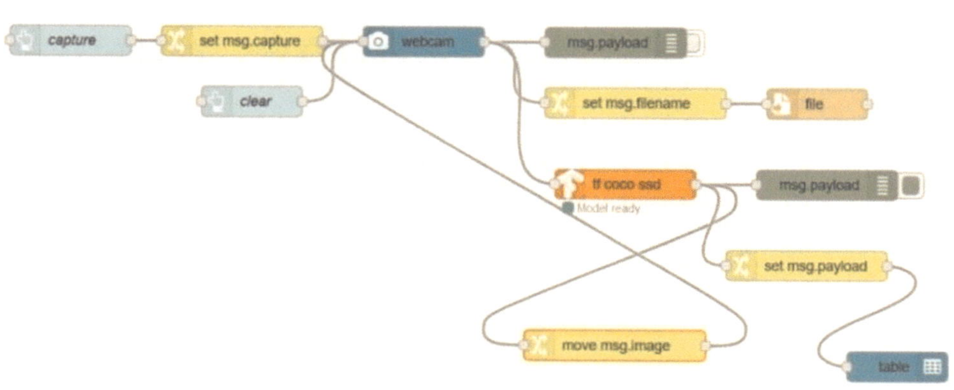

Figure 10.
Node-RED flow for live camera capture and object detection using machine learning (ML).

3. We connect the nodes by inserting button node = 2 (capture and clear), change node = 4 (set msg.capture, set msg.filename, set msg.image, set msg.payload), UI-webcam node = 1, UI-table node = 1, tfjs-coco-ssd = 1, debug node = 2 (msg. payload), file node = 1.

4. We check whether the camera of the PC/laptop is working or not.

5. After deploying successfully, we go to the hosting ip address followed by /ui, which opens another new webpage showing the output of the live web camera.

The object detection flow recognizes objects in an image and annotates objects with bounding boxes. An image can be loaded from a built-in camera, the file system, or by injecting the default image. We need to make sure that we have the node-red-contrib-browser-utils package installed for all these input nodes to work. This flow uses three of the custom nodes mentioned above (tf-function, tf-model, and post-object-detection). The loaded image is passed into the preprocessing node as msg.payload. The msg object is a JavaScript object that is used to carry messages between nodes. By convention, it has a payload property containing the output of the previous node. The preprocessing function node is an example of tf-function that directly calls the tf.node.decodeImage method with the predefined tf variable. The node produces a Tensor4D image representation as the payload and then passes it to the COCO SSD lite node, which is an instance of the tf-model custom node. This loads the COCO-SSD lite model.json from an external URL and runs inference on the model.

The result of the model goes through the postprocess node that returns an object array containing bbox, className, and score properties. The objects node combines an additional property, complete that is set to true, to the msg with the image object. Then, the bounding-box node draws bounding boxes on the input image and displays it in the browser.

4.2 Experimental results

Example 4.2.1 DHT11 Sensor Data on Node-RED using a Serial Port (ESP32).

Once after the successful deployment, we go to the hosting ip address followed by:1880/ui, which opens another new webpage representing the gauge readings of the temperature and the humidity of the DHT11 sensor. The temperature and humidity readings are directly sent from the serial port to the Node-RED directly. **Figure 11**

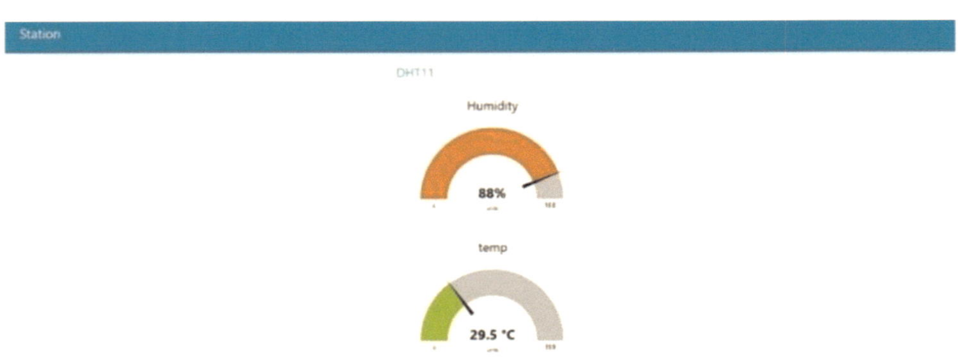

Figure 11.
Dashboard of temperature and humidity from DHT11 sensor (serial port).

shows an example of the dashboard showing temperature and humidity from the DHT11 sensor (serial port).

Example 4.2.2 MQTT Broker Service (ESP32) on Node-RED with DHT11 Sensor Data.

Once after the successful deployment, go to the hosting ip address followed by:1880/ui, which opens another new webpage representing the gauge readings of the temperature and the humidity of the DHT11 sensor. Temperature and humidity readings are sent from the sensor to MQTT broker (as a cloud), then finally sent to the Node-RED as a third-party service. **Figure 12** shows an example of the dashboard showing temperature and humidity from the DHT11 sensor (MQTT broker service).

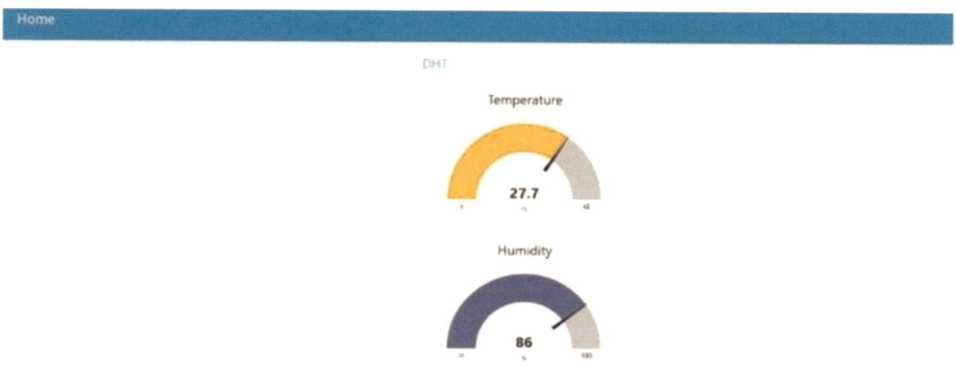

Figure 12.
Dashboard of temperature and humidity from DHT11 sensor (MQTT broker service).

Example 4.2.3 Live Camera Capture and Object Detection.

When the deployment is successful, go to the hosting ip address followed by:1880/ui, which opens another new webpage asking for the permission to allow camera

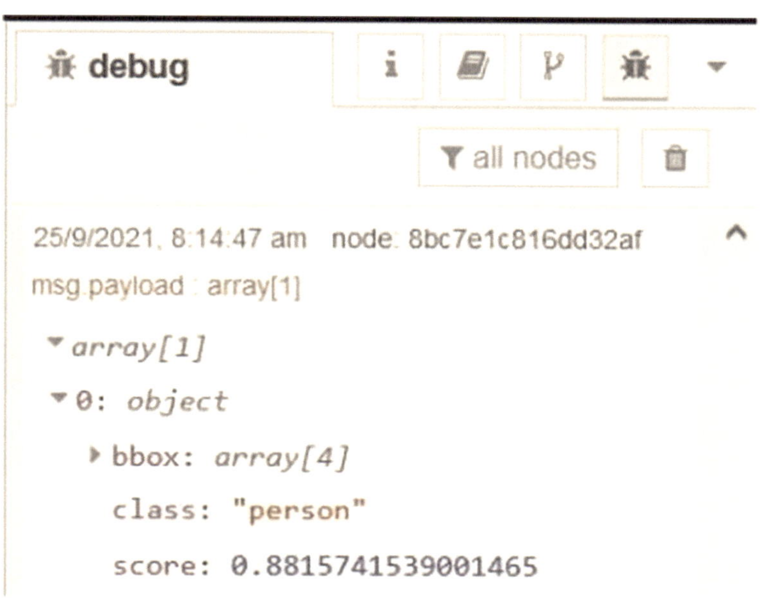

Figure 13.
Debug message showing single object class and accuracy score.

Figure 14.
Debug message showing dual object class and accuracy score.

(Press allow). Then, we can see the live camera working and press the capture button to capture. It detects the object with the help of TensorFlow analysis node as earlier describe and the output can be seen on the debug panel with the accuracy score of its correctness. The examples of the single object and the dual object detection are shown in **Figures 13** and **14**, respectively.

4.3 Implementing as a mobile application

From the given examples, they can also be made visible on a mobile phone for both iOS and Android. It is done through remote access just by installing the application named "RemoteRED" from the mobile app store. The steps are explained as follows.

1. Install the Remote-RED node in the Node-Red.

2. Open the Remote-RED settings and configure it to get the QR code.

3. Open the Remote-RED application from the mobile phone and scan the QR code.

4. Wait for a minute as it is asynchronous to get updated on the mobile phone.

Figure 15.
Connecting to remote-RED application (iOS/android).

5. Now we can see the same output of the Node-RED on the mobile phone Remote-RED application as shown in **Figure 15**.

6. This process is the same and it works for any Node-RED workflow.

5. Discussion

The results show that simulated systems developed using the Node-RED can be deployed in the real world without changing the system parameters. Moreover, the simulated system can be connected with hardware platforms easily. VPL-based hands-on tools are effectively smoothing the beginner's learning curve on IoT. The stranded network protocols and IoT protocols are easy to understand using hands-on experience and deploy in the Node-RED environment. Node-RED system models are easy to debug compared with the traditional programming debug methods. The platform works well in both Internet and Intranet mode as all the components are virtually presented in Node-RED. After all, the laboratory instructors can effectively convey the basics of network and IoT concepts to the students through a VPL language including the Node-RED.

6. Conclusion

The book chapter described a complete outlook of Node-RED that can be applied for an IoT based virtual laboratory. The configuration, the flow development, the requirements, and the usage of the Node-RED were explained with respect to handling all the various types of errors. We modeled, implemented, and tested the IoT virtual laboratory using Node-RED. The implemented virtual laboratory system is currently serving for flexible postgraduate programs and broadcasting completely online. Students obtain great encouragement and motivation toward virtual IoT hands-on practices as they can manage their own and convenient time and a location. The virtual laboratory concept utilizes the available hardware (Wi-Fi IEEE802. 11 b/g/n routers, classical Bluetooth hardware, and system-on-chip (SoC) like MCU) at the student location. The virtual IoT laboratory concept was proved to help students to learn faster than a classical theory class or a video-recorded lesson. With the simplicity of Node-RED and its built-in entities a few examples, which can be used for an IoT-based virtual laboratory, were done to evolve innovative platforms with less coding complexity. It provides flexibility such that the remote laboratory can run on several operating systems or on a mobile application. The proposed solution is platform-independent, and therefore, it can be implemented on low-cost hardware for smaller systems, and the clients can run on mobile devices. The first and second examples are typical scenarios in IoT on Node-RED platform including Arduino and third-party cloud service, whereas the third example is live camera capture with object detection capability. Finally, it was also shown about how Node-RED can be used as a mobile application remotely. After the completion of the book chapter, the readers are supposed to be able to develop IoT systems using VPL-Node-RED, integrate IoT with Node-RED, to design various workflows for IoT on Node-RED, develop real-time IoT applications, and apply security features for IoT and Node-RED while using cloud-based services. Hence, IoT with Node-RED has the capability to change the entire education system, which makes better learning with good interaction and flexibility.

The variety of IoT devices in the future is expected to dramatically grow. Our Node-RED IoT platform was designed to be extendible. To model these future scenarios, we expect to support new IoT device types by using the generic framework for creating new devices. An example of such devices could be wearables that generate movement data. This type of data can be emitted at high volumes but small size. Another device type, which is expected, is an IoT device that is configurable at runtime. This would give us the ability to change the behavior of the device according to an operation plan. An example of this type of device would be a smart home thermostat. Furthermore, we also want to improve the intelligence of our smart testing framework providing machine learning libraries that can continuously learn from past data to improve prediction accuracy. Finally, empirical research can be done collecting a large amount of data in order to know the impact of virtual IoT laboratories on the students with their involvement as it helps the instructors to improve their laboratory sessions further.

Conflict of interest

The authors declare no conflict of interest.

Author details

Kalapatapu Venkata Sai Krishna Raja Shiva Kumar, Attaphongse Taparugssanagorn* and Arunya Prasantha Senadeera Senadiri Dumunnage
School of Engineering and Technology, Asian Institute of Technology, Phatum Thani, Thailand

*Address all correspondence to: attaphongset@ait.asia

References

[1] Ray PP. A survey on visual programming languages in internet of things. Scientific Programming. 2017; **2017**:1-6. DOI: 10.1155/2017/1231430

[2] Chaczko Z, Braun R. Learning data engineering: Creating iot apps using the node-red and the rpi technologies. In: Proceedings of the 16th International Conference on Information Technology Based Higher Education and Training (ITHET'17); 10–12 July 2017. Ohrid. Macedonia: IEEE; 2017

[3] Node_RED Node-Red Contribution [Internet]. 2017. Available from: https://flows.nodered.org/node/node-red-contrib-pdf [Accessed: 2022-02-28]

[4] Rajalakshmi A, Shahnasser H. Internet of things using node-red and alexa. In: Proceedings of the 17th International Symposium on Communications and Information Technologies (ISCIT'17); 25–27 September 2017. QLD, Australia: IEEE; 2017

[5] Debauche O, Mahmoudi S, Mahmoudi SA. Internet of things: Learning and practices. Application to smart city. In: Proceedings of the 4th International Conference on Cloud Computing Technologies and Applications (Cloudtech'18); 26–28 November 2018. Brussels, Belgium: IEEE; 2018

[6] Alejandro A. Pycom Launches World's First Triple Network Low Power WAN, WIFI and Bluetooth Dev Module on Kickstarter [Internet]. 2016. Available from: https://pycom.io/worlds-first-triple-network-dev-module/ [Accessed: 2022-02-28]

[7] Giang NK, Blackstock M, Lea R, Leung VC. Developing iot applications in the fog: A distributed dataflow approach. In: Proceedings of the 5th International Conference on the Internet of Things (IOT); 26–28 October 2015. Seoul, Korea (South): IEEE; 2015

[8] Abdel-Basset M, Manogaran G, Mohamed M, Rushdy E. Internet of things in smart education environment: Supportive framework in the decision-making process. Concurrency and Computation: Practice and Experience. 2018;**31**(10). DOI: 10.1002/cpe.4515

[9] Veeramanickam M, Mohanapriya M. IOT enabled Futurus smart campus with effective E-learning: i-campus. GSTF Journal of Engineering Technology (JET). 2016;**3**(4):81

[10] Elyamany HF, AlKhairi AH. IoT-academia architecture: A profound approach. In: Proceedings of the IEEE/ACIS International Conference on Software Engineering, Artificial Intelligence, Networking and Parallel/Distributed Computing (SNPD); 1–3 June 2015. Takamatsu, Japan: IEEE/ACIS; 2015

[11] Marquez J, Villanueva J, Solarte Z, Garcia A. IoT in education: Integration of objects with virtual academic communities. In: Proceedings of the World Conference on New Advances in Information Systems and Technologies; 02 March 2016. Recife, Brazil: Springer; 2016. pp. 201-212

[12] Chin J, Callaghan V. Educational living labs: A novel internet-of-things based approach to teaching and research. In: Proceedings of the 9th International Conference on Intelligent Environments (IE); 16–17 July 2013. Athens, Greece: IEEE; 2013

[13] Wang Y. English interactive teaching model which based upon internet of things. In: Proceedings of the

International Conference on Computer Application and System Modeling (ICCASM); 22–24 October 2010. Taiyuan, China: IEEE; 2010

[14] Bagheri M, Movahed SH. The effect of the internet of things (IoT) on education business model. In: Proceedings of the 12th International Conference on Signal-Image Technology and Internet-Based Systems (SITIS); 28 November-1 December 2016. Naples, Italy: IEEE; 2016

[15] Aldowah H, Ul Rehman S, Ghazal S, Naufal UI. Internet of things in higher education: A study on future learning. Journal of Physics: Conference Series. 2017:892012017. DOI: 10.1088/1742-6596/892/1/012017

[16] Akiyama K, Ishihara M, Ohe N, Inoue M. An education curriculum of iot prototype construction system. In: Proceedings of the 6th Global Conference on Consumer Electronics (GCCE'17); 24–27 October 2017. Nagoya, Japan: IEEE; 2017

[17] Marquez J, Villanueva J, Solarte Z, Garcia A. Iot in education: Integration of objects with virtual academic communities. New Advances in Information Systems and Technologies. 2016;**444**:201-212. DOI: 10.1007/978-3-319-31232-319

[18] Torres D, Dias JP, Restivo A, Ferreira HS. Real-time feedback in node-red for iot development: An empirical study. In: Proceedings of the 24th International Symposium on Distributed Simulation and Real Time Applications (DS-RT'20); 14–16 September 2020. Prague, Czech Republic: IEEE/ACM; 2020. pp. 1-8

[19] Kodali RK, Anjum A. Iot based home automation using node-red. In: Proceedings of the 2nd International Conference on Green Computing and Internet of Things (ICGCIOT'18); 16–18 August 2018. Bangalore, India: IEEE; 2018. pp. 386-390

[20] David V, Ragu H, Duraiswamy RK, Sasikumar P. Iot based automated indoor agriculture system using node-red and ibm bluemix. In: Proceedings of the 6th International Conference on Inventive Computation Technologies (ICICT'21); 20–22 January 2021. Coimbator, India: IEEE; 2021

[21] Thuluva AS, Anicic D, Rudolph S, Adikari M. Semantic node-red for rapid development of interoperable industrial iot applications. Semantic Web. 2020;**11**(6):949-975. DOI: 10.3233/sw-200405

[22] Ferencz K, Domokos J. Rapid prototyping of iot applications for the industry. In: Proceedings of the IEEE International Conference on Automation, Quality and Testing, Robotics (AQTR'20); 21–23 May 2020. Cluj-Napoca, Romania: IEEE; 2020

[23] Fox J, Donnellan A, Doumen L. The deployment of an iot network infrastructure, as a localised regional service. In: Proceedings of the 5th IEEE World Forum on Internet of Things (WF-IoT'19) 15–18 April 2019. Limerick, Ireland: IEEE; 2019. pp. 319-324

[24] Mohammad MA, Musard B, Daniel H, Lars EO, Andrei S. Securing node-RED applications. In: Protocols, Strands, and Logic. Sequence Number 1: Springer International Publishing; 2021. DOI: 10.1007/978-3-030-91631-2_1

[25] Clerissi D, Leotta M, Reggio G, Ricca F. Towards an approach for developing and testing node-red iot systems. In: Proceedings of the 1st ACM Sigsoft International Workshop on Ensemble-Based Software Engineering;

November 2018. New York, NY, USA: ACM; 2018. pp. 1-8

[26] Clerissi D, Leotta M, Ricca F. A set of empirically validated development guidelines for improving node-red flows comprehension. In: Proceedings of the 15th International Conference on Evaluation of Novel Approaches to Software Engineering (ENASE'20). SciTePress; 25-26 April 2022. Online Streaming Conference: 2020. pp. 108-119

[27] Jost B, Ketterl M, Budde R, Leimbach T. Graphical programming environments for educational robots: Open roberta - yet another one? In: Proceedings of the IEEE International Symposium on Multimedia; 10–12 Dec. 2014. Taichung, Taiwan: IEEE; 2014. pp. 381-386

[28] Kuhail MA, Farooq S, Hammad R, Bahja M. Characterizing visual programming approaches for end-user developers: A systematic review. IEEE Access. 2021;**9**:14181-14202. DOI: 10.1109/ACCESS.2021.3051043

[29] Repenning A. Moving beyond syntax: Lessons from 20 years of blocks programing in agentsheets. Journal of Visual Languages and Sentient Systems. 2017;**3**:68-91. DOI: 10.18293/vlss2017-010

[30] Johnston WM, Hanna JRP, Millar RJ. Advances in dataflow programming languages. ACM Computing Surveys. 2004;**36**(1):1-34. DOI: 10.1145/1013208.1013209

[31] Rekers J, Schürr A. Defining and parsing visual languages with layered graph grammars. Journal of Visual Languages and Computing. 1997;**8**(1): 27-55. DOI: 10.1006/jvlc.1996.0027